ONE THOUSAND WAYS
TO MAKE $1000

ONE THOUSAND WAYS
TO MAKE $1000

■ ■

Practical Suggestions, Based on Actual Experience,
for Starting a Business of Your Own and
Making Money in Your Spare Time

■ ■

Edited by
F. C. MINAKER

AN INC.
ORIGINAL

Published by Greenleaf Groups, PO Box 92664 Austin, TX 78709

Previously published by Dartnell Press

FIRST EDITION 1936

SECOND EDITION 1937

THIRD REVISED EDITION 1940

FOURTH EDITION 2010

FIFTH EDITION 2016

ISBN: 978-0-9991913-0-9

Printed in the United States of America

Fifth Edition

To THOSE *pioneers in American business who had the wisdom and tenacity to stay on their course until they arrived, this book is dedicated*

Publisher's Note

*O*NE THOUSAND WAYS **to Make $1000** *was first published in 1936 by The Dartnell Corporation. For many years, the book has been out of print and difficult to find. Yet Warren Buffett, and his biographers, credits it with shaping his business acumen at an early age. So in 2008, we decided to make the book available again. Working from the 1940 edition, we made every effort to reproduce the content exactly as it was originally presented, except for the photographs, which were not in the public domain.*

Since 1940, the business world has changed dramatically, yet the core concepts in this book still hold true today.

CONTENTS

OPPORTUNITY KNOCKS

By JOHN CAMERON ASPLEY

Publisher, AMERICAN BUSINESS

N EVER in the history of the United States has the time been so favorable for a man with small capital to start his own business as it is today.

For some time now the world has been slowly but steadily recovering from the disruptions and economic shocks that came in the wake of the World War. The ratio of debts to incomes is rapidly being equalized. Farsighted monetary reforms, especially in the sterling group of countries, have been made. While we are by no means back in the hectic prosperity days of 1929, and there still exists considerable unemployment, even the most pessimistic man must concede that the last two or three years have put us all on a firmer footing. In fact, a great number of companies have managed to reach their sales peak since the black days of 1935. Business does exist for the man who will work and plan for it.

Here in the United States, legislation has been enacted that is particularly favorable to the small business man. Obstacles, inadvertently put in his way by early activities of the administration, have given way to a sincere desire to help the small business man, who is the real backbone of American industry. Agencies have been set up especially to protect and help him. He is the "white haired" boy of the new order of things.

We have all heard a great deal about the opportunities of bygone years. We envy the men who discovered and settled the West. We wish that all the railroads were not built so that those opportunities would still be open. Why, the opportunities of yesterday are as nothing compared with the opportunities that await the courageous, resourceful man today! There are fortunes to be made that will make those of Astor and Rockefeller seem picayune.

Ever since the beginning of time the world has made way for the determined man with a real idea for serving his fellow men. In ancient Egypt, in classical Greece, in legalistic Rome, as in every succeeding stage of civilization, society has rewarded those who served it best. It will continue to do so for many thousands of years to come.

So if you have the urge to go into business, or to lay the foundation for a future business by capitalizing your spare time, delay no longer. If you wait for conditions, conditions may leave you in the lurch. Determine upon some plan of action that will enable you to render a needed service to your community. Put your whole heart and soul into rendering that service. Face the disappointments that go with starting in business resolutely and courageously. Cultivate courtesy and consideration of others. Work as you never worked before, and you will succeed. But you cannot possibly succeed until you start. Nor can you succeed unless you serve.

Good luck to you in the most fascinating game in all the world—the great game of business.

CHAPTER ONE

HOW TO START YOUR OWN BUSINESS

WHEN Gustavus Swift, a youngster in knee breeches, dressed and sold his first calf to the fisher folk of Cape Cod, he laid the foundation of the largest meat packing business in the world. The desire to make money—to have a business of his own—was a driving force in the make-up of young Swift. In Barnstable he was known as a chap with a lot of "get up and go" to him. So it was not surprising that when he felt the desire to make money, he didn't waste his time wishing, but took his courage in his two hands and started in the dressed beef business in his dad's back yard.

No doubt there were other young men in Barnstable who wanted to make money too. But while they were wondering how they could make it, Gus Swift cut the Gordian knot. It meant work for him. It was not a pleasant way to make money. There was the possibility of his not being able to sell his calf after he had dressed it. He had to walk miles in order to market his veal, for Cape Cod in those days was a "spread out" sort of place. But Swift didn't care. He wanted the money. The work, the walking and the adventure were fun. And because he regarded making money as fun instead of work, he later was able to come to Chicago and start the great Swift packing business. How different from the average young men of today! They are usually more interested in having a good time than they are establishing themselves in a business of their own. Being in business is so confining! So they concentrate on enjoying themselves, serene in their philosophy that tomorrow is another day. If these people, and they are not all young people either, worked half as hard at making money as they do at having a good time, they would be rich.

Then there are people who are willing to work and do work hard at making money, but they are not successful because they lack a target. They are like the chap who hunts big game with a shotgun. They do a lot of shooting, but they bag very little game. Next to being willing to pay the price of success in hard work, the most important thing is to have a definite, clear-cut *objective*. Since it is necessary to crawl before you walk, it is suggested that you make that objective $1,000.

Now you may say, why stop at $1,000? Why not make it $100,000? While there is merit in the idea of setting up your sights high, there is such a thing as shooting at the moon. Set an objective that you know you can attain. Having attained your first objective, you can then consider what your next objective will be. Remember that after you start in business you are going to run afoul of many discouragements. While it looks easy now, it may not two months from now. If you have as an objective a mark that you can almost reach out and touch, it will help you to carry through this period of discouragement.

The Story of Money

Since this is a book about making money, and money will be mentioned frequently, it might be in order to get it clearly fixed in our minds what money is. Money itself is no good. You cannot eat it. You cannot wear it. You cannot use it for much of anything except to exchange for things which you need. That is why it is called a "medium of exchange." Money can be anything. In the early days of the West whiskey was used for money. A farm was advertised as being worth so many barrels of whiskey. Beads were used by the Indians as a medium of exchange. The island of Manhattan was bought from the Indians for a few beads. The first use of coins as money antedates Christ. To save people the trouble of having to weigh each coin to determine its value, the government stamped them with its mark. They could then be passed in exchange without using scales, although even today the banks in Great Britain weigh all gold coins presented to them to determine the wear.

One of the first countries to use credit money as a medium of exchange was England. People took their silver to the Exchequer and received in exchange a tally stick. Notches were cut in this stick according to the number of "pounds" of silver loaned to the government. These tally sticks were about three-quarters of an inch square and about ten inches long. After being notched, the stick was split in half, and one-half was hung in the Exchequer, and the other half given to the person loaning the silver. At first these tally sticks were used as receipts only, but after a time people exchanged them for things they needed. Then the Exchequer issued tally sticks notched for even number of pounds of silver—one pound, five pounds, twenty pounds and so forth. These were much more convenient than carrying around the actual silver. Eventually the tally stick was superseded by paper receipts, the forerunner of our present paper money. The big advantage of the tally stick was that no two sticks were notched in the same way, so that when the owner of a tally stick called at the Exchequer to collect, the notching on his tally stick certified to his ownership of the silver. It remained for John Law, the eminent Scotch banker, to carry money to its next stage of development—pieces of paper secured by various kinds of assets, and too often by nothing at all.

It is important to know how our present system of money grew, so you will understand its true place in our scheme of business. When you determine to make $1,000 you are not thinking of ten one-hundred-dollar bills so much as you are thinking in terms of what you can buy with those bills. And the same is true of those from whom you get money. You both talk about money as though money was all important, but actually you are exchanging services. So your success in making your first $1,000 will depend upon your ability to make or do something, of definite value to society, which people want more than they want the money it will cost them.

In the years gone by, there was money in making and selling carriages. Based on figures alone it might seem like a good thing to start in the carriage business. But even the most casual investigation will show the folly of doing so. The public today needs low-priced aeroplanes, automobiles operated with fuel oil, and similar things. So other things being equal, if two men started in business today, one making carriages and the other making Diesel automobiles, it is probable that while the man making carriages might make a bare living out of his business, he would never make any "big" money. He might be every bit as smart, even a better business man, but society is not willing to exchange money for better horse-drawn carriages. But it will for automobiles which will run one hundred miles to the gallon of crude oil!

The First Step in Making Money

It is easier to make money in some localities than in others. There is, for example, the Ogden hardware merchant who became rich selling shovels during the California gold rush. He was quick to see that with people pouring into the West digging everywhere for gold, they would need a lot of shovels. So he wrote back east and bought all the shovels he could get. It was no trick to sell them. All he had to do was to advertise that he had shovels to sell, and the prospectors took them away from him at fancy prices. That kind of merchandising does not require any skill. Neither does it require any knowledge of business principles. But the gold rush is over. The West has been settled. To be successful in business today you need more than a stock of merchandise. You have to know how to sell goods at a profit. Nine out of every ten men who start in business today fail because they cannot measure up to those requirements—especially the last part of the formula.

So the first step in starting a business of your own is to know something about it. You need not know all about it. But you must know something about it. Fortunately much of the knowledge you need may be found in books and trade periodicals. The manufacturers of the equipment which you will need to get started are usually able to furnish you with essential information. The federal and state governments have publications of value to you. This is all experience which you can buy very inexpensively, yet it is experience that has cost others much time and money. So read everything published about the business you intend to start, to get the combined experience of others, and begin your plans where they left off.

15

You will find many people who will laugh at the idea of learning how to make money in books. They will tell you that business success depends upon inherent trading ability and action. They will cite men who never read a book in their lives and still made lots of money in business. Do not be influenced by these views. No man ever started in business for himself, who did not short-cut the time it took him to become established, by reading about what others had done. When you read a book about business it is just as though you were invited into the home of the author and sat down with him and talked over your problems. Only those who think they know all there is to be known—and more besides—consider such an exchange of ideas foolish. Why spend hundreds of dollars to find out that a business idea or plan will not work, when another who has tried the plan tells you in a book or a magazine article *exactly* why it is not a good idea? At the end of this volume you will find references to books, pamphlets and magazines which may be consulted for further information on some business problem. Consult those references. They may save you much grief and loss.

But understand this: Reading alone won't enable you to succeed in business. The best idea ever conceived for making money is utterly worthless until somebody puts it to work. You, no doubt, know many brilliant men, fellows with more ideas for making money than a dog has fleas, yet who never get enough money together to buy a second-hand automobile. What is wrong with them? They are probably like the inventor who never stops inventing long enough to make and sell his invention. One good idea, at work making money, is worth a thousand ideas just buzzing around in the head of the smartest man in America.

How to Begin Making Money

The way to begin making money, is to begin. That may sound foolish. But the hundreds of thousands of people in this country who would like to make a lot of money are not making it because they are waiting for this, that, or the other thing to happen. Some are waiting for business to get better. Others are waiting for the right moment. For the most part, however, they are waiting for no reason in the world except that it is easier to put off until tomorrow those things which should be done today. Business is a game of "put and take"—you can't "take out" until you "put in."

People often put off starting in business for themselves because they cannot see clearly ahead. So they go to friends for advice. It is characteristic of people, when advising friends, to be super-conservative. Benjamin Franklin, you will remember, asked his friends what they thought of his chance to succeed in publishing a newspaper in Philadelphia. Without exception they advised against it on the grounds that there were already too many newspapers. They did not take into consideration Franklin's ability nor his capacity to succeed. Had they stopped to analyze the situation they would have advised him to go ahead by all means. The fact that there were so many newspapers made the opportunity for a better newspaper that much greater! As a rule most of the advice to those contemplating a business venture is "don't." If you ask the advice of enough people you are almost sure to end up by doing nothing.

The only person really qualified to advise you as to what you can do is *yourself*. You know yourself better than any one else does. You, and you alone, know how determined you are to make a success of the undertaking. And in the last analysis, about 90 per cent of being successful in business is that indefinable thing which for lack of a better name we call "guts." If you have the "guts" to work eighteen hours a day if need be; if you have the "guts" to go without pocket money in order to carry your business over the rough spots; if you have the "guts" to stick when others say you are just wasting your time, it is a pretty good bet that you will succeed, because that is the stuff from which success is made.

So do not be overconcerned with the real and imaginary difficulties that loom up so large at the outset. It is not necessary that you see the harbor at the other end of your course before setting sail. If you sail straight, and keep moving, you will get to your destination. But you won't get there, or anywhere, unless you *start*. Once you have started, most of the difficulties will give way before your enthusiasm and determination to succeed. You may end up in an entirely different business from the one you started. You may have to change your plans a number of times. But what does that matter? The all-important thing is that you have started.

In the following pages you will read about hundreds of people who, like yourself, had the urge to make a thousand dollars. Some earned it making things, and others selling things. Some made it quickly and others slowly. But you will find one thing true of every story in this book. Each person began making money *when he or she started*. Had these people not come to a decision, and started in a business of their own, they would never have made any money. Their success began with their decision to start— and so will yours.

Raising Money to Start a Business

Many a man with a good idea hesitates to start in business because he lacks capital. Capital is important, and it cannot be denied that a lack of it is one of the principal reasons for business failures. However, lack of capital need not hold back a determined man. The old saying, "Where there's a will, there's a way" still applies.

Sometimes a money-making idea is so good that men who have capital will "grub stake" you in starting your business. Many famous businesses were started in just this way. Hires root beer is a case in point. Charles

E. Hires discovered the formula for his root beer in a farmhouse back in 1877. One morning George W. Childs, publisher of the Philadelphia *Public Ledger*, sat down beside Mr. Hires in a street car. "Mr. Hires," he said, "why don't you advertise that root beer of yours?"

"How can I advertise?" said Mr. Hires. "I haven't any money."

"Advertise to get money. Come around to the *Ledger* office and I'll tell the bookkeeper not to send you any bills for advertising until you ask for them."

Mr. Hires was a man of action. He knew that without venture, nothing could be gained. He accepted Mr. Child's offer. An inch advertisement ran daily from that time on in the *Public Ledger*. Slowly, but steadily, it began to pull. When at last the profits from the advertising were sufficient to justify Mr. Hires' asking for his bill, it amounted to $700. But it was a good investment. It provided the capital upon which the Hires' business was founded. For ten years Mr. Hires plowed all his profits back into advertising, keeping only enough out for a bare living for himself. He became one of the largest national advertisers in the country, with annual appropriations amounting to more than $600,000.

When a product has good repeating qualities it is sometimes possible to interest advertising agents in extending credit in order to get a business started. If an idea offers mass advertising opportunities, some of the larger agencies may accept stock in a company to offset the advertising bills. Among the well-known products now on the market which have been started in this way, or which are partly owned by advertising agencies are: Pepsodent, Barbasol, Bon-Ami, Sapolio, Palmolive soap and Van Camp's beans. It will be noticed that all these products have two things in common: (1) They are articles which can be sold to the general public, and (2) they repeat quickly. This last qualification is important, because generally you have to spend an amount equal to the selling price of the first purchase in order to induce a person to try a product. Your only chance, therefore, of making a profit on your advertising is the repeat factor of the article. It must have real merit, and it must have an outstanding feature that will lend itself to mass exploitation, either over the air or through the press.

Another way to finance a business is to organize a stock company and sell the stock to friends and local business men who have surplus funds to invest. In following this plan, it is important to keep the voting control yourself, otherwise you may find that after you have the business out of the red and into a money-making position, you have been eased out of the picture. Incorporate your company for twice as much as the capital required, and keep 51 per cent of the common or voting stock in payment for the idea or the patents or whatever it is that makes the business attractive. It is better, however, to finance a business out of its earnings, on a payas-you-go basis, rather than to organize a stock company. The reasons for this are: (1) When you sell stock to others you are in effect taking them in as partners. The more partners you have, the less control you will have over the policies of the business, and the greater the danger of dissension. (2) Minority stockholders, unless they are employees, contribute little to a business beyond the initial capital. There is no reason why they should be given 49 per cent of the profits. They are entitled to a "rental" for the use of their money, and the risk they take, but in the case of a successful business, common stock dividends often represent a return of several hundred per cent a year.

The best way of raising the money you need to start your business, and the way which in the long run will prove most profitable to you, is to find something that you can sell. Let the commissions accumulate in a bank until the balance is enough to enable you to start in a small way. Then, by the simple process of putting back the profits into expansion, as Mr. Hires did, let your business grow. In this way you will keep control and will not have to share an unduly large proportion of its earnings with others.

In this connection you will find on pages 341 to 359 of this book a number of suggested items which you can sell. If you lack the necessary capital to start in business, you will probably find something described in that chapter which can be successfully sold in your community. By this plan you can soon accumulate a thousand dollars or more for business capital.

■ ■

The Story of the Cash Register

ONE of the outstanding examples of American business successes is the National Cash Register of Dayton, Ohio. It is a monument to the genius of its founder, John H. Patterson. It is a demonstration of what a man with an idea and a lot of determination can accomplish, because probably no product ever made had such poor prospects for success as the cash register when it was introduced in 1884 by Patterson. That it was a useful invention no one denied, but because its value depended, so it seemed, upon the assumption that a business man's employees were dishonest, it encountered terrific opposition from retail clerks.

Mr. Patterson's success was due in a large measure to taking what seemed to be an insurmountable objection, and turning it into a reason for buying. Cash register salesmen were taught to turn the opposition to their advantage by pointing out to employers that when they put temptation in the way of their clerks, *they shared the guilt* of any clerk who pilfered the cash drawer. They brought the issue to the proprietor of the business by pointing the accusing finger at *him* rather than at his clerks. And as so often happens, once the right approach to the selling problem was found, the business began to grow. Even to this day, the leadership which this great company enjoys in the field of selling all over the world, can be traced to its policy of turning objections into reasons for buying. In the words of a famous cash register salesman: "Sell your man with the weapons he hands you."

John H. Patterson did not invent the cash register. His early experience had been in the coal business. When he was 40 years old, he came to Dayton and paid $6,500 for the controlling interest in the National Manufacturing Company, which held basic patents on a cash register. It was a crude device that functioned by punching holes in appropriate columns on a strip of paper. There seemed to be no demand for the machine at all and Patterson's investment in the enterprise came to be a standing joke in the community. In fact, Patterson's old associates made so much fun of the cash register, he offered the seller of the stock a bonus of $2,000 to release him from his contract. However, the seller wouldn't take it back as a gift! When his offer was refused, Patterson made up his mind that he would go into the business and make it a success.

Perhaps it was fortunate that Patterson knew nothing about manufacturing. For, if he had, he probably would not have touched the proposition. He would have known the difficulties of running a business without an established demand for the product. But Patterson didn't know that "it couldn't be done." In December, 1884, he changed the name of the concern to the National Cash Register Company and from then until his death at 78, he "slept, ate and drank" cash registers. No one else could see a future for cash registers, but he refused to change his vision just because others could not see ahead. He started absolutely from scratch. He had to improve the cumbersome old machine; he had to find and develop a market; he had to create advertising to sell his product; he had to develop salesmen to do the selling. One might say that he invented modern salesmanship, because until that time, most selling was just order taking.

By 1888, the company was beginning to make itself a power. It weathered the panic of 1893 and later depressions. Patterson worked day and night against almost insurmountable odds. There were times when, had he admitted to himself the possibility of being bankrupt, he would have failed. He wouldn't recognize failure—*he could not fail*. By constantly improving his product, his sales methods, and his manufacturing facilities, he built up in Dayton a world-wide business that has earned millions of dollars for the Patterson family. It shows what a man with an idea and a lot of "guts" can do.

How J. C. Penney Made His First $1,000

JAMES C. PENNEY'S first job paid him $2.27 a month. Thirty-two years later, he was the successful head of a great business, with more than 1,000 partners. He was just the average small-town country boy. Was it luck? Not at all. It was a combination of enthusiasm, vision, and singleness of purpose, backed up by *work*. He admits that hard work alone will not bring you success. But hard work and a definite goal will do the trick.

After clerking for some time in a store owned by T. M. Callahan and his partner, young Penney was offered a chance to become a partner in the business, with a new store to manage. His savings amounted to $500—not nearly enough. But the two partners agreed to lend him the additional amount needed at 8 per cent. However, Penney was shrewd for his years, so he shopped around and found he could borrow the amount from a bank at 6 per cent.

The new store opened April 14, 1902, with a capital of $6,000, a third of which was Penney's. It was a success from the start. The sales for the first year amounted to $28,891.11 and Penney's share of the profit was well over $1,000. While the long hours and the incessant work connected with selling customers and buying stock may have seemed like drudgery to many, it was fun to Penney. Merchandising was his field. This was the work he wanted to do, and here was the opportunity. All he needed was the energy to put the business over, and he had plenty of that and to spare.

By 1904, J. C. Penney had opened his third store. It was about this time that T. M. Callahan and his first partner decided to separate. They offered to sell their interest in the three stores to Penney. He lacked the needed amount to buy, but such was their confidence in him they accepted his note for $30,000.

The stores were known at this time as the Golden Rule stores. The unusual idea J. C. Penney developed from the very beginning was the building of managers. He built up his men and sent them out to open new stores. They in turn likewise built up managers and sent them out to open still other new stores. In this manner, each new store would accumulate enough capital to start the next store. Each manager who opened a new store, of course, shared in the profits of that store. Thus each man selected by J. C. Penney to branch out developed not only business, but men to handle the business. Here was the idea and the vision. One look at the recent sales figures, running well over $250,000,000, shows it succeeded.

The Story of "Morning Glory" Tomato Juice

THE Snead family of Evanston, Illinois, were up against it, just as thousands of other families were in the early days of the depression. Two sons ready to go to Dartmouth and Father Snead out of a job. A less determined family might have decided that "luck" was against them and let it go at that. But the Sneads are not quitters.

So they put their heads together and decided to get the agency for some lime drink which would mix with native gin, and see if it could not be sold to the supposedly well-to-do people along Chicago's North Shore. But the North Shore did not get very much excited about the Snead family's lime ricky.

One day when the Snead spirits were down close to zero a friend on a down-state farm sent the family a case of very fine seed tomatoes. Not knowing what better to do with them Mrs. Snead decided to convert them into tomato juice. Being a good neighbor she sent a few bottles next door. The neighbors made a great fuss over it. Mrs. Snead began to wonder if perhaps her husband and the boys might not be able to do better selling tomato juice the way she fixed it, than they were selling lime ricky. The family went into a huddle, and since the lime ricky business was getting no better fast, they decided to try Mother Snead's idea. They would call it "Morning Glory" Tomato Juice—because it made you feel glorious, regardless of how badly you may have felt the night before.

The idea of fresh, homemade tomato juice, squeezed from choice seed tomatoes took hold in great shape. The Sneads charged more than the grocery stores charged for tomato juice, but nobody complained. People are that way. The late Colonel Simmons used to say: "The recollection of quality remains long after the price is forgotten." The Sneads were careful to keep the quality up by making arrangements with a chap who grew tomato seeds, and therefore had the choicest varieties. They took over his entire crop and squeezed and seeded it for him. In that way they not only obtained juice that had a superior flavor, but they got their raw materials at rock bottom prices. Most important, however, it gave them a talking point—and a good talking point may mean the difference between success or failure.

It was not long before the Sneads were selling all the tomato juice they could make in their kitchen factory, and had to enlarge their facilities. They rented a plant alongside the railroad tracks and began to think in terms of a nation-wide market. They considered all the various ways of getting distribution. They thought of selling through brokers, as so many food product manufacturers do. But the brokers told them their price was too high. They thought about employing college men to sell house to house. But that idea would take too much capital. Finally, they determined to stick to the plan they had so successfully used on the North Shore.

So they picked out a few social leaders in selected cities, people like the Drexels and Biddles of Philadelphia, and wrote and told them about "Morning Glory" Tomato Juice. The idea of serving tomato juice that was made to order had a real appeal. The orders began to come in. When Mr. Snead had the endorsement of these prominent people, he went to the exclusive hotels in those cities and gave them the opportunity to serve the same brand of tomato juice to their guests as the first families in the city served on their breakfast tables. With the hotels lined up, the idea of serving "Morning Glory" Tomato Juice was next suggested to the railroads. The Pennsylvania Lines, always alert for something better, ordered a trial supply and featured it on the menus of their crack trains. Next the Illinois Central fell in line. In that way "Morning Glory" Tomato Juice got advertising worth thousands of dollars, without the Sneads having to spend a thin dime. Before long the Snead business was going "big guns." Today, what started out as a stop-gap during the worst period of the depression is now a full-fledged business handling not only tomato juice but other food products as well. This family's hard-earned success simply proves the often overlooked truism that to sell the masses, *first* sell the classes.

■ ■

How the Great Wanamaker Business Started

JOHN WANAMAKER had saved $1,900; his brother-in-law, Nathan Brown, had $1,600 that he was willing to risk in a partnership. "Why not begin?" said Wanamaker to his brother-in-law. He figured that any time was a good time to begin—provided you really did begin. Business conditions were bad—the national depression, that had followed the closing of many banks in 1857, had caused unemployment, low wages, and the demoralization of manufacturers and wholesalers. Philadelphia, especially, was saturated in gloom. It was 1861, the threshold of the Civil War. However, Wanamaker's mind had been made up and in February, 1861, he signed a lease that put his store into business. At 23 he was ready to assume the responsibilities of a business, regardless of national affairs, business conditions, or the well-meant advice of friends who had tried to discourage him from the undertaking.

The store fixtures cost $375 and some clothing fabrics $739. The store opened April 8, but little was sold for several days. Plenty of people passed the store, but very few entered it. Then the books showed an entry of $24.67 worth of "gentlemen's collars, cuffs and neckties," sold April 18. In the meantime the $3,500 which John Wanamaker and his brother-in-law had scraped together was fast disappearing. It was just a question of how much longer they could hang on.

Fortunately, there was an opportunity to buy the stock of a clothing manufacturer who was nervous over the effect which the war might have on business. Wanamaker took over the stock on thirty days' dating and invested all the money he had left—$24—in six advertisements in the Philadelphia newspapers. This happened on April 27, 1861. The advertisements did what was expected of them and the entire stock was sold in two weeks.

From then on the business grew, under the Wanamaker policy of putting every dollar that could be spared into advertising. By 1869 Wanamaker & Brown were the largest retail dealers in men's clothing in the United States. With the death of Nathan Brown, John Wanamaker & Company was organized to do a general business. Today it is one of the great stores of the world, and a monument to faith in advertising.

It was Wanamaker's method to expand constantly and depend upon advertising to fill in the open spaces. What his rivals called his foolhardiness was grounded in a supreme faith in the power of advertising to build volume, and the realization that volume attracted volume. When business came upon any dull times or during a panic, it was always Wanamaker's policy to increase and expand his advertising appropriation as his sales increased.

■ ■

Mrs. MacDougall Turned
$38 into a Million

WHEN Alice Foote MacDougall, of New York City, was left a widow in 1907, with three little children to support, she turned to the only work she knew outside of handling her household duties—coffee blending. With a capital of $38, she decided to continue her husband's coffee-broking business. It was uphill work. There was much antagonism on the street, and coffee-men in the business gave her just six months to last. However, she gradually became established and the six months passed. Her little office included a borrowed desk and a second-hand chair. Not only did she have to overcome the prejudices against a woman in this business, but she had to learn the simplest routine of running a business.

Most of Mrs. MacDougall's accounts were clubs, hospitals and sanitariums. In the beginning, she solicited orders by mail, but she realized that she would have to make personal calls to secure more business. She mapped a radius of seventy-five miles from New York and traveled this territory for several years. Two years after she started in business, she was taking in $20,000 a year. However, the profit on this amount was small as the net profit on each pound of coffee was only about four cents. Several years later, having built up a reputation for good coffee, she opened a small coffee shop in the Grand Central Terminal, serving coffee and simple foods.

Within a year from the time the shop opened, she was serving 8,000 customers a month. Gradually this shop led to a chain of six eating places, each patterned after a typical European scenic spot. Mrs. MacDougall was a success; people flocked to her restaurants. They liked the leisurely, foreign atmosphere. Her tea rooms at this time earned as high as $1,684,000 a year.

Then came the depression! In 1932 like many another, Mrs. MacDougall went broke. The six restaurants went into receivership. Mrs. MacDougall, however, had fought business difficulties before and came out ahead. She didn't cry "stop" now. At the age of sixty-five, she made a comeback and is now the mistress of a chain of three restaurants. She is again stressing "atmosphere" in her restaurants and the public is once more putting its stamp of approval on her undertaking by giving these restaurants its patronage. Once more Mrs. MacDougall is on her way to making an outstanding success.

■ ■

How Otto Schnering Made His First $1,000

IT WAS back in 1914 that Otto Y. Schnering, then twenty-one years old, went into business for himself. He had only a few dollars capital. He rented a little office and established himself as a manufacturers' agent, struggling along against unpredictable odds, but gaining business experience. Then came what he thought to be his real "break." In 1916 he learned of a candy-making machine he could buy for $100. "Fortunes have been made in the candy business," thought Schnering, so he bought the machine.

The first day the machine was delivered, he put it into operation. He worked until midnight and made a batch of what he believed to be very fine candy. The next day he took this candy and arranged with a few shopkeepers to sell it for him on consignment. Then he returned to his office and made up a second batch. He was to discover that his candy did not go well. When he made his second call, very little of it had been sold. This did not discourage him. He had embarked upon a career as a candy manufacturer. The thing to do, he figured, was to find out why his candy didn't sell, and then make candy that would sell.

Unwittingly, Schnering had made a mistake that thousands of others have made when they decide to go into any kind of manufacturing business. He made a product that *he* liked, instead of one the *public* liked. There are thousands of manufacturers today who are slowly going bankrupt because they do not follow this simple principle. They often try to force their ideas on the public, when it would be so much easier to make something that the public actually wanted.

It did not take Schnering long to discover his mistake. He found out that three types of candies sell best, namely, chocolate, caramel candies and candies containing peanuts. He concentrated on making candies of this type, and his candies sold, though not as well as he anticipated.

Schnering then experimented with many kinds of candy bars. It took him three years before he had hit upon the ideal combination, one blending chocolate, caramel, and peanuts, and the way the candy-public took to this bar justified his experiments. He later decided to call the bar "Baby Ruth," because the word "baby" was familiar to every small child and adult, and because the common name, "Ruth," was easily pronounceable by man and child. He priced it at five cents. The success of this bar was immediate.

To make a candy bar that will sell successfully does not require a candy-making machine. You can start in your own kitchen, and by following the principles outlined above, may, in a few days, work out the formula for a successful selling bar. Candy formulas are not subject to copyright, but the trade name of the product may be registered in the Bureau of Patents and Copyrights, and its use denied to anyone but yourself. The experience of every candy manufacturer, however, would indicate that the best kinds of candy to make would be candies made from chocolate, since chocolate candies are always in demand. Kitchen-made candies, chocolate creams, dip caramels and other types sell better because they are fresher, and there is an unlimited demand. A market is always ready in the local stores, where goods placed on consignment, that is, with the understanding that you will take them back if not sold within a specified time, are generally accepted.

CHAPTER TWO

SELLING AS A BUSINESS

IN LOGGING camps the cook shouts, "Come and get it." In the army the bugler sounds mess call. In either case a horde of hungry men come running for their meals.

In business it would be simple if a manufacturer or a merchant could bring all his customers within earshot, shout, "Come and get it" and be rushed by a crowd of customers eager to buy his product. However, as we all know, people are not that anxious to buy. They must be educated, persuaded and shown how and what to buy. That is the job of salesmen and saleswomen.

There is always a demand for people who can sell. Salesmanship draws its manpower from every other profession and trade. Lawyers have closed their law books and turned to selling; some have grown rich. Surgeons have put aside their white coats and become salesmen. Bankers, grown tired of sitting on tall stools, or behind fancy desks have thrown up their jobs and turned to the more satisfying job of selling. Farmers have walked away from their plows to take up salesmanship; men from machine shops, from schools, churches, stores and offices have sought the greater freedom and wider opportunities for profit offered by a career in salesmanship.

There are many reasons why so many men desert other types of work to take up salesmanship. One of the first reasons is that you can write your own ticket when you become a salesman. You do not have to wait until the boss gets ready to grant you a raise; a good salesman can give himself a raise in pay almost any time. You do not have to work long, dreary hours, Sundays and holidays as the druggist, the restaurant owner or the garage employee must.

In selling you are almost entirely your own boss. You set your own rate of pay and, like the captain of a ship at sea, you rely on your own judgment and ability. There are many other things that go to make selling real fun. You meet the community's most successful, most interesting and influential people. You are in constant touch with what's going on in the world, and you are laying the foundation for success and increasingly bigger pay checks.

There is almost no other man who is so thoroughly independent and secure as the salesman who has built up the confidence and friendship of a group of customers. A merchant may suffer fire losses that will wreck his business or he may make mistakes in buying that will shatter his profits for an entire season; a surgeon may lose the delicate skill of his hands as he grows older, and the loss of one important case may send a lawyer straight down the path to obscurity. A farmer may lose an entire season's work in one heavy downpour of rain, or an overflow of the creek or river. But no fire can burn, no flood destroy, no thief can steal a salesman's stock in trade which is, as you know, the confidence and friendship of his customers.

Of course, there can be no doubt that most men take up selling to earn money. But there are other satisfactions and compensations in addition to the money earned. In 1928, a salesman almost jammed a life insurance policy down the throat of a certain New York newspaper man. The policy had an accident and sickness clause which paid $100 a month in the event of illness and disability. When he signed the application and paid the premium he was in the best of health. Less than two years later he was in a hospital, drawing $100 a month compensation. Was he grateful to that insurance salesman? You *know* he was. Had it not been for the salesman's insistence, he would have suffered the loss of ten months' earnings, and there would have been no funds to pay the heavy hospital expenses. Yet it seemed to the buyer when he took that insurance that he was doing the salesman a favor. As it turned out, the salesman did the newspaper man a favor for which he has been grateful ever since.

A salesman who sold a radio receiver sometime ago to an old lady who is crippled and confined to her home said that he wondered if he had done the right thing. It was an expensive set and she was dependent on a very small income. "I thought perhaps I ought not to have sold her, because it was obvious that her home needed repairs and painting. But as she made the payments I realized that the radio set had brought the world right to her armchair. She has since told me that her radio receiver, next to her husband and children, has been the greatest joy in her life."

There are literally millions of people who owe much of their happiness to salesmen. Think of the people who might never have owned a home if some real estate salesman hadn't "pushed them over." Think of the thousands of mothers whose lives have been made easier by some salesman who sold them a washing machine, a vacuum cleaner, or an ironing machine. There's a president of a big advertising agency in New York who traces his upward rise back to the time when a salesman sold him a correspondence course in advertising. Numberless cases could be pointed out where salesmen, through their ability to educate, to persuade, and to induce people to act, have brought new prosperity, happiness and satisfaction into the lives of millions of people. That's why it is so much fun to sell things.

Qualifications of a Good Salesman

One of the best salesmen in his field was a big, blonde fellow who was a great handshaker and backslapper. He never missed an opportunity to make a friend or to push himself forward to meet the right people. He joined all kinds of lodges and clubs. He wore pink shirts, too. He was a typical salesman—the kind we read about. And he was a big success. Another topnotch salesman was a fellow who was totally unlike the first man. He never slapped any backs; he was quiet, reserved and almost diffident in his relations with people. But he could sell. When he sold an order he made a customer, and often a lifelong friend.

These two men are mentioned to emphasize the idea that you don't have to be an expert storyteller, a gin-hound or a great handshaker to be a good salesman. There are thousands of good salesmen who never take a drink of hard liquor. There are other thousands who are quiet, unassuming, modest fellows who do not feel the necessity of joining a lot of clubs or lodges, or painting the town red. It isn't even necessary for a man to have the "gift of gab" to be a successful salesman. Experience has proved that more salesmen have become failures from talking too much, than from too little.

Because a man doesn't have to be a good "mixer," in the usual sense of the word, don't jump to the conclusion that a miser can be a good salesman. But there is a whole world of middle ground between being a "mixer" and a miser. If you enjoy meeting people, if you are not scared in the event a man becomes a little gruff and grouchy with you, if you are not afraid of hard work and study, and if you have a grim determination to succeed, you have most of the important qualifications of a good salesman.

Of course, if you are imaginative, can see the inherent value in a proposition quickly, if you have the knack of explaining values in interesting and forceful terms, if you have any natural qualities of leadership—so much the better. But, important as these qualities may be, many men who have them in only the smallest degree succeed in selling.

You may ask what is meant by "natural qualities of leadership." Were you ever the captain of a sandlot or high school baseball team? Are you invariably appointed to some office in any little group, lodge, association, or club you join? Do people gravitate toward you and go out of their way to see you or please you? If these things are true, you are a natural leader and there is no better way to capitalize your inherent abilities than in a career as a salesman. But if you like to be alone, if you would rather read about a football game than go to one and yell your head off, if you would rather sit by the fire of a winter's night and read a good book than go to a party, perhaps you had better not try selling—unless you are willing to fight hard to overcome your natural inclinations.

To add one word of caution: Don't pay too much attention to what your friends tell you. Many a potentially good salesman has been ruined by the well-meant, but mistaken, advice of wives, friends, mothers, or schoolteachers. After all, it is up to each man to decide for himself what he wants to do, whether it is running a retail store, building up a manufacturing business, farming, selling or anything else. You know in your own mind whether you want to sell or not. Once you have made up your mind, go ahead. If you are the sort of person who is constantly swayed back and forth in your opinions and your desires by the advice of friends, then perhaps you had better not try to be a salesman.

Getting the Name on the Order Blank

When you begin to sell you are almost sure to find nearly everyone will promise you some business. You will be told, "I will keep you in mind," or "I will let you know when I need anything." People really mean these pleasantries when they say them to you, but they seldom bother to remember them after a salesman is out of sight. You must learn, and learn quickly, too, that a promised order pays no commissions, turns no factory wheels.

The ability to close sales without a long, drawn-out series of "call backs" is the greatest asset a salesman can have. Without this ability you are just a solicitor, not a salesman. There's an old saying, "Anybody can solicit business, but it takes a salesman to close orders."

The first thing to remember in closing a sale is that most people need a little pushing to bring them to a decision. The natural inclination of every prospect is to put off buying as long as possible. Even a woman, a few days before Easter, will want to put off buying a hat or a new outfit, until she has seen what every store in town has to offer. Yet she *wants* that new hat or dress as badly as she ever wanted anything. She'd be heartbroken if she knew she couldn't have it. But she wants to wait, wait, wait and see if she can't find something she likes a little better.

Keeping this human trait uppermost in your minds, as salesmen, you can understand the necessity of persistence and pressure in helping people to make up their minds. Take the case of a man buying a new automobile. He may have decided to buy a Ford, a Chevrolet or a Plymouth. But which one? All three cars are presented to him in the most favorable manner. He is a bit confused. Each car has certain special features which appeal to him. The salesman's job is to bring him to the point of deciding. There are definite methods of doing this. For example, one salesman may say: "Mr. Prospect, if you will just check your preferences as to color, tires, and body style, I'll put your order through, so you can drive this car next Sunday."

See how this salesman has simplified the prospect's problem of making a decision. See how much better this attempt at closing is, than: "Think it over and let me know what kind of tires and wheels you want." The washing machine salesman may say, "Mrs. Jones, if you will sign this memorandum you can have this machine in your basement by Monday, and finish your washing long before noon, leaving you free from worry and work all Monday afternoon."

In closing an order make everything as simple as possible, and get the prospect to take some first, easy steps toward signing. A typewriter salesman had the president of a large company convinced that his machine was right. But there were some twenty-five old machines to be listed for trade-in and a contract to be drawn. The salesman saw that the president, who was accustomed to "okaying" memoranda which had been prepared for him, was busy. Had he waited for the president to ask someone to list all the old typewriters to be traded in and to draw up the contract, he would never have obtained the order.

The salesman went out of the president's office, tore off a sheet of wrapping paper. On it he listed the serial numbers of all machines which were to be traded in. Under the list he wrote, "$21 allowance on these machines." Back into the president's office went the salesman. He showed the president the memorandum and said, "Just okay this and I will have your purchasing agent prepare the order." The president scribbled his initials and his okay in a jiffy. Later the salesman went to the purchasing agent who prepared a formal purchase order for the twenty-five new typewriters. The salesman had made the job of buying as simple as possible.

At the first sign of agreement on the part of the prospect, the wise salesman *"asks for the order."* If he can't close at this point, he goes right on explaining, even in some cases, repeating things he has said before. Then he asks for the order again. More men make the mistake of asking for the order too late than too soon. Remember this point when selling—ask for the order five times before you give up. Very often a prospect will spar and feint by saying he will check his stock and let you know. Or he will tell you that he will find out what color, or what size, or what quantity is needed. Here is where the salesman shows whether he is really an order getter, or just a solicitor. If he is really a salesman he'll say, "That's fine, Mr. Prospect, just okay this order with the color (or size or quantity) left blank and I will have your clerk (assistant bookkeeper, or secretary) fill in the details."

Not long before this was written a salesman was trying to sell a landlord a Kelvinator electric refrigerator. Two other refrigerator salesmen were after the order too. The landlord couldn't make up his mind, so he said he would talk to the tenant and find out what make the tenant preferred. The Kelvinator salesman went straight to the tenant and explained all the good points of Kelvinators. The other two salesmen waited a day or two and then came back. "Sorry, but I bought a Kelvinator," said the landlord when they approached him. The Kelvinator salesman had "cinched" the order by seeing the tenant and then going right back to the landlord and saying, "Your tenant will be delighted with a Kelvinator, because I have just seen him and told him all about it."

31

Deciding What to Sell

What do you want to sell? Don't make the mistake of thinking, "I would sell *anything* if I had the chance." The first step in going into sales work is to decide what you want to sell, and what you think you *can* sell. You might do a splendid job of selling electric ranges, yet fail miserably in selling electric motors. Or vice versa. You could conceivably make a big success selling life insurance and fail completely to sell accounting machines. Your own previous experience, your interests, hobbies, education, and background, all should govern the selection of something you like to sell. If you like the feel and touch of materials; if you have an eye for style, line, color; if you are a natural trader who loves to see money changing hands, by all means get into selling something that is sold over the counter in retail stores. But if you are the kind of fellow who thinks that a retail merchant is just a "shopkeeper," and you can't get excited about a piece of merchandise and the possible profit it carries, then forget about selling to retailers.

Do you like automobiles? Are you interested in all the new models that come out from year to year? This interest may be turned into profit by selling automobiles. Are you of a mechanical turn of mind? There are a thousand mechanical devices to sell. And so on through the long gamut of everything that is made. There are a thousand things you could sell. But find the one thing you *want* to sell, and you've made your first step toward a career in selling.

In the following portion of this chapter you will read how other people who, like yourself, had a real desire to sell, satisfied their desire and made good money to boot. You will notice that in nearly every instance the adventure proved successful because the product offered for sale rendered a definite *service* to the buyer. It is not enough that *you* are enthusiastic about selling a product or service; it must be something for which a need exists. When you are searching for something to sell, make sure that it not only appeals to you, but that it will appeal to those to whom you must sell it. In this connection you will find in the supplement in the back of this book a list of products, which offer such opportunities. From this list you can make a selection with every assurance that the product is salable.

Every Woman Is a Hosiery Prospect

LUCILE ANTHONY, forced to shift for herself and her six-month-old baby when her husband had deserted her, turned to selling silk hosiery. The fascination beautiful silk hose held for her was, she admitted, almost an obsession. She points out that her chief reason for selling connection with a hosiery manufacturer was to enable her to go from home to home and meet people.

"Besides a genuine love for sheer silken hose, I had practically no other enthusiasm," Lucile explained. "I received samples of six different colored hose in a light folding case from the company, and was so eager to tell my friends about the hose that my first calls didn't seem like selling at all. I visited friends first. Most of them gave me orders in units of three or more pairs. But I soon ran out of friends, for you know no matter how many people you're acquainted with, sooner or later you've told the story to everyone. So when I had seen every friend I had, I started selling to strangers. This proved more difficult than I expected. When the women came to the door, they didn't expect to see a saleswoman and were not in the mood for buying. Many scowled. None asked me in, as my friends had done, and I thought while making my initial call on strangers that the world was hard and cruel. In three days I made only two sales. Something was decidedly wrong.

"I realized that I was not using a scientific approach when calling on these women—I was saying the first thing that came to my mind. Since I wasn't getting anywhere, I thought something was wrong with my product. Then, like many others, I blamed my inability to make sales on the kind of work I was doing. Indeed, I was so sure it was because I was doing house-to-house selling that housewives wouldn't give consideration, I was annoyed and upset. Yet the idea of selling hose, of handling them, of talking about them to everybody was strong enough to overcome the impulse to quit. Out of my first impressions about selling, there emerged a few clear ideas on salesmanship. I began to realize that my trouble was the way I went about making sales; that it wasn't exactly what I said at the door that mattered, so much as the way I said it. There are no magic words that admit one to homes.

"Presently I was aware of being more successful getting in when I kept on talking. Women who opened the door to tell me they wouldn't buy anything, usually waited until I made a move to leave before closing the door. So I began to use strategy. Standing several feet from the door, at the edge of the porch, I would talk loudly. I would tell the woman about the beautiful hosiery I carried.

" 'No. Nothing today,' was the usual answer. 'But if you would only give me a minute—.'

" 'I'm busy. Not today.'

" 'It won't take any time at all. Won't you let me come in?'

" 'I have no money. Not today.'

" 'But if you once saw them, Mrs. Smith, I know—'

" 'Call back again next week. I won't buy a thing today.'

" 'But I'm not asking you to buy, won't you even take a moment to look?'

" 'Not today. I'm sorry. I'm very busy.'

" 'I understand you're very busy, Mrs. Smith. I really won't take up any time at all. Won't you let me in?'

"After some moments of this type of conversation, the housewife would invite me inside. That gave me a chance to do some real selling. My enthusiasm for silk hosiery usually proved infectious and the woman would let me have an order."

Mrs. Anthony's method of getting past the door is used by many successful salespeople with good results. She makes an average of forty-five calls daily, and during her second six-month period of selling for this company earned commissions which totaled eleven hundred and seven dollars. Her biggest day's income came just before commencement exercises at the University of Chicago, when she called on two sorority houses and sold fifty-six pairs of hosiery in two group demonstrations. Her commission is fifty cents a pair, collected as a deposit from the prospect at the time the order is given. The balance due the company is collected C.O.D. when shipment is made.

This type of work is ideal for women who are anxious to turn their spare time into money. Working hours may be suited to your own convenience and no investment is needed to start in this remunerative business.

■ ■

Overcoming Price Objections

IT IS typical of merchants and others engaged in smaller businesses to feel they cannot afford most of the things they would like to have. It seems to be a sort of complex with them. But as Henry Ford once said: "Every man feels much poorer than he really is." This is a good point to remember when selling to storekeepers. You have to anticipate this objection, by presenting what you may be selling in a way that will turn the price into a reason for buying. Very often this "can't afford it" feeling can be made the key point in a sales presentation and capitalized to advantage. This is especially true if you are fortunate enough to be selling a product which looks "expensive" but which actually costs much less than the prospect imagines he will have to pay for it.

Take the case of George Conrad, for example. He has developed a sure-fire plan of selling slicing machines around this very idea. When he enters a store he doesn't say a word, but lays a big broadside on the merchant's counter showing a colorful illustration of the slicing machine he is selling. He leaves the machine outside in his car.

"What do you think of that?" he asks his prospect, who in this case is the proprietor of a small meat market.

"It looks good," the butcher replies after looking at the colored advertisement for several minutes. "But I can't afford an expensive slicing machine such as that. It costs too much."

"But you need one, don't you?"

"Yes, but I'm not doing very much business and can't afford to lay out a lot of money for a slicing machine."

Conrad smiles, goes out to his car, brings in a sample machine, hooks it up behind the counter, and requests the butcher (who is still protesting that he can't afford it) to try the machine.

"Like it?" Conrad asks after a few minutes. "Certainly, but I simply can't pay . . ."

"I understand. This machine is a low-priced slicer, however, and looks and works just like the expensive ones. Guaranteed too. How much could you afford to pay in cash for a slicer?"

The butcher shakes his head. "The way business is, I couldn't go over $10."

"Well, if you can pay that much get out your money," is Conrad's standard reply. "This slicer will cost you only $7.50."

This is typical of the interviews Conrad has with grocers, butchers, and proprietors of lunchrooms, restaurants, delicatessens and taverns when he calls with his hand-slicing machine. It is this approach which is responsible for his averaging $75 a week for the past two years.

"This slicer looks like an expensive machine that costs a lot of money," declares Conrad. "It is a sturdy, rotary type slicer with a stainless steel blade adjustable to any thickness, so that it will slice ham as thin as tissue paper, or bread any thickness you desire. Before this came out, though, the average grocer and delicatessen proprietor had to pay around $150 for a slicing machine. Naturally, when they see this one, which looks every bit as good as the expensive machine and is quite as satisfactory, it is hard for them to believe it's not an expensive outfit. I let them think that. I let them build up as much resistance as they want toward paying a big price. Then, when I've finally got them to make a demonstration and admit the machine is good, I crash this opposition with the low-price offer. And I seldom lose a sale."

To those who like to sell to stores, a good slicing machine offers a real money-making opportunity. Conrad's commission on each sale is two dollars, and he has sold as high as eighty machines in one week. His average week, however, is about thirty-seven slicers.

■ ■

How to Sell "Tailored-to-Measure" Suits

IN THREE months, John Gleason "cleaned up" well over a thousand dollars from the sale of men's tailored-to-measure suits. But Gleason had been making little or no profit from his selling activity in the previous months. Indeed, as he himself put it, he was just another doorbell pusher. He had difficulty overcoming the objections raised by prospects. He had trouble finding men who were in a position to buy suits. And he experienced disappointment when getting in to see prospects. As a salesman, Gleason admits he wasn't so "hot."

To believe that he suddenly turned over a new leaf would be too much. He didn't. He did change some of his selling methods, however, and taught himself to be at ease with people. It was due to his willingness to let an older hand show the way, though, which enabled Gleason to climb into the big money-making class.

"Living in the apartment above was a salesman I greatly admired," explained Gleason. "This fellow was a polished, suave chap, who had been selling for years. When I got pretty well acquainted with him, I asked him for pointers on selling. It was difficult for me to understand all the points he made. At first I thought they were only theories so I did not take them seriously. I grew more and more discouraged. I mentioned this to him. 'I'm awfully sorry,' he said, 'I'd like to do something to help you.' 'You can if you wish,' I answered quickly. 'There's a lot that you could teach me, if you would make a call or two with me.' He agreed to do so.

"It was arranged to call on some prospects together. I made the first interview but didn't get very far. It was a call upon a doctor who got rid of me in a hurry. Outside the office, on the way to the next call, my friend was very thoughtful and made no comment. When I lost the second sale, he said softly: 'Let's drop down to the lunchroom and talk this over. You've made an effort to make two sales, and have avoided letting anyone know what you're trying to sell.' He made no further comment on the matter until we faced each other across a table in the lunchroom. Then he pointed out an obvious error in my tactics. 'When you got in to see those fellows, they knew you came to sell something. Why do you talk about representing a large responsible house selling high quality merchandise? Why not try to sell them a suit? These men are busy. They know what they want, when they see it. Cut the introduction and get down to business.'

"'You've got to begin, you know,' I said in defense.

"'Sure you do,' he retorted. 'That's my point. Begin at once. When we go to see your next prospect, I'll give you an idea of what I mean.'

"Half an hour later, we entered the office of a real estate dealer. 'I'm offering some of the greatest suit bargains you ever saw,' said my friend, but the realtor shook his head. 'That's a fine looking suit you're wearing. Isn't it one of our twenty-two fifty line?'

"'Nope,' replied the realtor, 'I bought this in a store.'

"My friend moved over to the prospect and closely examined the man's coat. 'Hmm,' he murmured, 'that is certainly a fine piece of goods, isn't it, Gleason?'

"I stepped up and admired it. The realtor smiled. 'Let me show you the same goods here—' and my friend held out his hand as a sign for me to show a sample. I opened my case and brought out a sample swatch. Quickly this was placed in the prospect's hand. A moment later he was fingering it.

"'Do you like your sleeves that short? They seem a trifle short to me,' my friend said critically.

"The prospect admitted the sleeves were a little short. I got my friend's idea at once. Quickly I measured the prospect's sleeve and marked it on the order blank. Then I went through the entire measuring series myself.

"After taking this prospect's measure, I asked him if he wanted us to have a suit made up for him. He hesitated, but my friend saved the situation.

"'Here's a fabric that certainly will make up beautifully, and it'll look fine on you.' The prospect was guided back to a consideration of fabrics once more. Finally his choice was narrowed down to two fabrics and soon the sale was closed.

"My friend pointed out the following errors in the method I had been using: (1) My opening arguments were not natural or interesting. (2) I did not tie up the prospect with the idea of owning another suit. (3) I did not show how good my suits were in comparison with those being worn. (4) I did not picture the prospect wearing the suit. (5) I was voiding all the previous interview by a negative suggestion at the close, when I should be writing the order.

"Closely following the tactics used by my friend brought results. I now sell an average of four suits daily, netting commissions of $12.95 a day which is better than $3,000 a year!"

Gleason calls on business men and workers in shop and office; he does not waste time on men who are not working. Calling at the factory entrances of plants about lunch time enables him to make a demonstration to a group of men and arrange evening appointments at the homes of those interested. He sells from a sample. The order blank is so arranged that anyone can easily follow the directions for taking the accurate measure for a suit. The deposit, made by the prospect at the time the order is taken, is the salesman's commission. The balance is collected C.O.D. by the manufacturer when the shipment is made.

To sell clothing successfully does not require selling experience of any nature. It does require a sales plan and some initiative in working the plan. Many made-to-measure tailoring companies, selling their suits through direct salesmen to the wearer, supply detailed instructions for salesmen.

■ ■

The Right and Wrong Way to Sell Nursery Stock

WILLIAM WERNER got his first thousand dollars from trees. There were financial worries in the Werner household, and the need of additional cash led Werner, who clerked in a men's furnishing store, to sell nursery stock in his spare time.

"One day," he said, "I happened to mention my nursery line to a teller in the bank. He was building a new home and wanted a few trees and shrubs. But he cooled off when I said that our stock was small and that it took some years for the trees to grow big. 'What will they look like then?' he asked. I tried to explain and he said he would think it over. When I called back, he was still in doubt whether to buy from me or from a local greenhouse. 'The greenhouse man has such a beautiful story about how nice and shady a fir tree would be in one year that he has almost sold my wife. But if you want to tell your story to her, it's all right with me.'

"When I called at the teller's home, I asked his wife to step into the yard and look at the old brick wall of the apartment house they were living in. Then I tried to picture to her how much more attractive that bare wall would be with English ivy clinging to it, and the foot of the wall gay with flowers. This seemed to make an impression on her. We talked a lot about the different kinds of bushes and shrubs. She preferred lilacs, it developed, and said she always liked the scent of the lilacs in the air. I kept telling her about the way the place would look when it was finished and the shrubs and bushes planted and fully grown.

"I got an order for $207 before I left, but it took me from two that Sunday afternoon until six-thirty to get it. My commission was $29. Elated, I wrote the firm about the way I made this sale, and got back a letter containing some very good advice. This letter complimented me highly, and said: 'Always remember that when people buy nursery stock, they expect definite results. It's results they want, not a tree a foot high. Sell them results.' I've thought about that many times since. The other day, when I was talking to a farmer about buying 100 apple trees of a new variety, I knew he wanted to know how many apples the trees would bear. I pictured a whole orchard for him, with fruit hanging on the trees. Of course, he realized as well as I did that the trees would be tiny when he planted them, but he knew they would grow big with the passing of time, and that eventually they would bear fruit. He wanted to see a vision of results, and I helped him see the vision.

"Merely to quote prices on berry bushes, fruit trees, shrubs and other nursery stock would never get an order for me. Most people, I've discovered, are totally lacking in imagination. They are able to picture a thing only when it is shown to them. It is up to me to do their imagining for them. Orders vary in size, and the commission varies greatly, of course. I sell every kind of shrub, and sell in quantities of from one tree for the backyard of a city dweller to a whole orchard of perhaps a thousand. The first six weeks after I sold that banker's wife, I earned commissions well over $1,200."

Werner, after this success, left his regular position and devoted all his time to selling nursery stock. He makes many calls, but succeeds in interviewing only seven prospects in an average day. The commission earned on each sale he has made since he started selling nursery stock is $9.10 an order. He averages two orders daily. His commissions are paid to him weekly, as orders are verified, this being the nursery's established policy. This policy does not apply to all nurseries. Some concerns insist the salesman collect his commission in the form of a deposit, at the time the order is given. Prospects are found everywhere, in small towns and big cities, suburbs, and rural districts. Some nursery salesmen make a practice of calling at regular intervals upon county school boards, playgrounds, churches and like places, where there is frequent demand to replenish or replace trees and shrubs. No money is needed to start in this profitable field.

Selling Frocks Brings Back Prosperity

WHEN S. P. Liest lost his job, his family became panicky. They had no savings, and the prospect of Liest getting another job quickly was remote. But his plucky wife did not despair. She had read about a manufacturer of women's frocks who appointed agents to sell his products. She wrote to him asking for a local agency, and presently received a number of style cards and a selling kit, with some practical suggestions for getting started. The plan was to call upon housewives in their homes. Determined to make money the first day, Mrs. Liest started out.

"I was lucky on my first call," Mrs. Liest declared. "When I approached the door I felt the porch would open up and swallow me, I was so frightened. When the prospect opened the door and smiled good morning, I couldn't talk, and I believe if I hadn't been so desperate for money, I might have quit right there. This prospect was very gracious, however. She seemed to feel sorry for me. She asked me to step inside, and by degrees I recovered from my stage fright. Then I started to talk about the frocks, and the dresses I was selling just as though I were visiting a friend. We talked styles and colors and fashions. I showed her the style cards, pointing out that they featured the latest Parisian fashions, and that she had probably seen similar designs in a current woman's magazine. We got the magazine and compared the style features of my frocks with those illustrated in the publication, and I soon forgot I came to get that woman's order, having become so absorbed in talking about clothes. When she presently told me that she would take each one of three numbers the manufacturer was pushing, I was not a little surprised. My commission, $4.30, was the exact amount of the deposit required, the balance being collected by the manufacturer C.O.D. I was elated. I didn't make another call that day. I hurried home, stopping at the grocery on the way to get things for dinner, and entered the house loaded with bags of groceries."

Mrs. Liest was not so successful the next day, however. She made several calls, but failed to get an order. Analyzing that day's selling effort made her wonder why it had seemed so easy to make her first sale. "I couldn't help believing that my first sale was prompted by the charity and kindness of my first prospect," Mrs. Liest pointed out, "and that was disappointing, but the more I thought about it, the more inclined I was to change this view. I saw after some time, that when I started out I didn't make a conscious effort to get an order. I talked dresses and dress styles. I was just one woman talking to another woman about clothes. This touch, present in the first interview, was lost in those that followed, and I was making a stilted, unnatural effort to build interest. I changed my method. Now when I call to see a woman about frocks, I talk as most women would talk about clothes. I get my selling points over in this way, and it's natural. I make a point to wear my sample, and the prospect then can visualize the way it hangs and looks when being worn. I ask the prospect to note the depth of the hems, the French seams, the latest style features, and the washable guarantee that is sewn into each frock. In this way I build the prospect's interest to the buying point."

During her first nine months, Mrs. Liest made a profit well over $1,000 from frock sales. Commenting on this, she said: "All I do is talk woman to woman about clothes." She was not required to invest in a sample kit or style cards. Her entire selling outfit was furnished by the manufacturer. She makes an average of thirty calls a day, and sells not less than four frocks daily, on which her commissions total $5.17. Mrs. Liest has had days when she sold as many as fifteen frocks, and more than one day she has sold from ten to thirteen. She has found that the best time for calling upon housewives is between nine-thirty in the morning and three-thirty in the afternoon.

Because women like to talk about clothes, they willingly admit the representatives of dress and frock manufacturers who call at their door. You may readily become a representative for such a manufacturer who sells on the C.O.D. plan. The deposit, or initial payment, made at the time the order is taken, is retained by the salesperson as the commission on the sale. The balance is collected C.O.D. when the parcel post shipment is made.

■ ■

A Good Way to Sell Radios

ENTERING the lobby of a small hotel frequented by salesmen and guests who resided there permanently, James Winton placed a radio on the clerk's desk and said to him: "May I connect this to a light socket? No ground, no aerial is necessary."

The clerk obligingly permitted Winton to connect the radio and several men in the lobby gathered around him out of idle curiosity. In a few moments a local station was tuned in and music floated over the heads of this group, across the lobby. For some minutes Winton contented himself with a demonstration of the radio, moving its volume control from a whisper to a loud clear tone, without saying a word. When he felt that he had secured the undivided attention of his audience, he took a punch board from his brief case, and addressed the men in the lobby.

"This radio retails for twenty-nine fifty," said Winton.

"It is one of the best small sets you can buy. The fellow who punches the right number gets it." He extended the board to one of the men, and in

41

ONE THOUSAND WAYS TO MAKE $1,000

less than thirty minutes, the board, passed from one to another, was completely punched out. A guest in one of the rooms on the third floor started away with the radio, smiling. Winton, pocketing the proceeds, suggested to the clerk that he take a punch board. "You keep 25 per cent of what you take in on the board," said Winton, "and the radio will be free." The clerk agreed, so Winton left a board with him and then went on to his next call.

"I made twenty dollars profit on that first punch board in the hotel," said Winton. "On the board left with the clerk, I made five dollars. I delivered the radio when the board was punched out. The radios were sold to me at the usual discount to dealers by the manufacturer, so I had a nice profit from those two boards. But small hotels are not the only places where I sell radios. You'd be surprised at the number of barber shops, cigar stores, billiard halls, and other places of this nature where you can put in these radios and do a nice business. Some of the more popular barber shops, lunchrooms, and recreation parlors use as many as three boards weekly. I had a little difficulty getting the hang of lining them up at first though. I thought it was only necessary to sell the proprietor or a clerk. I was fooled. You have to show them how to make money on the board. That's why I connect the radio first. No one is interested in a demonstration that doesn't demonstrate. They want to hear the radio as well as look at it. My present method proves the money-making possibilities to the clerk and shows the crowd just how good the radio is."

Winton pointed out that trying to talk up the sale isn't effective with him. He buys his radios from a wholesale company, specializing in this type of radio distribution, and during his first four months his profits were well over a thousand dollars. He builds up his business by establishing an "agent" in a barber shop, pool room, or tavern, in the manner described above. Each agent, so appointed, uses between three and six boards monthly. He pays for the boards and the radios he uses when delivered by the wholesaler, and the cost of the first radio is the extent of his original investment. This amounts to twelve dollars.

It is possible for anyone who will really work to make a good profit supplying the hotels, restaurants, lunchrooms, cigar stores, drug stores, barber shops, and billiard halls with this sales plan. By making about twenty calls on prospects daily, Winton averages over nineteen dollars a day when he is working.

A Storeless Shoe Business

WHEN J. W. Hawkins, of Cleveland, Ohio, who had been representing a wholesale shoe company for twenty years, had his territory taken away from him, he decided to turn his knowledge of the shoe business to his own advantage. He made a connection selling shoes direct to the wearer and five months later he had earned a thousand dollars.

"I simply took advantage of a situation with which the trade is familiar," Hawkins said. "Every experienced shoe salesman knows people have only a vague idea of the size of their shoes. You'd be surprised to know how many times the average person buys ill-fitting shoes in his lifetime, believing he is properly fitted. That's because it's impossible for a shoe store to keep a complete stock of sizes, widths, styles and colors of the lines it handles, all of the time. When the store is out of the proper size, the clerk substitutes a size close to it, and the average person doesn't know the difference.

"I have trained myself to tell at a glance if a person is properly fitted. Prospects, wearing ill-fitting shoes, usually complain of being hard to fit and doubt that I can give them shoe satisfaction. I tell them: 'I guarantee the fit. If they don't fit, you don't pay.' Shipment is made C.O.D. but I make certain to call up my customers about the time their shoes arrive. I know there won't be a substitution as my orders are filled at a wholesale warehouse."

It took about four weeks before people became fully aware that the shoes Hawkins sells would actually be better fitting than store shoes. He sold his first order to an engineer of a railroad, and the engineer was so pleased that he told his fireman. When Hawkins called back upon the railroad man, he had two orders waiting for him. The fireman bought, so did one of the trainmen. Later he got orders from thirty-three men working in the railroad yards, all traceable to the first order. Meanwhile, he called upon a local foundry and machine company, and got an order there from the foreman. When this man received his shoes, he phoned Hawkins.

"I've never had a better fitting pair of shoes," the foreman declared, and Hawkins was told to call back later. He received orders for sixteen pairs of shoes on this one call. Hawkins makes an average commission of one dollar and twenty-five cents on a pair of shoes, which he collects in advance. The shoes retail at less than three dollars. The commission is deducted from this price and the balance is collected on delivery by the mail-carriers. Hawkins carries no stock of shoes, but sells from a sample. A special order blank measure supplied by the company assures accuracy in getting the proper size.

"It doesn't take long to learn the knack of fitting, and when you get the knack and sell a man a pair of shoes that fit him, he will gladly recommend you. Most of my sales come that way. From my first fifteen sales, I have obtained ninety-seven orders. It took about two weeks for my first order to be delivered. After that first two weeks, it was plain sailing. It was almost four weeks before I got a real break in repeat business, and up to that time I only sold twenty-nine pairs of shoes. Then, orders piled up fast."

Hawkins declares it is possible to get orders from women and men on a straight canvass every day. He, however, specializes on selling men's shoes, and calls only on men who are working in factories, shops and offices. While he makes few calls—about fifteen a day—he does a large volume of business.

■ ■

James Horner Became a "Premium Specialist"

IT IS human nature for the average person to want something for nothing James C. Horner knew that and decided he could make a thousand dollars easier selling premiums to merchants than he could by doing anything else. And this belief seems to be justified by his results. His success is due to the plan he uses which is so simple and practical that it is surprising others have not tried it.

"The plan," explained Mr. Horner, "is to call upon the best merchant in town. I give him about two hundred coupons to start and also some printed signs for the windows, circulars to he given store customers, and a sample premium for display purposes. The merchant gives out these coupons with five-, ten- or twenty-five-cent purchases, and when the customer has saved up a certain number, she is given a premium. The success of the premium as a business stimulator depends upon its quality—it must compare favorably with items of the same sort which are sold in the store and it must be something the housewife wants but feels she can't afford to buy at the regular retail price. Offering premiums that do not meet these requirements won't develop much business for you. I usually suggest electric clocks or silverware. The clocks come in radio, mantel and wall-clock styles and have proved to be particularly good business stimulators.

"When the clock premium idea gets under way, I secure a surprising amount of repeat business from the stores. Frequently they re-order twenty-five or thirty clocks at a time. After the clock premium has been used for a while, I suggest that it be followed by another premium, such as silverware. A good quality silverplate can be given in the same way as the clocks, and those store customers who have had clock premiums, begin saving for silverware. This keeps them trading at the store and builds up a steady business for the merchant.

"I call back upon each merchant several times, not only to keep him friendly but to show him the right way to use the premium. I have found practically no objection to premiums by the merchant. The idea, as every merchant knows, is essentially sound and about the best sales stimulator he can find. Many merchants, I point out in my sales talk, have found that the use of premiums saved their business from suffering serious losses during the worst periods of the depression. The public's popular acceptance of the premium principle bears out this contention and helps me close orders. I call on the smaller towns exclusively. I don't object to cities, but it takes too much of my time waiting to see the store manager in a city store."

Horner works in Wisconsin. He calls on the stores in Watertown, Madison, Kenosha, Racine and Janesville. He restricts his premium deals to one store of each kind, and his commissions average seventy dollars weekly from calls on twenty stores a day. Every merchant feels the necessity of increasing his sales, and is ready to listen to you when you call to tell him about a method that will bring in new customers as well as keep old customers coming back. Premiums can be used by the filling station, drug store, small department store, variety store, jeweler, grocery, meat market, hardware dealer and restaurant. You need no capital to start. Companies which make a business of supplying premiums will send you the full details of their plan, and its sales possibilities.

■ ■

$1,000 from Selling Fire Extinguishers

IF YOU were to ask Frank DePries how to make a thousand dollars, he would answer without a moment's hesitation: "Sell fire extinguishers." That answer would be drawn from his own experience too, for DePries has made that much money in a six-week period. It was about two months after he became connected with the fire extinguisher manufacturer's organization that he set his record. During his first month he didn't earn much. He made a number of calls, but his percentage of sales was low. "Here was my trouble," said DePries. "I was calling upon people who were not good prospects. In addition, I had no selling experience when I started and was lost in a maze of conflicting notions about selling. Soon I discovered I wasn't getting anywhere. My earnings were sometimes five, sometimes ten dollars a week. There were two weeks when they didn't total twenty dollars. However, I decided that if someone else could make big money, I could.

"I knew I was selling about 50 per cent of the prospects that had a use for the extinguisher, but nine out of every ten people I called upon had no real use for it. Many calls and interviews, therefore, were a waste of time. One night I discussed this situation with my wife, and she said the sensible thing to do would be to call only on prospects that needed an extinguisher. This had not occurred to me, but it sounded good, so I spent the next day studying the classified telephone directory and made up a list of firms which I believed needed extinguishers. I listed twenty-seven firms in one business district. These calls were fairly close together, and I routed them so I wouldn't waste time going from one to the other. That day's commissions totaled thirty-six dollars."

DePries sets a quota of twenty-five calls a day. Out of these twenty-five calls he averages sales of twelve fire extinguishers. This does not mean that he sells twelve different concerns, for one small factory may give him an order for ten or twelve extinguishers. There was one week when his commissions amounted to a little over three hundred dollars, and in one ten-week period he earned nearly a thousand dollars in commissions.

DePries concentrates his calls on small factories, wholesale houses, warehouses and garages. Fire insurance underwriters have approved the extinguisher he is selling, and, as a consequence, he is able to point out to prospects that possession of his extinguisher will reduce the cost of their fire insurance.

The company which manufactures the equipment which DePries sells does not require experienced salesmen, nor does it demand a cash investment from salesmen. Any ambitious man or woman may make a salesman's connection with the organization.

■ ■

A Business Selling Mending Fluid

WHILE visiting a friend, Dwight C. Ritchie, of Pablo, Montana, noticed a tube of mending liquid lying on a table. "What's that for?" asked Ritchie. "Why, it's for mending small holes in shirts and socks. It's great stuff. Takes but a minute to mend a tear, or a hole in a silk stocking," the friend replied. Ritchie made note of it. He wasn't married and had to mend his own clothes, so he bought a tube. Later he wrote to the manufacturer, and requested a connection as a local representative. Never having sold house-to-house, he found much to learn in the first few weeks of his new job. However, he soon learned the importance of a good demonstration and before long, his earnings from daily sales were averaging around twelve dollars.

Ritchie's sales averaged six dozen daily. There were days when his sales ran between ten and twelve dozen tubes, from which his profit, clear of all expenses, was as much as twenty-two dollars. He didn't have an easy time, however. He admits being lucky the first few days for, as time went on, problems of many kinds confronted him which made selling difficult.

"A product people want, and have a daily need for, is important. More important, however, is the way it's sold," Ritchie said frankly. "I knew the product was all right. I experienced difficulty convincing many others, until I began to sell systematically. When I tried to sell one woman, living on a farm just out of town, she told me she had no money but as I was willing to accept farm products in payment I suggested that she trade one of her chickens for two tubes. Another woman lacking money offered to trade eggs.

"Many have to be shown what the product will do. So I have a demonstration book which I use when making a brief demonstration. To this demonstration book, I add such items from current magazines and newspapers as will help clinch sales. In this book I also carry pieces of silk stockings, cotton cloth, linen and other fabrics, which I have repaired with this product. Turning to pages of this book, I point to these fabrics and remark: 'When you get a run in a silk stocking just touch a little mending fluid with a toothpick or a broom straw to the top and bottom of the run, and if you want to patch it, you can do so in one-fourth the time.' I clinch my points like this: 'You see you can make repairs much quicker and better than with needle and thread,' and when the prospect nods agreement, I go on. 'Now, you'll want two or three tubes. The price is twenty-five cents.' I hold out the tubes. Few women turn me down. Many take three, and some buy as many as four tubes. Others just take one. So many women say, 'No, I don't want anything,' when they open the door. At first this remark would stop me. Now I answer. 'That's all right. I just want to show you how to stop a run in silk hose.' My demonstration starts from there."

Ritchie is a hustler. Making an average of sixty-seven calls daily keeps him on the go from early morning until almost dark. But he declares that if you want to make money you have to get out and work for it.

To get started with a small specialty, such as Ritchie is selling, requires no capital investment. The product may be sold anywhere. A search for many new uses for the product broadens the possibilities of its sales, and is rewarded by increased profits.

Selling Protection Against Death

IN DENVER, Colorado, T. J. Devers startled his friends when he earned a thousand dollars in five months by selling memberships in a mutual benefit association. When he started, Devers was broke. He had answered an advertisement and received instructions on how and where to get new members. Devers thought little of the "canned sales talk," as he styled it, which the company sent him. However, he did need cash badly, and since the proposition offered a way to get it, he decided to give it a chance.

"Don't let anyone tell you it was easy," he said, talking about his first sale. "It was anything but easy to find a man who was willing to pay five dollars to join this benefit association. That membership fee, collected at the time the application is made out, was my commission. At first I made the mistake of overselling my prospects. I was talking with an old man and promising him everything I could think of, when he said sharply: 'Young fellow, you're a liar. You might sell me if you'd stop lying and tell the truth.' I said, 'All right. I'm starting out with this proposition. I don't believe you're in good health. If you are, and you want to join this association, sign the application and give me five dollars.' He didn't sign. He said no doctor in the county would say he could live more than a week, but if I saw his son, I might get an order. Although I had no assurance the boy would buy, I located him, explained that his father sent me, and this time, told the truth about my company. The boy took one of my policies, and paid me the initial membership fee. That was my first sale. I had learned one important thing. That was the importance of telling the truth about the mutual benefit policies. Later on, I learned another and that was to learn all there is to know about the policies and the protection they provided. I spent almost seven weeks learning everything I needed to know about them. Meanwhile, I wasn't selling many memberships.

"As time passed, though, I became convinced that I could sell them. The thing that was holding me back was not knowing where to find prospects who needed protection. Usually, the man who is able to carry old line insurance is not a prospect for mutual benefit policies. But those who have been forced by circumstances to drop their old line policies are in need of some protection. The mutual benefit plan is a godsend to them, inasmuch as the cost of this protection is relatively small, compared with the cost of regular life insurance. These benefit policies require no medical examination, and pay benefits up to a thousand dollars. The monthly cost is only one dollar, which most people can afford to pay.

"I struck up an acquaintance with an old line insurance solicitor one afternoon, and we talked about business. He told me that many of his customers were forced to give up their big policies, and were carrying only small industrial policies. That made me curious to see these people. I asked him if he would tell me the names of a few new lapsed policies on his debit, and he did this readily. I called on them. Being careful not to say anything that would be looked upon as knocking the old line company, I explained that this mutual policy was actually replacing the larger old line insurance in many instances, where the family could not afford to keep up their premiums. I then pointed to the low cost, and the safety features of the benefit policy I was selling. I sold each one of them and in a day or so called back offering two dollars commission for each policy I sold to friends they recommended. They took advantage of my offer and gave me the names of friends and relatives. Within a week I had signed up fifty-four memberships from those recommended. These in turn recommended a number of others and within a short while I had all the prospects I needed."

■ ■

Unique Cigarette Dispensing Humidor

"**I MADE** my first thousand dollars placing cigarette humidors in apartment hotels and homes," Charles Dagmar told a Dartnell staff writer in search of money-making ideas to include in this book. "Since both women and men smoke cigarettes these days, I figure making an average sale of two packs of cigarettes daily from each humidor. At an average profit of four cents this pays a good return on my investment. Getting locations for these home humidors is no more difficult than getting locations for any coin machine. There is this difference, however, you don't pay any commission to the owner of the location.

"When the home humidor first came to my attention, I thought it was a good idea. Carrying some photographs of the humidor with me, I called upon the owner of three big apartment hotels, and 'sold' him on the idea of letting me place a humidor in each apartment. 'It's a self-merchandising machine,' I argued, 'saves the tenant's time, and offers him the convenience of fresh cigarettes day and night. If he runs out of cigarettes he doesn't have to go out to the store to get them.' That argument, and the beauty and utility of the humidor, appealed to the apartment hotel owner. He said that he would have to place a piece of furniture in each apartment similar to the humidor anyway, and as long as he didn't have to pay anything for the use of the machines I could install them. In his hotels there are a hundred and four apartments and I placed a humidor in each. As my average profit is four cents on each package of cigarettes sold, my earnings run close to $375 monthly for these three hotels.

"These humidors are excellent pieces of furniture. They come in various styles such as end tables, occasional tables, telephone stands, magazine and newspaper racks and card tables. The humidor is so constructed that it keeps cigarettes fresh for an indefinite period. It can be loaded with fifteen packages of cigarettes, which are enough for the ordinary household at one time. If more than two in the family smoke I make two trips weekly and refill the humidor. Service is the keynote of success with this product. I take my money from the cash box on each trip.

"The convenience of the humidor is quickly apparent to the average man or woman who uses cigarettes. The favorite brand of the user may be placed in the humidor so that there is no objection to the cigarette itself. Almost everyone has had the experience of smoking his last cigarette late at night, during a party in the home, or while listening in on a distant radio program. I remind hotel men of this experience if any additional argument is needed to place the humidors."

Dagmar paid one-third cash and agreed to make a monthly payment of a small amount of his earnings for the humidors which, when bought in quantities, cost $13.50 each. He has placed these humidors in several apartment hotels and in many homes. There seems to be an unlimited field for this machine, especially in large cities where there is a tendency for families to live in small furnished apartments. There is also an opportunity to make money with this coin machine in the small community. Collections are made weekly, and a steady income is assured from each humidor, once placed.

■ ■

Selling Printing Specialties to Business Men

IT HAD been raining all morning, and when Johnson McCloud entered the office of a doctor in Akron, Ohio, he found the physician gloomily looking out the window at the rain. "Nasty weather, isn't it!" commented Johnson. "A day like this is a good day to write letters to delinquent patients." Turning from the window, the doctor nodded, moved to his desk and slumped into a chair. He waited for the doctor to say something, but he remained silent. Johnson opened his portfolio, and produced an assortment of sample letterheads. "What do you think of these?" he said, handing them to the doctor. The doctor admitted the letterheads were good. "I couldn't use anything quite so expensive, however," he said evasively, "there's no need for it in this business. I use only a few cards, envelopes, bills, and letterheads and I get those from one of my patients who is a printer."

"It's a good idea to patronize the local printers. However, I think you'd be surprised to know how little it would cost to print up your letterheads and give you a better quality. My house specializes in standard forms. We handle big runs of job stuff too, and some small runs, where we can work them in, but the prices I can quote on letterheads, billheads, cards and envelopes will surprise you."

Meanwhile, the doctor was considering the paper stock of the letterhead. His attitude was that of a man bent upon killing time, rather than that of a person keenly interested. The price, evidently, didn't seem so much of a factor. Johnson watched him closely. He handed him an envelope. "Feel that paper!" The doctor took it and nodded. "What do you pay for your letterheads, may I ask?" inquired Johnson. "Oh, I don't know exactly. Offhand, I'd say it wasn't much. Two and a half, or maybe three dollars a thousand. My, but it's raining."

Johnson ignored the doctor's last comment and handed him a third printing sample. "Do you order in quantities of five or ten thousand?" he inquired. "Lord no! Five hundred or a thousand is about all I need." "Fine," said Johnson, "now, which of these sample papers do you like best? Some prefer a high-grade tinted stock; others like a heavy white paper like this. I can fix you up with this stock, a thousand letterheads and envelopes to match, with your name and address printed as on the samples in bold, modern-faced type, for $20.90—and that price includes both the letterheads and envelopes. That represents a saving of about two or three dollars on these two items. Shipped express collect from the plant. You pay me only a small deposit now and the balance when the job is delivered."

"How do I know that I'll get this same quality printing?" the doctor demanded. "Here is the guarantee," replied Johnson, "it covers everything. See? It's printed on your receipt. I'll leave it with you—it's a part and condition of the order."

Johnson McCloud left that doctor's office with a small order and a recommendation to three other physicians with offices close by. That day he sold $57.00 worth of printing and his commission amounted to $17.11. During the first six months at this work, Johnson's commissions totaled $1,400. While it may seem that he must have made some rather large sales to earn commissions such as these, he claims that all of his sales were made to men who ordered in relatively small quantities.

"My orders vary in size," he said, "some being as low as $1.50, others up to $35.00 or $40.00. I've never had an order for more than $45.00. Commissions vary on this line, and on some jobs I make more money than on others. My efforts are concentrated on business men, but I never overlook a store, restaurant, factory, doctor, lawyer or dentist. I had some

ONE THOUSAND WAYS TO MAKE $1,000

difficulty during my first two months in finding just how to approach my prospects, but I solved this problem slowly. I have found almost every prospect I call upon requires a slight variation of selling method, and that a standard sales talk or method of approaching prospects does not do the trick. There are basic fundamentals, however, that apply to every case. It is important to place samples in the prospect's hands quickly after getting in, and keep him fingering samples throughout the interview. If you can focus the prospect's attention on samples and keep it there, you will usually sell him."

Johnson McCloud never brings up a subject which may cause the prospect to think of anything but the sale under consideration, during the interview. Selling standard forms, letterheads, billheads, envelopes and circulars is made easy because there are a number of concerns, with special machinery, which can handle such orders at unusually low prices. The quality of such printing generally is higher than that of a local printer and the cost to the prospect is much less. These are two strong arguments which can usually be depended upon by the salesman to close sales quickly.

■ ■

Bringing the Store to the Customer

CHARLES GRAVES pulled his green sedan to the curb, took a package containing a dozen towels from the rear seat, and hurried to the door of the white cottage. A woman answered his ring. Graves said: "You told me, Mrs. Markham, that if these towels were the size and quality I said they'd be, you'd order other goods. And I have some real bargains." Mrs. Markham invited Graves into the house. There she opened the package of towels and inspected them carefully. "They really are wonderful. And so cheap," she remarked.

"Certainly," Graves returned quickly, "and you'll find everything you buy from me is of the same high quality. Remember, Mrs. Markham, you don't pay for anything until I deliver it and you inspect it here in your own home. You see, I operate on a small profit from my car. I don't have the tremendous overhead a merchant has. And you know the merchant figures up his rent, light, wrapping paper, cost of fixtures, interest on money invested in the store and stock, taxes, and all that sort of thing, and adds that to the price of everything he sells. If he didn't he wouldn't make a dime. He's entitled to it. But I eliminate this cost, and pass the benefit on to you in the form of bigger values. Now here's something you'll appreciate: Picot topped, 320 needle silk chiffon hose. Silk from top to toe. A dozen to a box at only $5.20 a box. Can you beat that?" "That does sound reasonable," replied Mrs. Markham. The prospect feels the sheer silken material, mentally makes an effort to determine the price for each pair, and concludes it's about forty cents or a little over. And Charlie Graves is off on a new sale!

He's been selling merchandise in this way for three years. He makes a point of offering good quality at fair prices, and does a big business. During his first six months, he made a very good living and put almost a thousand dollars in the bank.

"I believe that you must merchandise to make money," Charlie declared. "I mean by that you must be able to show value and build a sales talk to make the most out of it. It is true that I sell most items under the regular store prices and that my costs are less. My profit runs a little higher on each sale, however, than the store operator's. That's because I've been buying from wholesalers who deal in bankrupt stocks. They buy up an entire stock of bankrupt goods at a price. They sell it at small profit to themselves, and turn over their money quickly. Seldom can they supply a variety of items that would enable a store operator to stock up on a line of one item large enough to interest most store people. But they have enough high quality merchandise for small fellows like me to keep going on. My big talking point, of course, is *price*.

"I use the 'sandwich' method of building up orders. When talking to a customer I ask what she is paying for, say, her husband's socks at the local department store. She tells me. 'I have a very fine sock that I know would please him, and the price is only $1.59 in dozen lots,' I say. 'What are you paying for towels? I mean the large-size Cannon turkish bath towels?' She tells me and I go on, 'I can sell you a package of one dozen Cannon bath towels, the large size, at $2.10 a dozen—less than twenty cents each.' These are two low-priced items in constant demand. I don't make much on them, but I make a good profit on most of the other items I carry. So after throwing two low-priced items out to catch interest, I whip in a profit maker. Say it's soap. I get this hand soap, a regular ten-cent item, at one and a half cents a cake, and offer it at four for a quarter. Then I mention another profit maker, such as a house dress. After that, I mention a low-priced leader item, and by that time the prospect has the impression that every item I have is very inexpensive. That's what I mean by merchandising the goods."

Some of Graves's orders run as high as $30.00, and his average is $4.75. His average profit is $1.69 an order. Graves has built up a regular route, calls on this route once every three weeks, and makes an average of twenty-three calls daily. He closes orders in twelve out of the twenty-three homes he calls upon, and his daily earnings average close to $19.00.

His entire equipment consists of his stock, in which his original investment was $50, and the car he drives, which cost him $300 at a used car lot. You can build up a business as profitable as that of Graves in your own community with a small investment.

■ ■

How Cord Earned His First $1,000

E. L. CORD, president of the Cord Corporation, who built up the Auburn Automobile Company, and is the directing head of many important business enterprises, made his first money rebuilding Ford cars.

He bought a $75 second-hand Model T Ford. He geared it for high speed, added a homemade racing body, gave it a coat of paint and sold it for $675.

The plan worked so well that he bought twenty Fords, put them through the same rebuilding process and sold them all for an average profit of $500 per car.

Of course, this opportunity is gone today. But there are other similar opportunities. Second-hand goods of all kinds are constantly being traded in on new goods. Washing machines, radios, vacuum cleaners are frequently traded in long before their life usefulness has ended. A few new parts, a coat of paint or enamel will put them into a salable condition.

There's a real opportunity in almost every town or city for the man who is mechanically inclined, who has a few tools and isn't afraid to get his hands dirty, to make a good living reconditioning second-hand household equipment.

Almost every dealer who takes in second-hand equipment offers a pitifully small allowance on it. To get rid of it he is often willing to sell it for just what he paid. At times even less. There is a steady market for rebuilt and reconditioned household equipment. Hundreds of people who do not want to pay the price of new equipment are good prospects for rebuilt equipment.

All you need to start is a few tools and one second-hand machine, such as a washer, vacuum cleaner or refrigerator. The first step is to take the equipment apart, clean it thoroughly, replace worn and broken parts, refinish where needed. Then you are ready to make your first sale. Offer your first rebuilt piece of equipment to your next door neighbor. If he doesn't buy, offer it to the next nearest neighbor, and so on until sold. As you make each sales call, ask them if there is some other piece of equipment in which they are interested. After you have made a few calls, you will have taken orders for some other equipment which you can buy second-hand, rebuild and sell. Some men who have tried this plan have orders for all the rebuilding they can do for weeks ahead.

A safe plan to follow is to add the cost of the equipment and the cost of all the parts and materials to a fair price for your time and labor in rebuilding. Then add 50 per cent to this figure to arrive at your selling cost. Thus, if you paid $7.50 for a used washing machine, spent $3.25 for new parts, enamel, etc., and two days' labor, your price would be, figuring your labor at $4.00 a day, $7.50, plus $3.25, plus $8.00. This totals $18.75. Add 50 per cent and your selling price is $28.12. This would leave you a gross profit of $9.37, after paying yourself $4.00 a day for your work. Some rebuilders pay a commission of 20 or 25 per cent to others for selling. To do this, you should double your costs after paying yourself wages. For example, on the washer which cost, including your labor, $18.75, the selling price would be $37.50, which would carry a 20 per cent commission for selling. This price would net you $30, or a profit of $11.25. The extra profit is to pay you for the time your salesmen will inevitably take up, and the necessary help you will be forced to give them.

■ ■

Using Old Customers to Get New Ones

CHARLES ANGLE, of Milwaukee, Wisconsin, raised his extract business from an ordinary $20-a-week enterprise to one which paid him $4,000 annually by developing a customer cooperation plan among women who bought extracts. It is a plan that might solve your problem, just as it did his.

Mr. Angle explained his plan as follows: "There isn't a big profit in extract sales. My special four-bottle deal, selling for ninety-nine cents, with a generous-sized package of dessert thrown in free, is a quick seller. However, there is only a thirty-cent profit for the salesman. You have to sell a lot of these special offers to make any real money. I went along for a while up here in Milwaukee doing a big business but not getting much profit. Then I interested a woman in boosting my flavoring extracts to friends, promising her four bottles and the special dessert free for each five she sold for me. This worked out so well that I made the same offer to another woman living two blocks away. She promptly got busy on the telephone and turned in orders for 39 specials in less than a week. I rewarded her by giving her a pair of silk stockings in addition to the promised bottles of extract.

"After that experience, I made more effort to secure customer cooperation than I did to make direct sales. In two months, I had established 34 cooperating customers on this plan in the Milwaukee area, each of whom averaged 12 sales a week for me. I gave them some inexpensive prizes for their efforts.

"I have discovered that women will gladly do their best to recommend a worth-while product if they feel their efforts are appreciated. They like to believe you are not going to forget them. A card at Easter and Christmas was sufficient to line up several women who had fallen out of the habit of cooperating with me last year. One woman, who had been very active helping me get business, but who had given up for several weeks, was once more added to the active list when I sent her little girl a birthday card."

Angle has always been a hard-working salesman, but admits that without the cooperation of his women customers, he would never have climbed out of the small earning class. He points out that the cost of the gifts distributed to the women cooperators seldom exceeds one-third of the commission, an amount he can well afford to pay. He declares that were he to appoint these same women as subagents, however, they would not secure the same amount of business for him.

The extracts and flavoring Angle sells are of good quality. He buys at wholesale, and the bottles come in special containers. He is not required to buy any definite quantity to secure the wholesale price. The company supplying him gladly ships in any quantity, regardless of the size. For this reason, Angle, without capital, has been able to build up a good business. Today, there are 46 women boosting his sales in, and near, Milwaukee. They phone in their orders after five-thirty, when he returns home from making his canvass of the district. An average of two sales daily is turned in by these women, which, with Angle's personal sales, brings daily profits between $14 and $19.

■ ■

Antiques Are Coming Back

JACK OVERHAUSS drove a truck for a Chicago retail furniture dealer. One day he was instructed to take the truck over to a railway warehouse and pick up a spinning wheel, said to be an expensive antique the dealer had difficulty acquiring. Later when he unpacked the spinning wheel, Overhauss recalled having played with a similar spinning wheel, when a boy, in the attic of his mother's home at Jackson, Minnesota. He mentioned this to his employer.

"If you know where there's another spinning wheel like this and can get it for me," the dealer told him, "I'll pay you fifty dollars." Overhauss promptly replied he knew where there were at least a dozen near Jackson, and was told to get them. Overhauss went up to Jackson, inquired among his mother's neighbors about their spinning wheels, and in less than a week obtained seven at an average cost of four dollars each. Before returning to Chicago he secured a total of thirty-nine spinning wheels from residents of Jackson and surrounding territory, who were glad to dispose of them at the price Overhauss offered just to get them out of the way.

During his stay in Jackson, Overhauss kept on the alert for other items. While seeking spinning wheels, he noticed a number of articles in the attics and barns of the homes and farms he visited, such as flint lock pistols, flint lock muskets, bowie knives, bows and arrows used in Indian warfare, spears, hatchets, unique caskets, and other objects which had been kept by the families for many years but which no longer possessed sentimental value for their owners. Overhauss listed these articles and sent copies of the list to several furniture and antique dealers. Within a few days he received an order from one dealer for the entire lot and realized a profit of over $300.

Very little capital is required to make money from antiques. You can start this fascinating business right in your home community. In every town there are ten homes or more whose attics contain furniture and various articles collected over a period of years. Before buying any of these, make a list of every article you find that is worth while and send copies of this list to furniture manufacturers, furniture dealers, antique shops, and collectors in larger cities. When replying, the dealers will mention the amount they will pay for each article. Those who have prospects for the articles listed will gladly pay good prices.

While the demand for antiques fell off during the depression, it is coming back with the return of better times and the revival in building. During the period of prosperity we are now entering, thousands of homes are going to be remodeled and refurnished. Many of these home-owners will refurnish in the early American style, because of its charm and distinctiveness. This will bring back with a bang the demand for all kinds of antiques and those who tie in with this movement are bound to reap profits. It's an interesting business, too, and may lead to your becoming an interior decorator with a shop and factory of your own.

Sullivan's Collection System Portfolio

IN SEATTLE, Washington, H. J. Sullivan made $1,080 in fifty-three days. He did it by selling a collection system to local business men during the worst months of the depression. "My commission runs about two-thirds of the selling price," Sullivan said. "On a $7.50 unit I make a profit of $5.00, and on the higher-priced units the commission is relatively higher. My biggest advantage was my list of acquaintances. I knew most of the first 200 business men I interviewed, and had enough selling experience to understand how to handle prospective users of the system whom I didn't know personally. To clinch the sale after I had a man interested, I used a portfolio of letters of endorsement supplied by my firm. This portfolio was a gold mine. It contained hundreds of letters from business firms in every line of business, from a small grocery store or market to a big public utility corporation. These companies were located in every state in the Union.

"I was broke when I started out with this system, but it wasn't long before I was making real money. My first call was on a small factory where the owner knew me from the old days when I sold him merchandise. I said: 'I've got something here which I'm sure you'll agree is a mighty wonderful collection stunt. There are a number of concerns which owe you money you think you will never get. Well—look at this." I opened up this mammoth portfolio of reference letters and picked out the names of several leaders in his line of business. He read the letters—every word of them. There isn't a business man in the country who doesn't perk up with real interest when he sees what his competitors are doing. 'What's the system you are selling?' he asked. I explained it to him, pointing to my samples and letting him examine the entire method. 'If you collect only one old account with this method,' I said, 'the system will have paid for itself.' He agreed with me on this, and gave me his order. The commission on this sale was the easiest money I had ever made.

"My next six days were devoted principally to thinking up answers to objections. Then I saw that it wasn't an answer that was needed. These objections became selling points when properly analyzed. I hadn't been inquiring about the total amount of the prospect's bills receivable, but I changed my canvass a little, and early in the interview brought up that point. Most business men do not know how large an amount of money they have coming until they look at a balance sheet. Then they are a little surprised and often worried about it. When I'd ask a prospect what the total of his bills receivable amounted to, he generally called the bookkeeper and requested a statement. Intently he would consider that statement. 'I guess we should use some kind of system. How much did you say that one cost?' he would usually remark, and the order followed."

Sullivan pointed out that he doesn't make many calls in a day, since it often requires as much as an hour for his selling interview. He averages ten calls daily, however, and of these sells six, giving him a high percentage of closures. His commissions run better than $8.00 a sale.

Collection systems are much in favor during the present era of tight credits. While you may not make as much money as Sullivan did selling this system, it does offer an opportunity for the inexperienced man who prefers calling on business men in factory, office, shop or store. A store unit, declares Sullivan, runs about $7.50. The others are in larger amounts. The commission is either collected in advance, or the full amount of the order may be collected C.O.D. upon delivery, and the commission sent to the salesman.

■ ■

How the Waffles Sell Moth Tabs

JAY WAFFLES and his wife together earned twelve hundred and seven dollars in six months selling deodorants in and around Rockford, Illinois, and near-by small towns.

Waffles, forced to quit his job in a Rockford factory because of his health, was sent to Mayo Brothers Hospital in Minnesota, where, after several weeks' treatment, he was discharged. At home he didn't improve as well as was expected, and was told that a trip to California would hasten his recovery. Waffles hadn't enough money to make the trip. "We must get some money quickly," declared his wife. One day the following week they made a sales connection with a manufacturer of moth tabs.

"We sold a few moth tabs to our neighbors during the first week," said Mr. Waffles, "but not enough to increase our bank account. The usual excuse offered by most housewives was 'I have no money.' Every woman in town seemed to be just out of ready cash when we called. It stumped us. Mrs. Waffles would go down one side of the street and I down the other. We'd meet at the end of the block, and compare notes. 'There's nothing in it,' I said disconsolately one day. She didn't agree with me, and reminded me that the company had mentioned one man who had made a success. I said frankly that I doubted it. That night we were feeling pretty blue when we got home. We were eating supper when the doorbell rang, and Mrs. Waffles answered the bell. I heard her say to the man at the door, 'Not today, I have no money.' The salesman didn't seem to hear her at all. He went right on with his sales talk. She kept repeating over and over that she had no money, and finally he went away. When she rejoined me, she said:

'I think if he had remained another moment I would have bought from him. He certainly had a good-looking can opener.' 'Maybe people would buy from us, too, if we stood at the door a little longer,' I remarked absently, and she stared at me. 'That's just it. It must be!' she exclaimed. 'Do you know what? We don't make half as effective a sales talk as that man did. We must improve it.'"

The Waffles went into a huddle and came out with a brand new canvass. They tried it out on each other that night. Long after midnight, they retired and awakened the next morning enthusiastic over their new plan. "We'll check it as we go along," they decided. That morning's sales were better. Their combined profits amounted to six dollars and ninety cents. But better than that, they began to discover the weakness in their sales presentation. It was then that they started the habit of writing out what the prospect said, and what the Waffles answered after each interview. This took a little time and reduced the number of calls, but within a week it increased the percentage of sales to interviews from 10 per cent to 60 per cent. They saw another weakness in their method. They were carrying five items, the leaders of which were the moth tab, bowlitzer, and refrigerator deodorant. The three items together paid them a seventy-five cent profit. They had been talking up only one item. Now they found the way of selling the other two after getting the order for the one. The result was more income from every sale. In two weeks, they had increased their profit from six dollars a day to twelve dollars daily.

"If every woman who raised an objection were counted, I guess the total would include every woman in the country," declared Waffles. "Certainly they object. But a skillful turning of the objection and a little selling pressure will make them buy. I was told fourteen times by one woman that she didn't have any money in the house, but each time I smiled, agreed with her, and then pointed out how much money could be saved by using the moth tab. After ten minutes, she invited me inside to let me show her how easy it was to hang the tab in the clothespress. I told her, meanwhile, I did not expect her to buy a thing, but if she knew about the products, and wanted them later, she could phone me. I told her about a special preparation for keeping moths out of her overstuffed furniture and she led me to the living room to demonstrate. Here we sat down while she examined and bought every item I was selling."

Waffles makes the delivery of the products when he makes the sale, and collects the total selling price. He buys the deodorants from the manufacturer at a low rate and resells to his prospects at a good profit.

Possibilities of Industrial Uniforms

WHEN Chester Burton walked from the office of the White Front Service Stations, Inc., he had an order in his pocket on which his commissions totaled $69. That order, the result of an hour and a half interview with the purchasing agent and the general manager of a chain of 17 gasoline filling stations, was for 107 work uniforms, on the front and back of which the name "White Service Stations" was to be embroidered. It wasn't the first order Burton had taken. It was the second he had that day, the first being for a smaller number of garments from a local garage. It was typical, however, of the kind of money he was able to make selling industrial uniforms to gas stations, hotels, auto agencies, moving companies, dairies, factories, restaurants, druggists, laundries, bakeries, and offices where industrial uniforms have come to be considered a necessary thing.

It took Burton, who didn't have a moment's selling experience before he became connected with the manufacturer of these uniforms, exactly five months to earn his first $1,000.

"Don't think it was easy for me to get my first real week's salary out of this line. I puttered around with it for several days before I got the right idea. I called on prospective users of industrial uniforms, of course. I showed them the samples of materials and explained the methods used in making up the garments. I talked wear, strength and durability, and I didn't get to first base. Something, I thought, was wrong with me, with the line, or with the method I was using. Determined to find out what was wrong, I devoted my next three days to an exhaustive quizzing of buyers. And I found out why I wasn't getting business. In my desire to impress durability and wearing qualities, I had been making a comparison of my garments to overalls. I had completely overlooked one of the strongest selling points in connection with the uniform.

"These concerns do not want overalls. They want a uniform which looks neat, is properly styled, and in some cases, tailored, and which lends dignity to the appearance of the workman. Gasoline stations were particular on this point. 'Our men come in constant contact with the public,' I was told by a big chain buyer, 'and we must insist that they have an alert, snappy appearance in dress. An appearance that may be kept uniform in all stations is necessary to identify attendants of this company.' Here then, was the new idea I was seeking. I took the answers to my questions and made up a sales talk, using the buyer's own arguments and showing where my uniforms served every requirement. I photographed some gasoline service station attendants who were wearing the uniforms. I showed these photographs, together with drawings in my portfolio, to the buyers for other companies. I added photographs of doctors, druggists, and others to make the collection complete. I didn't pay a lot of money for these pictures, but took a small kodak with me everywhere I went. When I recognized one of our uniforms on an employee, I stepped up and got a snapshot.

"All this proved to be valuable when closing a sale. Some big companies want to see what a uniform looks like when a man is wearing it. I can quickly show a photograph, which is just as good as showing a uniform. They get the idea."

It might be pointed out that Burton finds little competition in his sales work, and has systematized his calls to make the most of his time every day. His average daily earnings are close to $17, and he calls on about twelve companies each day. There appears to be no real reason why any aggressive and ambitious person should fail to make money with this line.

■ ■

Five Dollars Starts Stamp Exchange

WHEN James Wallen was graduated from high school, he went out to look for a job, but jobs were scarce. So he decided to go into business for himself.

Rummaging around in the attic, he found in an old trunk a letter addressed to his mother. The letter was written back in 1870. The envelope bore a two-cent black stamp with a portrait of Andrew Jackson on it. He took the envelope (known to philatelists as a cover) to a stamp dealer and sold it for $5.00.

With the money thus secured Jimmy purchased a Scott's stamp catalog and three packages containing about three thousand mixed "missionary" stamps—that is stamps sent in to dealers by church missionaries from all over the world. Jimmy had long been interested in history and geography and found the stamps held a great fascination for him.

He conceived the idea of selecting one particular stamp and finding out everything he could about it. He wrote an interesting story about the man on the stamp. He then went to the history teacher in the local school and sold her the idea of using stamps to teach history. In that way he started a stamp "craze."

Jimmy tied in with the "fad" by getting five students to act as his agents to sell stamps to other boys. He went to a printer and had stationery and approval sheets printed with his name. It wasn't long before he had turned a large portion of the original three thousand stamps at a nice profit.

With this money he purchased a larger supply from a wholesale stamp house in Boston. He began putting up small packets of especially sorted stamps which he sold through several stores in town on a consignment basis. When these assortments failed to move fast enough, he changed them about until they did sell.

Jimmy now sends stamps to all parts of the country and a number of foreign countries. The number of his boy agents in near-by towns is constantly increasing. He has made his first thousand dollars and is on the way to his second thousand.

■ ■

A "Killing" on Carded Merchandise

WHILE talking with a customer about his regular line, Carl O'Neil, a cigar salesman, got an idea which enabled him to earn better than $1,000 within nine weeks! Just as the storekeeper stopped talking with O'Neil, a young man entered the store. The cigar stand proprietor asked him what he wanted. The young fellow took two display cards of five-and ten-cent merchandise from a sample case, and showed them to the cigar man. "There's 120 per cent profit on this card for you," said the newcomer, "these carded products sell themselves." One card was filled with envelopes containing aspirin, and the other had packages of razor blades attached. The lithographed cards invited the store patrons to serve themselves. There wasn't much of a sales talk needed to show the store man the advantage of an open display from which a customer could take small items without bothering a clerk. In less than two minutes, the cigar man bought one of each of the cards, paid the young salesman and returned to O'Neil who had been listening meanwhile. When the other salesman left, O'Neil made note of the name and address of the manufacturer of the carded products from the card left with the cigar man, and that night wrote a letter inquiring about the possibility of selling carded items as a side line.

"I got the connection right away," said O'Neil, "bought a few cards to carry with me, and decided to introduce them to my regular cigar dealers. Being acquainted with every cigar man in my county, I was sure I could make extra money which I badly needed. I had no trouble selling my first twenty-five cards, and reordered twenty-five more. The goods sold themselves from the cards in a store when they were displayed in the proper place.

"Usually I placed the cards where I knew they would attract attention. Sometimes the store man moved the cards around, however, and would complain that the merchandise didn't sell. Others said they had carried such merchandise, but hadn't been able to do much with it, and refused to buy. This complaint was pretty general for my first two weeks and held down my sales. But wherever the store man left my cards in a good spot in the store he sold a lot of this merchandise. That got me thinking. I couldn't force a store man to keep my card where I wanted it. But if I knew enough about displays, I could teach him to leave it where I put it. I studied store displays. A good place to put the card is close to the cash register. Another good place is on the top of the glass display case in which the low-priced cigars are kept. I told this to my customers and figured out for them in dollars and cents exactly what the value of this space was to them when they displayed my merchandise. The results were surprising to me. In less than a week most of my customers ordered additional cards and told me to place them where I thought they would do the most good."

O'Neil did so well that soon he gave up selling cigars and concentrated on the sale of carded merchandise. Loading his car with fifty cards each morning, he drove through the country, established regular routes, and placed cards with every kind of store. He makes ninety calls a day, and sells an average of one card for each two calls. His profit is never less than twelve dollars daily. During one stretch of nine weeks, he worked intensively on a plan to get merchants to display three cards where they had been displaying one and his commissions for the period were $1,019.20.

Inexperienced salesmen who do not relish house-to-house selling, may find calling on stores with carded merchandise unusually profitable. Cigar stands, drug stores, grocery stores, bus stations, railway stations, magazine stands, hotels, and restaurants offer a ready outlet for carded merchandise.

■ ■

"Taking a Chance" on Soap Wins for Fitze

CARL FITZE, a house-to-house soap salesman calling on housewives in Dayton, Ohio, uses what he calls a "gambling system" for getting business which has enabled him to earn handsome profits. The effectiveness of his selling method may be appreciated when it is considered that he started out with practically no capital, investing only one dollar and fifty cents for a supply of soap to start his business. When this was sold, Fitze took the entire proceeds and reinvested them in more soap, and pyramided his purchases until he had built up a large soap inventory. His first week was a disappointment. Most women, he knew, had enough money in the house to pay for a box of soap. The price he asked—thirty-nine cents a box—was reasonable for a box of soap, generally priced much higher.

Nevertheless, it took him two days to sell his first ten boxes, although he worked hard at the job.

"Wherever I called I was usually given the same story," he explained. "'I won't have any money until Saturday when my husband gets paid,' is what I heard many times each day, and I'd turn away from the door, to be greeted at the next door with the same 'reason.' On my third day as a soap salesman I told one woman who gave me that excuse, 'All right. I'll leave the soap now, and come back, say Monday. If you wish, you can pay me a small deposit now, or you can pay the entire amount Monday. Just as you prefer.' She thanked me, and said that would be all right, so I handed her a box of soap, wrote her name and address in a book, and went on to my next call. Here again, I met the same objection in the same way by leaving another box of soap. At the next three calls, however, my readiness to trust the housewife brought out the cash, and by early afternoon I had sold fifteen boxes of soap for which I was to collect later, and collected the full amount for ten more. I was then all out of soap so I took all the money I had collected to the company that supplies me with soap and reinvested it in a fresh supply. The next morning I used the same argument I had used the previous afternoon when women told me they had no money. Within two hours I left twenty-five boxes, fifteen of which were cash sales. Again I returned to the company and this time secured thirty boxes, which I disposed of before dark.

"When I called back to make collections for the soap on the following Monday, only one woman refused to pay me. My profit on the sales up to that time was forty-six dollars, so I could stand the few cents loss nicely."

Fitze continues to use his "system" with remarkable results. Each morning he starts out with a sack containing twenty-five boxes of soap, and along about noon returns to get another twenty-five. Sometimes he sells as high as seventy-five boxes a day. In one four-month period, he averaged a daily sale of sixty-two boxes and made over a thousand dollars. By making about ninety-five calls daily, Fitze averages around fifty sales. As his profit is twenty cents a box, he makes an average income of about ten dollars a day. The beauty about a business such as Fitze has built up is that he is dealing with necessities. Everybody uses soap. Everybody buys soap. They buy it in hard times, and they buy it in good times. It repeats, too, which makes it possible for a man to build up an established business quickly.

If you find in selling house to house that you are constantly running into the objection, "I have no money today," try Fitze's plan. Leave your product on the payment of a small deposit or, if it is an inexpensive item, without any deposit. About 99 per cent of the human race is honest and you probably will never have any difficulty collecting your money when you call back. And remember—it is one way to get past the door and to put your product into the customer's hands!

Every Man Wears Shirts

CLARENCE B. TRAVIS wondered how he could make $1,000. He found a good line of shirts which he sold direct to the wearer, and soon had the money he needed. Last month he put another $1,000 in the bank. Travis, who lives in Port Arthur, Texas, was disappointed at the beginning but once he developed the plan he now uses he began making money hand over fist.

"I won't say this plan differs materially from the plan of other fellows," said Travis. "I believe a good many men are using similar plans. In brief, it is to forget about the call, and think about a connection. Not long ago I called upon a prospect occupying an executive position in a cheese factory. He told me he had given an order to a direct salesman a year or so before, and was 'swindled' so badly he was determined never to buy from a house-to-house salesman again. All the other salesman had thought about was an order. The prospect said that he had to wait an unreasonable time before his order came and when it did arrive, his shirts were not as he had ordered. I admitted the justice of his complaint, but pointed out that because this one man had broken faith all others would not also. I didn't get his order then, but after many calls I succeeded in convincing him he would get his money's worth from me. That was sometime ago. Today he is a satisfied customer and has recommended me to many of his friends.

"Shortly after I started selling, I entered a local garage to see if I could interest some of the men in a medium-priced shirt. I was confronted by a hard-boiled, grim visaged superintendent who informed me I was wasting the men's time. Hurriedly I explained it wasn't my intention to interfere with his men, and that the error was undoubtedly due to my lack of experience. I then urged him to tell me when it would be convenient to return and interview them. I made a point of being very courteous to this fellow, and as I agreed that he was right, he calmed down a great deal, his gruff manner softened, and he asked me what I was selling. I showed the samples, explained and demonstrated them, and he gave me his order. Then he said that if I talked to only one man at a time, it would be all right. His men who had witnessed this scene were impressed by his purchase, and I left with orders for fifteen shirts. I tried this same idea half an hour later in the office of an express company with good results. That started me calling on industrial plants and offices, and led to many sales. While a majority of such calls resulted in firm turndowns, there are enough offices and factories where the foreman or superintendent will let me talk to the men to make this system profitable."

Travis makes most of his sales in units of three shirts. He carries shirts of various prices, however, and his commission varies between sixty-five cents and a dollar on each. Specializing on factories, offices, and stores, he maintains an average sale of fifteen shirts daily, although he only makes seven interviews a day. Some shirt salesmen concentrate calling on business and professional men, and carry socks, ties, and underwear as additional lines. The shirts, such as Travis sells, are made to measure from material selected by the prospect, and shipped C.O.D. The deposit, required when the order is placed, is retained by the salesman as his commission.

■ ■

Gifts for Young Men to Give to Girls

THERE are certain specialties manufactured today that open a wide range of money-making opportunities for men and women. Some of these are luxuries; others combine utility with novelty. George Lehman decided a cigarette case, which kicks out a lighted cigarette when you press a button, was a good money-making idea. His commissions from the sale of this lighter exceeded $1,000 in three months! Here is his story:

"This cigarette case appealed to me as one of the things many men would go for, but I'll admit that my first efforts to sell it were a washout. Everyone liked its appearance. They thought it was novel and all that, but they didn't seem to have the money to buy. Then I realized I was not calling on the right people. Those I talked with were men working on a small salary and barely making a living. I sought out younger men. One gave me a cue by buying a case for his 'girl friend' as a birthday gift, and she was delighted with it. He was so pleased that he phoned me and said a pal of his wanted one for his girl. I followed up the idea of selling the cigarette case to young men for gifts and began immediately to make money.

"I found that the fellow about twenty or twenty-five, who isn't married, likes to flash a novel cigarette case of this kind. No matter where you are, you're sure to have someone ask to see the case when you press that button and a lighted cigarette jumps out. I soon exhausted most of the young men prospects I knew, but by that time I had decided to go after sales in a more efficient way. Any man who has driven a car knows how awkward it is to light a cigarette in traffic. With one of my cases, the auto-driver merely presses the button, and a lighted cigarette immediately pops between his lips. So I devoted most of my energy to showing this case to auto-drivers. I didn't have to do much talking. I'd stand at popular gasoline stations and, when a man stopped for gas, show the lighter and explain it. One out of every twelve asked me the price of the lighter, and when I mentioned it, bought without any further urging.

"Experience taught me that the best place to show the lighter was at the gas station while the man was behind the wheel. He is most easily sold then because he is driving. He, no doubt, wanted a cigarette and in fishing first in one pocket for a package, and then in another for a match, probably came near going off the road. Naturally, he welcomed a cigarette case such as I was selling. It is quite a different matter in his home or office, however. The motorist at home forgets all about the inconvenience of lighting a cigarette while driving, and when in his office his mind is on other things. Thus, the best place to catch him is at one of the many gasoline stations at busy intersections. The gas station attendants usually don't mind having me hang around. There's always some little thing I can do to help around there, and I am someone to talk to when business slumps off."

Lehman sells as high as sixteen cigarette cases daily, netting him a profit of $17.37. On days when the traffic is unusually heavy, he sells as many as thirty-five cases. The selling price, $2.50, does not seem too high to prospects.

Lehman's success with this case is typical of the success of many specialty men, once they find the right spot to sell their products, and the right way of introducing and demonstrating them.

■ ■

Greeting Cards Made Money
for Ettinger

LAST year, James J. Ettinger needed some extra money. He knew that hundreds of men and women make good money around the holidays selling greeting cards. But instead of trying to sell his cards house to house, he concentrated on two special fields—the professional and the service station field. By concentrating his calls on these types of prospects, he not only made a maximum number of calls in a minimum of time, but he spent his efforts on two practically unworked fields.

His campaign was mapped out to cover only the office buildings in his town—particularly those buildings which housed doctors' and dentists' offices. For these prospects, he carried two kinds of cards—one for personal and another for business use. In order to get in to see the doctor, he concentrated on selling the office girl first. When he had sold her, he would ask to see the doctor or the dentist. Usually the office girl was impressed with his sincerity and his evident desire to please, as well as with the excellent line of greeting cards he carried. Having reached the doctor or the dentist and succeeding in making a sale, the next step in his campaign was to sell the wives of these men. Generally, he would get permission to telephone from the doctor's office making an appointment to show the line of greeting cards.

His success with this "endless chain" method of selling was due to making the prospect feel that he was an important customer and impressing him with his need, as a professional man, of the right type of greeting card. After making a few sales, he found it fairly easy to size up his prospect and decide whether he would like something conservative, something radically different or something showy. Most professional men do not like to be rushed and when they are not busy they like to talk. This talkativeness gives Ettinger a chance to get the names of other prospects, and he never fails to ask whether the doctor's brother, or uncle, or sister, or aunt, or any other member of the family he may mention would be interested in selecting Christmas cards.

It wasn't long before Ettinger found that most of the doctors' offices are pretty busy in the afternoons. Furthermore, they close early. So he decided to cover the service stations in the afternoons, evenings, Saturdays and Sundays. This was a field that also needed what Ettinger was selling and a field that few salesmen approached. Nearly every service station in a residential section depends upon the business received from the immediate area surrounding it. This steady day-after-day trade is the backbone of the business and, naturally, the operator wants to keep in touch with his customers. Ettinger found that these men were glad to buy greeting card remembrances from him.

The first efforts Ettinger made to sell greeting cards at the holiday season netted him $295 in five weeks! He doesn't believe he could have made this much money selling house to house, although others have done well with the house-to-house plan. Ettinger prefers the highly specialized field and the quick sales results. This year he expects to make considerably more money because he not only knows how to go about getting prospects, but he has a number of customers' names on his calling list. He will also start earlier and get in another week's work.

CHAPTER THREE

MAKING THINGS TO SELL

OVER in Oberammergau, Germany, there is a colony of people who, for generations, have been wood carvers. They specialize in religious carvings. Years ago, when the only outlet for works of art was the church, the founders of this little colony began carving religious statues and selling them to churches. They became so much interested in the history of the men whose likenesses they portrayed in wood, that they conceived the idea of re-enacting their lives. Thus out of one art developed a greater art and soon the Oberammergau Passion Players became famous the world over. But the Passion Play was the result and not the cause of their success as wood carvers. Today, in ritualistic churches all over the world, the religious carvings of Anton Lang and his associates have become very valuable. Proud indeed is the church, whether it be of the Roman or the Anglican faith, which boasts a wood screen or a crucifix carved in Oberammergau.

Now if the Oberammergau wood carvers were only one or two people it would be easy to dismiss their great success on the grounds that they had a natural gift for carving. But nearly every person in Oberammergau carves, and carves unusually well. Which simply goes to prove that being able to make anything well is not so much a matter of being gifted, as it is being interested enough in what you make to be willing to *acquire* through patient practice the skill that success requires. There is a world of wisdom in the old saying that genius is one-tenth inspiration and nine-tenths perspiration.

You frequently hear people say: "How I envy So-and-So; if I only had his gift of being able to write." It is true some people have more natural ability than others when it comes to expressing themselves on paper. But you will usually find that the permanently successful novelists and short-story writers got where they are because they liked to write in the first place, and then wrote, and wrote, and wrote until they perfected a style or specialty which made their work stand out above the crowd and catch the imagination of the public. It has been said, with a good deal of truth, that if you have aspirations to be a successful short story writer, the way to begin is to write a hundred stories, and throw them all into the waste paper basket. Then send your one hundred and first story to a publisher. The point is that no matter what you elect to make or do, skill requires *practice*. It is better to practice on yourself than on those whom you hope will some day buy the things you make.

But don't let the need of practice discourage you from trying. Rather let it steel you against the discouragements which always go with selling things you make. Remember that even Anton Lang, the Oberammergau wood carver, was once a beginner. At one time in his life he was just as inept as you are so far as wood carving is concerned. True, he had the help and inspiration of the more experienced men in the village, but just the same he was a *beginner*. So was every great artist. Remember then that you can never arrive until you begin. And having begun, never for a single moment allow yourself to become discouraged or to depart from the straight course you have elected to follow. For that is the all-important thing in success—staying on the main track all the time.

Naturally, you are going to be most skillful at the things you really like to do best, so it is easier to be successful when you work with materials you like to handle. If you like the feel and the smell of wood, you will be happier—and probably more successful—making things of wood than working with metal. If your mind is precise, exact, and mathematical, cabinet making may be your forte. What kind of tools do you like to use? Do you feel at home with a scroll saw, lathe or forge? Or tools such as a knife or chisel may interest you more. If you have the "watchmaker's mind," you are likely to be more successful making intricate little models of ships, designing engines or building model houses.

It may be possible that you are not now successful selling what you make because it is not the sort of thing you like to do. A man may work for years in a certain field and find that long after his prime, he could have made a better living working at the thing he really enjoyed doing. If necessity has made it impossible for you to make a choice in your vocation, keep up your hobby that you really enjoy, and sooner or later you may find an opportunity to turn it into money.

Free Training in Handicrafts

If you have tried to make things and have given up, feeling that you could never acquire the necessary skill to turn out a good product, perhaps you just lack a few pointers in handling your tools properly or selecting the right designs. In most of the larger cities, the public schools give free courses in handicrafts. The Young Men's Christian Association also holds classes in the applied and fine arts. Students of either sex, of any age, may enroll in these classes for a small fee. There are several magazines on the newsstands which cater to the craftsman, and the U. S. government publishes bulletins which will give you exact plans and instructions in making many things for use on the farm or in the home. The public library in your city has dozens and dozens of books that tell how to make things.

Manufacturers will send you instructions for the use of their products. There is plenty of help for the man or woman who is eager to acquire skill in his work.

With a few good books or other material to guide you and plenty of practice, you can develop skill in practically any type of work you really like. When you have reached the point where your work begins to look professional, then you must start thinking of ways and means of marketing your product. For no matter how well you make a thing, you will not make a profit from your labor until you find a market for it. Even before you begin making things, it is a good idea to find out what your community needs and likes. A walk through the department stores, the gift shops, the woman's exchange, and other sales outlets will give you some idea of what the public is buying.

The trend today leans toward the "streamline" effect in practically everything—from automobiles to kitchen knives. Keep away from the outmoded designs. Look through the women's magazines and the periodicals on interior decoration and furnishings to find out what is in good taste today. The present trend toward the "classic modern" in furniture suggests that you omit excessive ornament from any cabinet work, but it means that your work must be superior in design and execution in order to achieve that clean streamlined effect. Linens, rugs, glassware, china, jewelry, lamps, picture frames, ash trays, kitchen implements and equipment, as well as furniture, all have more or less of a tendency toward the modern in design. This does not mean the hideous *art moderne* which cluttered up the country a few years back. Beware of any designs that border on that short-lived "epidemic" in house furnishings. In a number of magazines you will note a tendency toward the "Victorian" in furnishings. However, this style of ornate furniture and decoration will undoubtedly prove to be more or less of a fad. We live in a modern, machine age and a modern style of design seems to be more fitting. The old colonial type of furniture and decoration is in demand today, but even the colonial is being produced by manufacturers in keeping with the modern lack of ornamentation and simplified lines.

Suiting Your Product to Your Market

What is your community like? Is it a suburban section where people are interested in garden furniture, rose trellises, fireplace equipment, bird houses, dog kennels, door knockers, sun dials, hooked rugs, handmade quilts, handmade furniture, pottery and other beautiful things for their homes and gardens? Perhaps your community is an apartment district, where people have little time to make good things to eat. Try selling your bread, or cake, or doughnuts, or baked beans to these householders. Or your painted tin ash trays, parchment lamp shades, cocktail tables may suit their fancy. If a great number of children live in your community, whose parents have medium to good incomes, then toys, nursery furniture, colored cutouts of animals, and similar projects may be money-makers.

When your product is ready for the market, it can be sold through the gift shops, the woman's exchange, through advertisements in your neighborhood newspaper, by word-of-mouth advertising, by opening a small shop in your home or in an inexpensive location, or by taking space in a successful shop selling something unlike your product. You may also be successful selling it house to house. If it is possible at all, have your product on display in some spot where people shop. Let people know what you are making—tell your merchant, your neighbors, people you talk to on the street car or at a ball game, the service station attendant, your doctor, the milkman—in fact, tell the world. You can't expect people to search you out—you must go to them with your product.

■ ■

Billy B. Van and His "Pine Tree" Soap

BILLY B. VAN used to be in the show business. His job was to make people laugh. Just as he felt that he was making some progress toward becoming established in his chosen profession he developed tuberculosis and had to leave the show in Boston. He had little or no money at that time, so the members of the company and other friends financed his period of recuperation in the White Mountains in New Hampshire. Here he regained his health and in two years was able to go back to the theater for six months. His long stay in the pine forests gave him two ideas: One, to take the fresh, fragrant odor of the pines to people who had neither the time nor the money to get to the pine woods; the other, to build up a business that would support him comfortably as soon as he could leave the theater.

He decided that soap was the product that would suit his purpose, and he experimented with many formulas before he found one which would actually hold the fragrance of the pine needles. After searching around a bit, he discovered a man who would make the soap for him in quantities. However, he, Billy B. Van, would have to go out and sell it. At first, he laughed at the idea of a comedian becoming a salesman. Then he realized that this was what he had been doing all during his show life—selling; he had been selling himself to his audience night after night. It should be easier to sell soap, he reasoned. So each morning he filled his pockets with samples of his soap, his heart with hope, and started ringing doorbells.

74

There were difficulties. There always are. The druggists didn't know his soap and wouldn't stock it; the jobbers wouldn't move it, and he had no money for advertising. Suddenly the idea came to him that he could introduce his soap through the hotels. Most of his life had been spent in hotels and he knew hotel managers from one end of the country to the other. But the hotel managers thought it a huge joke—Billy B. Van selling soap! He soon found that there was no short-cut to prosperity selling to friends. He finally secured permission to place a trial order in a hotel. Around each cake of soap he wrapped a circular stating: "This soap will keep everything clean but your conscience." A coupon was attached to the circular which read, "Dear Billy: I like your soap. Send me six cakes. Here's your dollar." The idea worked like a charm. Many orders came from the hotel's guests. In this way, Billy B. Van had put the reverse English on direct-mail advertising. As he had no money to write to prospects he arranged for them to write to him! This was the opening wedge in the merchandising of the Pine Tree Soap. From that time on, little by little, he progressed with his merchandising plans. Eventually he built up a lucrative business in the White Mountains where the pine trees send out their clean, healthy fragrance.

The point to this story is not, however, that Billy B. Van, one-time showman, became a successful soap manufacturer, but that by doing the obvious thing he made money. So many people foolishly suppose that the only ideas that are any good are the clever ones, which nobody ever thought of before. The truth is that the ideas that make the biggest money are usually those which are only waiting for somebody to pick them up, just as Billy B. Van picked his Pine Tree Soap idea out of the air of the New Hampshire mountains. There were many brands of soaps on the market when Billy B. Van started to sell his soap, but as he found out, there is always room for another product—if it has quality and answers a specific need.

■ ■

Knapp Specialized in Pressed Chicken

IN EVERY farming community there is an opportunity to start a "pressed" chicken business. No skill and very little capital is required. You simply contract with the farmers and poultry raisers in your community for their chickens when they become too old to lay and too tough to eat. Because they are such tough old birds you don't pay much for them. Then you buy or borrow a steam pressure cooker, and you are in the pressed chicken business.

That there is good money to be made quickly in such a business is demonstrated by the experience of the Knapps, The Knapps have a poultry farm in Eaton County, Michigan, not far from the State Capital. In addition to selling eggs—there is a capacity of 2,000 laying hens at the farm—quite a few chickens are also sold, mostly broilers. However, at the end of the breeding season there are, of course, a number of old hens and stags which must be marketed for which only the lowest prices can be obtained. After handling the left-over stock in this manner for some time, the idea occurred to them that they might be able to make a profit by cooking the old birds and selling them as "pressed chicken."

The chickens for this purpose are best cooked in a pressure cooker as cooking under pressure requires only from 30 to 40 minutes, whereas cooking in an open kettle requires from two to three hours. In addition to reducing the time spent in cooking, the pressure method of cooking produces a much richer product than the open-kettle method as the additional water required in the latter method naturally reduces the rich stock. With a pressure cooker Mrs. Knapp was able to save the cost of the extra cooking time. After the chicken is thoroughly cooked, the meat is cut into cross sections (to reduce the length of muscle shreds), seasoned to taste (some seasoning is added during cooking), the chicken stock is added, and a tablespoonful of plain gelatin. The extra gelatin helps to keep the mold firm and makes for easier slicing of the loaf when it has set. The molds should be greased to prevent the contents from sticking and when filled they are placed in the refrigerator to set. In addition to making plain loaves, Mrs. Knapp also adds sliced vegetables, olives, the riced white and yolks of hard-boiled eggs, etc. By preparing the loaf in layers a very attractive summer dish can be made. To form this loaf, the chicken should be cooked in the usual way, the white meat separated from the dark meat and each kind cut fine or run through a food chopper. The yolks and whites of several hard-boiled eggs should be chopped up separately and each seasoned well. Then the four ingredients, the white meat, dark meat, egg yolks and egg whites, should be mixed with the chicken stock which has been cooked down thick enough to jell. The white and dark meat and the yellow and white egg should then be arranged in layers, pressed in a pan or jar and allowed to set overnight.

Adding water to the stock results in a larger quantity of food, but, of course, the product brings a lower price. In a quality market a loaf should sell for 50 cents a pound. As a five-pound male bird, at the usual 45 per cent loss, should dress out to about two and three-quarter pounds, the return on one bird would be about $1.28. By adding water and doubling the amount, a product would result which could be sold for about 25 cents a pound. Although the addition of water would make a loaf not nearly so rich, the return per bird would be the same. Whether to dilute the product or put up a richer loaf depends entirely upon the market. If a quality market can be developed and you can secure 50 cents a pound for the loaf, it means making as much money on fewer customers and, therefore, less selling effort. However, if the trade prefers a lower price and the diluted product, there is nothing to do but cater to your market.

■ ■

Handkerchiefs for the Chinese

FLORENCE ROCHESTER was a secretary in the attorney general's office at Topeka, Kansas. But Mrs. Rochester needed more money. To appease both the need for more cash and to do something more artistic than copy legal briefs, she began making dainty little lace handkerchiefs in her spare time. She found a ready sale for them among her friends. She spent as much time as necessary to turn out just the kind of handkerchiefs she liked, bought as expensive material as she wanted, and charged for the handkerchiefs accordingly. That was back in 1926.

It was not long before these friends began showing their handkerchiefs to their friends. The demand for Rochester handkerchiefs grew. Before she realized it, Mrs. Rochester was in the handkerchief business!

When orders began to pile up and she no longer was able to make the handkerchiefs and hold her regular job, she talked over the matter with her husband, a civil engineer for a railroad company, and he advised her to quit her job and concentrate on handkerchiefs. She did. She saw that if she built up the business she now was determined to have, she must sell to stores rather than depend on sales direct. She called on two near-by department stores with samples. She sold orders to both. She went back home and opened her "factory" in her own home.

It was the same old story of the world beating a path to the door of the person with quality merchandise—except that Mrs. Rochester did not wait for this path to be beaten. She went out and told merchants about her handkerchiefs.

Today Mrs. Rochester not only sells handkerchiefs to merchants in every state in the country except three, but to foreign countries as well. Foreign orders grew so fast she opened a branch factory abroad to expedite export business.

Start a Pie Bakery

FIVE years ago in Benton Harbor, Michigan, the John Mayers started a pie bakery. If you want to buy cake, cookies, bread or doughnuts, you have to go elsewhere to make your purchases; the Mayers' idea was to do one thing superlatively well and they have succeeded in baking pies that are good enough to keep people coming back for more. The market for their pies consists of hotels, restaurants and the near-by summer resorts. Quite a few are sold direct to consumers at thirty-five cents a pie.

The usual demand in any American community for good pie has enabled the Mayers to build up a profitable business, keep up a nice home which they own, have a car, and provide a comfortable living. There is a limitless market for pies as practically every other man who enters a restaurant orders pie even though he knows it may not be particularly good. Just why there are so few good pie bakers in a country where dessert generally means "pie," is one of the great unsolved mysteries. There is really no competition for the person who has the knack of baking pies like those "mother used to make."

■ ■

$100 per Month with Felt Work

RUTH G. JONES, a widow living in San Antonio, needed money and needed it quickly. She had had no commercial or business experience of any kind prior to her marriage; she had no special ability or talent. What could she do?

One day she heard the son of a friend complain that he was unable to find anyone who could cut out letters properly and sew them on his baseball uniform. That gave Mrs. Jones an idea. She investigated and found that none of the sporting goods stores in the city had equipment for furnishing this service. There was, she found, a little shop that did this felt work so she went over and had a talk with the proprietor. The outcome was that she took over the shop, equipped it properly, and went out after business.

The only experience Mrs. Jones had had in cutting or designing felt was when she cut out a few pennants for herself and friends at college. Yet with a modern sewing machine, a pair of good shears, some sharp razor blades and a small assortment of felt, she was ready for business. She called on all the sporting goods dealers and sporting goods departments in the city. She told the managers about her service and asked them to cooperate with her, pointing out that they would be rendering their customers a service by sending them to a place which was equipped to design and sew on any sort of letters or emblems wanted on uniforms.

Most of the dealers simply send the uniform purchasers to Mrs. Jones and the transaction thereafter is entirely between her and the uniform owners. However, one or two stores prefer to deal with her direct and make a small margin on the deal. The best season for the little shop, of course, is just prior to opening of the baseball season; but there is always some work to be done on swimming suits and both basketball and football create some business. Sweater emblems and letters contribute to year-round volume.

With an investment of less than $100, Mrs. Jones earns on an average of $100 per month the year round, with peak months going to about $150. She believes the idea would be good in any city where there is no such shop, or where there is no uniform factory which provides this service.

■ ■

Starting a Food Specialty Business

WHILE making bread one morning, it occurred to a widow in New England that the one thing she liked to do most of all was to bake, and she decided to give some thought to developing a "Food Specialty Business" in order to add to the family income. The next day she made arrangements with one of the local shops to handle her coffee cake and doughnuts and nut bread on a commission basis. She secured an order from the lunchroom near the station for a daily order of doughnuts, the first orders being put in on trial. A tea room which had a rather good business each day—and especially on Sunday—wanted rolls and pies as well as nut bread. These orders were, of course, not all placed in a day, but as she found a growing demand for her products, and her confidence increased, she had the courage to solicit additional business. Out on the edge of town was a tourist camp which like all such places had little facilities for baking. One afternoon she sent her son out on his bicycle with his basket filled with doughnuts, cookies, pies and coffee cake. It was all sold without difficulty and Johnny came home with orders for more. All summer long this proved to be a fertile market for her products.

That fall and the winter following, she turned her hand to catering and developed a good business during the "party season." Occasions such as the hard-times party at the club and a big Halloween party also at the club called for dozens of doughnuts. She secured both orders simply because the committee responsible for the refreshments knew where to get the best doughnuts in town. That was the secret of her success—everything did taste so good that people came back for more and more. She found that gingerbread was another favorite with the young people in town and she made a specialty of it by adding a fudge sauce to be poured over the slices. After her business had developed, people got in the habit of calling her when unexpected company arrived, and she generally managed to provide something delicious that would fill in for a tea or a luncheon or a Sunday night supper. She remembered that bridge party hostesses liked to serve such dishes as creamed crabmeat and creamed chicken in patty shells. As good patty shells were hard to obtain in their town, she added this item to her list and succeeded in working up a good demand for this specialty by recommending it for Sunday night suppers as well as bridge parties.

"Word of mouth" advertising sold most of her products naturally, but the small cards enclosed with her bread, cakes, coffee cakes, and other items helped to advertise her business. These cards were about three by six and contained on the reverse side a number of suggestions for special "treats" for luncheon guests, bridge parties, Sunday night suppers and children's parties. Many a hostess turned these cards over in an emergency and found a happy solution to "what to give the Joneses after bridge tonight." The cards were carefully typewritten by a friend of the family for a small fee. During the Christmas season, Easter, Fourth of July, and other holidays, cards containing a list of foods which were especially suitable for holiday parties were mailed to her customers.

When large orders were received or when a catering order came in, it was, of course, necessary to secure extra help. Frequently this was a young woman who had just completed high school and not having secured a position was eager to make a little pin money. Her work was simple and consisted of such jobs as icing the little cakes, putting the icing or powdered sugar on the doughnuts, beating the eggs with the electric beater, putting the cakes or doughnuts in boxes, washing dishes and pans used in baking, and frequently delivering special orders when Johnny had too many to handle. The actual preparation of the various specialties was never turned over to anyone else, however—the special goodness of these products could not be entrusted to any assistant.

For a woman without business experience this unusual success might seem phenomenal. However, she succeeded because she put into her business what everyone has to put into business if he is to succeed—knowledge, hard work, ingenuity, and personality.

Making Money from Worn-Out Tires

AMONG the unclaimed goods in James Hadley's storage warehouse in a middle-western town were a number of worn-out tires. He couldn't collect rental for their storage space, and he couldn't sell them for more than a few cents. So when he heard of a machine which made doormats out of the used tires, Hadley decided to investigate.

"I had a good many old tires on hand, and if I could make them up into mats, I thought I could get a little profit from them," explained Mr. Hadley. He invested three hundred dollars in the mat-making machine and incidental equipment, made up a number of mats, stacked them in his warehouse, and then advertised them in the local newspapers.

"I believed I would sell a number of mats from the advertisement," said Hadley, "but didn't. There were no crowds clamoring for mats, and I was disappointed because only a few came to buy. I didn't sell enough to pay for the advertising. I reasoned this was because people did not know enough about the mats, and my problem was to get people acquainted with them. So I tried a window display. But it was hardly noticed. I tried calling from door to door, and sold a good many, but I couldn't down the feeling that there was a better market somewhere."

James Hadley kept thinking about this better market. He went around to office buildings and talked with managers. They used mats in the entrances of the buildings, they told him, and admitted his mat was better than the one they were using, but they were supplied. "I walked my feet off for two weeks," continued Hadley, "before it occurred to me that I wasn't using the right kind of merchandising tactics. I changed them. Concentrating my calls upon business concerns, I adopted a policy of leaving a sample mat with each concern, to be used for a short period. I then pointed out that since the mats were made from old tires, each mat was much tougher and stronger than an ordinary mat, and built up a demonstration to prove the long life of the mats.

"One firm, manufacturing twist drills, wasn't impressed by this argument. The purchasing agent told me that if the workers operating surface grinders preferred my mat to the one being used, I'd get an order. He put my mat on the floor in front of a surface grinder. If the solution used in operating grinders gets on the bare floor accidents are inevitable; so when my mat proved its ability to avoid such accidents, the workers wanted it. Before the day was up, the purchasing agent phoned and asked me to bring over forty-five mats. That cleaned me out of mats and out of tires, too. I got another order for one hundred and thirty feet of mat from a chain of grocery stores the next day, and had to scour around town to find old tires."

James Hadley paid five cents each for the old tires, and got an average of three square feet of matting from each tire. He sold the mats at seventy cents a square foot. His total cost including production cost and overhead was twenty-five cents a square foot, giving him a net profit of forty-five cents. With the mat-making equipment he was able to turn out three hundred square feet of matting daily. Operating thus for the first ten months gave Hadley a profit of more than a thousand dollars.

There is an unlimited field for mats made from old tires in most cities. Laundries, taverns, roadhouses, saloons, cemeteries, churches, office buildings, machine tool manufacturers, electric power houses, dry cleaning plants, stores, restaurants, printing plants, factories of all kinds, and every home, are prospects for sales. The mat-making machine is small and operates on house electric current from an ordinary light bulb. It may be set up in your basement, or some unused room. The mats turned out are unusually durable, being woven together with heavy spring steel wire.

■ ■

Community Marketing of Handicrafts

ONE of the difficulties sometimes experienced by those who make things to sell is that they are more or less at the mercy of buyers when it comes to marketing their products. If there are several people in your community who make similar things, it may be possible to organize a community marketing agency, with one person acting as an agent for the products of all members. This, of course, has been done successfully in agricultural communities, and the idea is beginning to find favor among those who make things that are usually sold through such outlets as gift stores, department stores or wholesalers.

A typical organization of this kind is the Willow Cottage Weavers, of Nantucket, Massachusetts. After several members of this group experienced difficulty in marketing their handicrafts, a central sales department was established, which devotes its entire attention to building up and maintaining a year-round market for the products of members.

Deference to the style factor is most important in holding a clientele which must be persuaded to pay premium prices for quality products. Next to shortcomings in design, lack of conformity to color trends has been the most serious drawback for many a venture among arts and crafts groups. To overcome these serious obstacles, the sales agent for the Willow Cottage Weavers goes scouting several times a year to the style centers to study fashion trends, and more particularly, color preferences.

As 95 per cent of the output is original in design, it is most essential that the merchandise conform to apparel trends to hold customers, many of whom buy on sample.

The direct sales campaign is two-pronged. On the one hand, there is the solicitation of old customers by mail. This has lately been coupled with a "traveling exhibition" which is counted upon to muster new prospects as well as to contact the old customers in the cities visited. Some of the producers of hand-woven textiles have simplified their display problem by staging demonstrations in department stores. The head of the Willow Cottage organization prefers an exhibition sale at a hotel, club, vacant store, or other location that permits an atmosphere of detachment. Invitations to hand-picked lists are relied upon to coax potential buyers.

A second line of attack by the Willow Cottage Weavers is a distinct departure from the usual handicraft marketing methods. Several times a year, representatives of the twelve-loom plant visit leading cities to contact interior decorators and other volume purchasers of hangings, upholstery fabrics, etc. This plan has been richly productive of new business in sizable units. For example, a record-breaking order came in for fabrics for a new dormitory at Cornell. Because of the demand in modern upholstery and interior decoration for period designs, most of the work must be done to order to insure color conformity.

These master weavers have found one secret of tying the steady customers which seems to have eluded most exploiters of handmade products. This trick is to fill the gap between orders of yardage for suits and coats with specialties such as scarfs, neckwear, runners, mats, bureau and dresser sets, etc. In addition to creating many additional orders for the weavers, this activity cultivates gift side lines that, in a sense, serve a sampling purpose in respect to weaves, patterns and color combinations.

■ ■

An Architect for the Birds

THE name of Joseph H. Dodson is so well known that when you see it you immediately think of little wren houses swinging from trees or commodious apartment houses for martins.

This flourishing business had its beginning years ago when Joseph Dodson worked for a Chicago bond house and much of his spare time was spent in the basement of his home making bird houses. These little bird houses were unique in that each one had a tiny piece of shiny metal tacked to the outside. He had discovered that many birds like to primp and preen themselves before mirrors and that by simply attaching this little piece of metal he could entice more birds to spend their summers with him.

Before long his neighbors began to ask him to make bird houses for them. Then the friends of his neighbors sent in orders and soon he realized that there were commercial possibilities in this hobby. From this simple beginning a good business has developed and today, Joseph Dodson is still making bird houses and shipping them all over the country from the little town in Illinois where he lives. It is an idea that might appeal to you as one way to make that $1,000 we are talking about. There is a good market in nearly every community for "de luxe" bird houses and especially martin houses. They are easy to make and all you need to get started is a clever design and a few tools.

■ ■

Building a Business on Homemade Fudge

MRS. BENTLEY, who had a family of four children of school age, found herself faced with the necessity of adding to the family income. Near her home, in Chicago, was a district zoned for light manufacturing. Girls who worked in these offices liked candy, she reasoned; the men did, too, for that matter. So she made up a quantity of fudge, wrapped it in cellophane, and made the rounds of the offices. She sold out her box of fudge before noon the first day and scheduled a return the next Tuesday to those offices she had called upon. That night she made another batch of fudge and the next morning called on the offices on the other side of the street with the same result.

It wasn't long before she had built up a steady trade. She had divided the zoned section into areas and devoted one half a day to each area. In that way people in the offices in each area could plan on getting fudge if they wanted it on a certain day of the week. The girls—and men—arranged to leave their orders at the switchboard and it took but little time to fill them and be ready to go on to the next office.

For special occasions, such as Mother's Day, Valentine's Day, parties, week-end trips, anniversaries, hostess gifts, etc., she packed fancy boxes of the fudge, alternating light and dark pieces to form a pattern. She booked orders ahead for these boxes and the children delivered them after school.

She had arranged for two school stores and one bakery in the neighborhood to handle her candy and a tea room also gave her space for a small box of fudge which sold at a penny a slice. Through her cousin, who was the cashier in a large cafeteria in the neighborhood, she secured a good display of the candy on the counter near the cash register. Additional orders came from the teachers in the grade and high schools her children attended. These orders amounted to a nice little business, especially at Christmas time when many teachers went home for the holidays and wanted to add several boxes of candy to their Christmas gifts for the family. Another sales-making idea of Mrs. Bentley's was to put a card bearing the name "Honey Fudge," her name and address, telephone number, and the price a pound, in each package. The boxes had to be inexpensive to keep costs down, so she chose plain, deep cream-colored boxes and with a hard brown crayon wrote the words "Honey Fudge" in a distinctive backhand script on the covers. A little practice was required, of course, to acquire the proper swing to the writing. At first she found it difficult to get the right pressure when using the crayon on the cover, but this problem was solved by placing the box cover on a block of smooth wood. A little touch such as this in packaging merchandise often means the difference between success and failure in marketing your product.

■ ■

Where to Sell Candied Popcorn

STANDING in a crowd of three hundred and fifty people who stopped to watch a prairie baseball game, James Barlow, of Waterloo, Iowa, got an idea. Barlow wanted some popcorn and the nearest store was about two blocks away! Here were a hundred or more people all wanting popcorn. What a chance for making money! So he decided to test the possibilities of his idea the following Sunday. He bought a corn-popper and went to work.

His wife's cookbook furnished a recipe for making caramel from corn syrup and water, and from that recipe Barlow made up a quantity of syrup which he poured over the corn. Then he pressed this caramelized popcorn into balls, wrapping each ball with red waxed tissue. Just before the game began he filled a clothes basket with popcorn balls and carried it into the crowd gathering to watch the game. Slowly moving up and down the side lines, he soon sold all his popcorn at five cents a ball, and returned home three times during the game to refill the basket. His total sales were one hundred and seventy-nine popcorn balls.

Expensive equipment is not necessary for successfully caramelizing popcorn. You may secure satisfactory results by pouring a thin caramel syrup over the corn shortly after it is popped, and letting it stand for a few minutes. Either corn syrup or molasses will make a good caramel when mixed with water and boiled. The syrup should be thin, however, so it will spread easily and dry quickly.

Popcorn, always a fast selling item, retains its freshness for two or three days, and sells readily wherever people gather to enjoy themselves, such as beaches, picnics, summer resorts, parks, and tourist camps. Opportunities for quick sales are sometimes found among the crowds who wait outside of public buildings, fair grounds, and the theaters.

Once you get the "hang" of making the popcorn, you can hire for a small commission a few "live wire" boys of high school age to help you do the selling and the first thing you know you will have a thriving business. It means a little work to get started, but it is more than worth it.

■ ■

Ivory Carving Proves Remunerative

YEARS ago when Frank Foster of Atlanta, Georgia, was a boy, he learned to carve ivory. As he grew older it became his hobby and as the years went on he became more and more expert. Like many skillful arts, ivory carving can be learned by almost anyone who can handle simple tools. It only requires patience and much practice to become expert.

There are degrees of fineness in ivory carving just as in wood carving. Frank Foster turns out many different kinds of objects, from a plain billiard ball to the finest, most delicate bit of lacy carving.

Since his retirement from business, Frank Foster has built up another business with his unusual hobby. Dominoes, billiard balls, beads, fancy boxes of all types, chessmen, bracelets, earrings, brooches, letter openers, book ends, small picture frames, quaint replicas of birds and small animals, figurines, and of course, elephants of various sizes, all are made by his skillful fingers. His chessmen are particularly beautiful. A fine set of thirty-two chessmen brings him from $50 to $75; a de luxe set as much as $250.

Ivory is rather easy to work with because of its resiliency. The ivory used by Mr. Foster is elephant ivory. The tusks cost about $1,000 each, but he manages to buy scrap ivory around one-tenth the original cost. Piano factories have hundreds of pounds of material that are useless for making piano keys because the curve in the tusk makes it difficult to secure long pieces of ivory. Therefore, the amount from a tusk that can be used for keys is comparatively small. This scrap ivory is of excellent quality and can readily be used to form small objects.

Potato Chips Made Hibbard Independent

ROY C. HIBBARD did not relish the long hours and uncertain income driving a taxi. He realized he was getting nowhere. So he kept his eyes open for some way to make extra money. He made many stops to pick up fares at beer taverns, and in this way became acquainted with the tavern owners. Sometimes they talked to him about their business in a general way. To make people drink more beer, he learned, salty food specialties, such as potato chips, were given free to tavern patrons. So Hibbard thought it would be a smart idea to supply taverns with potato chips.

He obtained a machine that turned out a high quality potato chip, and made up sample packages which he left with each tavern owner he knew. His first sampling produced a total of fifty trial orders. The quality of the chips was excellent, and the day following he was gratified to secure reorders totaling seventy-five pounds of chips. Hibbard quit his job driving a taxi to devote his entire time to his potato chip business.

Hibbard's initial investment was about $100. He bought the machine on a deferred payment plan, paying $85 for it. Potatoes averaged ninety cents a hundred pounds, and grease for frying cost fourteen cents a pound in twenty pound cans. By setting the machine up in the basement of the apartment building where he lived, he had no additional rent to pay. He made good money right from the start. His success was in the selection of the right kind of potatoes. At first he used a thin-skinned cobbler, which is inexpensive, but he later learned that all potatoes do not fry into good chips. The more expensive Idahos, recommended by the maker of the machine, were found to be much more satisfactory.

Hibbard figures the cost of frying potato chips at nine cents a pound and by bagging them in five-, ten- and twenty-cent sized bags, he averages fifty cents a pound on retail sales. Sales in bulk to taverns bring him thirty cents a pound. He averages a net daily profit of better than $11, and his business is steadily growing.

A potato chip machine similar to Hibbard's can be set up in your own home. It is operated from gas, and fries potato chips of uniform quality. Ready outlets are found in taverns, lunchrooms and restaurants, and you may wholesale them at fifteen cents a pound to grocery and delicatessen stores. When put up in bags, such as the five-cent bags, an additional charge should be added.

Doll Hospital Pays for Operation

MOLLY WINDER, the wife of a textile salesman, had been in an automobile accident which had injured her right foot. An operation would cost around $800. How could she get that much money? Of course, there was her husband's salary, but payments on a home, insurance premiums and living expenses, pretty well used all of that. Mrs. Winder had often dressed dolls at Christmas time for her friends' children from the textile samples discontinued by her husband from his line. Perhaps making doll clothes was the answer.

She found her friends quite willing to buy the doll clothes for their children's birthdays and as gifts. Her doll clothes sold quickly because she patterned them after the current styles in women's and children's clothes. A doll dressed in the current fashion always makes a hit with children. She had started to make the doll clothes in September and in November and December she concentrated on getting as much business as possible for the Christmas season. It was at this time that she found herself not only dressing dolls for Christmas, but also mending them. The dolls brought in by the mothers would have a broken arm or leg, a scratch on the face, a cracked head or a badly torn wig. Of course, these damages would have to be repaired before the doll could be dressed.

It was easy for her to make these simple repairs. A little glue here, a bit of sewing there, the wig recurled and the new clothes would make "Betsy Ann" or "Sally Lou" look brand new again. Molly Winder is the genial type of woman who has a large circle of friends and acquaintances and almost before she realized it, the word had gone around and she was in the Doll Hospital business. However, she did not stop at repairing dolls—toys of all kinds were brought to her to mend and even china and little pieces of bric-a-brac. She also found—perhaps "cultivated" would be a better word—a market for character dolls and dolls dressed in the costumes of the various nations. These dolls were raffled at church bazaars and charity affairs held by societies, lodges, etc.

By the following June, Molly was able to make arrangements for her operation. She had enough money to pay the hospital bill and more than half of the doctor bill, Now that she had built up a good list of customers, the second Christmas was so profitable the work required all her time and she delegated the household activities to her eldest daughter of high-school age. Mrs. Winder was fortunate, of course, in that she had most of the materials needed in her work and but little money had to be spent for supplies. However, even with the added expense for materials, operating a community hospital for dolls can be made a profitable venture.

Brown Bread and Beans Pay the Taxes

THE woman who lives in or near a section of apartment dwellers will generally find a market near her home for breads, cookies, cakes and similar products if she but searches her neighborhood for prospects. One woman living on Chicago's south side developed a market for brown bread and baked beans by calling on homes in her neighborhood on Friday afternoons. Many homes that serve baked beans, creamed codfish and similar Friday foods, find that brown bread is just the needed item to make a perfect meal. However, most women will not bother to make brown bread and it is one of those special foods that the commercial food firms have not been able to reproduce with all its fine flavor.

She started out with the idea of selling brown bread only but the tie-up with baked beans was so obvious, it was not long before she was selling both. Her method of introducing the brown bread was to carry a small case similar to a typewriter case containing several whole loaves of brown bread and one sliced loaf. The slices which had been cut in half were offered to each prospective customer as a sample. The bread was exceptionally good as the sample proved and before long she had several Friday customers. The baked beans were deliciously brown and put up in brown earthenware of two sizes, small and large, depending upon the size of the family ordering. Most of the women welcomed the idea of a home-cooked meal without any of the fuss of preparation. They could arrive home from their bridge parties, put the pot of beans in the oven to warm, slice the bread, fix up a substantial salad, bring out the pickles and catsup and serve the dessert prepared in the morning before leaving for the party.

Being a wide-awake person, this woman made up a list of foods with which brown bread tasted good, such as baked beans, codfish, potato salad, finnan haddie, etc. She also suggested it for the children's lunches with a big glass of milk, as well as sliced, cut in circles or other fancy shapes, and spread with cheese, to serve at luncheons and parties. Her name, address and telephone number were typed by her daughter in high school on regular recipe-size cards and a list of the ways of using brown bread was typed on the back of the card together with prices. These cards were mailed to friends of customers (names she secured simply by asking for them), given to prospects who had shown an interest in her products, and to customers. She also mailed them to tenants in the buildings where she had customers. Incidentally, she never missed an opportunity to call on other tenants in a building where a customer lived.

In addition to this type of business she opened up another field for her brown bread by calling upon the three hotels in the immediate vicinity, as well as selling four other hotels in an adjacent neighborhood that catered to more or less permanent guests who were fussy about their food. Her high school daughter and 12-year-old son delivered the orders near home while she herself drove the old family car and delivered the hotel orders and other orders outside her immediate neighborhood. As the business grew she began to put aside a tidy little sum of money which paid the taxes on her home each year and helped to dress the children as well as herself.

■ ■

He Made "Snake Snaks" Popular

SEVERAL years ago George K. End, of Arcadia, Florida, helped his two small sons kill a rattlesnake and skin it. The reptile's flesh, which was a pale, salmon pink, looked inviting and Mr. End decided to taste it as an experiment. To his surprise he found that it had a delicate flavor and was exceedingly tender. Sometime later he served the meat at a convention at Tampa and those who tried it agreed that it was delicious. A number of friends also tried it on his recommendation and pronounced it a real delicacy. He decided that there might be a market for the product and as the immediate vicinity has more rattlesnakes to the square mile than any other part of the United States, he had an unlimited meat supply for his odd business. He established a canning plant and started to prepare and market his product.

The main difficulty, of course, was overcoming the prejudice people have about eating snakes. However, Mr. End found enough people who considered his product a delicacy to enable him to build up a good-sized business. People eat eels, snails, and frog legs, so why not clean, palatable snake meat, a product much cleaner than the oyster which so many people enjoy?

The snakes are captured alive by means of a noose at the end of a bamboo pole about six feet long, then they are swung into a wire cage and taken to the cannery. Here they are killed the same day if possible, as they will not eat in captivity and, consequently, lose considerable weight. The snake catchers are paid at the rate of twenty cents a foot averaging about $1.25 a snake. The meat is prepared with or without a sauce and orders for raw rattlesnake meat are also filled. The average snake weighs about nine pounds when brought in but much of this weight is lost through shrinkage in cooking and with the removal of the head, bones and rattles. Not cheap by any means, the meat sells for $1.25 for a four and one-half ounce can; the uncooked meat bringing $2.50 a pound. The meat is also smoked in the same fashion ham is smoked and marketed as "Snake Snaks" in small bags. In view of the fact that the meat has a very delicate flavor, it is especially delicious served as canapes. Other parts of the rattler such as the head, the rattles, the fangs are made up into ornaments and a rubbing oil is made from the fatty tissues. The skin, of course, is made into hat bands, belts, pocketbooks, book covers, etc.

You may not be keen about the idea of starting a snake cannery, even though you live in a snake infested area. However, the way Mr. End made his $1,000 may suggest to you the many opportunities for making money that exist right in your own back yard, so to speak, if only you look for them.

■ ■

What You Can Make from Clam Shells

MARY COOPER, who lived with her two small children in a cheap rooming house, had lost her job. However, being an ingenious person, she had soon established herself in a nice little business of her own making novelties from clam and oyster shells. She secured the shells without cost from a near-by sea food shop and made them up into novelties. She took them down to the beauty parlor where she had been working and the owner of the shop gave her display space in a window for a commission on all that were sold. Such novelties are inexpensive to make. The materials used consist of common pipe cleaners, clam, oyster shells, and other shells. No particular skill is required. Here is how to do it:

Drill a hole in the small end of an oyster shell. Insert one end of a pipe cleaner through this hole and fasten it securely by twisting the wire over and around the edge of the shell, letting most of the pipe cleaner extend upward. Now repeat this operation with a second oyster shell of the same size. Place the two shells alongside each other. Halfway up the length of the pipe cleaners, bend and twist them together for the rest of their length. Next select two small oyster shells. Match and fit them together about the twisted single portion of the pipe cleaners. That portion of the pipe cleaners which protrudes above the shells becomes a neck. Now drill a hole in one side of a small conical shell. Attach this to the top of the pipe cleaner. You now have the figure of a comical man, with two large feet made from oyster shells, a body made from oyster shells, and the legs and neck from the pipe cleaners. The small shell on top is, of course, the head. Arms may be added by cutting a pipe cleaner in half, and attaching to the neck at the juncture of the oyster shells. A small brush and ten cents' worth of paint will enable you to tint your figures any color. Ash trays and a score of useful items may be easily made in this way.

■ ■

Tosdale Sisters Saw Paris on Fancy Pillows

THE Tosdale sisters had just finished college, and after the usual round of parties had been given for them in their home town, they developed a bad case of wanderlust. Somehow or other Helen and Mary Tosdale meant to make some money for a trip.

There was one thing in which both girls excelled and that was sewing. Both of them had made all their dresses and many of their suits and coats since their high-school days. They knew colors and fabrics and they had style sense. However, neither one of the girls had any desire to develop a dressmaking trade. It would have to be some other type of sewing, they decided. And then they hit on the idea of fancy pillows. The years of sewing in the Tosdale home had resulted in trunks and boxes of both used and unused fabrics and ribbons and edgings. After a check-up, they found they would have enough for quite a number of pillows before they would have to buy any new material.

That summer they worked over pillow designs and by November, they had made several dozen unusual and beautiful pillows. Ribbons in matching tones were woven together to make interesting squares; bands of contrasting material were appliqued in modern effects; porch pillows were made of sturdy chintz and cretonne, their edges bound in contrasting colors; fine linens were daintily embroidered to fashion baby pillows of softest down; scraps of lace and silks were used to make boudoir pillows, and jewel-colored squares of velvet and satin were trimmed with looped fringe edgings or with pipings of a contrasting material to make plain, tailored cushions.

Three weeks before Christmas they were ready to display their work. They persuaded a local laundry agent to rent them his window space for the three weeks for five dollars. After the mad Christmas rush was over, they found that they had sold every pillow they had made up and had orders for about two dozen more to fill. They charged good prices, too. As a matter of fact, they discovered that people seem to appreciate handwork in direct proportion to the price.

While a handsome profit was made on the Christmas sale there wasn't enough money in the travel fund to take them both to Europe that year.

So they designed, and planned, and sewed all spring and summer. The magazines were scanned for ideas, and the silk sales eagerly watched for bargains. They managed to buy a lot of kapok and down-filled pillows in muslin covers from a wholesaler at a price cheaper than they could make them. During the spring, the two girls had orders from a half dozen local families for pillows and draperies and they sold pillows steadily through the summer for porch use. One of the local gift shops gave them an order for pillows which the proprietor admitted were more attractive and better styled than any she could purchase elsewhere.

Late that fall they worked busily to get enough stock ready for the Christmas sale. They figured that even if they made too many they could be sold during the next year. By the time the Christmas season arrived they had more pillows than the laundry agent's window could hold. So a vacant store on a busy street was secured for a month and it was so attractively arranged that people came in just to look around. The majority of them, however, evidently left with pillows under their arms, because when two tired girls figured up their sales after the last mad scramble Christmas eve, they found only two pillows left, one of which had been stepped on and soiled and the other wedged behind a counter out of sight.

So the Tosdale sisters saw Europe the next year and evidently it won't be their last trip for they have decided to open up a shop. Now that they have an idea of what people want, their shop will carry pillows, curtains, quilts, padded throws for the chaise lounge, pads for dresser drawers and shelves, padded dress hangers, equipment for wardrobes and closets, etc. To have enough stock on hand, they have secured the part-time services of two women who do exquisite needlework.

■ ■

Makes Miniature Reproductions of Antiques

VISITING George Cona's shop in San Francisco is like traveling with Gulliver through the land of Lilliput. Time and space are eliminated by this craftsman's wand as he fashions miniature models of antique furniture. In orderly rows above his workbench, hang diminutive planes and saws, and tiny little hammers that drive still tinier nails into bits of wood of matchlike thickness.

With these tools Mr. Cona fashions tiny cabinets no higher than an orange. Every detail is finished with minute precision even to the lining of the drawers, for no cabinet-maker ever delved more intensively into furniture lore or applied his knowledge with closer attention to authenticity.

As a boy in England, Mr. Cona studied period furniture and cultivated his talent for reproducing it. Later, in California when his health failed after many years in the ministry, he turned to cabinet making for a livelihood. There were fat years during which he became notable in San Francisco for antique furniture reproductions so clever that only an expert could tell the copy from the original. Then came 1929 and lean years. He was past three score and ten, yet his agile fingers still held their cleverness. When business languished he turned to his hobby—the modeling in miniature of Chippendale chairs, Duncan Phyfe tables and Heppelwhite sideboards. Of course, this does not mean doll furniture. These bits of furniture are real miniatures. To give a cash basis of differentiation—a Cona bedroom set sells for $5; a doll's set of similar proportions for 25 cents.

Former patrons straggling in with odd jobs noticed the exquisite little models and bought them. They sent friends who "wanted a set just like it." Gradually a *little furniture* business filled the *big furniture* void. One day a woman with a pre-depression bank balance asked Mr. Cona if he could build a doll house to fit the furniture. The answer was yes, Mr. Cona having studied architecture along with antiques in England. He drew plans and built a house that clicked and brought more orders. Now he makes to order houses that, as he puts it, are "just a little better." These range from a $10 cottage for a real estate firm to a $300 mansion for a wealthy client's child.

Just now he is working on a house complete with furniture that will bring $550. The house stands in his window and the furniture is being added piece by piece as finished. Every day interested observers pause before the shop window to ascertain the progress made. The five-room colonial house is white with green trimmings. It has parquetry floors of oak and mahogany and a delightful oak staircase, with banisters, that leads to the bath and bedrooms above. The rooms contain electric switches of postage stamp size and the chandeliers are fitted with tiny globes. The finely wrought window frames enclose real glass windows instead of the usual mica.

The interest in miniature reproductions of antique furniture during the past few years has been largely stimulated by the exhibit of Mrs. Ward Thorne's exquisite miniature rooms at the Chicago World's Fair, and by the $500,000 doll house exhibited for charity by the moving picture actress, Colleen Moore. Another beautiful example of this work is the priceless collection of Helena Rubinstein, the well-known cosmetic manufacturer. Some of the tiny little furnishings of these rooms have been acquired by their owners during years of collecting little objects of glass, brass, wood, and bits of furniture. However, most of them have been made by modern craftsmen. Many a man with a workbench in his basement and a flair for design can turn out these tiny bits of furniture. Books and periodicals on furniture design will help him in getting the lines of the tiny pieces of furniture as authentic as the originals.

■ ■

A Rattling Good Income from Rattlers

CATHERINE C. REIDY, of Tucson, Arizona, became interested in snakes while homesteading twenty-three miles from the town where Mr. Reidy worked. She began studying the local wild life and vegetation as a pastime and became so interested that she started to write on nature subjects. This meant getting together more or less of a reference library, cameras and other equipment. Then the depression came along and slashed the family income rather badly. She wrote a few letters and found herself engaged to collect bugs for several biological supply houses. She also sold cactus and wild flower seed.

It was while collecting notes on native foods of the Indians that she found the Indians not only use the meat of the rattlers for food, but they made ornamental necklaces from the bones. This aroused her curiosity and the next time she captured a rattler, she popped him into a kettle and the next day she had a business. The ornaments include costume jewelry, buttons, buckles, necklaces and bracelets. "The bones," explains Mrs. Reidy, "resemble carved ivory, and achieve a startling whiteness after a lengthy cleansing and bleaching process. They are then matched carefully and strung in various ways, some naturally and some in combination with colored beads of many kinds and sizes." The rattlers' skins make lovely billfolds, bookmarks, cigarette cases, check-book holders, pocketbooks and even boots and jackets. During the Chicago World's Fair, a tailored suit of rattlesnake skins made by Mrs. Reidy was displayed in the Arizona exhibit, and attracted a tremendous amount of attention.

Business became so good, the Reidys moved back to town and fitted up a studio where their handicraft could be displayed more easily. She now has several hunters to secure the snakes and has put in a stock of meat. She has found that there is always a small demand for the skulls and fangs and the rattles. In addition to maintaining the studio, Mrs. Reidy exhibits her wares at tourist camps and dude ranches in the West.

He Specialized in "Hamburgers"

A FEW years ago, Henry Fisher lost his job in a restaurant. He took fifty dollars from his small savings account, rented space in a Chicago Loop office building, and opened up a hamburger shop. In three months, Henry's business became so profitable, he opened two more shops, which he now operates successfully.

"The space secured for my first location was hardly big enough to turn around in," he said. "I hoped to be able to get additional space later, add a regular line of restaurant food, and serve coffee, tea and milk. But I decided against this policy during my first week and specialized in hamburger sandwiches. These were a little larger than ordinary, and I sold them for a dime. People working in the building crowded around at noon, and it was at once apparent that they wanted quick service more than anything else. As news of my stand got around the building, I had considerable difficulty keeping up with the crowd's demand during the noon hour.

"My investment in equipment amounted to sixteen dollars. Rent for the six-by-ten-foot space was thirty-three dollars a month. I did no advertising. I hadn't figured on it, for I hadn't planned on staying in that small space very long. As I was serving a better hamburger sandwich for a dime (one covered with relish in which a little mayonnaise dressing was mixed on a rye bun—sometimes known as 'Vienna' style), they sold themselves. On my first day, I took in twenty-four dollars. My expenses ran to fifteen. The second day was a little better and by the end of the week, I figured I was on my way. My wife, who was as excited over the success of this first stand as I was, urged me not to be satisfied with one location, but to open a second stand. However, we had difficulty finding a spot for it, since few office buildings had suitable space available and those having such space wanted too much for it. So we chose a small room on the second floor of an industrial building which was almost entirely devoted to the printing industry. One typesetting company employed a hundred and twenty men, and a printing company occupying two floors employed six hundred men and girls. Our success in this spot was immediate. The workers patronized us because we were convenient and gave them a satisfying sandwich for a dime, which was about all many wanted to pay for a lunch. Those who didn't want to leave their shop or office, often asked someone to bring back a hamburger. Office and errand boys from the offices in the building take back as many as fifteen or twenty hamburgers for the girls and men in their office at one time. I could have sold coffee at our first location, but that would have meant a delay in service. People who want coffee generally want to sit down at a table and I didn't have room for tables there. Those who bought the hamburgers didn't seem to mind not having coffee.

So I saved the rental on larger space and the cost of fixtures, and did just as big a business as if I had them. In the second shop, however, we sold coffee, because it seemed to be a custom for working men to send out a boy for enough coffee for eight or ten at one time. Our profits in this building were almost as large as in the first place. When I decided to open the third location, I chose a spot in another industrial building. Here rent was cheap, and there was a large and highly concentrated market for coffee and hamburgers."

Henry pointed out that he did not consider locations outside of the business or industrial districts as suitable for hamburger stands. His success, he declares, was due to offering a convenience to working people with limited time. If he can get 30 per cent of the workers in a building, he is able to keep one stand going in great shape, and have the evening for himself.

His first equipment was one second-hand griddle, thirty by eighteen inches, for frying the hamburgers, a large tin box for his supply of "giant" rolls, and a large bottle of relish. A trick in making hamburgers especially delicious is to mix the meat with crumbled stale bread. No ice is required since the hamburgers come ready for the griddle on two daily deliveries from the local packing house warehouses. A stand of this kind may be opened with very little capital in any small space on the lower floors (not necessarily the lobby or street floor) of an industrial or office building. Potato chips bagged, small pies, and similar specialties might profitably be carried as side lines.

■ ■

Etched Bottles and Boxes Sell Easily

WHEN Harry Brown finished college, he decided to see if he couldn't make some money with an idea he had been mulling over for some time. In his chemistry course in college he had learned how to etch glass by coating it with beeswax, lettering words with a steel point, and then exposing the surface of the glass to the fumes of hydrofluoric acid.

With a little practice Harry found that he could produce some rather neat looking bottles suitable for the medicine cabinet. He purchased a carton of standard-sized bottles of good clear glass and etched them with the names of the usual medicine cabinet remedies such as boric acid, witch hazel, hand lotion, glycerin, etc. He made up several sets of four bottles each and sold them to friends and relatives. Later he sold them from house to house. On every call he tried to sell a complete set of bottles. However, when it was plainly evident that the housewife did not need the entire set, he would suggest her taking a pair of bottles. Sometimes he could get her to suggest other labels for two more which he would etch for no additional charge. He also took orders for special sets of bottles for the invalid in the family or for the baby's medicines.

Harry made it a point to deliver the orders in the evening. Generally, the "man of the house" would be home and there would be no delay in getting the money for his work. Furthermore, he frequently found that father would be interested in securing for his "private supply," a uniform set of bottles with names such as Rye, Bourbon, Scotch, etc.

Another idea that sold well was a little mirrored-top match box. He bought these by the dozen and etched numbers from one to eight on the mirrored tops. Women bridge fans were delighted with them as they could use them for bridge prizes. When these went over so big, he purchased some larger mirrored cigarette boxes and etched the names of the popular cigarette brands on the tops. Women bought these novelties for bridge prizes also as well as for their own homes.

Before long, Harry found himself so busy that he not only had to secure assistance in handling the work of etching the bottles, but also had to hire someone to follow up inquiries.

■ ■

The Vogue for Wrought Iron House Numbers

WHEN the depression took away his office job, Leander Hvale of Deerfield, Illinois, turned to his hobby, the making of hand-wrought knickknacks for homes. Word-of-mouth advertising along the fashionable North Shore section has brought Mr. Hvale many orders for handmade iron home-markers (swinging signs at the gate or on posts near the entrance), wall plaques, weather vanes and other handicraft. His son, a Chicago Art Institute graduate, makes the designs. One home-marker, which he worked out for a dog shelter (an enterprise of one of Chicago's society leaders), shows a little dog up on his hind legs, begging. Two other little dogs are sympathetically listening. Another design was a lovely madonna for the wall of an outdoor living-room of a North Shore estate.

The home-marker had its origin in the Middle Ages before the invention of house numbers. In order to identify one's home it was customary to use some sort of distinctive sign. Thus people came to speak of Mr. So-and-So who lived at the sign of the "Green Rooster" or the "Yellow Lantern."

Among the nobility the crests from the family coat-of-arms were used as home-markers. Fighting cocks, spread eagles and unicorns were popular. The modern vogue of naming homes has brought with it the demand for markers to symbolize hospitality and good-fellowship.

Mr. Hvale realized that he would have to let people know what he could do with wrought iron if he were to have any kind of success. So, although he had no money to spare, he planned to have an exhibit at the Garden Club flower show held at Chicago's Navy Pier. The money for the display space was earned by doing odd chores and shoveling peat for a month for the club. The display did bring his work to the attention of those who appreciate the beauty of wrought iron and created no little business.

There are any number of things to be made of wrought iron and those who have a hankering for this type of work will find innumerable designs in books on the subject. The wrought iron gates and balconies of New Orleans, made in the colonial days, are known all over the world for their beauty. For years these examples of art and skill have endured. The intricate, lacy designs are really the work of artists and are not easy to equal. However, there are many simpler designs which can be made by the average craftsman. Home-markers, colonial lanterns for entrance lights, railings, small balconies beneath windows, fireplace equipment, grills, hinges, door knockers—all are in vogue today due to the revival of interest in colonial architecture and furnishings. Prices charged for wrought iron things should, of course, be high enough to put a proper value on original design and expert craftsmanship of this sort.

■ ■

James Mack's Sandwich Bar

FOUR years ago, James Mack, in search of a better climate for his health, drove to Florida and stopped for a while in Miami. Now James Mack was a connoisseur of good coffee. He was fussy about the kind of coffee he drank, and well he might be for he made a good cup of coffee himself. According to Mack, there was no good coffee in Miami. He tried all the restaurants, the hotels, and even the refreshment stands. The coffee was terrible!

Well, if he couldn't get a good cup of coffee in Miami, he would make it himself and show these Florida cooks how the people from up north liked their coffee! No sooner said than done—James Mack opened up a sandwich bar. The menu included only two types of sandwiches—fish and hamburger—and the best coffee you could buy at any price. Yet he charged only a nickel a cup for it. Milk was added to the menu as a concession to those who couldn't drink coffee. The fish used in the sandwiches was always whatever was in the market that morning in quantities sufficient to be purchased at a good price. The hamburger was always strictly fresh and prepared so that it really was good enough to accompany the best cup of coffee in town. No pie, no cake, no cookies, no ham and eggs—nothing but the sandwiches and coffee and milk were served.

People were skeptical at first, but the few who tried his coffee were back soon with other customers. It became the habit to brag to newcomers, "I'll take you over to Mack's where you will get the best cup of coffee you ever tasted." There were seats for only twelve at Mack's place and he refused to enlarge. "I don't want a great big place with lots of overhead," he remarked to a visitor who asked him why he didn't enlarge the place. "The customers really like it this way—it's cozy and different from the average restaurant or hotel dining room. If I enlarged and had to have waitresses and tables, the place would look like every other food 'emporium.'"

People did like it as it was—they stood four deep in line to get their coffee, and thought it fun. They ate their dinners at the hotels and came over to Mack's for their coffee. It became a fad and he was wise enough to know it and to keep it so. Once he had made his reputation for having the best coffee in town, he did nothing to change it. That coffee had to be good! He bought the berries himself, blended them, and ground the coffee fresh each time it was prepared. The few things he served were all fresh and good quality. The place was immaculate and so was Mack and his assistant in their white coats. There was no noisy clatter of dishes and silverware—the service was quiet, the place cool and shaded from the sun by awnings. Mack was proud of his coffee and sandwiches—he expected you to enjoy them, and you did.

Mack's emphasis on quality succeeded. He has turned in his old car on a new one, paid his doctor bills back up north, improved his place, paid for all his equipment, and has money in the bank!

■ ■

Doughnuts Bring Profits

UPON leaving his job in the circulation department of a Chicago newspaper, S. D. Lavely retired to Watervliet, Michigan. Idleness soon palled on him, and he decided to start a small business of his own. He rented a store and invested $250 in equipment for making greaseless doughnuts. The first batch of doughnuts baked was given away as samples to people passing the store. That first day Lavely sold seventy dozen doughnuts at twenty-five cents a dozen. The second day went even better as a majority of those who bought the first day repeated, and brought others with them.

Before the first week passed, Lavely had reached an average daily sale of over 150 dozen—all he could bake. He expanded his business and added more equipment. As Watervliet is but a short drive from Paw Paw Lake, Lavely figured he could do a brisk business with the summer resorts around Paw Paw. So he hired a woman to help his wife bake doughnuts while he packed sixty dozen in his car and drove down to the lake. Within two hours he sold the entire lot to vacationists in cottages. After that he drove down to the lake at least once every day. Later, he established a regular route to the near-by towns of Marcellus, Lawrence, and Hartford, where he sold the doughnuts at wholesale for fifteen cents a dozen to most of the restaurants, retail stores, tea rooms, soda fountains and lunchrooms.

The cost of baking greaseless doughnuts averages under six cents a dozen with the equipment Lavely used. His small machine bakes eight dozen in an hour, or eighty dozen in a ten-hour day. Lavely started with two of these machines, giving him a daily output of 160 dozen doughnuts. During the first week, his sales totaled 900 dozen at twenty-five cents a dozen. When he had deducted all his expenses he found that he had made quite a nice little profit—about $161.

Greaseless doughnuts are baked in electrically operated bakers. They are not fried like ordinary doughnuts. The doughnut batter used is exactly the same as is used when baking the "greasy" doughnut. When packed in waxed paper containers, greaseless doughnuts remain fresh for six to eight days. This type of doughnut is quite easily digested and may be eaten without harm even by chronic stomach sufferers.

Equipment for baking greaseless doughnuts may be set up in your own kitchen and operated from a light socket. Demand for this product is always good, and stores, lunchrooms, and restaurants are excellent outlets. You may retail some to your friends and neighbors, as Lavely did, and before you know it you will have a thriving business of your own. It has the great advantage of being a business where satisfied customers draw others. The average American takes to doughnuts like a duck takes to the water, and it does not take the people in town long to make a beaten path to the door of the man who can make better doughnuts.

Motor-Driven Chairs for Invalids

LUZERN CUSTER, of Dayton, Ohio, makes motor-driven chairs for people who are incapacitated—invalids or cripples. His plant, in Dayton, turns out about three chairs a week, at an average price of $200 a chair. Until recently, all the chairs were driven by electric batteries. Now, however, some of them have gasoline motors and will run along at 15 miles an hour. Some of these chairs have built-in showcases to enable their users to sell candy or notions. One Southerner had a chair built to carry himself and his Negro attendant. Many of the cripples for whom he makes chairs like gay colors, so he paints their chairs fire-engine red and equips them with powerful headlights and loud horns.

Twenty years ago Mr. Custer started to make chairs for board walks. Putting motors in them revolutionized the business for him and he made good money for several years. Then he saw a market for motor-driven chairs for invalids and the incapacitated. It wasn't long before most of his business was catering to this market.

■ ■

100 Other Things Easy to Make

WOOD—Start with the simpler things such as book ends, a book-stand, bird houses, garden trellises, picture frames, racks for garden tools, window boxes, footstools, flower stands. When you have developed some skill and ease in handling tools, try folding screens, end tables, cupboards, hanging bookshelves, coffee tables, toys, etc. The modern style of furniture is simple and easy to make. Keep clear of elaborate ornamentation which does not add to the design of the product. There is also a good demand for the rustic type of lawn and garden furniture. This furniture is made of small logs and branches upon which the bark is left. The construction is simple in the extreme. Blueprints can be had from such magazines as *Popular Science Monthly, Popular Mechanics,* and the government.

CEMENT—It requires much less skill to make things of cement than of wood. Forms of wood or metal may be bought or you can make them yourself. There are government bulletins explaining how to mix and use the cement; the cement companies will also send you instructions. Get a catalog from some company making this type of product and see just what items are in demand. Bird baths, sun dials, aquariums, benches, urns or large jardinieres, and other garden and lawn equipment are popular. When you have acquired some skill, you can also make clever little figures and ornaments such as frogs and mermaids for the lily pond; rabbits and squirrels for the lawn; fauns, birds, etc.

PAPER—So many things can be made with paper it is almost impossible to enumerate them. With pastepot and shears, or shears alone, clever hands can fashion an endless number of things that can be sold in the gift shops, in your own shop, from door to door, or at fairs and exhibits. One of the most interesting things to do with paper is to make silhouettes. There are books on silhouette making and many magazine articles have covered this art. With practice and a certain dexterity, you can make a good living with this work. The usual practice is to set up your worktable in a gift shop, a department store, a greeting card shop, a county fair, a street fair, or any place where many people congregate. The silhouettes are sold at from 50 cents to $1.00 each. Double your paper and cut two of them at once. Then offer them to the customer at two for 75 cents or two for $1.25, depending upon your price per silhouette. A little "showmanship" will add to your sales. With wall paper you can create some beautiful folding screens—look over those on display in your local department store. You can also make closet accessories from boxes and wall paper— hat boxes, blanket boxes, shoe boxes, etc. These should be matched, or ensembled. With wall paper you can also make scrapbook covers, cover waste-paper baskets, tin cooky boxes, cigarette boxes, etc. These should be shellacked when finished to protect the paper. Many decorators have had unusual success with cutting designs from wall paper and making an applique border for bathroom, kitchen or bedroom walls. These borders can also be used to decorate kitchen cabinets, bread boxes and other containers, valances for windows, etc. Colored cut-outs of animals, fairy tale characters, fruit, flowers, etc., can be made for children's rooms, as wall or furniture decorations. Make these in sets, put them in glassine envelopes and sell them for 50 cents and up a set. With crepe paper you can make fascinating favors and decorations for parties. The Dennison Company's party books will give you directions for making favors, party decorations, and paper costumes.

OILCLOTH—Oilcloth may be used in much the same way as wall paper. It is excellent to cover folding screens (especially for kitchen or nursery use), to cover boxes, to cover scrapbooks and schoolbooks, as cut-outs for wall and cupboard decorations, for valances, etc. In addition, oilcloth makes attractive breakfast and luncheon sets for the summer cottage, table mats for children's use, porch cushions, kitchen aprons, beach bags, table runners for the porch, babies' bibs, laundry bags, as coverings for kitchen articles (the scouring powder can, match box, etc.), racks for pot holders, waste basket, etc.

WOOL, YARN—The craze for knitted things of all kinds presents an opportunity to sell knitted garments for babies and adults. Knitted suits and dresses sold through the department stores start at around $50. The vogue for colonial furniture in the last few years has brought a demand for hooked rugs which are in keeping with colonial interiors. These rugs are also suitable for summer cottages. One young woman who made several rugs for herself, not only achieved considerable skill in making the rugs, but speed as well, and could make the small type of bedroom rug in her spare time in a few days. Through her friends, the local gift shop, and an advertisement in the neighborhood paper, she secured orders which netted her enough profit to pay half her household expenses. Her rugs sold because they were well made and were of unusual designs. Modern designs can be hooked as well as the colonial type. Knitted garments for babies, needle-point chair seats or footstool covers, all suggest ways of making money. Skill in this type of work always comes with practice.

TEXTILES—Aprons and house dresses offer a fertile field for a woman's clever hands. Many a small business has been built up by someone who started making aprons and selling them to her neighbors. Nelly Donnelly is today one of the most successful makers of women's dresses and aprons in the United States. She started this business in a little workroom in the attic of her Kansas City home. Most manufacturers thought then that women would not pay more than 69 or 79 cents for wash frocks to wear about the house. Nelly Donnelly knew better and proved it by building a success with $1.00 wash dresses. Many women have found that men like their shirts made to order and will pay a little more for a well-tailored garment. Handmade handkerchiefs for men and women, curtains and draperies, slip-covers for furniture, hand-quilted comfortables and "throws," smocks, shoe and dress bags, infants' and children's garments, fancy costumes for parties and school plays, collar and cuff sets, are other suggestions. The secret of success in this field is not to try to compete with cheap merchandise now on the market. People are willing to pay a price for handmade things. Make your dresses, aprons, shirts, and other things of excellent material and good workmanship and put a good price on them.

METAL—There is a vogue just now for articles made of tin. Almost any type of tin can be used to make such things as candlesticks, book ends, vases, boxes, sconces, and toys for children. All that is needed in the way of equipment is a work bench, a pair of leather gloves, a pair of heavy shears, a block of wood, a wooden mallet, a pair of dividers, a half round file, a vise, and a soldering outfit. The finished product should be given two coats of paint. In addition to making useful and ornamental objects of this metal one may use other metals such as embossed copper, brass, and pewter. These require a little more skill in handling. Tin may also be embossed. Hand-wrought iron equipment for fireplaces, home-markers (swinging sign at the gate), foot-scrapers, lanterns for colonial doorways, and other such items are in demand today, due, no doubt, to the revival of interest in the colonial mode of decoration. Lighting fixtures of wood and copper or wrought iron and wood are simple to make. Not long ago a woman inventor in Chicago grossed $6,000 a month, making hair curlers out of lip stick containers. Sheet metal is another material which can be handled dexterously by the amateur craftsman. This material makes up into good-looking stands, baskets, racks, shelves, fire screens, bird cages, lawn ornaments, stools, tables, lamp bases, book ends, cigarette boxes, ash trays, toys, novelties, and innumerable other things. Until recently, this work meant tedious hours with soldering irons and other hand tools. Now, however, with the new sheet metal working outfit on the market, the home craftsman can use the same methods as the modern factory does. With this equipment, a simple piece like a metal waste basket can be completed in less than half an hour and the total cost, including the paint, is less than twenty cents. The makers of the metal working equipment furnish books of designs and patterns as well as the necessary materials.

OTHER MATERIALS—Parchment lamp shades (particularly shades for wall lights) are always in good taste. The parchment may be purchased in the stores and many department stores have trained women on their staffs who will help you with designs. Handmade baskets, pottery, beadwork, batik work and hand-loomed fabrics are not difficult to learn to make and bring good prices. Raffia makes beautiful table mats and coverings for wine bottles. Shells make droll little figures. Sheet celluloid makes costume jewelry, buttons, silhouettes, etc. A scroll or jig saw is necessary for this work. Old inner tubes can be used to make marionettes—the rubber helps to make the dancing figures more realistic. Leather covered boxes, desk pads, letter cases, telephone book covers, book carriers, and many other articles made of leather sell well in the stores today, especially at Christmas. Tooled leather work is not hard to learn—a surprisingly small number of tools are needed to carry on the entire work. Some of the plastics on the market today can be used to make ornamental and useful items that are money makers. Practically all the companies making this material furnish directions for the beginner.

CHAPTER FOUR

RAISING THINGS TO SELL

THE next time you complain about making a living in the United States, think of that little party of Pilgrims who landed at Plymouth Rock in 1620. Think of what they were up against. They had come to a new country, about which they knew very little, seeking religious freedom and an opportunity to prosper. The country to which they came had no currency. There was no government to guarantee their livelihood. There was no police force to protect their property. All they had was a lot of courage and as much ground as they required *to raise the things they needed.* And Mother Earth did not disappoint them. What they planted grew. The live stock which they brought from England multiplied. And by barter and trade, they laid the foundation of the New England Confederation—that group of states north of New Amsterdam which has since become known as New England.

Any American who has a patch of ground, no matter if it be only the back yard of a city lot, is infinitely better off than his Pilgrim forbears. At least he has close at hand a market for what he raises. He has the benefit of a medium of exchange, so that he can sell the things he raises for money. He enjoys the security and protection of the armed forces of the state in which he lives. He does not have to get out of bed in the middle of the night to fight off marauding Indians. And if he can devise a way of raising things that are in demand, he can expand his activities until he has built up a large and profitable business. No other country of the world, unless possibly it might be Canada, offers such opportunities to the man who is not afraid of work and who has a desire to raise things to sell.

Under our present complex system of living, however, it is important that careful consideration be given to what you raise. It is not just a matter of planting corn and potatoes, as it was in the days of the Pilgrim Fathers. Corn and potatoes may be a drug on the market in the community in which you live, so it might be much smarter for you to raise something else. What that something else ought to be depends upon a lot of things. It depends upon what you are best qualified to raise; it depends upon what you would enjoy raising; it depends upon the needs of the people to whom you must sell the things you raise, and upon what can most profitably be raised in the particular locality in which you operate. A widow in Victoria, British Columbia, made thousands of dollars raising tuberous begonia bulbs. She started raising the bulbs as a hobby in the back yard of her Victoria home.

Today, she has a big business and the begonias are shipped all over the world. Much of her success was due to the mild climatic conditions of that part of Vancouver Island. It does not follow that you would be as successful in a community less favored by nature.

In the same way there is a man in Florida who raises alligators for leather. He used to hunt them in the Everglades, but found he could make more money raising them. By raising them himself he was able to get skins of just the right age and size, which is quite important. This man has made a great deal of money raising gators. But in order to conduct such a business successfully you have to seek a locality which is favorable for the growing of alligators. An alligator farm would not go in Maine, but a mink farm might do amazingly well. So one of the first things to consider when you set out to raise something to sell is to fit your product to the climate. Then, too, give consideration to style changes. A chap in California spent a lot of money to start an ostrich farm. He made a great success of ostrich farming so far as raising the birds was concerned. But soon after he got things going well, ostrich plumes went out of style and he went broke.

People who have not had much experience in raising things are inclined to look with favor upon various land development schemes. As a rule these are not practical. Some years ago a company was formed to plant and develop 7,000 acres of orange trees on Lake Pontchartrain, within the limits of the city of New Orleans. The land was cleared, drained, and planted in five-acre groves. They were sold to people of moderate means in the North. The development company undertook to plant the trees, and cultivate the groves until the trees reached bearing age, then they were to be taken over by the grove owner and personally operated. In theory the plan had many attractions. But it turned out to be a failure because the scale of operation was too big. When a freeze comes in a climate like New Orleans, an orange grower living on his land can get on the job and take precautions against the frost, either with oil heaters or smudge pots. It is an individual responsibility. There are today a number of small orange groves in lower Louisiana which produce remarkably fine oranges, but almost without exception the owners live on the groves and are in a position to go into action quickly upon the first frost warnings. While there have been instances where these development schemes have worked out successfully, as a rule it is much better to put your money in an improved place of your own rather than in a big scale development.

The price of farm land is still low, but it is steadily increasing in value. Many business men are buying foreclosed farms as a hedge against inflation. If you are looking for a small place of your own on which to raise the things you intend to sell, you may find just what you are seeking from one of the insurance companies or land banks. Other things being equal, the man who is going to raise things to sell, and whose capital is limited, should get as close as possible to his market.

■ ■

He Cultivates Violas for the Market

IN TREE-STUDDED Lafayette Square, a spacious park a little over a mile from San Francisco's business center, F. W. Davis' hobby of viola growing has become a profitable business, a business which has unsuspected money-making opportunities for all those who love flowers. The viola looks like a pansy except that instead of the pansy face thin dark rays spread out from a yellow center. A hundred years ago the Swiss viola found in the Alps was blended with the pansy bringing forth a blossom resembling both the violet and the pansy.

Mr. Davis, a graduate of the Royal Horticultural Society of England, has been interested in flowers for sixty years—all his life. He has had charge of nurseries and chose viola raising as his hobby because of the opportunity it gave him to experiment and bring forth new creations in size, shape and color. For twenty-five years, while in charge of the Balboa Nurseries in San Francisco, he put all his spare time into the development and evolution of the viola. He finally had one that he thought worth while and when a sufficient supply was ready he took them to a leading florist.

The viola was an immediate sensation. So instead of a hobbyist Mr. Davis became a commercial grower with a demand constantly exceeding the supply. He soon needed more ground and was fortunate in leasing the historic place up in the heights of Lafayette Square. While the park is owned by the city, the mansion and its grounds are still under private ownership.

There are twenty-five plots four and one-half feet wide and from thirty to eighty feet long, tier upon tier, a solid acre of violas blending myriads of colors. As the cut flowers are ideal for decorative purposes the entire output is marketed to San Francisco florists. Some of the plants are sold but Mr. Davis makes no effort to sell them. At first people begged for a plant for their garden and cheerfully paid $5.00 for one. Prices now range from 50 cents up.

Sixty varieties are under cultivation but the grower works continually on them and each year a new one is added. Getting new varieties is not exactly simple. It sometimes takes a thousand seedlings to produce one worth cultivating. To bring out a red one is Mr. Davis' ambition.

As a new variety appears a name suggests itself. A pure white with gold center, for instance, is called *Shasta* after the Shasta daisy, the *Rainbow* is radiantly colored, and one brownish purple is named *Othello*. Another purple suggests "When Irish Eyes Are Smiling," and is naturally *Colleen*. Then there's *Cocktail*; its browns and yellows indicate the reason.

There was no backsliding in the viola business during the depression. Mr. Davis went right on selling all he and his daughter—his only assistant—could raise. Like anyone who has found his right work, he's happy in it. A wiry, sparse, gray-haired man with a skin as bronzed as his khaki breeches, he conducts you through the grounds with quiet contentment. If you ask him whether he is kept busy, he answers: "Oh yes, I generally work ten hours a day and sometimes fifteen or twenty."

■ ■

A Map Salesman Learns How to Raise and Sell Broilers

THOUSANDS of people have started poultry farms. But not everyone has been successful. One who did succeed was Howard Whitely, a salesman for a map publishing company. During the years he had been a special representative for the publisher, he had made a good salary and had saved his money. The doctor told him he had to give up his job and get outdoors in the sunshine as much as possible. So he decided to buy a 15-acre farm near Indianapolis. The former owner had tried to make a living by growing produce, but Whitely decided to raise chickens.

Not knowing a great deal about raising chickens, he sent to the U. S. Department of Agriculture for bulletins and studied them carefully. Then he visited a farmer in the neighborhood who had been raising poultry with indifferent success. Here he learned what not to do if he wanted to make money. Inquiry revealed that the farmer had little or no idea how to feed his chickens and practically no ideas on marketing them. His poultry house was filthy, and it was obvious that the chickens had little or no attention from one day to another. The farmer thought government bulletins and poultry magazines were a lot of nonsense. "As if," he growled, "you can learn to raise chickens from a book or a magazine."

However, Howard Whitely had his own ideas on this subject which he discreetly kept to himself. On his little farm there was a poultry house which he thoroughly cleaned and fumigated. He built a poultry run and then purchased a second-hand incubator and a brooder from a dealer in town. From another dealer he bought ten dozen eggs and then he started his poultry business. Some of the eggs, of course, did not hatch. Of those that did, he kept about half for breeding, and the rest were raised for the

110

market. In raising the chickens, he followed the government bulletins religiously. He found that cleanliness was the most important thing in keeping the chickens free from disease. By preventing all possible contamination, he not only saved himself a load of trouble but considerable expense. Naturally, he made a few mistakes, but none of them serious. He found, too, that he liked raising poultry.

In the meantime, Whitely had been thinking about his marketing problem. Having been a salesman he realized it was one thing to raise a good product, but unless you got busy and sold it, there would be little profit to bank. By the time he had his poultry ready for market, he had secured orders from a number of old customers in Indianapolis as well as from two hotels and three restaurants. When his customers saw the plump, milk-fed broilers he had raised, they were sold to the hilt and he had no difficulty in getting reorders. He and his wife made a great effort to pack the birds attractively. Each capon was wrapped separately in white, moisture-proof wrapping paper, and packaged four to a box. His prices were slightly above the store price, but not a kick was received. He was supplying the market with what he knew the market wanted—a superior product. And the market was willing to pay for it.

The hotels and restaurants gave him regular orders for poultry which he delivered every two or three days. His customers telephoned him when they wanted a broiler and often drove out for it. He kept a card record of all his orders and when he failed to hear from a customer in a reasonable period of time, he followed him up by phone. Several friends of his old-time customers telephoned him orders and he also added a fancy food shop to his list. This shop, which catered to Indianapolis' "400," took only the very best of his broilers—and at very nice prices, too.

Another good order he got was from the country club which was situated about half way between his farm and Indianapolis. He had heard that the club was planning a gala affair one week-end so he interviewed the club manager, sold him a nice order of capons, and made a regular customer of him.

Howard Whitely made no attempt to market eggs as he realized that he could not develop a good egg-breed as well as meat-breed type and do justice to both. Whenever he had a surplus of eggs, he endeavored to sell them along with his poultry, but he never made any effort to secure a market for them.

Mrs. Fox's Mink Ranch

GERTRUDE FOX, the wife of a busy doctor, tried to settle down to a peaceful, quiet life among the Westchester hills. But like so many energetic, enthusiastic people, an inactive life was impossible for her. She began looking around for a hobby and having previously raised domestic animals, decided that raising fur-bearing animals might be interesting. Her first idea was to develop a fox farm, but it had features that did not appeal to her. Somebody suggested mink ranching and she decided to give it a "whirl."

Knowing nothing about raising minks, she spent a whole year studying the subject, reading every available book published and every government pamphlet on it. She also visited the few mink ranches scattered throughout the East and the Middle West. Most of these ranches, she found, were stocked with Mississippi minks, whereas, the finest type of mink comes from the north shore of Labrador. The pelts of these animals are as dark and glossy as sable. A coat made of an inferior grade of mink may bring only from $500 to $800, whereas, a coat made of Labrador skins brings from $6,000 to $12,000. She reasoned that she might as well raise the best as long as she was going to risk her time and money into the venture.

She purchased her breeding stock, consisting of 11 males and 19 females, from a rancher in northeastern Quebec. These animals were pure Labradors just one generation removed from the wild. She set up her pens on the South Salem estate and began experimenting, becoming so far as is known the first woman in this particular work. This was in 1929. In 1930 she was asked to exhibit her pets at the Woman's Exposition of Arts and Industries, and it was this event which marked the turning point in her career. Not one visitor in ten at this exposition had ever heard of a mink ranch and interest ran high.

From that time on, she was kept busy supplying breeding stock to people who wanted to start their own mink farms. As a matter of fact, while she started mink raising to sell the pelts, she has never been able to pelt any of her animals. They have all been sold as breeding stock to amateur mink ranchers.

From raising minks she has drifted naturally into teaching others how to raise them. The beginners are instructed in methods of constructing pens and runways and in proper ways of handling and feeding the animals. Her interest in her customers, or students, as she terms them, extends a year after they have purchased their herds. During this time they may write to her about their problems and she will advise them on points of feeding and handling.

As keeping the minks free from vermin is one difficulty in raising them, Mrs. Fox emphasizes the importance of building pens so that they are raised from the ground. With the exception of death from pneumonia, there are almost no fatalities from disease and if their bedding is always dry minks are not likely to have even this disease. The minks are fed a varied diet of beef, horse meat, ground bone, eggs, milk, cereals, tomatoes, cod liver oil, and fish. Each animal must be segregated from his fellows as the mink is a vicious little beast and will attack any other mink that comes near him. Fighting must be prevented at all costs, as in addition to possible deaths which may occur, the pelts may be severely damaged. The mink mates once a year, in the spring, and the litter consists of about five or six young. The young are born about fifty days after mating and are hidden by the mother in her nest until they are about four weeks old. When an excessive litter occurs, the young are raised by another mother mink or by a cat.

Besides managing two ranches of her own, providing breeding stock for amateur ranchers and publishing a monthly bulletin on fur trade conditions, Mrs. Fox owns and edits *The Black Fox Magazine* and has published a very practical book by the title of *Raising Minks in Captivity*.

■ ■

Goat Dairying—a Coming Business

ROBERT FEARN, Norbeck, Maryland, is a goat dairyman, and a very successful one. He seldom raises any kids, as he finds it more economical to buy new milking stock each fall and sell his culls in the spring. When he began business he had 125 does for which he paid $10 a head. But he learned it paid to buy better stock. Now he has about 30 for which he paid from $50 to $75 each. From these 30 does he gets four times as much milk as from the 125 inferior ones. In December and January, he gets about 70 pints daily from 25 does; in summer, 200 pints. The six- or eight-quart does, so eagerly sought by the beginner in goat keeping, are of little interest to Mr. Fearn. He considers a doe, even when she is giving but three pints a day, a profitable one. Animals which give around six to eight quarts a day are very rare and are hardly ever for sale. Generally speaking, a production of two quarts a day is fair, three quarts good, and anything over that, excellent.

The does in Mr. Fearn's dairy are not permitted to run about as they please. They must lie down, chew their cuds and make milk. At milking time they go in groups of ten to the milking room, stand in stanchions and are fed. Great care is taken to see that the milk is pure. It takes about thirty minutes to prepare them for milking and to milk them. By that time they have eaten their feed. By milking three times a day, he finds that he gets more milk. "Soy bean hay," states Mr. Fearn, "produces the best milk. Lespedeza is, without doubt, the coming roughage. The goats are very keen about it when they can get it."

Feeding rations vary considerably and each breeder or dairyman must experiment until he finds the proper combination of feeds for his stock. Information on this subject can be secured from the U. S. Department of Agriculture, Washington, D. C.; from *The Goat World*, Vincennes, Indiana; the *Dairy Goat Journal*, Fairbury, Nebraska, and the American Goat Society, Inc., Herkimer, New York.

The goat selected by most breeders for stock today is a pure-bred, imported type. The American or "scrub" goat does not give good milk production and its kids command very low prices. It is, undoubtedly, to the best interest of the goat owner to purchase pure-bred animals only and to see that all the kids are registered. The types usually purchased by breeders and dairymen are the Toggenburg, Saanen, Nubian, French Alpine, Rock Alpine, and the Murciana. The Toggenburg is the biggest milk producer and the Nubian is noted for the richness of its milk, the butter fat content being much higher than in any of the other breeds. The price of pure-breds will run not less than $35 for mature stock or $15 for kids. Certain stock for breeding may run somewhat higher than these prices and, naturally, outstanding breeding stock will bring very fancy prices just as any other kind of fancy live stock does.

Goat milk sells for 25 cents to 50 cents a quart. As it is the nearest animal milk to human milk, it is an excellent food for babies. However, being much richer than cow's milk, it must be diluted by more than 50 per cent before a baby can assimilate it. Goat milk is alkaline instead of acid (cow's milk is acid), so it is an excellent food for invalids, old people, and those suffering from stomach disturbances. Goat milk also contains one important mineral which cow's milk lacks—iron. The taste of goat's milk is very palatable if the animal has been fed correctly. There will be absolutely no disagreeable odor or taste if the doe's stall is kept clean, the milk is handled in a sanitary manner, and the bucks are kept in another stable altogether. As the goat is practically free from tuberculosis, its milk does not carry that dread disease germ. But to make certain that the goats are not likely to contact tuberculosis, they should be kept separate from cows.

Mr. Fearn's merchandising methods are particularly interesting. Instead of selling to hospitals and doctors, he has placed small refrigerators in drug stores in Washington and Baltimore. They are attractively labeled and have glass doors that give a view of the pint-size paper bottles of goat milk. Each pint bottle sells for 25 cents and they have a ready sale.

The dairyman may also find a market for goats' milk in the canneries which are now putting up a brand of evaporated, unsweetened goats' milk. This retails for 20 cents a can of 11 ounces, which is equivalent to about 30 cents a quart for the original milk.

A doe averaging two quarts a day for 10 months produces 600 quarts. At 25 cents a quart, this returns an income of $150. Feed for the doe for 12 months at 10 cents a day would be $36. The profit less the labor cost would be $114. A three-quart doe would give about 900 quarts at 25 cents or $225. The feed would probably cost a little more, say 12 ½ cents daily or $45. This would make a profit less the labor cost of $180. This little comparison between the two- and three-quart milker easily shows how much more profitable the better milker can be. It is conservatively said that a good doe will pay her purchase price back in milk each year and an extra dividend in kids.

Cheese As a Source of Income

A great many goat owners have failed to recognize the opportunity existing to make additional money producing and selling goat cheese. Some of the finest imported cheeses are made from goat milk. Tons of these cheeses are coming into this country every year and finding a ready market. There is a good market for domestic cheeses also, but the public must be taught the value of good domestic goat cheeses. Among the cheeses made from goat milk which are finding favor today are cottage, cream, Neufchatel, cheddar, Roquefort, Swiss, Parmesan, and primost or brown whey cheese. Directions for making these cheeses can be secured from your state agricultural experiment station, the U. S. Department of Agriculture, or from the *Dairy Goat Journal*, Fairbury, Nebraska.

It is well for the amateur to begin with soft cheeses such as cottage, cream and Neufchatel, as these are easy to learn to make. The first thing to know about making cheese is that your does must test pretty high in butter fat or you cannot make a quality cheese. Good cheese simply cannot be made with poor quality milk.

Where is the market for goat cheese? If you already have a market for milk, everyone of your customers is a prospect for cheese. Take samples to your regular customers when you deliver your milk. Also place samples in the stores in your locality.

Advertise locally and don't forget to have some signs on the roads approaching your dairy as well as a large sign on the dairy itself. Passing motorists are frequently good prospects. Your neighbors, your friends, and the friends of your friends are all prospects for your products. Tell them about the value of goat milk and cheese. If you make good cheese, "tell the world about it"—word-of-mouth advertising moves a great deal of merchandise.

■ ■

A Different Kind of Poultry Farm

A CHICKEN farm, organized along factory lines, has been a great success in the East. This poultry farm near Cockeysville, Maryland, covers only one acre of ground. The 61,000 chickens handled by this farm would require 610 acres if they were being raised and fed in the usual manner. On this farm, however, the chickens never touch the ground—never go outdoors. They live in tiers of wire cages, in large, air-conditioned, disinfected, thermostatically heated and cooled, photoelectrically-lighted rooms. There are no nests for the 2,500 laying hens, as the cages are so arranged that eggs, when laid, roll down into a little rack outside. Here the eggs are picked up by attendants on hourly collection rounds. Under these conditions, the daily production of laying hens is 58 per cent as against the usual 50 per cent figure.

The chickens' food is within easy reach of each cage, being supplied on a conveyor belt which runs on each tier. A constant drip of water is provided from a metal nipple at the top of the cages. A second conveyor belt, running under the cages, catches the waste matter which is carried to a bin and there removed periodically to be used in making a high-grade fertilizer.

As any infection would be disastrous to the entire flock of 61,000 chickens, the utmost cleanliness prevails. Each room is disinfected once a day and, at short intervals, all cages are subjected to live steam. The twenty-one employees wear spotless uniforms—the women being dressed in white and the men in striped linen trousers and coats.

This factory-operated farm has created such interest that not only have farmers in adjacent communities made trips to the farm, but those from distant lands, such as Egypt and Africa. In fact, so numerous are the visitors during the week-ends, that the cages have been separated from the onlookers by walls of glass in order to minimize the danger of infection.

Selling "Fighting" Fish by Mail

WHEN Bill Klaiber, of San Francisco, took up the hobby of breeding Siamese fighting fish and other tropical varieties, he little realized he was starting what has since turned out to be a "national" fish business.

Bill's regular job is a glass worker for a paint manufacturer. He began raising tropical fish three years ago, having bought some fish from a friend who was going out of business. As usual, Bill delved deeply into his subject, reading everything he could find; even buying expensive books unobtainable in the library. He applied what he read and added constantly to his stock. Fanciers heard of his fine collection and came to buy. Bill Klaiber was amazed at the marketing possibilities and the eagerness of people to secure a coveted specimen. So he became a dealer as well as a fancier before many months passed.

He had made contact with seamen to secure rare fish for him when they went inland for fresh water in the tropics. Today he maintains tanks on a number of boats that reach the tropics, paying seamen to look after his interests.

When an opportunity came three months ago to buy a small hatchery complete, Bill moved his outfit to a larger store which he remodeled and called "Kay's Aquarium." His wife spends part of each day there and he keeps open evenings and Sundays.

There's a tropical atmosphere about Kay's Aquarium. Innumerable tiny fish, streaks of iridescence and brilliant color, dart about in small tanks. Aquatic plants furnish both oxygen and decoration.

Caring for the fish is easy. The real work is in breeding, but therein lies its fascination. It means time and patience and often disappointment, but Bill Klaiber never tires of hybridizing and trying for perfect specimens. Some species, such as the Scalare, are particularly difficult to handle. "These fellows," he explains, "won't marry unless the bride pleases them and it takes finesse and many females to induce them to become breeders." The fact is that Bill is one of the two or three fanciers in town who have succeeded in making benedicts out of the Scalare. Another rare specimen deposits its orange colored eggs in an even row on a long reed, and the male and female "spell" one another guarding the eggs and foraging for food.

The *Betta* or Siamese fighting fish, in which he specializes, are kept singly in mayonnaise jars because if placed together they would fight each other to the death. In Siam, *Bettas* are used for gambling, and fortunes have been won or lost on the outcome of staged battles. The little savage is correspondingly tender in courtship, however, guarding the fertilized spawn against would-be devourers, including its erstwhile mate.

Volumes might be written about the tiny tank dwellers. Bill's initial stock of thirty that cost him two dollars has increased to several hundreds. He receives orders from Texas, the Middle West—even Canada, and his weekly profit sometimes exceeds his salary. How does he get his trade? News, of course, travels fast among fanciers and much of his new business comes from friends of old customers.

One reason for his success is his practice of selling only healthy stock. He believes that while "sluffing off" sickly fish is easy, it is a foolish thing to do. Another reason for his success is because he sets up the aquarium, if desired, keeps in touch with customers, and gives the buyer help whenever he can.

A map in his outer room illustrates his thoroughness. Patiently he worked out a list of tropical fish and their habitats. On a map of the world he printed the names of various fish in the section where they are to be found. The map, besides being informative, is an aid in selecting stock.

■ ■

Breeding Dogs for Fun and Profit

DO YOU like dogs? Do dogs like you? Then why not turn that liking into dollars? Why not combine business with pleasure and raise dogs? Perhaps no business offers better opportunities for making money in your spare time or to develop a national reputation in your field. For instance, Mrs. Harold Cluxton, of Chicago, regarded as one of the most successful breeders of Russian wolfhounds in America, started her kennels as a hobby.

It was not until Mrs. Cluxton was given a very fine pair of Russian wolfhounds by a friend living in Canada that she decided to establish her own kennels. She became intensely interested in the breed and studied everything she could find on the subject. She subscribed to all the dog magazines published both here and in England and even went so far as to study the Russian language, so that she could read what had been published in that country on wolfhounds. She has carried off nearly all the prizes for wolfhounds in most of the shows, and has obtained as high as $5,000 for a single dog.

One of the nice things about breeding and raising dogs is that you can start with as little as $100 capital. True, you cannot get a "blue ribbon" dog for any such sum, but with a little shopping around and good judgment you can get a likely bitch for that amount in a number of popular breeds.

118

First of all decide upon the breed on which you intend to specialize and get a registered bitch of the best blood lines possible. The bitch should be healthy and should not vary in type from the breed she represents. In other words, if the breed is supposed to be heavy of bone, select breeding stock with this characteristic. Check up on the breed carefully and find out the main points upon which the animals are judged, then try to get as many good points in your breeding stock as you possibly can. If possible, purchase stock from a line in which there have been blue ribbon winners as this gives you a good selling point to talk about to prospective purchasers.

As in every business, there are hazards in dog raising. Worms and distemper take the greatest toll of puppies, but both can be controlled if the breeder is careful. At the beginning it is wise to invest money in the services of a good veterinary to handle the first few litters, to worm the puppies and take care of any other problems with which you are not familiar. This will, of course, cost you extra money and must be figured in your overhead. In addition, you will need the services of a veterinary to guard your kennel against distemper. Every breeder who wishes to protect himself, as well as his customers, against losses from distemper, has his puppies inoculated against this dread disease at the proper time. If you take chances with this disease, you are sure to regret it as the expense of bringing even one puppy through it is considerable. So many times the veterinary cannot save the dog and then the expensive treatments, plus the loss of the dog, will eat up your profits.

If you like dogs, you probably have attended the dog shows and know something about the various breeds. Of course, the most popular dog appears at the dog shows in great numbers. One year it will be the German shepherds (commonly called police dogs), another year, wire-haired terriers, another year Airedales or Scotties. Then there are certain breeds that never seem to go out of style. Over a period of time these have been the Boston bull terrier, the Pekingese, and the cocker spaniel. Certain types of hunting dogs are always popular. The setter (both English and Irish) is favored by those who never shoot game as well as by the sportsman. The German shepherd has been another unusually popular dog, but as he is not quite suited to city life his popularity is beginning to wane.

For the city type of home and especially for those who live in apartment buildings, the following dogs are the most suitable, due to their size and their adaptability to city life:

Boston bull terriers, French bulldogs, dachshunds, wirehaired fox terriers, smooth fox terriers, cocker spaniels, Scottish terriers, Irish terriers, the Pekingese, the Pomeranian, the sealyham, miniature schnauzer, Japanese spaniel, and the Yorkshire terrier.

For the suburban home, the dogs just listed and the following are the most suitable breeds:

English and Irish setters, Irish water spaniels, the springer spaniel, Airedale-terriers, collies, Dobermann Pinschers, German shepherds, Dalmatian hounds, chowchows, German schnauzer (medium size), pointers, beagle hounds, Gordon setters, bull terriers, and bulldogs.

For the large estate or farm, the following dogs may be added to those listed for the suburban home:

Russian wolfhound, Irish wolfhound (the largest of all dogs), St. Bernard, mastiff, Great Dane, Newfoundland, Labrador retriever, Shetland sheep dog.

If you are in a section where there is considerable hunting each year, the following hunting breeds may sell well:

Springer spaniels, Irish water spaniels, beagle hounds, rabbit hounds, coonhounds, deerhounds, foxhounds, Labrador retrievers, English and Irish setters, pointers, Llewellyn and Gordon setters.

Regardless of the fact that in your locality there may exist a market for the larger breed of dog such as the St. Bernard, mastiff, Great Dane, etc., the beginner may do well to cultivate another market in which he can sell the smaller breeds. The reasons for this are obvious. You need a large amount of ground to maintain kennels for the larger breeds, and the food bill for these breeds is an important item in your overhead as you will realize once you have seen a St. Bernard eat.

Raising dogs naturally entails a great deal of work—kennels must be kept immaculate to ward off disease, the dogs must be brushed and combed, their food must be carefully prepared and they must be fed at regular periods. When ill they must be segregated and carefully tended not only for humanitarian reasons but for financial reasons also. The dam must be cared for especially at whelping time and the puppies must be given a great deal of attention. Then there is weaning which means more work. However, if you really like to handle dogs, all this work will be interesting and therefore not drudgery.

For advertising you will need to have some cards printed for prospects who come to see the pups, the local paper should carry your advertising, and every merchant in your vicinity should know that you are a breeder of Scotties, Bostons, or whatever breed you intend handling. An advertisement in the Sunday morning edition of the largest circulation newspaper in your city, or if you live in the suburbs or country, the nearest large city, will often bring prospects. Be sure to include your telephone number.

Many small breeders raise dogs as a side line and manage a full-time job also. In this case, someone else in the family must have the routine care of the dogs. One interesting example is that of a laundry driver in

Chicago who worked six days a week for one of the largest laundries in the city. He and his wife lived in a little cottage on a three-acre place on the edge of town. Both of them were unusually fond of dogs and hunting. Having purchased a fine English setter for their hunting trips they decided to put him at stud. The charge made for this was $25 and in addition they received two male puppies from the litter, each of which sold for $35. The dog was bred again at the same charge and two pups again were sold for $35 and $40. With this money, they purchased a cocker spaniel of good blood lines and placed him at stud. The first two pups they received, a male and a female, sold for $35 and $30, respectively (the female usually brings a lower price than the male puppies). Later a female cocker spaniel was purchased which came from a blue ribbon line and the litters from this pair sold from $35 to $45 a puppy.

Fresh eggs from his own chickens, rich milk from a near-by farmer, careful feeding and plenty of sunshine gave his puppies good bone and muscle and shining coats. They practically sold themselves "on sight." Naturally, his customers were told about these puppies when they were available and many orders were received through their "word-of-mouth" advertising. A friendly arrangement with a "training school" for hunting dogs gave him some good leads and at the same time provided the school with the names of those who had made recent purchases of puppies.

■ ■

Bee Keeping for Profit

GEORGE JESSUP, Council Bluffs, Iowa, began raising bees as a side line. Before long, this side line returned enough profits to more than take care of expenses, and today his income from bee keeping exceeds a thousand dollars annually. In fact, bees not only pay all his household expenses, but enable him to put a good round sum in the bank every year.

"Few occupations," says Jessup, "offer the interest and relaxation bee keeping affords, and for the office worker it has the additional incentive of being carried on out of doors. I started with one colony in a large hive, which I was told would provide ample room for brooding and winter storage, eliminate swarming, and provide large combs for the queen bee thus making her more efficient. My initial expenses for bees and equipment ran about twenty dollars, and my cost of producing honey that year was five dollars. The colony produced a hundred pounds of honey, all of which I sold locally to retailers at an average price of sixty cents a bail, a measure which contains five pounds.

"The second year the colony was increased greatly by a winter brood, so I split it, and made a second colony, which also came in with a hundred pounds of honey. That, I found, was about the average yield for each bee colony. Meanwhile, I was so pleased with the way the bee keeping was going, that I increased the number of colonies to ten, and sold some of the honey at wholesale, getting an average of forty-five cents a bail for it. There is, of course, more work connected with the ten colonies, but not a great deal more as about all there is to do is gather the honey. Bees do not require much attention. You can leave them alone for several days and they will feed themselves and work for you while you are away. Last year, I added fifteen more colonies, to bring the total number to twenty-five, and my profit increased proportionately.

"Most of the honey I produce goes to local grocers. Some of it I ship to Dubuque and points not too distant. I sell to local grocers at sixty cents a bail as a general rule, and get fifty-five to seventy cents from outside markets. When I sell to the consumer, I get twenty cents a pound, and I did a lot of consumer business last year. It's in that market most of the money is to be made. However, I haven't been able to take the time to develop consumer demand properly, although I've been determined for a long time to go after it.

"Bee keeping is fascinating as well as profitable. You can keep bees in any place—the cellar, barn, garage, attic or even in a closet which has an outside window, and be perfectly sure that as long as you have a good queen in charge, the colony will stay 'put.' If the colony is permitted to get too large, however, there is a chance that a queen coming out of the winter brood will lure a portion of them to swarm in a hollow tree somewhere. So it is good policy to watch them and separate them, giving the queens from your brood a house of their own so they won't lure other bees to swarm.

"I believe much of my success has been due to the use of the Caucasian bees exclusively. These bees are gentler and permit you to work among them faster than you could with other types. They seem to be less inclined to develop disease, and their crop of honey is fully as good as the Italian bee. Experience has taught me the disadvantages of the big hive, however, and I now use standard ten frame equipment, with full depth hive bodies for supers. I simplify the provisioning of the brood chamber by slipping in a frame of honey from another super, assuring ample winter stores. Combs with patches of drone are easily removed by exchanging with combs from supers and allowing the brood to emerge above. When the comb is filled with honey at the end of the season it is handled right along with the rest of the crop until extracted. A mark across the top bar, made with a hive tool, makes its identification simple and disposal sure."

A bee apiary may be started with a few dollars. A small colony will more than pay for itself in a short time, and furnish a hobby or a side line that is immensely fascinating. Housing equipment may be made by yourself, or may be purchased for as little as ten dollars. The equipment is designed as a permanent colony home, and is built to withstand freezing temperatures.

Bees may be secured at very reasonable prices. You may buy a two-pound package of baby bees, with a young queen, for as little as two dollars. Two or three of such packages will start a very fine colony for you, and will soon be producing a hundred pounds of honey annually or better. It may be pointed out that the existing demand for honey far exceeds visible supply, and that a good price may be obtained for your entire honey yield all the year round. Wholesale prices vary somewhat in different sections of the country, ranging from thirty to fifty-five cents a bail. Retail prices range between forty-five cents and eighty-five cents a bail. In most sections, however, neither wholesale prices nor retail fluctuate much more than ten cents a bail.

■ ■

There's a Big Demand for Ornamental Birds

"I TURNED sixty acres, not suitable for farming, into pens for raising ornamental birds," said John Keller, of Kenosha, Wisconsin. "This land has a pond at one end and a shallow creek runs through it, but the rocks and marshy spots make it bad pasture. It was the pond that made me think of trying my luck with swans. These sixty acres, being handy to the house, would be ideal for swan raising I figured, because I could easily watch the birds. I paid sixty-five dollars for a pair of white swans, fenced off pen space for them at the edge of the pond. I read a good deal about the swan's habits and found it is an affectionate bird which, once mated, will never leave its mate. They lay in March, April and May, prefer to live by themselves, and must be kept away from animals. My first brood was seven young swans and by the end of the summer, I had eighteen swans. The swan, being very hardy, is not difficult to raise. It requires less care than a turkey or a chicken, and brings higher prices. My original investment was sixty-five dollars for the first pair and thirty dollars for fencing. By Christmas, I had sold eight pair of young swans, at seventy dollars a pair. I kept the others for breeding. In two and a half years, I've raised and sold a hundred-and-fifty pair of swans at an average price of sixty dollars.

"Shortly after I started the swans, I decided to experiment a little with peacocks as I had plenty of room. The peacock, I soon discovered, needed a high fence around the entire area used for raising him, since these birds have the habit of roosting on housetops, trees, and other high places, and refuse to sleep in a coop. They are quite hardy birds, almost as easy to handle as swans and are not bothered much by the cold. They are more prolific than the swan, and because of the beauty of their plumage sell for big prices. I get up to ninety-five dollars for a pair of well-matched green peacocks, and last year sold seventy-six pair at this price.

About the only thing I have to watch closely is that no dogs or other small animals get into the big pens. While the swan and peacock are large birds, well able to take care of themselves in any battle with a dog, the presence of a dog or the threat of one visiting them is sufficient to keep the birds from laying. Frighten a peacock or swan and it seems to lose all desire to lay. The swan is not subject to disease such as attack chickens, hence loss through disease and sickness is practically nil. The peacock and the swan mate for life and care should be taken to discover how they mate up, and not to break up mated birds. I figure the cost for raising a swan to be about three dollars, and three twenty-five for a peacock. This includes the cost of making the pens, feeding, incidental expenses, except labor. The work of looking after the birds, which is done by my wife and myself, takes only an hour or two each day."

The raising of ornamental birds takes more space than would be required for other fowl, inasmuch as these birds like to strut and preen themselves a good deal. There are many farms having marginal land that might profitably be devoted to raising these birds. A ready market is always at hand, as the demand for peacocks and swans by public parks, zoos, private estates, playgrounds, public and private institutions, and universities is greater than the existing supply.

Other ornamental birds may be raised along with swans and peacocks with little added cost. For example, the Chinese Mandarin duck, wood duck and Red Billed Tree duck will get along well with the swans, while Golden and Silver pheasants and Pearl Guinea fowl will thrive with the peacocks.

■ ■

A Smart Way to Market Broilers

WHEN Mrs. Alice Moffet, who lives on the outskirts of Blue Island, Illinois, decided it was up to her to help balance the family budget, she turned to raising broilers to make money. After several months of experimenting with marketing ideas, she hit upon a method that enabled her to earn more than a thousand dollars from her venture.

"Like many others who start a chicken ranch, I thought all one had to do was feed the little chicks, keep them warm, and when they were twelve weeks old, sell them to the butcher. I knew nothing about marketing poultry. I soon found out, however, that to make a big profit from broilers, they should be dressed and packaged attractively before marketing.

"I followed the accepted practice of buying one-day-old chicks from responsible hatcheries. Putting them in brooders, I carried them along until they were twelve weeks old. In developing the pullets for market, I made many mistakes which I have since corrected. I had permitted the chickens to run in a large pen which made their flesh tough. Now I no longer let them run about but keep them in a special 'broiler plant' and they bring better prices. Keeping the chicks in the 'broiler plant' enables me to feed and care for 500 day-old chicks in a small space. At twelve weeks they are ready for market and bring top prices.

"At first, I shipped the live pullets to the wholesale house, but I soon discovered that the loss from shrinkage in shipping, regardless of distance, is about 10 per cent, which cuts heavily into their market value. Pullets lose weight when shipped due to handling and irregular feeding. The first time I checked this loss against the price paid me by the commission companies, I couldn't understand it. I was doing a big business but wasn't making money. So I experimented with some marketing ideas. Instead of selling the pullets alive, I dressed them and packaged them in attractive pasteboard boxes labeled, 'Milk-Fed Broilers.' I sold them to the butchers who get a few cents a pound more for dressed broilers attractively wrapped in waxed paper than they can get for live pullets.

"Experience convinces me that cross-bred pullets make the best broilers. Their hybrid vigor makes them gain faster than pure-bred chickens, and they generally weigh 30 per cent more at twelve weeks than a pure-bred pullet. But in growing pullets for broiler purposes, the most important thing is the feed. Only a good feed can develop a broiler to the limit of its inherent capacity. A chick of the heavier breeds will gain up to thirty times its weight in a period of a few weeks if given a carefully selected prepared feed."

While Mrs. Moffet now has a chicken house forty feet long and eighteen feet wide, she started in a very small way; investing only $60 altogether. The present house cost $190 and her investment in equipment amounted to $160. This total of $350 was part of her profits. She pays four cents for one-day old chicks in 500 quantities. Five hundred chicks, when twelve weeks old, cost a total of $120. "When dressed, packaged in pasteboard containers, and wrapped in waxed paper, they bring Mrs. Moffet a profit of about $50. The cost of packaging of the pullets runs almost four cents each. Chickens for broiler purposes are not difficult to raise. As many as 200 may be developed in a comparatively small space, with a small broiler plant. A ready market is furnished in every fair-sized city, especially during the spring. Prices for broilers vary with the season. Only chicks from disease-free stock should be used for broilers. Sickly chickens do not have the necessary stamina, and the high percentage of loss through death wipes out the profits.

■ ■

Raising Rabbits for Their Wool

DO YOU know that rabbit fur is dyed and used in the manufacture of synthetic sealskin coats? Well, it is, and it offers one more way for a wide-awake person to make a thousand dollars. Blanch Krabill, of Toledo, Ohio, had been raising rabbits for their pelts which she had been selling to a tannery at a profit. However, she discovered that she could make about as much money by shearing the rabbits for their wool instead of using the whole pelt. Her hutches now contain nine hundred rabbits which supply rabbit wool for commercial purposes.

"I hated to kill the rabbits for their pelts," Blanch said, "because I became so attached to them. But I had so many of them and they multiplied so rapidly that I could not afford to keep them. I had to get money out of them some way and when a friend suggested shearing them and selling their fur for wool, my problem was solved. Rabbit fur is softer than lamb's wool, and not so greasy. My problem was to find out if there was a demand for the wool and, upon making inquiries, I learned about the rabbit's commercial value as a wool producer. The Angora, with its unusually long silky hair, is the ideal rabbit for wool production. There are regular markets for this wool in all big cities, such as Detroit, Chicago and New York. Upon making this discovery, I sheared the rabbits and shipped the wool to the nearest market.

"Rabbit wool is used for any number of things, such as knitting sweaters, baby clothes, muffs, scarfs and dresses. It makes a beautiful yarn which has the strength and durability of regular sheep wool although it is much finer and softer. I receive a dollar and forty cents a pound for this wool and shear the rabbits four times a year. The Angora rabbit is unusually large, and each one produces about one and one-quarter pounds of wool yearly."

The rabbit is one of the most easily raised of all the furbearing animals and as many as five hundred rabbits may be successfully raised in your own back yard. They are not subject to vermin of any kind, and resist practically all ailments. Success requires only ordinary attention to sanitation and cleaning the rabbit hutches regularly. The cost of raising rabbits in quantities of a hundred or more is about ten cents a rabbit.

Miss Krabill gives this suggestion on breeding to those interested in raising rabbits. Secure two bred does and a buck from a reliable breeder who will guarantee them to be healthy, pedigreed stock. Specify that the buck must be from a different litter than the does, so he may be used when breeding the does' litters later on. This precaution will enable you to mate the rabbits in the first and second litters without danger of inbreeding. Rabbits reproduce prolifically, and with good stock to start, you soon will have a number of animals with salable pelts. You can dispose of them through a tannery or, if you prefer, shear them for their wool.

■ ■

"Glad" Garden Brings Joy and Profit

EIGHT years ago Lucretia Kays Hanson, of Mill Valley, California, was confronted with the problem of supporting five children and a husband whose ill health had forced him to quit business. Mrs. Hanson is five feet tall and weighs a hundred pounds but she shouldered the burden without flinching. At first she was a "jill" of all trades. Finally she applied for a job with the *Mill Valley Record*, a newspaper edited by two capable women. Perhaps women editors are soft-hearted; anyway Mrs. Hanson got work in the office and has been there ever since. Evenings she typed letters for a blind business man, coached in French, English and mathematics, and looked after her brood and her nine-room house.

Meanwhile, Mr. Hanson busied himself with his hobby of raising gladioli. He had the knack and the "glads" responded by blossoming in gorgeous profusion. People were enthusiastic over their exceptional beauty and wanted to buy, but Mr. Hanson gave the flowers away in great armfuls until his wife suggested: "If they want to buy why not sell?"

They discussed commercial distribution and Mrs. Hanson called on the owner of the town's swankiest market. Would he put their gladioli in for sale? He consented, saying that flowers like theirs would be an asset. His only stipulation was that they be arranged before the store opened.

Mrs. Hanson got up still earlier six mornings a week and while the fresh produce was being set out she arranged masses of "glads" in tall vases. Fifty dozen were sold the first month which added twenty-five dollars to the Hanson income. As the grocer refused a commission, Mrs. Hanson insisted that he take home all the flowers he wanted on Saturdays and whenever his wife gave a party.

The sale of bulbs followed naturally. Customers wanted certain varieties for their gardens. One big seller was a pale yellow which has been named *Billionaire* because of its great stalk and the profusion of blossoms, sometimes twenty to a stalk. *Billionaires* were popular for wedding decorations and floral sprays.

It wasn't long before she found there was another outlet for the flowers. Although several large nurseries are located in outlying districts, there is no florist in Mill Valley; consequently the undertaker sells sprays. In return for services rendered he taught Mrs. Hanson how to wire sprays and she began getting orders which brought from two dollars up.

Soon other ideas for getting orders presented themselves. A donation now and then to the leading tea room brought orders for decorations when banquets were held there. A bouquet presented to the owner when a new store opened in town increased trade; so did an occasional advertisement in the *Record*. On one outstanding occasion red "glads" banked the platform of the San Francisco Civic Auditorium where ten thousand people gathered at the International Convention of the Christian Endeavor to celebrate that society's Golden Jubilee.

"Selling 'glads' has been fun, and although it hasn't meant a fortune the money has often been a godsend," Mrs. Hanson remarks. "Besides, being gainfully occupied has saved Mr. Hanson much worry and unhappiness."

■ ■

Making Money from an Herb Garden

ALTHOUGH herb gardens are as old as history, the last generation in America seems to have neglected this type of gardening entirely. Of course, we use sage and celery salt in seasoning our cookery, but most of us have forgotten the herbs our grandmothers and great-grandmothers knew and used daily in their kitchens.

Recently, however, there has been a revival of interest in the herb family and once again kitchens are giving off the delicious odors of foods seasoned with thyme, marjoram, basil, and tarragon. While these herbs may not add to the food value of a dish, they do give it a savory flavor. Certain herbs, notably lavender, are also used for scenting linen closets or chests. There are also the medicinal herbs which constitute a study in themselves.

Most herbs can be grown with little care if they are planted in good, well-worked soil in a sunny spot. Midsummer is the time for collecting herbs from the garden. If cut before the flowers open, all the fragrance is retained in the dried herbs. Not only is herb gardening a pleasant way to make money, but the study of herbs is a most fascinating subject. A woman in the East has made an excellent living with her garden of the rarer medicinal herbs which she sells to the pharmaceutical houses. Not only is her garden a financial success, but she has become an authority on medicinal herbs.

One does not need a large space for an herb garden. Miss Helen Lyman of Oakland, California, has an herb garden, approximately 25 feet in diameter which holds 30 varieties of herbs. Her little booklet entitled, "30 Herbs Will Make an Herb Garden," tells others how to succeed in this interesting enterprise.

Marshall Field & Company, Chicago, the largest department store in the world, now has a department devoted entirely to herbs for use in cookery, medicine and perfume. The herbs are imported from an herb farm more than a century old which is located near Kent, England. Among the products handled by Field's herb department are the old-fashioned pomander balls just like those our grandmothers hung in their clothespresses. All the well-known herbs are available, several types of vinegars, jellies with special herb flavoring, and cosmetics prepared from certain beneficial herbs. A small shelf of 10 selected kitchen herbs is sold as a unit. Mixed salad herbs are also sold by ounce or half ounce.

Many a woman who has a sunny corner in her garden could develop an herb garden specializing either in medicinal or in kitchen herbs. If she is known for her jellies and jams, she can combine two interesting occupations and, incidentally, make jellies so unusual that they will bring higher prices. The better food specialty shops offer an outlet for such products.

There are several books on the subject of herb growing and most of the garden magazines have published articles about people who "herb garden." The details of such gardening are simple enough for any man or woman to follow and success in this field is dependent only upon the energy and initiative of the individual gardener.

■ ■

Raising Goldfish for Premiums

BACK in 1900, Eugene C. Shireman was selling washing powder for a company which had hit upon the bright idea of offering a small bowl and a pair of goldfish as a premium. This premium idea worked so well that they soon ran out of goldfish and Shireman decided to turn a swamp, which he had received as a legacy years ago, into a fish farm and sell his crop to the company. He stocked his pool with two hundred goldfish which multiplied rapidly. But by the time he was turning out sufficient fish to sell, the company had gone out of business. However, there were other outlets, and today the fish are sold through five-and-ten stores, pet shops, chain stores, drug stores, florists, department stores, etc. The various State Departments are also a market for goldfish which are used extensively in mosquito control work. The goldfish, which belong to the carp family, are exceedingly fond of the mosquito larvae and will clear a stagnant pond of water of these pests in no time.

From a small start with 200 fish in 1900, Eugene Shireman has developed the famous Grassyfork Fisheries at Martinsville, Indiana, and has raised over 75,000,000 fish. Grassyfork Fisheries consist of 1,500 acres of gently rolling hills and give employment to 125 persons. There are 615 ponds as well as 216 hatching tanks. The ponds and tanks are terraced so that they can be fed with a continuous circuit of fresh water from the numerous springs located on the property.

One hundred and sixty thousand carefully selected goldfish are reserved as breeding stock at the Grassyfork hatcheries. Branch shipping points are maintained at Chicago, Illinois, and Saddle River, New Jersey. From Martinsville the goldfish are shipped via a fleet of tank trucks. From Chicago and Saddle River the fish are shipped to the customers, via express, in peculiar, globe-shaped shipping cans. In addition to the goldfish, the Grassyfork hatcheries also raise some forty varieties of toy tropical fish which have recently become so popular, such as Gouramis, the live-bearing Guppies, Helleri, and other species. As these fish are less hardy than the common goldfish, the tanks in which they are raised are located indoors in greenhouses. An important part of this business is the aquatic plant department. About sixty varieties of water lilies are raised, besides perennials, marsh and bog plants, and all the other items necessary, to add beauty to pools and rock gardens.

The price for goldfish runs from a nickel apiece for small common goldfish to $25 apiece for the relatively rare Moor "telescopes." The most interesting goldfish and also the most valuable specimen ever seen in America was the famous Liberty Bond fish which was exhibited during the World War. The colors of this fish were red, white and blue and it was used to attract crowds during Liberty Loan drives of 1917 and 1918. The value placed on it at that time was $10,000.

There is still a big market for goldfish among merchants and other business men who use them as premiums. The L. Fish Furniture Company, of Chicago, built its business, one of the largest in the world, that way. Fish furniture is sold on the installment plan. When a customer gets her account almost paid up, she is called upon by a salesman who presents her with a bowl of goldfish with "Mr. Fish's compliments." That breaks the ice. The salesman then proceeds to find out if the customer has an electric refrigerator. If not, he sells her one—on the installment plan, of course. If she has a refrigerator, he sells her a washing machine or some other electric appliance. In this way the company's customers are kept on the books year after year.

■ ■

Cleaning Up on Turkeys

WHEN Mrs. Paul Engle, of Pulaski County, Indiana, decided to raise turkeys instead of chickens, she didn't realize the "clean-up" she was going to make. "Everybody was raising chickens," Mrs. Engle said, "but only a few were paying attention to turkeys. So I began with turkeys on a small scale. In 1933 we had a thousand turkeys which we sold at Christmas time at twenty cents a pound, and we were well satisfied with our profits." As the average turkey ran to a little over ten pounds and her cost for each of the birds was about 50 cents, she had a profit of about $1,400 for that one season.

The work connected with the care and raising of the turkey poults did not bother Mrs. Engle in the least. "Work," she said, "is a tonic for anybody." She converted the former chicken house on the farm into a large turkey house. It was a big job but proved worth the effort. As she places day-old poults in this turkey house, everything connected with it must be kept safe and sanitary. Before placing the baby poults in the old chicken house, the floor, which is cement, was scrubbed with lye water. Every piece of equipment was cleaned and scrubbed, and the house fumigated. A sun pen was built just outside this chicken house. The sun pen was a collapsible affair, arranged so that it could be quickly taken down, and put out of the way. It consisted of frames covered with wire, and cost but little to make. In good weather, the young poults were permitted to run in this sun pen. After the oats harvest was completed, the turkey poults were turned into a small oat field, which was used as a turkey range.

The entire cost of rearranging the chicken house and building the turkey pen was less than $100. Mrs. Engle did not buy brooders and incubators for the turkey poults, but utilized the equipment on the premises which had been used for raising chickens.

Sanitation, Mrs. Engle believes, is an all-important element in successful turkey raising. Too much care cannot be given the pens to keep them free from infectious diseases. Once a week she has clean straw spread on the floors of the turkey house after soiled bedding is removed. When anyone enters the turkey house where the young poults are kept, he must put on rubber boots that have been thoroughly disinfected just before entering. "We cannot be too careful about this," Mrs. Engle explained. "Without such precaution, blackhead infection could be tracked in from the ground over which the chickens have run."

Although Mrs. Engle has increased the number of turkeys on the farm to about three thousand, the cost of raising each poult has steadily decreased until now it is close to 27 cents each. She emphasizes the fact that it is not the cost of feeding which checks profits, but careless handling. Careless handling causes the poults to die from disease and then the crop goes "into the red."

Day-old poults may be secured from one of the big poultry farms at very small cost. A small turkey flock does not require a big area for ranging, for as many as 100 birds may be brought to maturity on an average city lot. Such birds are carefully shipped either by parcel post or by express, and with ordinary care 90 per cent will mature for market, giving a high percentage of profit to the raiser.

■ ■

Raising Irish Terriers

WHAT you can do with the hobby you have acquired has been demonstrated by Jules Beaumont, who a few years ago acquired the lease of a garage on the rear of a building lot near Chicago's "Gold Coast" and started his own kennels. Beaumont had been given two pedigreed Irish Terriers, and was so attached to them that he had rented the vacant garage property as a home for the dogs and their puppies. People in the neighborhood noticed the fine breed and form of the animals, and stopped to buy the puppies. He held his prices high, not caring whether he sold them or not. Before he realized it, he was in the money in a big way, averaging better than three hundred a month from the sale of blooded dogs and supplies to dog owners.

"I am touching on a controversial subject when I mention dog intelligence," declared Beaumont, "but I believe the owners of Irish Terriers will agree that they are about the most intelligent of the dog kingdom. These terriers I had at the beginning had good pedigrees, and they never failed to attract the attention of anyone passing the kennels. One day a woman wanted one so badly for her boy, then about fifteen, that I couldn't resist selling it, though I didn't want to. In the end she paid a hundred and fifty dollars for it. I thought that was a lot of money at the time, so let her have it. I had four puppies of the Irish Terrier breed, but within a week, friends

132

of that woman had called, and each insisted on getting one of those puppies. As orders came in for the pups of the next litters, I decided to go into dog breeding. At this time, I didn't have any money left that I could invest in additional dogs, so I cared for and watched over those I had. When the litters came in, I noticed the people who had ordered. I made enough from the sale of the dogs to break even during the first six months, and got a good profit out of the sale of accessories, such as dog food, harnesses, leashes, and dog medicines.

"There were other sources of profit. Few people can see a cute puppy without handling it a great deal. Some make it play until it's tired. Others feed it too much. The pup, therefore, from well meant overdoses of kindness in one direction or another, becomes run down, and suffers from various types of illness. In addition, pups are subject to worms, and frequently the owner neglects to worm them. The result is a sluggish, sick puppy. These are but a few of the abuses a dog receives almost from the day it is bought. As the kennel from which the dog was secured is the first place the owner goes for advice and treatment, one soon accumulates side lines that are profitable, and cost but little. For instance, many dogs that are seemingly ill only need to be placed in a warm dry spot and left without food for a day or so. This treatment means little or no expense to the kennel, but, of course, the owner is glad to pay well for getting his dog back in good condition.

"As a rule, a litter will have two males or more and one or two females. The males are always in big demand and bring good prices; the females are generally lower priced. The females from my first litters were sold, but I kept those from subsequent litters for breeding, and in two years have greatly increased the productivity of the kennels. Later I added other popular breeds as I found there are certain breeds of dogs which capture the public favor and for which people will pay more money than others. In this group are the Sealyham, Pekingese, Pomeranian, Wire-haired Fox Terrier, Dalmatian, and some Collies.

"Many believe that it requires a lot of money to start a kennel. This, however, is a myth. I never had much money until after I had a good start in the kennel business. As a matter of fact, my total investment for blooded stock was less than three hundred dollars. It cost me about seventy dollars to turn the abandoned garage into a suitable kennel for dog breeding. I discovered that while you may have little trouble selling a few puppies to people who pass your kennels, you have to do a little merchandising to sell a good many dogs. I use the easiest method, which is holding a dog show at the kennels. I don't place dogs I have for sale in these kennel shows, but enter only the dogs of my customers and their friends. Those who condition their dogs properly are the owners who receive the blue and gold ribbons. These dog shows not only attract new customers, but also increase the sale of supplies and accessories. They are open to all blooded dogs whose owners care to enter them."

You may start an Irish Terrier kennel in your home. A good female is usually all the stock you need to start, and may be purchased for around forty to fifty dollars. When old enough, she may be put at stud with a pedigreed male at one of the first-class kennels. The fee for studding is usually one male of the litter. By retaining the females of each litter, you soon will be able to have a number of puppies for sale. If you are unable to get good prices yourself or want to sell wholesale only, any kennel, recognized by the American Kennel Club, will buy your puppies and resell them for you.

■ ■

Quick Profits from Mushrooms

WHEN Laz Lewin made up his mind to start a business of his own he decided to do something different. Learning that mushrooms may be profitably grown in cellars, sheds, barns or garages, Lewin bought a small quantity of mushroom spawn, rigged up a mushroom bed in his cellar, and started to raise mushrooms. This wasn't a new idea. Home cultivation of mushrooms has been attempted for many years, but during the past few years new methods have been developed which greatly increase the profits in this business. It was a new idea in Memphis, Tennessee, Lewin's home town, however, and his venture won quick approval from local storekeepers, restaurants, cafes and similar establishments.

"I never saw a mushroom grow before I started raising mushrooms," admitted Lewin. "I was somewhat surprised at the suddenness of their growth, and realized the meaning of the old 'saw'—'grows like a mushroom.' I started with a mushroom bed one hundred feet in area. It cost me two dollars to make this bed, ten feet by ten. Then I ordered the seed, or 'spawn' as it is called by mushroom growers. When it reached me, it looked like a mass of tangled white threads. I planted it, carefully following instructions, and two weeks later a white substance, appearing like cobwebs, covered the bed. Over this I spread ordinary back-yard dirt, and waited for another three weeks. One morning, upon going into the cellar to look at this bed, I was amazed to see it covered with baby mushrooms. This was a surprise, for nothing had been there the night before. ,I wondered how long it would take to develop these baby mushrooms for market, but the next day, when I saw the mushrooms had increased in size ten times, I picked them. I averaged a little over two and one-half pounds per square foot for the one hundred square feet in the bed and sold this entire crop to local markets at an average price of forty-five cents a pound.

"My investment in spawn was slightly over eight dollars which, with the two dollars for making the bed, comprised my total cost. I received approximately $110 for my crops.

"It was then I fully realized what a profit there could be in raising mushrooms. I increased my mushroom beds with the profit from this first crop and soon had one thousand square feet in production. At forty-five cents a pound, I easily sold the entire crop. As I have no rent, overhead, special equipment, or marketing expenses, I enjoy an advantage over the commercial grower.

"Up to that time, the local market held up well, and there appeared to be no reason why I should not increase my growing space. Many of the companies from which spawn is purchased are also commission merchants with branch mushroom receiving stations located throughout the country. Some of the companies will agree to purchase all the mushrooms produced by home growers and resell them to local stores. This, of course, helps the grower to secure a ready market for his product at the current wholesale market price. Moreover, they pay the shipping charges on shipments of five pounds or more. With an assured market I increased the size of my mushroom beds, using more of the space formerly wasted about my home. The pure white variety of patented mushroom I have been raising brings top prices for my crops. I was lucky, I guess, when I picked out this particular variety."

Mushrooms are easily raised as they require but little attention. Sunshine not being essential to their development, they will grow as well under the cellar stairs as in a pleasantly lighted room. In fact, bright sunlight is really not desirable according to experienced growers. The market for mushrooms is wide and profitable. The ability to supply fresh stock at all times, and give quick delivery service, insures attractive profits.

The cost of "spawn" for raising a pound of mushrooms varies between four and one-half and six cents. Persons shipping to wholesale and commission houses find sufficient profit margin between the prices received and their actual cost, to operate profitably. Generally, the best plan is to sell some of your crop in your own community, at higher prices, and to ship the remainder.

Practically any mushroom spawn today will grow in ordinary cellars or sheds wherever it is possible to maintain a fairly even temperature. The temperature should be from 55 to 70 degrees according to the period of growth of the spawn.

Advertising Makes Farm Pay

IT WAS not until the Arthur Wolf Farms, Tippecanoe County, Indiana, erected "want ad" signs, that business really did pick up. These signs are the billboard type and bear the name, post office and telephone address of the farm at the top. Under this information are two columns with the headings, "For Sale" and "Want to Buy." These columns are so arranged that the farmer can insert listings which are painted on removable sheets of metal.

Whenever the farm has something to offer or is in the market to buy, Mr. Riley, the manager, inserts the proper metal strips under the correct headings. Under the "For Sale" heading will be such items as mules, sheep, clover hay, bred gilts, oats, alfalfa, shoats, feeding cattle, machinery, hay feeders, hay corn, etc. Whenever Mr. Wolf needs any kind of hay, live stock, clover or alfalfa hay, oats, hogs, etc., a sign specifying the need is put up under the heading, "Want to Buy."

As Mr. Wolf's live stock operations are rather extensive, and there are many cattle and hogs to feed, there are times when he needs hay or corn. Then he will buy from anyone passing on the highway who sees his sign and has the right product to sell him. When the farm is short of stock and long on feed, the truckers become the buyers. The last crop of turkeys and hogs was all sold by this sign. Whenever there is a surplus of any stock or produce, the sign usually sells it in a few days. From time to time, feeder cattle or hay may be auctioned in the field. The sign tells the passer-by several days ahead of time about the auction. Two signs are in use all the time on this farm of 1,050 acres—one on each side of the place where the highway intersects the property line.

Is there an idea here for a business of your own in selling and installing signs like these for the wide-awake farmers in your locality?

CHAPTER FIVE

THINGS TO INVENT AND PATENT

THE closer your business comes to being a monopoly the surer you will be of success. Here in America there is a good deal of confusion over the meaning of "monopoly." To some people it means taking advantage of small competitors by unfair practices. But since the days of Elizabethan charters and patents, a monopoly has meant protection against competition. Sometimes a monopoly was granted by the state in the form of a patent or grant, but more often it was obtained by the business man or tradesman by virtue of his membership in a "guild." The last official act signed by Queen Elizabeth was to annul the British Monopolies Act.

What forms of monopoly do we find in American business? First we have the "trust" or holding company which enjoys a monopoly by virtue of buying out all its competitors, thus giving itself a clear field to charge all the traffic will bear. Such monopoly is based on financial power. It is a pistol pointed at the heart of the small, independent business man. It is the type of monopoly which Theodore Roosevelt attempted to crush with his trust-busting activities. Some business men still believe his method is the answer to ruthless competition. The use of such power to obtain a trade monopoly is un-American in its conception, uneconomic if carried to its logical conclusion, and would inevitably lead to a monopoly of monopolies and finally monopolize the functions of government.

But there is another kind of monopoly fostered by the government, which is just as much in the public interest as the other sort of monopoly is against it. Under that classification comes the monopoly of skill. That is the best monopoly of all. It is the monopoly that is enjoyed by the man who can build a better mouse trap or paint a better picture, write a better book, design a better dress or excel in any field. The very fact that you can do one little thing better than anyone else in the world can do it, assures your success. And although the monopoly granted for one achievement is limited as to duration, the success will continue so long as you make good your monopoly by keeping ahead of the imitators who are always found in the wake of success.

Then, there is the monopoly that comes from location. For example, it is a well-known fact that on the Island of Bermuda, a certain group of people pretty well control the island. These "best" families protect native business men against the encroachment of newcomers who seek to exploit the island. How do they do it? Very simply. You go over to Bermuda on a trip, fall in love with the climate and decide to start an automobile agency there. It looks like an easy way to make a few thousand dollars. Statistics show that the number of inhabitants per automobile is higher in Bermuda than in any other place in or around the United States. It looks like a wide-open opportunity. So you get an agency and hang out your shingle in Hamilton. But nothing happens. The first thing you find is that only government officials are licensed to drive automobiles on the island, that residents there don't want the smelly things rushing about killing people. Next you learn that it is not considered good form in Bermuda to patronize any business that has not the approval of the "best" families. Bermuda is a small place, and one who lives there feels the need of social contacts. People who patronize the "wrong" business men suffer a sudden social catastrophe. In that way a monopoly is granted to those whom the older families wish to have succeed, and failure usually overtakes those who try to "muscle in."

Another form of monopoly is to get an exclusive concession at a fair, or the exclusive local agency for some advertised product. When Eskimo ice cream bars were first put on the market, men paid fancy prices just for a local franchise to make these bars and sell them to the public. The "rights" to sell Neon signs in a territory were sold to eager salesmen at prices ranging from $1,000 to $15,000. The Coca-Cola Company is another well-known concern which gives exclusive franchises to sales agents. It is worth noting, however, that in nearly every case where the sale of franchises has been used to finance a business, a large part of the money received for the franchises was used to pay for the initial advertising campaign. While there are cases of men selling patent rights to raise money it is a difficult and usually a disappointing method of financing a new business.

What Goes with a Patent

Most inexperienced people feel that if they invent something and are able to get it patented, they can make a thousand dollars very quickly, either by selling the patent on a royalty basis, or by selling the patent outright. They assume that because they have a patent, they have the federal government back of them to keep off poachers and pirates. There is danger in placing too much reliance on, and attaching too much importance to, a patent until it has been tested in a high court.

For example, a number of advertising men have "invented" trick mailing cards, letters which fold down from the top, or some other device, and have applied for, and been granted, patents on these things. In many cases they have, on the strength of such patents, collected royalties from printers and others for the use of the idea. One large lithographer paid several thousand dollars for a patent on a folded-down letterhead, the patent covering any letterhead which had printing under the flap. There was nothing wrong with the patent. But if this patent claim was appealed to the U. S. Supreme Court an infringement suit would probably be dismissed on the grounds that the patent covered an operation which was natural to a mechanic in the pursuit of his trade. English common law gives a mechanic definite protection, just as it protects business men from confiscation of capital without due process of law; and the question of whether a patent is for a real invention and not mere mechanical skill must be left to the judgment of the courts in view of evidence introduced on both sides of the controversy.

There is also the possibility of somebody being able to show prior use of anything you may patent. A patent was recently granted for a "pop-up" idea in collection folders. It appeared to be a perfectly good patent, and hundreds of companies are paying the inventor a royalty for the use of the idea. Yet it is possible that this idea was used in valentines many years before its present use in folders. If somebody wanted to go to the trouble of searching among collections of old valentines and found a sufficiently similar idea, the patent could be invalidated by proving that it was not an original idea, and therefore the inventor was not entitled to the benefits of a government monopoly.

Another hazard that goes with patents is the possibility of some person "improving" upon your patent or otherwise changing it just enough to get around your patent claims. The idea, of course, is to make the claim as broad and as inclusive as possible, but because of earlier patents or printed publications, the claims must be limited to only the advance in the art which the inventor had made. Sometimes the only thing that can be patented is an accessory. That is why in taking out a patent you should go to a reputable and experienced firm of patent attorneys and stay clear of quacks who advertise for "suckers." You will pay a reputable patent attorney a little more than the quack's advertised price, but the reputable attorney will tell you frankly if your invention is practical and may even be able to help you to market it.

Strangely enough, most of the outstanding inventions were made by "outsiders." The principle of the steam engine, as everybody knows, was discovered by James Watt, who got the idea watching the lid of a teakettle jump up and down. It suggested to him the existence of power in steam, and he set about in his crude way figuring out how that power could be harnessed. Out of that invention came our present industrial system.

Benjamin Franklin was not an electrician, but he invented the lightning rod. The Eastman Kodak Company paid a hundred thousand dollars to a man who invented the device which enables you to write on the back of a film after it is exposed. And even the humble brake on a baby carriage was not invented, as you might suppose, by a carriage manufacturer, but by an advertising man in search of an "exclusive" feature to advertise.

So do not feel that just because you do not know all there is to know about a particular product that you cannot find ways to improve it. Strangely enough, a person who is using a thing is often the one to think of an improvement, rather than the man who makes it, and the maker is eager to pay him either a lump sum of cash for the patent or a royalty on it. Improving the appliances and things that you use in your daily work is perhaps the easiest and most practical way to make money on patents. It is not much of a trick to get $1,000 from a large manufacturer for any worth-while improvement which you develop and patent. There are a hundred ways to make a thousand dollars right in the kitchen of your home. In spite of the thousands of existing patents there is still a need of a better can opener, a better clothespin, a better bottle opener, and other simple everyday things that are in daily use.

As a rule, simple inventions are the most profitable. The hump hairpin is a case in point. For years women had been using and losing straight hairpins. The pins fell out of the hair because there was nothing to hold them in. Then some bright fellow thought about putting a little kink in the wire. It was so simple it seemed unimportant. Yet a great business has been built up in Chicago, and millions of dollars have been made on "hump" hairpins.

On the other hand, this same chap might have spent years inventing a dish-washing machine, only to find after inventing it that people had to be educated to wash dishes by machine and that there were already a dozen on the market. If you are of an inventive or deductive turn of mind, and have an ambition to make some money on a patent, first be sure your market exists before spending time and money on an invention.

Of the large number of patents issued annually, many are taken out by corporations to protect their development work in improving upon their products, or their production methods and apparatus, which have already been more or less approved in the market. Often corporations will also take out patents on alternatives or substitutes which they do not intend to exploit, but merely to hold, to forestall competitors adopting them. But of the other patents—those issued to "free lance" inventors—perhaps nine out of ten patents are on inventions which prove to be of practically no commercial importance. Generally, this is not so much because the invention lacks merit as because there is an inadequate commercial field for it. There are many reasons why the commercial field for an invention may be inadequate. Expense of manufacture may be too great to bring the selling price of the invention down to profitable production. The cost of merchandising may be too great in cases where the article invented cannot be standardized and requires too large an assortment of stock.

Often the invention involves a meritorious idea for the particular situations for which it was designed, but the possible users are too few and too scattered to make it practicable to contact and sell them economically. This is particularly true of accessories usable only on particular makes and models of automobiles or on certain types and makes of domestic boilers.

In other instances the cost to a manufacturer of taking over an invention and developing it until it is ready for production may promise to involve so much expenditure that it is difficult to get a manufacturer interested. It is often the high cost of development (which along with the royalty to the inventor must come out of the manufacturing profits) which reduces the revenue an inventor might otherwise get on his patent. Thus, in inventions where the probable cost of development is the least, the inventor has the best chance of realizing a large royalty or lump sum payment for his patent.

These difficulties are reviewed not for the purpose of discouraging you from making money by inventing something, but rather to point out other factors than the merit of the invention itself or how well it works, in deciding whether you are going to devote your time and money to a particular invention you may have in mind.

The Cost of Taking Out a Patent

The cost of securing a patent is one factor of expense which ought to be balanced against the probable reward for your efforts in the event of success, and you must take into consideration that an invention is something of a gamble until the merit of the invention has been demonstrated, and your patent upheld in the courts. To a certain extent the cost of securing a patent depends upon how complicated the machine or device is. But, on the other hand, the very simplicity of some inventions makes them more expensive to patent because the attorney has to spend more time in presenting arguments to the Patent Office to overcome the objection that because the invention is simple it is seemingly obvious. It is seldom possible to have an attorney prepare and file an application for you for less than $100, including the cost of the Patent Office drawings and the government filing fee of $30. A worth-while patent nearly always involves some cost of prosecution in getting the patent through the Patent Office after it has been filed, and before the patent is finally issued another $30 must be paid to the government as a final fee. The total cost of securing a patent, on even the simplest inventions, will be at least $140 or $150 in most instances. Even the average invention will be a little more expensive than this to patent, and if the invention is unusually complicated, the cost of the Patent Office drawings and the time which the attorney will have to devote to the proper preparation of the application and claims, may increase the total cost of securing such a patent to $300 or even more. Because your income from the invention will probably be due almost entirely to the patent protection you get, it is well to have the services of a competent patent attorney in procuring your patent, as often the value of the patent depends largely upon the skill of the attorney. It is wise to have your patent procured by an attorney of recognized ability, although some other attorney might prepare your application for a lower fee. Incidentally, you will find that being able to confer directly with your patent attorney is going to be of considerable value to you.

■ ■

Improvements Are the Most Salable Patents

THE best way to make money on inventions is to devise improvements for things which you use every day. As a rule manufacturers are anxious to improve their products and will pay substantial sums for ideas along those lines.

Take the ordinary kitchen mixer, for example. It does many things, but it is safe to say that there are a hundred and one undiscovered uses for this common home appliance. There are several manufacturers of such appliances and competition between them is keen. An attachment to increase the use of the mixer, which one of these manufacturers could feature exclusively, would be a valuable sales point.

Similarly, it is possible to improve the most simple things. A good example is the ordinary tube of tooth paste. The tube was an improvement over the sift-top can, just as the sift-top can was an improvement over the can of soap which our fathers used. Yet the tube leaves much to be desired. It is unhandy, it is a nuisance, and it is unsanitary. What will the next improvement be? Will it be some simple dispenser, similar to the soap dispensers on Pullman cars, which can be built into a medicine cabinet or the washstand and always be ready for use? Somebody thought of wall dispensers for Italian Balm, and it became one of the most important parts of the sales plan of that company.

There are many other opportunities for improving the things that we use in the home, in the garden and office, if one is observing enough to see them and ingenious enough to figure out a way to add improvements. Of course, if you are experienced in a certain field, you have a particular advantage in being able to invent improvements that apply especially to that area of activity. There is nothing so perfect in this world that it cannot be improved; nothing so well done that it cannot be done better. The man who thinks that we have progressed so far that everything worth while has been thought of will awake to find that nothing is static, but that the fertile brain of man is constantly finding a way to do everything better.

Of course there are opportunities—many of them—for inventing new things to fill a long-felt want. But the development and marketing of such inventions is at best uncertain. The story is told of the man who invented a knife and fork for a one-handed person, and in his enthusiasm had thousands manufactured. He learned too late that there were not enough one-handed people to use them and that it would cost so much to create a demand that he would have to charge more for his product than the average one-handed person would pay. Had he spent the same time and effort on improving something for which a known demand existed the loss of both time and money might have been saved.

■ ■

Bert Pond's Hobby Ended Up in a Business

WHILE Bert Pond was still a high-school boy in Chicago, he became interested in model airplanes and joined the Illinois Model Aero Club. This airplane research group, he believed, was far ahead of the rest of the world in the study of miniature flying craft of all kinds. While he attended Illinois U, he continued to make many midget planes and often paid his fraternity house bills with cash prizes he won at national exhibits.

It was after Lindbergh's flight, however, when the country became aviation-conscious, that he began to cash in on his knowledge of model airplanes. He resigned his job with the Minneapolis-Honeywell Corporation and decided to build and help others build model airplanes. His first work was instructing classes in model airplane design at Y. M. C. A. meetings, Boy Scout camps, and at various schools all over Indiana. He next wrote a series of articles on model airplanes for *Popular Aviation, Popular Science Monthly,* and other publications of this type. It wasn't long before the students in all these classes and the readers of his articles wanted materials to make their own models. So his next step was to make these materials which were so much in demand.

In his model airplane shop, Peru, Indiana, he began to manufacture not only a midget motor and a 6½ ounce gasoline motor, but also the familiar rubber-band twisters and other parts and accessories for fans who build their own models. He later supplied the featherweight wood called balsa, which is used for airplane models, Japanese silk tissue, special cements, and fresh rubber to power the planes. He also manufactured a low-priced scale used to weigh parts for the models down to 1/1000 of an ounce, and a miniature true pitch propeller. Thousands of these little propellers were turned out for other miniature aircraft companies. His shop also designed model kits and made ready-built planes for other concerns. In the last few years, the shop has sold many hundreds of thousands of planes in the five-and-ten stores.

Regular orders kept this shop busy the year round, but during certain rush periods the shop ran night and day. During the three or four major national contests held each year, there was a gratifying increase in orders. Bert Pond's success with his hobby suggests the value of developing an interesting hobby which some day may provide your bread and butter—and perhaps a little jam.

Another hobby which later became a real vocation was that of H. E. Boucher. As a little boy, Mr. Boucher frequently made little boats which were the envy of his playmates. His parents had planned his entire education to the end that he would some day become a naval architect. He did reach this goal but his hobby persisted in taking all his spare time and soon he found that he was making many miniature ships for his friends. The demand increased and presently his "real" work was being crowded out of his life by his hobby. It was then that he decided to stop fighting against his interest in this hobby and he organized the H. E. Boucher Manufacturing Company. The market for his products was provided by the hundreds of other hobbyists interested in miniature ships and ship parts. Eventually what started out as a hobby became one of the largest businesses of its kind.

■ ■

Electrical Toy Sells Out State Street

FOR perhaps a year or more, an editor on a Chicago business publication had been working on an electrical toy. At first glance, there seemed to be nothing remarkable about this toy. When you picked it up you thought it just another "Jack-in-the-box." When the little hook holding "Jack" in the box was lifted, however, there really was a surprise in store for you. "Jack" had two big electrical eyes which lit up fiery red when he popped out of the box!

When the toy was ready for market, the editor, who had had considerable selling experience, decided to take it around to the store buyers himself. This was in September. By the middle of November he had sold every store on State Street, except the largest, whose toy buyer had been too busy to give the toy any real study. The small factory handling the production of the toy had made up the quantity the inventor thought would sell the first holiday season. But now demands for the toy came from outlying stores and also from the "big" store. However, he had made the profit he had set out to make that year and the other buyers had to wait until the following Christmas for stock. The next year a much larger quantity of the toys was made up and again he sold out.

The mechanical or electrical toy field offers a rich market for the inventor who can capture a new idea in toys or take an old idea that has been on the market and put it in a new dress. Every holiday, fond mothers and fathers, to say nothing of grandparents, aunts and uncles, search the toy sections for something new and different for Jimmie or Sally Ann. Their wants are insatiable and the inventor who can satisfy those wants will profit handsomely.

■ ■

Funeral Flags and Insignia

TWO years ago, Robert Hubbell was out of work. Then one day he went to a funeral with a friend. Before the procession of cars started for the cemetery, the undertaker's assistant clamped a metal device on the running board of the car to hold a white flag with a purple cross. When the funeral was over and the clamp was removed, Robert Hubbell's friend found the enamel scratched and the metal wrinkled where the clamp had been applied.

Robert Hubbell gave the matter a little thought and within two hours in his workshop had invented a flag holder that slipped on over the bumpers. As flags get bedraggled in the rain and snow, he decided that a paper flag would be better as it could be changed for every funeral at small expense. So, the new arrangement included a flag mast on which a paper flag could be clamped.

The idea was a winner and today, Mr. Hubbell has a factory where he makes holders, masts, and white flags. He employs a dozen people and spends most of his time out on the road selling to wholesalers. In addition, he has spent some time helping to lobby bills through a dozen states requiring the use of funeral flags in processions to prevent traffic from breaking into the line.

Toy Automobile Puzzles Onlookers

A LITTLE fifty-cent toy Ford automobile, which is bringing its inventor plenty of profits, creates interest by its trick of automatically turning in another direction. Just as it reaches the edge of the table and you think it will run off, a hidden third wheel, at right angles to the front wheels, turns the automobile in another direction. Everyone wants one of these toys because of its trick of fooling the onlooker. Such toys offer a fertile field for inventors.

■ ■

Profits from Whittling

IN 1915, A. O. Dinsdale (O'Dee to his friends) was an ambitious young man who had just been graduated from the California School of Fine Arts and the Berkeley School of Arts and Crafts. He was determined to become a painter equaling Michelangelo. But the war changed all that. After serving in France, Dinsdale returned to San Francisco restless and unsettled. He went up into the high Sierras and isolated himself in a crude cabin twenty miles upgrade. Here he aimlessly whittled out queer little animals and painted them. A hunter chancing on his retreat saw these animals and chuckled. "They've got personality," he said. "Send 'em down to the art shops. They'll sell."

Dinsdale followed this advice and his animals became a fad. He grew so busy painting pink elephants and purple lions that he had no time to bemoan shattered ambitions. Returning to town he purchased a band saw and cut his creatures out of three-ply pine, painting them in oils. Because his art education had included a thorough study of anatomy, his animals were proportionately right despite their whimsicalities and gaudy hues.

Business expanded. In his garage he worked out nursery interiors and store displays: "The Old Woman Who Lived in a Shoe," for instance, for a juvenile shoe department. Dinsdale called his workshop the O'Dee Studio and designed a black cat and blackbird trade-mark because his recently acquired wife considered black cats "good luck."

Years passed. Today the O'Dee Studio is located downtown and equipped with the latest machinery. Animals have been left far behind in Dinsdale's "March of Progress." His unusual profession takes in decorative relief maps for vast projects, mechanical displays timed to light and sound, caricatures, and unusual animated exhibits.

Strange assignments come to Dinsdale, one of these being his group of historical displays created for the Wells Fargo Bank Museum. True to scale and history these dramatic tableaux in wood vie in interest with the valuable collection of relics bearing on California's frontier days. One, for example, has for its setting Sutter's Mill, where gold was first discovered, and shows in five scenes the evolution of mining implements from crude pan and shovel to effective hydraulic methods. The superbly painted scene, correct in every detail, is enlivened by quaint figures of Indians, miners, Spanish *caballeros*, and others, each true to type and costume.

A clipper ship assignment was a hard nut to crack because these ships, which used to carry mail round the Horn, are out of existence. Dinsdale spent days talking to old waterfront characters and nothing has been omitted either from his clipper ship education or from the finished model.

But his greatest interest lies in synchronizing sound with movement in mechanical displays. He built the first Christmas window of this type in San Francisco: "Three Little Pigs and the Big Bad Wolf" acted out while a phonograph played the song. Delighted crowds almost blocked traffic.

But this is only a crude beginning to Dinsdale who is working with a radio engineer on sound controlled mechanics. Future animated displays will not be timed to phonograph records, he predicts; they will be moved by actual sound vibrations.

■ ■

A Shoe Pain-Killer Builds a New Business

ALBERT SACHS, who had been a retail shoe merchant in Salisbury, Maryland, for many years, long had an idea for another kind of business. He selected the tail-end of the depression as a favorable time to launch this other enterprise. His idea was for a device that would take the "pain" out of shoes.

Mr. Sachs had been experimenting for ten years with various methods of breaking in new shoes mechanically. He had always been interested in finding out how he could give his customers more foot comfort. It seemed a pity to him that many people had so much trouble with new shoes.

Finally, he developed a system consisting of a set of jacks in which holes had been punched. These jacks were manipulated in the balky shoe until the area of pressure was over a hole. Here the leather was hammered until a depression was created, thus removing the cause of discomfiture to the wearer.

These jacks were but the forerunner of Mr. Sachs's present system. Gradually he evolved a hydraulic press, based on the original principle that he used in Salisbury. A variety of brass forms is a part of the equipment. The machine presses a form into that part of the shoe that is causing the pain. This is done with such great force that the source of the trouble is permanently removed.

Mr. Sachs decided that the best way to handle his invention was to lease the machine to operators who would run the business according to the inventor's specifications. Already there are three SHU-EEZ Comfort Shops in New York City. Though these shops are conducted by lessees, Mr. Sachs gives the closest attention to their supervision.

A charge of twenty-five cents is made for breaking in each of a pair of shoes. So popular is the service that dozens of customers drop in his main shop daily to have their shoes made wearable with comfort. It seems that everybody has shoes with pains in them. Early in 1936, a man from England dropped in to have his shoes adjusted. He returned a few months later, on another trip to this country, with an armful of shoes to be broken in by the hydraulic pain eliminator.

Mr. Sachs's novel business is still a very small enterprise. But it is making money, and it holds a brilliant promise for the future. He is more than glad that he did not let the depression scare him from putting his idea to work.

■ ■

Coleman Made His $1,000 with Polish

SOME years ago, George Coleman came upon a formula for making metal polish. It sounded simple, so he decided to get the ingredients and mix up some. This first polish was in liquid form, and reasonably successful, but when he tried to sell it he discovered that it wasn't exactly what prospects required. Then he searched for a new formula. After a great deal of experimenting, he developed a formula of his own that was practical for use as an all-purpose metal and glassware polish, and has made hundreds of dollars as a result.

"While I found a widespread demand for a high-grade metal polish," said Coleman, "I had difficulty selling enough to make a worth-while profit. I knew practically nothing about selling or advertising in the beginning, and it took a little while for me to learn. For instance, the containers I used had no labels, and my product had no name. I sold a gallon jug to a large Chicago hotel one day, and they asked me the name of the polish explaining it was necessary to name the brand in their records. That stumped me. 'I haven't called it any special name,' I said, 'but, use it. If it's good, you'll want more.' The man laughed. 'I'll call it *Use It*, then.' About two weeks later, I got a phone call at my home for five gallons of *Use It*. That's how I came to give the polish that name. When I went around, I told my prospective customers to use *Use It*, and sales began to increase. The polish did its work well, but there was a good deal of competition. However, as I picked up additional business steadily and was holding what I had, it wasn't long before I was making real money.

"I could have done better had I given the polish a trade name and made up a week or a ten-day supply at one time. But being cautious I made up only as much polish daily as was needed to fill orders. Furthermore, I should have had some circulars printed but I did not think it was necessary to give directions to the purchaser. I have since found I was wrong.

"To sell readily, a metal polish must have certain features and these should be explained to the buyer. This explanation should be followed by instructions about applying the polish to glass and metal surfaces, and the effect demonstrated. Be sure that your formula does not contain poisonous or inflammable agents. While the danger from fire is not great, big users of polish will not have an inflammable or poisonous polish on the premises as they don't want any more occupational hazards than are necessary. You can make up just as good nonpoisonous and noninflammable polish as you can a combustible and poisonous polish and the cost is less. I would suggest to anyone starting in the polish manufacturing business that he make innumerable tests of the product. Find out whether it is simple or difficult to apply. Make it as simple as possible to apply to secure the best results. If your metal polish is safe to handle, easy to apply, and polishes all metal surfaces including brass, copper and chromium perfectly, you will have a wide sale for it. But it will be in greater demand if it can be used to bring sparkling luster to mirrors, chinaware and porcelain."

There are a number of formulas for making a good polish, meeting the above specifications. The demand by clubs, hotels, taverns, hospitals, restaurants, office buildings, factories, garages, steamship lines, railroads and for home use is regular and steady. The polish may be made up at small expense, and attractively packaged. The cost including packaging is about six cents for an eight-ounce size, which retails for twenty-five cents. Sold in bulk to large users, such polish may be priced at from a dollar to three dollars a gallon. For one who likes to make up formulas, there is no better way to get the "first thousand" than through making and selling polish.

Mrs. Royeton's Button-Eyed Lambs

THERE lived in Oakland, California, a young widow named Charlotte Royeton, who, having four children to support, turned to a federal government agency and was given a job as playground instructor, providing she could entertain a lot of youngsters sufficiently to keep them coming back. Just how could she fill these requirements? The children were from poor families, mixed races. They cared little for reading, they couldn't play in the court all the time, and sewing was "out."

Desperately the widow scoured the five-and-ten, mentally discarding jigsaw puzzles, dominoes, and dish towels for embroidering. Then she spied the little pig outlined on cambric to be cut out and stuffed! She pounced on him and took him to market—that is, she sat up nearly all night putting him together.

The next morning, behold! Piggie had the niftiest black cutaway jacket edged in yellow, a curlicue tail, and a rakish black hat slanted over one pink ear. Mrs. Royeton's children voted him "a knockout" and when her charges saw him they seconded the motion and were eager to make one like him. The woman had no money but she said, "Look, children, I don't know how we'll do it but we're going to make those pigs."

She purchased four yards of material and as much kapok as her thin purse would allow. She got seventeen pigs out of the goods but ran out of kapok. So she had the children bring discarded stockings which were cut up and used to stuff the rest of them.

She added other animals, purchasing some patterns and designing others, until there were fifty varieties. The children, more and more delighted, brought every available scrap from home. Two Chinese girls brought two uncalled-for sheets from their father's laundry and after taking what material they needed gave the rest to the others. The old striped trousers of Antoinette's father yielded some amazing elephants, while Kitty McCarthy's green chinchilla reefer became woolly dogs with green bead eyes. Over two hundred animals were made that summer by a class that had increased from fifteen to fifty to the wonderment of the playground director.

But here's where the fairy tale comes in. The widow sat up nights designing animals for the next day's session and that's how *the lamb* came into existence. He was white muslin with black hoofs and his flat, black button eyes made him the most innocent looking lamb that ever followed Mary. Unknown to his originator he was chosen for a National Exhibit of Handicraft held in Washington, D. C., where he blinked at the toy buyer of Saks and Company's Fifth Avenue store, New York. It was love at first sight. The buyer demanded that lamb and more like him. In due course,

Mrs. Royeton was flabbergasted to receive a letter asking for a dozen lambs and placing a large future order.

Daughter Eloise and the three boys fixed up a basement workshop for their mother who glowingly declared: "I feel like a flower about to burst into bloom." She hopes soon to be able to stay home and look after her family while earning a living. And even if she doesn't sell a million lambs and make a million dollars there is every indication that she will make a thousand.

Chapter Six

STARTING A ROADSIDE BUSINESS

IF YOU lack money enough to take your goods to your market—that is, open a store, advertise extensively, or hire a crew to sell house to house—you must bring your market to your door. That door may be just a roadside stand such as you see along the highways. Along these well-traveled routes, with their ever-increasing army of tourists, you have a great potential market. Jump in your car and run out on any highway. You won't go but a few miles before you run across at least one roadside stand.

This stand may be the usual type which sells farm products—eggs, poultry, fruits, vegetables, butter, honey, etc. It may be one of the thousands of stands scattered far and wide across the country's highways which sells hamburgers, hot dogs, barbecue sandwiches, citrus and other fruit drinks, pop, potato chips, candied pop corn, doughnuts, or custard ice cream. Souvenir and postal card stands are so common it is hardly necessary to mention them. Then there are the historical souvenirs which are sold around centers of historical interest.

Which one of these many stands might make money for you depends upon the particular need in your locality, the buying habits of those who pass your way, and your ability to attract customers. Know your community well for much of your business may come from those in your neighborhood as well as the tourists who pass through your town. Key your product to your section. The tourist who passes through the little towns of Vermont most likely will want maple syrup or maple sugar candy. You might convert the natives of Vermont to hot tamales, or make the tourist think he wants them, but you probably would lose a lot of money before you had done so.

So cater to your section of the country. In the Pacific Coast region, Atlantic Coast, Gulf or Great Lakes sections, fish (fresh and smoked) are sold at roadside stands. In the East, particularly in New York, you will find a number of "milk stations." The inhabitants of Texas are great consumers of ice cream and any number of stands sell this hot weather confection. Mexican candy, known as pralines, is in demand around New Orleans and certain parts of Texas. In certain western and southwestern sections, unusual rocks and semi-precious stones are sold. Indian handicrafts—bead work, silver and turquoise jewelry, and leather goods—are sold from stands in and near the Indian reservations. Throughout the Southwest, practically everything to wear, use, or to eat, is sold at roadside stands.

Hand-wrought jewelry, pottery, beads, lace, carved ornaments, needle-work, handmade baskets, handwoven blankets, hot tamales, and chili are a few of the many items you can buy along the roadside.

In addition to these sectional types of stands, roadside stands are successful selling bird houses, garden ornaments, fishing bait, pets of all kinds, shells, taffy candy, honey and honey candy, pies, pecans, taffy apples, antiques, trellises and garden furniture of the rustic type, objects made of birch bark, toys carved from wood, flowers, plants and shrubs, goldfish, dolls and neckties.

Next to getting the right product for your locality, there is nothing so important to the success of your enterprise as advertising. This may be in the form of signs placed in advantageous places on the routes to your stand, signs in tourists' camps and railroad stations. Or, a novel type of display stand may be sufficient to advertise your wares. One enterprising chap had a local builder make a huge "hot dog" for a stand and thus advertised to all the world his specialty. In Hollywood is a large iceberg which sells ice cream and cones to the youngsters. Out west there are also a number of huge "lemons" and "oranges," which serve citrus fruit drinks and sandwiches. If you want something different you might construct an ice cream freezer similar to one built in Los Angeles. This enormous freezer, which can be seen for miles, has a real handle on it that turns by means of a motor. In the East a successful refreshment stand, selling buttermilk, butter, ice cream, malted milk, sandwiches and similar products, is built in the form of a gigantic milk can. An awning extends over the counter built around the can. A stand designed to resemble a huge basket of colorful vegetables would make a most novel advertisement for the sale of farm produce. While the country is dotted with many a "coffee pot," one such refreshment stand is unusual in that it has an apartment above the store proper where the owner lives. A cider barrel or an old mill would tell the world that you sell cider, and an igloo would advertise cooling drinks and ice cream. Often these novel stands cost little more than the usual type to build and the advertising value is incalculable. Motorists will pass dozens of ordinary stands, but an unusual one is bound to command their attention.

The display stand is not the only type of roadside business that flourishes, however. Many proprietors of golf driving ranges are making a good living catering to the inveterate golfer who is "just out for a ride" in his car. The "pony ride" is just as popular today with youngsters as it was years ago, and children will clamor for a ride whenever they see a pony. One man in Chicago made a good living for many years with his little string of ponies. When he retired and sold out his concession and ponies, he cleared several thousand dollars. Since archery is becoming popular again, archery practice fields are springing up along the highways. Bicycle stands are common and also riding academies. A successful riding academy near

Chicago was once an old farm. The farmhouse has been turned into an inn and about two dozen riding horses are stabled in the barns. Groups of young people come out on Saturdays and Sundays for a gallop and dinner. Many students on vacations come out during the week.

Another rather novel roadside enterprise was developed by a young man just out of school who was finding it difficult to get a job. He bought several inexpensive cameras and rented them at the entrance to a large picnic grove. A deposit was required on each camera and a small fee was charged for rental. He added to his profits by selling rolls of film at his little stand. A small enterprise of this type is bound to succeed. The overhead is practically nothing, and it fills a need that no one else is bothering to fill, always an important factor in drawing customers. Candy bars, chewing gum, packaged nuts and other items can be added to increase profits.

■ ■

Good Profits from a "Sale Barn"

IN EVERY farming community there is an opportunity to conduct a sale barn and earn regular profits the year round. If there aren't now too many in your community it is worth trying. You don't even need a barn, although you can conduct the business better if you have a large lot and a building. You can, of course, rent one for the purpose.

These sales are conducted in the following fashion: The operator of a sale barn advertises that on regular dates he will conduct a sale of any and all property brought to the barn. Usually the sales are held regularly, once a week, or twice a month. Saturday is frequently the day selected, although one of the most successful operators of sales conducts his sale at a farm near Washington Court House, Ohio, every Tuesday.

Horses, mules, pigs, cattle, sheep, vegetables, seed, shrubbery, fruit and all kinds of farm equipment as well as furniture, stoves, and similar articles are in demand. In fact, almost anything you can name is sold regularly at these barns. Sales are for cash and the auction plan of selling is followed.

At the S. F. Snider Sale Barn, at Washington Court House, Ohio, each seller pays the operator of the barn a commission on all sales. The customary figure being 3 per cent on live stock and 10 per cent on miscellaneous equipment.

One of the contributors to this book attended a sale one afternoon at which a wagonload of grapefruit, a disc plow, cattle and several horses were sold. A six-year-old gelding brought $215.

The way to start is to select a good location. This may be a vacant lot, close in to the business section, or if you think you need more room for the buyers and sellers to park their cars, select a larger lot on the outskirts of town. It is better, of course, if there are sheds, an empty barn, or some kind of shelter.

When you have selected your location, visit the farmers of the community and explain your plan to them, telling them the date of the first sale. At first it may be necessary to persuade them to bring in things to sell. When talking with the farmers ask them if they haven't a horse, mule, calf, cow, some extra fruit or canned goods, a plow, rake, cultivator, manure spreader or something of the kind they would like to sell. Nearly every farmer has some surplus of one kind or another.

If your first sale is properly advertised and talked about you will have a big crowd. A good auctioneer can always get something for almost anything offered. After the first sales results are known in the community there will be little difficulty in getting things to sell and crowds to attend other sales.

If there is a county or community fairground near your town and you can arrange to use the fair property for your sale, you will have an ideal place. But any location on good roads, easily accessible, will do for a start.

Commissions are paid the sale operator at the time of the sale. Usual rules of bidding at auction sales are followed. Small advertisements in the local papers, and handbills or sale bills, as they are called, will be sufficient advertising until the regular day and date of your sale becomes established and known in the community.

■ ■

A Roadside Tire Repair Business

IT WAS a blown-out front tire, occurring while driving along route US 20 from Chicago to Michigan City, that started James Mowry in business. When the blow-out happened, Mowry did what many other motorists do. He replaced the flat with the spare, and threw the old tire in the weeds along the road. He decided to buy a used tire in Michigan City to carry as a spare on the way back. After calling upon several tire dealers in the Indiana city, Mowry was forced to pay $5.00 for one that wasn't much better than the tire he threw away.

Mowry felt he was cheated. The idea persisted in his mind on his way back home, and he wondered how other motorists felt in similar situations. He thought that a roadside tire service station offering rebuilt tires at low prices would make a lot of money. By the time he parked his car in front of his house, Mowry decided to go into the business himself.

He rented a roadside stand adjoining a three-pump gasoline station a short distance east of Gary and stocked it with fifty rebuilt tires secured from a Chicago jobber. He put up large signs 300 feet east and 300 feet west of his new tire station reading: "Tires $2.25 and up—300 feet," and another large sign on the service station, facing the highway reading: "Home of Jimmy's Guaranteed Tires—$2.25 and up." Mowry opened up for business. That was July second. Over the Fourth of July he sold out his entire stock and made a profit of $52. His initial investment was $145, including cost of the tires, rent, signs, and incidentals. The first month he operated this stand Mowry netted a profit of $203, after deducting the entire cost of his investment.

Rebuilt tires such as Mowry handles are standard brand tires which have been reconstructed by a special process at low cost. You can safely guarantee good mileage to customers who buy such tires from you. It is both a pleasant and a profitable business, requires little capital and there is practically no chance for loss.

■ ■

A Target Green for Iron Practice

IN ESTES PARK, Colorado, a man made a "barrel" of money last summer by renting a vacant lot on the main street of this bustling resort town and, on a sloping bank at the far end of the lot, arranging a giant putting green. The bull's eye in the green was a hole about four times the size of a hole on a golf green. Circles on the target green were made with ridges of stone, and were graduated so that they became narrower as they approached the cup. The green was about twelve feet in diameter, and pitched facing the driving tee at an angle of about fifteen degrees. The driving tee was about fifty feet away from the cup.

The idea, of course, was to give those who thought they were good iron shots an opportunity to prove it by pitching ten balls into the cup with a niblick. Each ball dropped into the cup counted one; balls that missed the cup but dropped into the second ring, counted five, and those which landed in the next ring counted ten, and so on. Par for the hole was twenty and when a player scored par, he was entitled to shoot ten balls free. The charge for shooting ten balls was ten cents. The names of those who "shot the course" under par were posted on a blackboard where they remained all day, and a daily prize was offered to the player getting the low score.

157

Such a shooting green can be built at a very small cost, the only equipment needed being a dozen iron clubs, both mashies and niblicks, and about fifty repainted golf balls. While the idea is somewhat similar to the miniature golf fad of a few years back, it has one decided advantage: It gives the player an opportunity to perfect his "approach" shots, since he is playing with regulation clubs and under conditions identical to those he will experience in an actual game of golf on any club course. The owner of such a target green can figure on the average person shooting about fifty balls at a time.

■ ■

Selling Bait at a Roadside Stand

BROKE, lacking any income, and in poor health, Ella Gaston, a widow of seventy-seven, living in Joplin, Missouri, wondered what she could do to make some money. It occurred to her that a great number of fishermen passed her home along the highway leading into the Ozark fishing country. Where did all these men get their bait? There were plenty of worms in the mud flat of a creek near by—perhaps she could sell them. It was worth a try anyhow. A friend built a roadside stand for her and hung a sign above it which told all passers-by that fishing bait could be purchased.

Mrs. Gaston filled kettles, pails, boxes and buckets with soil and worms. The passers-by did stop and buy and before long she had to hire boys to dig worms for her to supply the demand. The boys are paid 10 cents a hundred for the wrigglers and she sells them for 10 cents a dozen. Some days she has sold as high as 1,000 dozen. In two years, Mrs. Gaston figures she has sold over a million worms! Incidentally, in these two years, she has paid her own and her dead brother's debts. And because she has had an interesting and profitable bit of work to do, she has also regained her health.

■ ■

Making a "Stop and Sock It" Range Pay

JOHN GALWAY and Martin Sheffield, high-school graduates who couldn't find a job, put their heads together, rented a vacant corner of two well-traveled highways on the outskirts of Chicago, and started a golf-driving range that paid them $600 in five months. It could easily be made to pay $1,000.

"The idea wasn't original," said Galway, "but it was the best we could think of, and required practically no capital to start. We rented the corner for fifteen dollars for the entire summer season, that being the amount of the owner's taxes. The owner thought we were crazy, I guess, but told us to go ahead. We borrowed fifty dollars from our parents, got some second-hand lumber with which we built a stand, and had some signs painted. Then we measured off distances and put up the signs at fifty, one hundred, one hundred and fifty, one hundred seventy-five, two hundred, and two hundred and fifty feet from the tee-off. We leveled the tee-off ourselves, and did all our own labor, cutting the grass, and fixing up things. Our expenses for lumber and the signs came to twenty-one dollars. As we had a few golf clubs, we didn't need to buy any at the start. We bought the cheapest golf balls we could get with the rest of the fifty dollars, and were ready to do business. Our prices were twenty-five cents for driving twenty-five balls; fifty cents for driving seventy-five balls. We opened up on a cold Sunday morning in late April, and with high hopes sat in the stand. A few cars passed, but none stopped. Our first customer appeared about one o'clock that afternoon, and invested fifty cents in driving practice. The next customer pulled up while the first one was on the tee, and invested a quarter. Two more appeared, before the first two had finished, and all left about the same time. However, we pocketed two dollars, and weren't feeling very bad. Still, we were rather anxious. In the days that followed there wasn't much business. We heard of another practice range about five miles off and I went over to see what they were doing, but they weren't doing much either. I talked to the owner. 'Don't worry,' he advised, 'they come in bunches. When they see one or two people practicing on your course, a number will stop. The idea is to keep someone practicing as much as possible.'

Attracting Customers

"I agreed with that, thinking of our first day's experience. I felt the trick was to get the first motorist to stop and practice. When I got back, I talked the matter over with Martin, who said: 'Why not decoy them, like hunters decoy ducks? Get someone to hang around and practice when we have no customers. Then when people are passing they might stop.' We tried to get someone, but everyone we invited told us we'd have to pay them a salary. As we couldn't do that we took turns swinging at the balls ourselves. First I would swing for an hour, and then Martin would have a go at it. Whether this brought the customers or not, I can't exactly say, but business began to pick up. Women, out for a drive afternoons during the week, drove up and practiced for a little while. Many came regularly every day. Meanwhile Martin and I were learning things about driving, and how to take a good stance and get that little extra snap in the drive that gives added power.

Soon we were making fairly long drives, and began to attract attention from motorists. A golf professional, formerly with a small golf club came to see us one day. He told us he was out of a job, and would like to give driving lessons. We arranged to let him use our place on a fifty-fifty split, and put up a sign. He charged two dollars an hour, and helped Martin's form and mine, while he was around. When he got another job, a month later, we left the sign up which offered instruction and collected the two dollars hourly ourselves for teaching. Sunday is our big day. On a sunny Sunday afternoon we took in as high as thirty dollars from the practice range, and from the lessons. Week days ran about eighteen dollars on an average. Of course, there was no business at all when it rained."

A couple of hundred golf balls, a few clubs, a stand, and a good-sized lot along a highway is all the equipment needed for a driving course. Side lines such as cold soft drinks, sandwiches, and ice cream, coffee, cigarettes and bar candies will add to the total profits. There are few more attractive ways for young and active men to get a start and accumulate capital during the open season.

■ ■

A Roadside Bookstore

AN UNUSUAL business has been developed by J. C. Meredith, who operates a roadside stand near Traverse City, Michigan. This roadside stand sells neither hot dogs nor hamburgers, ice cream nor gasoline, but books. While rare in this country, this type of bookshop or stall is common in Europe, especially Paris. Mr. Meredith believes that the average person likes to browse in a bookshop and that not even a tourist can resist the impulse to stop and look over books and prints. A large sign over his stand states: "Why hurry? You'll enjoy visiting this roadside bookshop."

CHAPTER SEVEN

STOREKEEPING AS A BUSINESS

WHEREVER you live there are plenty of ordinary stores. In most towns and cities there are too many ordinary stores. Every week thousands of retail storekeepers go bankrupt, are closed out and shut up, with losses varying from $1,000 to $10,000 each. One Los Angeles wholesale house has one man who does nothing but attend to closing up stores, the owners of which can't pay their merchandise bills.

Various reasons are given by the mercantile reporting agencies for the failure of so many retail stores: Lack of capital, inexperience, credit losses, poor management, bad locations. These are but a few of the reasons given. Yet when you come right down to the final analysis, you will find that the chief reason is because the storekeeper did not render a needed or useful service to the community he served.

That should be your first thought in determining whether or not you want to open a store. Can you render a useful service to the town, community or neighborhood to which you will look for your patronage? Will you offer the people of your community some service they need, or want, but are not now enjoying? Or will your store merely attempt to duplicate some service which is already being well performed? Will your store simply become another unit in an already overcrowded field?

There are in the United States, as this is being written,

532,010 food stores	13,198 men's furnishing stores
56,697 drug stores	32,555 meat markets
26,996 hardware stores	11,741 variety stores
28,709 dry goods stores	17,043 furniture stores
18,967 shoe stores	21,975 women's ready-to-wear
9,568 millinery stores	12,447 jewelry stores

Between the time this is written and the time you will read it, thousands of these stores will have gone bankrupt, changed hands, merged, moved or made some other change which indicates that the owners are making little, if any, profit. From this summary it may seem to you as if storekeeping is a bad business; but it isn't. It is a fundamental necessity. Retail business suffers less, as a whole, than any other type of business during a period of depression. Of course, a depression clears out the unfit, the lazy, the slovenly and careless retailers. But the good ones carry on year in and year out, during good times and bad, with as great a degree of stability as is found in any other type of business.

In spite of the dismal record of failures, you may want to open a store. What kind of store? The chains have made it increasingly difficult to make a profit out of a grocery, drug, cigar, hat or shoe store. There are plenty of these stores, anyway, so why pick a field in which you must compete with the most astute merchandisers in the country? Because of factors over which no individual has any control, discussion of the ordinary types of stores such as grocery, cigar, drug, hat and shoe, is being omitted. Of course, independent storekeepers enter these fields every week and some of them succeed. But to operate a drug store successfully you must be a pharmacist; a shoe store requires a heavy investment; there are so many incompetents in the grocery field and so much bitter competition from the chains, there isn't much incentive to enter it.

Despite all the adverse factors that must be taken into consideration when contemplating storekeeping as a business, it is well to remember that some of America's greatest fortunes have been earned from store-keeping. There is always room for real ability. Thousands of new things to sell are being put on the market each year, each new item opening a new field for the storekeeper. Think of all the electrical appliances which were unheard of ten or twenty years ago; think of how much more is spent today than ten years ago for sporting goods, sports clothing and toys. Think of all the things now bought ready-made or ready prepared which only a few short years back were made in the home. Millions of women never bake a cake today, but buy their cakes, cookies and bread from stores. Think of all the things women used to make for themselves that they now buy from stores. There was a time when a woman bought a purse and used it until it was worn out. Now she buys a purse, a hat, gloves, stockings, and shoes to match every dress. The matched accessories or ensemble idea has added millions of dollars to retail sales in recent years.

It is easy to see there is no limit to the variety of services a retailer can render. A far larger share of our national income is spent today in retail stores than in the days when our own hands made most of what we eat, use and wear. This is one of the reasons storekeeping is growing and will continue to grow and expand.

Deciding What Kind of Store to Open

Having eliminated fields which are overcrowded and fields where special experience or training is a necessity, it is evident that you may not want to tackle any of the usual types of stores. But even with all these eliminations there still remains a vast field for the owner of a specialty store. What is meant by the term "specialty" store? In the usual sense of the word it means the little shops that dot every Main Street—the shops that specialize in lingerie, corsets, costume jewelry, $1.88 hats for women, novelty shops, etc. But there are hundreds of other specialty shops which have not yet penetrated all parts of the country.

Some of these are: Tropical fish shops, pet shops, exclusive hosiery shops, little shops that sell nothing but nuts and nut candies, bridge shops that specialize in bridge supplies and prizes, necktie shops, fountain pen shops, vacuum cleaner stores, washing machine (new and used) shops, portable typewriter shops, drugless drug stores, gift shops, butter-and-egg stores, milk depots, stamp shops or exchanges, potato chip stores, pop corn candy stores, greeting card and novelty shops and a score of other unusual stores.

Your previous experience, your likes and dislikes, your personal preferences, all should be taken into consideration when thinking of opening a specialty shop. Then there is the matter of finances. How much can you invest? How big a business do you want? Do you want to go into business on a fairly pretentious scale, selling on credit, delivering and handling a large stock? Or do you prefer a small shop which you can run with the aid of one assistant, with no delivery or credit expense? Take all of these factors into careful consideration before you decide what kind of store to open.

There is another factor too. What kind of people do you know? Do you have a following and acquaintance among factory workers? Then pick a store with merchandise they can buy. Or do you know the community's wealthiest and most stylish folks? If this is true start a store catering to them. Make use of every advantage you possess. Do you know automobile owners, or have you served them in some capacity in the past? Then perhaps you will want to consider a tire store. Whatever your past experience may have been, you should try to capitalize on it when you open your store.

There is another way to determine what kind of store to open. Find out what the people of your community must go out of town to buy. Suppose you were thinking of starting a fishing tackle store. Contact a number of fishermen and get them to tell you where they buy tackle. Do they have to go to some out-of-town store, or buy by mail? Would they patronize you if you handled a complete line? What items do they have the most difficulty in finding in local stores? These are some of the questions to ask around your community before you start a store.

In this book you will find specific and definite suggestions, based on the actual experience of others in starting specialty stores. From these suggestions, and a careful survey of the needs of your community, there is no reason why, if you really want to, you can't start a successful store.

Choosing the Best Location

There are two general types of store locations, popularly called "high rent locations" and "low rent locations." Of course, the high rent locations are the "hot spots" on the busiest downtown streets. Even a small store in such a location may rent for thousands of dollars a year. Without adequate capital such locations are almost out of the reach of the average beginner in storekeeping. But for the sale of certain "drop in" items these locations are almost essential.

People will not walk upstairs, around the block, or even across the street to buy convenience items such as chewing gum, cigars, cigarettes, popular drug items, soft drinks and similar merchandise. For stores specializing in this type of merchandise, location is the most important thing.

In selecting your location try to determine how much your type of store is actually dependent on location. Pick a location that is in a growing section of town. Beware of a section that is being overrun by manufacturing, garages, cheap rooming houses, or gives other indications that the neighborhood is going to seed.

Different types of stores require different locations. Be sure you know just what type of people you intend to cater to, and that the location you select is in a neighborhood frequented by such people. In every business section there is always one side of the street that is most popular; locate your store on this side of the street. Most of the busiest locations are now cluttered up with cheap chain stores, featuring "price" merchandise. A high-grade store sandwiched in between a $1.88 hat store and a "five-and-dime" store might fail, in spite of the heavy traffic passing it.

Don't be too sure that your store will attract people a block or so out of their habitual path. People have gone broke trying to change buying habits. Don't hamper your store by selecting a location where people have to walk up steps, or take a few steps down to a floor level, even a foot or so below the sidewalk level. Obtain a location with floor exactly level with the sidewalk. Beware of a store with a front that curves inward—people don't notice such a front.

Most young business men make the mistake of leasing a store that is really too big. Figuring out how much you think you want, then cutting the space in half, isn't a bad rule to follow when selecting a location. Remember that a large store requires more heat and light, more fixtures, and a bigger stock. Just because a landlord wants to sell you the entire store is no sign he will not divide the store and rent you half or two-thirds of it.

It may even be possible to lease space from a noncompeting store. Jewelers occasionally lease a space in one end of a drug store. Sometimes you will see a jewelry store in one section of a furniture store. Many expenses can be reduced or eliminated if you can start your store as part of another store which is already well established. In hundreds of department stores throughout the country there are independent operators who own certain departments, but operate them as a part of the big store.

Lobbies of office buildings, hotel lobbies, or even a small space in what would be one entrance to a large store are frequently used for small stores. Remember that every cent you save on rent and other expenses will enable you to hold out successfully just that much longer.

What Makes a Store Successful

Sidney Carter, of the Merchant's Service Department of Rice-Stix, the big St. Louis wholesale house, has made a special study for many years of the factors that make a store successful. He puts it this way: "I know a merchant who isn't very friendly, whose store isn't very neat, but who does a big business because he has merchandise in good quantities. I know another merchant whose store is neat, whose stocks are good, but who does a comparatively poor business, because he isn't friendly with people. I know another merchant who has a badly lighted store, and no fixtures to brag about, but who does a big business because he is a good salesman and knows how to teach his clerks to sell. So you see there are always many factors in determining what makes a store successful."

The National Cash Register Company, whose officials know as much as almost any group of men on earth about operating stores, reports in its excellent book, *Better Retailing*, that the things which customers like are:

A good assortment of well-arranged stock.
Prices right and in plain sight.
Quick, courteous, accurate service.
Exchange and money back without question.
Truthfulness about merchandise.
The same price to everybody.
An attractive, convenient, well-lighted, comfortable store.
Chairs for rest when selecting goods that take time.
Careful attention to children and servants.
Accurate filling of telephone orders.

There has been an enormous improvement in stores in the past few years. Customers are accustomed to better salespeople, more careful attention, an increasing amount of "service," better lighting, and far more courtesy than we once expected. They simply will not tolerate a slipshod, careless, unkept store any more. A store that isn't neat has no more chance than a frowsy debutante.

People will no longer argue about returned goods. No matter how "wrong" the customer may be, he is right in his own mind and expects to be treated accordingly. A customer may have no right to expect to return a hat after she has worn it, but no merchant ever got rich standing up for his "rights."

Overbuying is another cause for many failures. A successful, old-time merchant's secret of making a profit was simply: "Remember you can always buy more." In buying your opening stock keep in mind that the manufacturers are scarcely going to stop making merchandise that is in demand. In opening your store don't tie up more than half of your capital stock. Save some of it for unexpected expenses, for tiding you over a dull season, or for stock to replace slow selling merchandise mistakenly purchased when opening.

Keep Merchandise Moving

Successful merchants aren't afraid to sacrifice merchandise that is not moving. After you have kept merchandise more than a few weeks it has begun to "eat its head off." It should be sacrificed at any reasonable price just to get your money out of it, so you can put money into something that will turn and make profits. No matter how much merchandise costs, it is worth only what you can get for it.

Successful merchants have always gone slowly in committing themselves for heavy time-payments on costly equipment. Don't make the same mistake one merchant did who had an $800 stock of variety goods and a $750 cash register! While good equipment is essential, don't tie yourself up for payments on fixtures, scales, registers and signs. Even if you do a good business monthly installments on equipment will take all the ready cash you can obtain.

Last, but not least, move heaven and earth to satisfy your customers, and keep them coming back. If a customer buys only once, telephone him, see him, write him a letter, if you even suspect that he is buying elsewhere. Find out why he didn't repeat. Make any errors right. Make him understand that you are striving to please him. It is by such tactics that successful storekeepers are made.

■ ■

Starting a Stamp Shop

THE intense interest which has developed in stamp collecting led Phillip Carpenter, retired from the postal service at the age of sixty-five, to sell the stamps he had collected to philatelists in Portland, Oregon, where he lives. Although he had a limited supply of stamps at the start, he rented a portion of a store window, placed most of his stock on display, and waited for buyers to come along.

"My time was worth practically nothing," he explained, "so there was little to be lost by displaying the stamps and talking to possible buyers. I had quite a number of stamps which I had bought from the post office during the thirty years I carried mail. Other stamps had been given to me by relatives and friends who had heard that I was collecting stamps. Many of these were duplicate commemoration stamps, such as the Century of Progress and Harding; a number were foreign and air mail. All in all, they made a good display.

"However, as I had little merchandising sense, I made only $15 the first week, which was barely enough to cover expenses. After a few weeks, I got acquainted with other dealers. We met once a week in a little restaurant and talked business. From then on I began to get the right slant on the stamp business. They explained that the prices I was charging for some issues were too low; other prices were too high. They also pointed out that I needed some new stock so I got in touch with several wholesalers. I learned values quickly after that and shortly I saw the real possibilities of this business.

"I studied various stamp issues and found that I could buy from private collectors at more advantageous prices than I could from the wholesalers. One day a chap came in with a marvelous collection. 'I'm broke,' he said, 'I'll sell you this entire stock for $100.' He told me that these stamps had originally cost him almost $2,000. The other collectors, because of the depression and because he insisted on selling them the whole lot intact, had turned him down. When I glanced over the stamps, I discovered several that were rare, and I saw that I could easily make a good profit. So I took the lot. The next day, I called upon a customer who had been seeking some Danish West Indies, and sold him three blocks of four each at a good profit. Before that week was over, I had sold the entire collection to history professors, school teachers, and stamp collectors for $796. For sometime I thought about this sale and I came to the conclusion that if one person had a collection to sell, there probably were others. I ran a small advertisement in the newspaper offering to buy all or part of the stamp collections of the people in Portland. I secured several good collections in this way and presently I had a good-sized stock at a cost of only $460. I discontinued the advertisement and began to concentrate on selling this stock. Before long I had sold all but a few of the stamps at a profit of $1,400."

Carpenter contacts the universities, schools and even the museum in Portland. School teachers, especially those teaching high-school classes, are interested in stamps, since they are able to teach more colorfully such subjects as history and geography through their use. Foreign canceled stamps, especially those from France, India, England, Italy, Germany, Sweden, British South Africa, Honduras, China, and Japan, are, regardless of issue, in constant demand by school teachers. They bring as high as 300 to 400 per cent profit to the stamp collector.

Catalogs listing the prices at which stamps should be sold are available from wholesalers and some of the stamp listings give both wholesale and retail prices. A stamp shop may be started either by advertising in the newspapers for stamps, as Carpenter did, or by getting in touch with one of the many wholesale stamp companies. These companies will generally submit a large assortment of stamps on an approval basis, allowing the dealer a discount of 25 to 50 per cent. Hence he can start his shop with very little capital. An excellent location for this type of business is in a circulating library near a school.

■ ■

Making a Grocery Store Pay

IT IS a notorious fact that most people who open up a grocery store fail. The mortality rate is higher than in almost any other business. There are a number of reasons why this is true. Sometimes the man who opens up the store lacks industry. He is just plain lazy. He may have picked a poor location. Or he may have shown poor judgment in stocking his store. But the principal reason for the high percentage of failures is that the average man who opens a grocery store overlooks the importance of *sales* ability and sales knowledge.

Competition in the grocery business is so keen today that old methods of storekeeping won't do. In order to succeed you have to know why people buy, and how to make them buy. To some extent this knowledge comes natural to observant people. However, there are certain definite fundamentals about salesmanship which need to be understood to be successful in the retail business. Fortunately for James Brandt, he realized this when he began to think about opening a grocery store in Los Angeles. He could not very well give up two or three years to acquire the needed selling experience, but he learned from a friend that there were schools which taught the principles of salesmanship by mail. That, he thought, would make it easy since he could open his store and study while he earned. "One section of this course," he said, "was devoted to retail merchandising and, among other things, explained various methods of building retail sales. This section, of course, was intended for the wholesaler's salesman making calls upon retailers, and was designed to show him how to help the retailer move the goods from his shelves. Being a retailer, I read this section carefully and found a number of excellent suggestions which I later put into practice in my grocery business.

"From the day I opened the store, I realized the benefits of my salesmanship course. Not only did it teach me how to address a customer, but it taught me how to suggest things so as to build up the unit of sale. By applying the right merchandising principles, I found I could increase a sale by as much as a dollar. You see there's a difference in the way an additional item is suggested to a customer. Suggest it one way and the customer resents it. Suggest it another, and the customer is interested. This art of suggestion helped me get a good start. By applying this principle and others, I soon built up a successful trade here in Los Angeles."

Jimmy Brandt's course in salesmanship cost him eighty-four dollars, which he paid in small monthly payments. But it was worth considerably more than that to him. While most people may not be interested in a course in salesmanship, it is well to think of the many advantages of training if you want to succeed in business. Undoubtedly, such training does open new fields, and keeps you from making mistakes that often are costly and always avoidable. No better way of preparing yourself for a successful career in business may be found than is furnished by specialized training in business practice and business fundamentals. It certainly shortens the way to that "first thousand."

■ ■

The "Ins and Outs" of Running a Gift Shop

MRS. BARCLAY had $500. She wanted to start a business of her own. There were already two struggling gift shops in the town, but they carried mediocre merchandise. Any gift the least out of the ordinary had to be purchased from the department stores in the near-by city. Practically everyone played bridge the year round in this town and there was an active social life—plenty of "showers" for brides-to-be, baby "showers," announcement parties, children's birthday parties, etc. Here was a made-to-order market for gift merchandise. "What this town needs is a good gift shop and I am going to see that it has one," Mrs. Barclay remarked to an old friend one day.

The first step was to find the proper location. A vacant store, near enough to the business center to attract trade and not too near that the rent would be out of line, proved to be an ideal location. The interior was painted a pale yellow, and the inexpensive shelves and display tables made by a local carpenter were painted the same color. Sheer yellow curtains at the two display windows were drawn to the sides in order to permit the passer-by a clear view of the interior. This one-color scheme made an effective background for the display of merchandise which naturally comes in every color of the rainbow.

One wall of shelves held china, pottery and glassware. The wall across from it held brass, pewter, woodenware and silver gifts. The display shelves on the back wall were low and above them was hung a lovely piece of chintz and a colonial mirror. These low shelves held toys suitable for children from infancy up to the age of ten or so. The space above the shelves on the other two walls was large enough to permit the hanging of several pictures—etchings, prints, reproductions of oils and water colors. Two comfortable chairs with end tables at their sides, three display tables and the wrapping counter took up the remainder of the space but left sufficient room for a small crowd to get about.

One of the tables was sufficiently long to display a number of items suitable for bridge prizes from $1.00 to $3.00, the prices usually paid in this community for bridge prizes. A smaller table displayed playing cards, bridge tallies, pencils, table covers, ash trays, and a few books on systems of playing bridge. The third table held novelties which were the fad at the moment and for which there would be a certain demand for a short time. The display case, which was the bottom of the wrapping counter, held merchandise which is easily soiled. This merchandise included silk lamp shades, silk and velvet cushions, dainty linens and baby gifts such as bonnets, jackets, dresses, shoes, carriage robes, and pillows.

A cabinet at one end of the counter contained gift cards, fancy paper for wrapping gifts, ribbon and colored string, little candles for birthday cakes, larger candles in various colors for luncheon and dinner tables, paper napkins and tablecloths, and place cards.

The windows were kept shining and bright and the displays changed daily. Only a few things were placed in each window each day—perhaps a bowl and candlesticks, a picture and a piece of beautiful brocade, or a small lamp and and unusual cigarette box opened to show the cigarettes within. Each piece displayed was beautiful, distinctive, colorful, or perhaps all three.

Building Up a Clientele

A customer list maintained on cards gives the name of the customer, address, and telephone number and, on the back, a list of the things purchased with the date of purchase. A check of these cards from month to month brings up the names that are not buying and a simple announcement describing new merchandise received is mailed to such names. The telephone is also used to tell customers about new items. Subscriptions to gift magazines keep Mrs. Barclay in touch with new merchandise, and a visit to the more important gift shops and the department store gift sections in the large city near by also gives her new ideas on displays and gift items. Then there is, of course, the semi-annual exhibit of giftwares in the city, which she attends regularly. Magazines such as *House Beautiful, Harper's Bazaar, Vogue* are looked over carefully for suggestions which may be incorporated in displays or window arrangements. When talking to customers she makes a point of mentioning such and such an item or display as being similar to that shown in the current issue of *House Beautiful* or *Vogue,* or other magazine from which it happens to have been culled. This plan always succeeds in creating interest in a new display and at the same time helps to sell the customer.

After the first few weeks people began to take notice of this shop. They found that it wasn't just a place where you *might* find what you wanted; it was a shop that would have *just what you wanted.* This ability to create confidence in her selection of merchandise began to build up a nice clientele almost immediately. By the end of the first year, Mrs. Barclay had to hire an assistant and to add two new sections to her shop—a greeting card section and a "knitting corner." The assistant was an expert with the knitting needles and being also a young woman with ideas and a pleasing personality, she soon helped Mrs. Barclay build up a nice yarn business in the "knitting corner."

It is possible, of course, to start a gift shop with less money than Mrs. Barclay invested. If your home is one of the old-fashioned, comfortable residences built in the nineties, part of the space can be used for your shop. The room selected should be easily accessible to the passer-by and have suitable windows for display. The walls and woodwork should be painted a harmonious color if they are not appropriate in their present condition for the display of merchandise. If the room has a fireplace, so much the better. While some shelving will be necessary for the display of merchandise, particularly as the amount of stock is increased, many of the gifts can be displayed as part of the furnishings of the room. The mantel offers a suggestion for the display of vases, china figurines, pictures, mirrors, etc., and the display should be changed daily in order to make the most of this central feature. One or two gate-leg tables, a Pembroke table, a tilt-top, and a coffee table will aid in the display of gifts and a chest of drawers will hold much of the more fragile merchandise. A study of the types of interiors featured in the current magazines devoted to interior decoration will help you in the arrangement of this type of room.

An announcement in the local paper and printed announcements, suggesting appropriate gifts for all occasions, mailed to a selected list of names, will let people know that you have a shop and that it is open for business. Keep a list of your customers and the "lookers" as well, and use the telephone to keep in touch with them when new merchandise arrives. Don't expect this type of business to grow overnight—rather a slow, steady rate of growth should be your aim.

■ ■

How to Become a Corsetiere

IF THERE is a hospital in your town here is an idea that may be worth $1,000 to you. A woman who had been a corsetiere decided to open a shop with her savings. She selected a location in a busy outlying part of the city in which she lived. Two blocks away, the neighborhood was zoned for light factories and, of course, many girls were employed in the offices of these factories. There were also a number of young women employed in the offices and stores in the immediate neighborhood. But most important of all, just two blocks from her store was a large hospital. Having had considerable experience in fitting surgical corsets, she had selected this location in order to build up a business catering to post-operative cases in need of abdominal support, and in supplying the proper type of corsets for invalids and others in need of special corrective garments.

She arranged to carry the "line" of a well-known manufacturer of popular types of corsets, brassieres and girdles. This company was also noted for its surgical supports and offered excellent cooperation to corsetieres handling this sort of garment. Keeping in mind her market, she stocked her shop with girdles for the younger women who worked in the offices in the neighborhood, with corsets for the heavy matronly figures among the housewives in the residential section, with collar and cuff sets, belts, gloves, handkerchiefs, a good grade of hosiery, brassieres and other lingerie, boutonnieres, and notions such as darning cotton, tape, thread, hairpins, powder puffs, etc. Later when she began to know her customers' tastes better she would purchase ten to fifteen dresses in the moderately-priced line which she knew would be suitable for certain customers, and telephone them that the dresses were in stock. Frequently, all were sold in a day or two as the styles and prices were right.

Her first step in building up a business in corrective garments was to call on the doctors in the neighborhood and explain that she was a trained corsetiere and specialized in surgical supports. She also left cards with the hospital office. Through the nurses who purchased hosiery and other items, she secured further advertising.

172

A card record of every customer was kept on file giving the name, address, type of garment purchased, date purchased, and size. From time to time post cards were sent to these names announcing something special. A separate record was kept of the patients who had been fitted with surgical supports, and these names were followed up by special calls in order to determine definitely whether or not the garment sold had been satisfactory and, incidentally, whether a new one or a different type of garment was now required.

The store had only one display window but she made the most of it by keeping it spotlessly clean, by changing the displays frequently, and by displaying the latest fashions in lingerie or the most attractive seasonal items. Whenever she had purchased a few dresses she would place one in the window with a card stating that a new stock of dresses had just arrived. Within the store, the collars and cuffs, the handkerchiefs and silken lingerie were attractively arranged in display cases, brassieres were displayed on models in the corset section, and if dresses were in stock they were arranged on a long rack at the back of the shop. The surgical support section was located in a room at the back of the shop which was divided to include a fitting room and space for altering garments.

For ten years this little shop flourished and during good times and bad she made money. What competition did spring up quickly died down because she never made any attempt to compete on a price basis and very few merchants could match her ability to serve customers. The corset manufacturer whose line she carried saw that she had about exhausted her market and for some time had been urging her to move to a neighborhood with greater possibilities. Finally she decided to make the change and rented the shop the manufacturer's agent had selected. Two display windows enabled her to attract more passers-by and a larger stock with greater variety helped to build up more business than she could have handled in the old shop. Two hospitals in this neighborhood kept her busy with special fittings, and she still had many customers through the doctors at the hospital in the old neighborhood. As she located only about two miles away from the neighborhood where her other shop was established, many of those whose names were on her customer list still patronize her shop.

Even though you may not have the advantage of the special training which this woman had, that need not prevent you from starting a business of this sort. Most of the corset manufacturers conduct courses which you can attend to learn the business. You do not have to open a store at first but can start by soliciting orders from friends and others until you get a trade built up. Very little capital is required if you begin in that way, and then after you have earned a few hundred dollars you can invest in a stock and open up a store. If you like people, enjoy selling, and buy cautiously, you should soon be able to build up a business which will net you a good income—well over $1,000 a year.

■ ■

Start a Second-Hand Magazine Shop

"**WE STARTED** our magazine shop with a pile of magazines, a few dollars, an idea and a location," said Mrs. McIntyre, commenting upon the beginning of the business in which she and her husband made their first thousand dollars. "We had to live somewhere, so we rented cheap store space, moved in, washed the windows and partitioned off living quarters in the rear. Then we bought a pile of second-hand magazines from a storage warehouse which was selling out the stored possessions of people who had not paid their storage rental."

After starting this type of store, the next move of the McIntyres was to decide on where they were going with it. While the sale of used magazines might tide them over the depression, to make a big business of it and to build for permanence and the future required a definite objective. They considered ways and means and finally they decided just to be "different." They would carry a file of back numbers as far back as they could, build up this file as a reference file, and at the same time build up a wholesale business in used magazines. Of course, they didn't accomplish this aim overnight. Like so many beginners, they made many mistakes and, too, they had a great deal to learn.

Watching Out for Profits

"The most important thing I discovered," continued Mrs. McIntyre, "is that everything you sell must be sold at a profit. As long as you make a little profit on every sale, you can't lose anything. In acquiring the used magazines, we accidentally got hold of books, sheet music, and unframed pictures and sketches. We did not want these things, but they were often forced upon us. When we had a number of old books and pictures, we sorted them and placed price tags on them. People entering the store for magazines, often bought a book or two, or inquired about books. We also found that the old sheet music had a cash value. So we decided while building a file of back numbers of magazines for reference, to build a back number file of songs. This requires patience and everlasting work, but it is worth the effort, for soon you build up a reputation for your shop. We came to be depended upon to deliver back numbers of many magazines, and we received orders from bookstores, libraries and collectors for back issues, as well as complete files of magazines. The price ranges from a nickel to two dollars and a half for each magazine.

"We obtain the magazines from the janitors of apartment buildings, hotels, and rooming houses. We also make frequent trips to the furniture storage companies and pick up magazines at little cost—usually about a cent a copy. Some magazines may run a little higher but the most we ever figure on paying for a magazine is twenty-five cents.

"We aim to have as complete a file on each magazine as it is possible to get. We also try to carry as many different magazines as our storage space permits and we are able to secure. If a call comes in for a certain magazine title or a certain issue, we make every effort to secure it for the customer. For this service a slight extra charge is made which the customer is usually willing to pay if he wants the magazine.

"It took a little time to learn how to estimate values. I've sold books for a nickel that I later discovered were worth several dollars, and magazines for ten cents that had a current value of two dollars. But each time I made a mistake of this kind, I remembered it. In the beginning, it's best to stick to the medium-priced magazines and books, until you learn more about the valuable ones."

In less than six months, it was necessary to expand the size of the shop so more space was rented to care for extra business. Later, this store covered a whole block and eventually a branch store was opened to care for the extra business.

■ ■

Quality Sells—Even Hamburgers

THIS story of a successful enterprise starts out with a creaky old jalopy and eleven cents. Ted Lansmann, a young Californian, owned both the automobile and the grand capital of eleven cents. On his way to give the old auto wreck to a friend because he could no longer afford to run it, he came across a hamburger stand on the route between Los Angeles and Pasadena.

The owner of the stand had given up hope of making anything of the business and he was about to close up when the jallopy and its occupant came along. After some conversation, the owner offered the stand in exchange for the auto and the offer was accepted. When he took over, the new owner found himself with eleven cents in cash, a couple dozen buns, three cases of pop and, of course, the shack.

Ted knew that 11 cents wouldn't go very far so he succeeded in borrowing $50 from a friend. Then he began to think about how he could put this new enterprise over. In this particular locality hamburgers were 10 cents at the majority of stands; some even charged only 5 cents. Ted decided to go whole hog and put his price up to 15 cents. The hamburgers were worth it; only the best ground beef and the best buns he could buy were used. He found he had no difficulty in getting 15 cents but it took him six months before he was doing much more than making expenses. The upturn came when a customer asked for a hamburger with a thin slice of cheese added. Ted tried one himself and from then on specialized in cheese-burgers. The business began to grow. He soon started another place in Los Angeles, then a third place was opened and finally a steak house where he served the best steaks that money could buy.

In 1937, business increased 500 per cent and in 1938, just eleven years after he traded in the old jallopy for the stand, Ted sold out his famous steak restaurant and property to another restaurant man for $150,000.

There are thousands and thousands of hamburger and hot dog stands throughout this country, but on your travels how often do you come across one that can serve you a really good sandwich and a good cup of coffee? Quality brings customers to the little wayside stand just as it brings them to the big department store in the center of a metropolis. Quality is what Ted sold; the returns speak for themselves.

■ ■

Butter-and-Egg Stores Can Be Easily Started

BECAUSE Harvey Keller didn't want to give up his "girl friend," he moved to the big city to be near her, and there established a business selling eggs and chickens fresh from his father's farm, which netted him a profit of over $600 in less than four months.

Keller first brought two cases of eggs into Chicago. He called from door to door, selling butter and eggs at a fraction under store prices and guaranteed them to be right from the farm. When these two cases of eggs were sold, Keller drove back to his father's farm and returned with seven cases. His profit on each case was four dollars. Noticing that aside from groceries and markets, there was no place where one could secure eggs, and considering the friendly way in which the public received him, Harvey decided to open what he calls a "hennery." He rented a small store on a side street a few doors from a street car line for fifteen dollars a month, and stocked this with eggs and several crates of live chickens.

"I didn't have opening a store in mind at first. I saw there was money bringing in cases of fresh eggs, but it was apparent that I was wasting a lot of time driving to the farm and back. I arranged to bring in a truck load of eggs and needed a place to stock them. I had my father send the chickens, hoping to find a market for them. People passing the store stopped and watched me stack the crates of eggs in the store. Some came inside and asked if I was opening an egg store. I replied that I just brought the eggs from the farm, and would sell them at regular store prices. In a little while, I had sold fifteen dozen, and was convinced a store selling eggs and chickens exclusively would pay in that locality. I locked up and made my rounds of the neighborhood and when I asked for orders, told my customers about the line. I sold a case of eggs and three chickens before noon, and returning to the store, fixed the door so it would remain open. That afternoon, I put in a counter. But business didn't rush in as I expected.

Advertising Brings in Customers

"The corner druggist told me, when I dropped into his store for cigarettes, that if he were in my place he would have some circulars printed, explaining that I had opened the store and offered chickens and selected fresh eggs brought in by truck from my father's farm, and to distribute these circulars wherever I went. This sounded like a good idea. 'Don't put these in the mail boxes,' the printer warned me when I picked up the circulars. 'Hand one to the woman when she opens the door.' Most women I called upon didn't buy from me, you know, for only one in a dozen needed eggs at the moment I knocked on the door. But I left a circular at each home I called upon. Within a few days, I was doing a brisk business. Some people came out of curiosity, but everyone bought something. I also got considerable business by paying high-school boys a small commission to get orders from their friends."

Keller supplies country fresh eggs from this store to people from many blocks around. His total investment in the store and his first stock was less than seventy-five dollars. His sales now average four cases of eggs daily, and daily earnings from the sale of both eggs and chickens run about nineteen dollars. In order to handle deliveries on orders phoned in, Keller found it necessary to hire a clerk. He continues to go out from house to house picking up orders, which he declares is the backbone of his business.

A somewhat similar idea has been developed by a family in Glencoe, Illinois, who owned a big farm near Lake Geneva. In order to market the farm's products and compete with local stores in North Shore towns, they rented and fixed up two barns at locations near the main highways on the edge of town. The stores were advertised as "The Barn" and catered especially to automobile trade. "The Barn," as in the case of Harvey Keller's "Hennery," depended upon established trade, the telephone being used to keep in touch with customers. The pleasing thing about a business of this sort is the quick turnover. There is no stock to go dead on your shelves. Even though you may not own a farm, or have any relative who can supply you with fresh farm products, you can locate some farmer who will be glad to arrange with you to market his butter, eggs and chickens in this way. By specializing on those three products—possibly adding ducks and turkeys in season—you can build up a tidy business in short order. People are willing to pay well for really fresh eggs and farm butter.

■ ■

The Hosiery Bar

THE Hosiery Bar is an unusual way of making limited capital usable in starting one's own business. Miss Hannah Hilb, owner-manager of the Hosiery Bar, Denver, found that she could take advantage of a part frontage in the center of Denver's most popular downtown section. A lease was secured on an eight-foot-wide store at a nominal figure. A few alterations changed the front to a "baby store" with two miniature windows and a three-and-one-half-foot door. The store, extending back to a thirty-foot depth, was carpeted with a remnant "buy." Fixtures included the regulation side cabinets, two display tables, and a specially made "bar." The side cabinets and the tables were cut down approximately twelve inches in their widths, finished in glistening ebony paint, and trimmed in chromium.

The "bar," the main attraction in the place, was constructed on modern lines, being a single piece of compo-board covered with ebony linoleum and protected and supported on each side with heavy chromium strips. Fashioned in the form of an elongated "J," the curve or tail was placed to the front of the store so that it curved under, forming one end support. The arm extended back to serve as a twelve-foot service counter. All fixtures were purposely narrowed in their width to create the illusion of more space in the shop. These fixtures, which were purchased second-hand, ran around $90—exclusive of the "bar." The latter ran about $60, remodeling of interior $200, extras about $50.

The original stock was approximately $500. Stocks are purchased by Miss Hilb through an eastern buying agency, which enables her to get full discounts with small orders. An average inventory runs about $1,500. With this amount of stock, Miss Hilb can offer her clientele a full range selection and gross volume of approximately $50 a day.

The location of the Hosiery Bar is such a good one, Miss Hilb feels that it is sufficient advertising in itself. A special stimulant for introductory business is used, however, in the form of a card which is presented to new customers. When this card is punched out through the sale of twelve pairs of hosiery, it is exchanged for one free pair.

■ ■

The Fat Men's Shop

IN NEW YORK there is a men's shop on lower Third Avenue which has catered for some twenty years to a special clientele—fat men. Here the oversize man can select suits, shirts, socks, shoes, and hats without the usual difficulties of being fitted in the average store. Even the clerks themselves are of whopping dimensions in order that the customer may not be embarrassed by any suggestion that he is an unusual specimen of the human race!

Naturally, only in a large metropolis can a special shop such as this find a need for its very special services. Cities, size of Detroit, Cleveland, Philadelphia, Chicago, New York, San Francisco, and Los Angeles, would probably offer markets large enough for such a specialty store. The same cities would also offer a market for a similar store catering to the stout woman.

In smaller cities, a special department catering to stout women or men is usually located in the larger department stores. Any stout person will tell you, however, that there is much room for improvement in these departments. The alert retailer who can develop such a department to its fullest will find a corresponding increase in his income.

■ ■

Open a Drug-Less Drug Store

DURING the Florida boom a young woman was sent by her firm to West Palm Beach as assistant manager of a small branch. She found the new place delightful, made many friends and brought her mother to live with her. When the bottom fell out of Florida, however, the home office immediately closed the branch and recalled the staff. It was not pleasant to think of going north again, taking a clerk's job in the home office (she couldn't hope to step back in her old position) and giving up the companionship of the good friends she and her mother had made in the five years they had lived in West Palm Beach. She realized that she would have to find some way to make a living in Florida! But how?

While buying some cold cream in a drug store the day after the notice came to close the branch, Miss Oliver got the idea of opening a "drug-less drug store." She reasoned that there were a great many items that people went into drug stores to buy that could just as well be purchased in a small attractive shop that would cater especially to their personal needs. She had some money saved, and upon inquiry she found she could have a little shop immediately that would be quite reasonable to rent. She talked the idea over with her mother and the two of them decided to try it out.

She stocked three good lines of cosmetics—really three price lines—including face powder, rouge, lipstick, creams, etc. Other purchases were four brands of tooth-paste, two brands of tooth brushes, some well-known toilet waters, soaps, bath salts, manicure instruments, sun-tan lotions and oils, talcums, and hair tonics.

Her "drug" section included such daily necessities as boric acid, witch-hazel, iodine, mercurochrome, nationally advertised antiseptics, corn remedies, vaseline, sunburn remedies, rubbing alcohol, adhesive tape, gauze bandages, indigestion remedies, etc. In addition she stocked the four most popular brands of cigarettes, some chewing gum, razor blades, razors, shaving cream, playing cards, a good quality of plain white stationery, and the popular magazines. At the back of the store where it was cool and inviting was the soda fountain and sandwich counter. A good grade of ice cream was carried, the usual bottled goods, and a fine brand of coffee. Sandwiches were prepared only on order and the lettuce, tomatoes, and other "fillings" were kept fresh and crisp. No cooking was ever done in the store, consequently the place did not have that unpleasant odor so often associated with drug and other stores which serve light luncheons.

While they were not aware of it, nevertheless, both mother and daughter were the sort that are exactly suited to handle a small retail business. Both were nice looking, were immaculate in appearance, had cheerful, optimistic dispositions, were friendly. They liked meeting and talking with people. And they were not afraid of long hours or hard work.

Special Corner Sells Cosmetics

The exterior of the store was pale cream stucco and instead of the usual screen door, the screen and frame were painted chalk blue and the screen partially covered with lattice work also painted blue. This gave the store its name, "The Blue Door." Blue awnings over the windows and blue hurricane shutters added to its distinctive appearance. The interior was a cool sea-blue color and chairs at the tables were covered with flowered cretonne slip covers.

Convenient to the cosmetic corner were a low table, a reed settee, an end table, and a deep cushioned reed chair with a tall white screen behind it. These pieces of furniture were painted white and the cushions covered in the floral cretonne. In this corner face powders were mixed for customers and perfumes tested for their fragrance, or lipsticks examined for proper color. It was a new idea for customer and proprietor to sit down and discuss the merits of this or that product. Women who came into the shop for the first time were agreeably surprised by its charm and particularly by this cozy little corner where one could relax, smoke a cigarette and make one's purchases at leisure.

The first year was a struggle and the second year found her almost willing to give up and go back north. There was so much work to do, so many of the sales were small items on which there was little profit, and to make matters worse, during the first two winters the tourist trade fell to an all-time low. However, when she talked it over with her mother, they agreed to try it another year. They were making a poor living but they were not yet willing to say "die." The third year saw a pick-up in the winter tourist business which tided them over for another year. By this time they felt that if they could keep going at all it was better to be doing something that they liked than to be making a mediocre living up north doing monotonous clerical work in an office.

It is now ten years since the little store was started and the last three years have seen it grow into a real business. In spite of the depression, the store did enough business to enable the owners to make a trip north each summer, to dress nicely, to save some money and to buy a coupe. To the original departments have been added a rental library, a stock of greeting cards, and some inexpensive bridge prizes and favors. During the busy season, an attractive young girl helps out in the store part time for "pin money." She is also available when the daughter and mother wish to spend an evening with friends. While the store will never make either of them rich, they are both living well, saving money, free of debt, and are happy in their work and independence. That's the big thing in having a business of your own. It makes you feel that you are somebody after all. So even though you may not be an apothecary, you can start a drug-less drug store in your town if you have the will and a little capital to carry you through the first few months.

"Dollar Pups" Make Pet Store Pay

IT DOESN'T take much money to start a pet shop. It does take a good idea to bring people inside the pet shop, however, and this, C. Kinowski learned when he opened his pet shop two years ago in South Chicago. The store space was so large that when he moved in his stock of pets, cages, and accessories, the space was far from being filled. So he built a cage along the wall from the windows far back into the store. This 25-foot-long cage is built entirely of wooden frames covered with a fine mesh screen and cost only $36.

"I covered the floor of this cage with linoleum on which I spread a thick layer of bird gravel," Kinowski said, "and then turned a number of canaries and other small birds loose in it. The birds were provided with nests and perches and the whole display attracted a great deal of attention. People from the neighborhood stood and watched the birds flying around the big cage. Some came in to ask questions, and bought canaries and parakeets, generally known as love birds, on the spot. When I saw how much attention was being given this big cage I decided to make it more attractive, and placed some tall palms around the outside to create a woodland appearance, partitioned it into sections, and told my customers I was using it as a flight breeding cage. I don't sell birds from this cage but let them breed. The young birds are removed and placed in small cages as they mature. The display value of the big cage with its nests and birds fluttering about, however, is incalculable.

Display of Puppies Adds to Profits

"Birds were going well, so I partitioned a section of the window space into rough and comfortable pens. In these I placed puppies. I put puppies of ages from three weeks to two months old in the window, and you'd be surprised at the interest shown in them. This display was so effective that I was soon hard pressed to get enough puppies to fill the demand for them. Children, especially small boys, stand for hours with their noses pressed against the glass, watching the puppies play. When these children get seventy-five cents or a dollar, they bring it in and buy a pup. Most of these dogs are just dogs. Of course, you couldn't sell a pedigreed dog for so low a price. But these dollar dogs go so fast that handling them pays more than enough for my rent and lights.

"To secure enough puppies was a problem until I placed a small advertisement in a neighborhood paper, offering twenty-five cents for puppies. In a few days, people came from near and far with puppies. These were dogs that would have been drowned or otherwise destroyed, so the owners were glad to get something for them, and to know that the pups would get a good home.

"One of the most important points to remember in starting a pet shop of this sort is the need for cleanliness and sanitation. Unless your shop is thoroughly cleaned once a day, it will begin to have an unpleasant odor which will repel customers as soon as they enter the door. In addition, lack of cleanliness will add to the danger of disease of both birds and puppies and once disease has gained a foothold, you may lose your entire stock. Cedar chips sprinkled among the newspapers in the dog display window or cage will help considerably to eliminate odors; cedar oil may also be used. In summer time, a ventilating fan at the back of the store will help to clear the air.

"The profits accumulating to the pet shop owner do not stop with the profits on birds, dogs, and other pets, however. There is a good profit in bird seed, bird cages, bird gravel, dog food, medicine of various kinds for young dogs, and accessories for pets."

Many pet dealers include in their stock a number of aquariums containing tropical fish, and the accessories which go with aquariums for home use, such as aquatic plants, fish food, and ornaments for their home aquariums. A pet shop may be started with as little as $100 for stock and equipment, and space may be rented at a reasonable figure in a good location. Too much emphasis cannot be placed upon attractively displaying pets and accessories since the average American's love of animals forces him to stop and watch them, when they are displayed in a window. There are few easier ways of making money.

■ ■

Cashing In on the Tropical Fish Vogue

A FEW years ago Ralph Watkins, a tropical fish enthusiast, opened an aquarium in Chicago's South Shore district. He had eight kinds of fish at that time, and ten small tanks. At the end of three years, he had one hundred and thirty tanks containing one hundred and twenty varieties of fish, was growing his own fauna, and netting well over a thousand dollars a year in this fascinating business.

"I started with two hundred dollars," said Watkins. "My rent was not high. My investment in fish amounted to a hundred dollars. Tanks, fauna, and accessories took my second hundred dollars, and when I turned the key in the door the first morning, I didn't have a red cent in my pocket. A few children passing on their way to school early that morning, had stopped to ask the price of goldfish and went on their way. I forgot them. Late in the afternoon they returned with several others. They were eager, curious and

fascinated with the few tropical and goldfish I had in the tanks. One youngster wanted to buy a goldfish. For a moment she studied it, then solemnly
said: 'What will I call it?' 'What's your name?' I inquired. 'Sonya.' 'This goldfish should be called Sonya,' I replied. That went over big. Before they left,
each had bought one or two fish which they named after themselves or other
children in the neighborhood, and I 'rang up' three dollars on the sale.

"Because the children liked the idea of naming the fish they bought,
they came back again and again. When a fish appeared sick or died, they'd
come in and say 'Alice has a tummy ache,' or 'Henry died.' Their parents
took up the idea and laughed about it. When 'Alice' or 'Henry' passed out,
I wouldn't know what type fish it was, so to make sure, I'd go over to their
homes to see the fish before replacing it. This gave me an opportunity to
explain the proper care of fish to the mothers and fathers of the children,
and to point out the decorative possibilities of the more expensive fish.
Soon I was getting calls for tropicals that ran into money. Many of the
species ordered were hard to get. Furthermore, I did not have even those
tropical fish that were easily obtained. I had acquired some colored photographs of tropicals during the previous months, and carried them with me,
showing them to the parents. These contacts proved valuable. As the average person knows little about fish and their care, I took this opportunity
to explain how the fish should be handled. Few at first were ready to buy,
stating that they had little luck with fish. So I adopted the policy of guar-
anteeing every fish, from the lowest-priced *Guppi*, to the highest-priced
Angel or *Scalare* in the shop. In each interview, in addition to telling how
fish should be raised, I emphasized the fact that tropical fish of most varieties will really live for many years, if cared for properly.

"I interested the neighborhood in tropicals as a feature of home decoration. To add to the species I had in the store, I bought some *Red Helleri*,
Silver Tetra, *Blue Gularis*, *Red Platy*, *Blue Gourami*, twenty varieties
of the *Angel* or *Scalare* which retail from fifty cents to fifty dollars each,
Calico Cichlidae and many others. When a man wanted to place a beautiful aquarium in his living room, I was able to show him a good assortment
from which he could make selections. The buyer seldom wants a common
fish when he is convinced tropicals will live. He will not hesitate to buy
rare varieties, after he starts an aquarium, and buys them as readily as he
buys a new chair. The advertising value of having in stock rare tropicals
which sell from fifteen to a hundred dollars a pair, is incalculable. Even if
I never sold one, I'd think they were well worth keeping on display in the
store. They do not cost me much more than the *Guppi* to raise, and bring
very high prices.

"Different kinds of fish require different kinds of water. Water is conditioned by plant life growing in the aquarium. Most races of tropical fish
require tropical marine fauna, and because I'm one of the few dealers in

my city having a large, well-stocked store selling nothing but tropical fish and supplies, I grow in my own tanks the fauna which I sell to my customers.

Raising Tropical Plants

"I may upset some common notions about tropical plants when I say that almost all tropical fauna necessary to conditioning tropical fish are native Florida plants. Even the so-called *Madagascar Lily* comes from Florida. This plant is easy to raise, and is pretty hardy. Some plants, however, are difficult to raise and until you hit upon the right method of growing them, you will have little luck. For example, almost every aquarium man thinks it impossible to raise the *Sagittaria Guayanersis*, a Florida plant. They have tried it in many public aquariums with little success. It fooled me, until I accidentally discovered that this particular plant requires a great deal of room for its roots to spread out. When the roots are cramped a little, the leaves become speckled, turn brown at the edges, and presently the plant dies. After learning what it required, however, I have had no trouble with it at all. The *Cryptocoryne Griffithii*, which thrives only in sand, is the only plant from the South Seas I use. I have four varieties of it, and have heard there's a fifth, which I'm trying to locate. One can obtain the seed or the cuttings of plant life at a very small cost, and in a year or two build up a surprisingly profitable stock of marine fauna. The plants cost practically nothing to raise, but as they require a great deal of light, I keep a lamp burning over each tank all the time. I determine the price for plants and fish by the demand and the time I've had them. The longer I have them, the more I get for them. The fifty-cent *Angel* is my bread-and-butter fish. I raise this fish right in my shop at no expense and it sells very fast.

"In selling tropical fish for home aquariums, there is one point that should be stressed. The water should be conditioned by tropical flora for several days before the fish are placed in it. Water should never be changed by emptying the aquarium and putting in fresh water. Salt should not be placed in the water. Water should be turned into the aquarium only when necessary to replace evaporated water. Water just out of the spigot is such a shock to tropical fish they will die overnight."

A good plan for getting your store known in a district is to appear before the natural history classes in grammar and high schools several times annually, giving a talk upon the care and feeding of fish, and the many interesting features of owning fish. Such talks might profitably be given at church gatherings and women's clubs also. Handling as a side line such items as home aquariums, plants, fish food, decorative shells and aquarium ornaments add greatly to the profits of this interesting enterprise.

CHAPTER EIGHT

PROMOTING A SMALL BUSINESS

IT IS a precept of business that goods well bought are half sold, and that any man who builds a better mouse trap than his neighbor will have a path worn to his door. Like most business maxims these are only half true. No matter how desirable the thing you are selling may be, your ability to sell it is in direct proportion to the number of people who know what you have to offer. The job of spreading that news is, for want of a better expression, called "promoting a business."

It is only within the last few years that the possibilities of "promotions" have been fully realized by business men. For a decade or more before the depression business men talked a great deal about the power of advertising. Advertising was held up as the modern Aladdin's lamp that brought success to all who touched it. Advertising still is a powerful business force. But gradually men have come to appreciate that advertising alone is not enough. It is just one of a number of ways to promote a business. And so we find in the up-to-date business not only a man in charge of advertising, but working hand-in-hand with him, a man in charge of promotion.

The use of "promotions" as a means of short-cutting the good-will building process, and increasing what is called "store traffic," has reached its highest state of development in the department store field. Here we find the management always searching for new ideas and thinking up all sorts of things to bring people into their stores, and to get themselves talked about. One Chicago store, for example, spent thousands of dollars to put on a "Quality Exposition." A section of the store was set aside for a display of quality products featured side by side with inferior products. The differences in value were made clear by tags and charts. Another store drew thousands of people into the china department by having prominent society women and leaders of civic organizations set dinner and tea tables, which were displayed in strategic locations. Big stores do not overlook a single trick when it comes to turning the public eye their way, and getting people to talk about them. These promotional activities are becoming increasingly important and it behooves the smaller business man, whether he is the proprietor of a small store in a small town or a manufacturer, to use showmanship as well as advertising in promoting his business.

Showmanship in Business

It is not necessary to spend thousands of dollars to put on a show that will make your business the center of interest and attention. During the depth of the depression a small jeweler in a little Indiana town found himself in a tight spot with his creditors. His "working capital" was tied up in diamonds, and at that time diamonds were a drug on the market. How could he turn these diamonds into cash and pay his bills? He found the answer in a "diamond contest." This contest was based on the inherent interest which people have in diamonds, and the general lack of knowledge concerning them. The jeweler arranged a display of diamonds in his window, and announced that he had prepared a series of questions about the stones. He further explained that he would award, on a certain day, a valuable diamond ring to the person who submitted the most complete answers to his list of questions. He had some handbills prepared, which were distributed door to door announcing the contest. He advertised in the newspapers. He got the school-teachers interested. In fact, so great was the local interest in the promotion that he was asked by the Rotary Club and the Chamber of Commerce to address luncheon meetings on the subject of diamonds. But in order to participate in the contest it was necessary for you to go to his store twice; once to get the list of questions and again to deposit your answers to the questions. That was the hook. What happened? Not only did this jeweler make his store the main topic of conversation in town for more than a month, but hundreds of people became interested in diamonds as an article of jewelry and as an investment. He quickly sold out his stock of stones and had to buy more. And that happened in 1932 when the banks were closed, and it was more or less fashionable to be "broke."

Another sure-fire way to promote either a small or a large business is to hitch your wagon to a star—some celebrity who is visiting town. Then there is that old reliable stunt of balloon parades. Recently Shell Petroleum opened a new filling station in St. Louis. Seldom, if ever, was a Hollywood opening more colorful than this service station opening. Clowns were on hand to service an old model T Ford; executives in full-dress clothes serviced other cars and girls from the local Shell offices, dressed as chorus girls, helped entertain the crowds. More than two thousand cars were serviced in twenty-four hours. Giant spotlights lit up the premises, bands played and speeches were made; St. Louis was fully conscious of the new station's opening.

One of the cleverest and best planned pieces of showmanship was the stunt staged in big department stores by Westinghouse to promote refrigerators. This company arranged with department stores to hold a style show. As the audience assembled in the auditorium there appeared a row of Westinghouse refrigerators. Suddenly, from behind the refrigerators appeared a group of beautiful girls in negligee; the idea was that this scene represented milady's busy day. From the refrigerator she took the "makings" of breakfast. Breakfast over, the girls disappeared behind the refrigerators, and from out of sight of the audience the filmy, lacy garments they had been wearing were thrown over the refrigerators; by this time the audience was shivering in anticipation—perhaps the girls would appear next in attire suitable only for a nudist party!

But the next appearance showed them attired for a morning activity of one kind or another—riding, tennis, or other sports. After showing the sports costumes the girls retired again behind the refrigerators, changed to a costume suitable for luncheon. Each appearance called for a visit to the refrigerator. This program was carried out through a typical day of a busy woman, until supposedly late at night when the wives appeared with their husbands, ostensibly from a late theater party or a bridge game to raid the refrigerator for a midnight "snack."

Here was a double-edged promotion. First, Westinghouse got over the essential idea that a refrigerator was about the most important tool in a busy woman's activities, always on the job, always ready to serve in any emergency food crisis, always saving time for the busy woman. Second, it provided a new idea and a new background for a style show, gave several departments of the store an opportunity to display many different costumes, including negligee, sports, afternoon, dinner, evening, and bathing, besides dozens of accessories, so important in modern fashions.

A particularly spectacular stunt in showmanship was the famous transcontinental trainload of movie stars and electrical equipment which General Electric hauled across the country early in 1933. A brilliantly decorated train, with coaches equipped with demonstration kitchens, and loaded with movie stars such as Leo Carillo, Bette Davis, Lyle Talbot, Tom Mix and others, visited many towns and was thrown open for public inspection. Thousands of people thronged through the train and visited the dealers' showroom where the stars were in the reception line.

This train pointed up the General Electric sales campaign and took the dealers' minds off the bank failures which became nationwide, just when the train reached Cleveland on its eastward journey.

While the smaller business man cannot, of course, undertake promotions of this magnitude himself, it is usually possible for him to "tie in" with national activities and thus bring to his business whatever local sales value they might have.

Promoting a Business with Premiums

Everybody likes to get something for nothing. Even though it is a fact that there is no such thing in business as getting something for nothing, this time-honored method of attracting customers is as good as ever. Among the great American business institutions which have been built up on "gifts" are the William Wrigley, Jr., Co., makers of Spearmint gum, the Jewel Tea Co., food products, and the Jas. S. Kirk Co., makers of American Family Soap. Each of these companies was started the same way—giving away something with every sale made to the consumer.

The story is told of a small soap manufacturer who made a powdered soap that was especially good for washing dishes. When he tried to sell it to dealers they all gave him the "run around." They said, "Our shelves are loaded with a dozen brands of soap powder. We cannot afford to tie up any money in soap. Go out and create a demand for your powder, and then we will stock it." That was a stickler. How could he create a demand without capital? It took far more money than he had to put on an advertising campaign, and it was difficult to get enough volume selling door to door. That night he talked his problem over with his wife who was a practical sort of person. "I'll tell you what," she said, "we have enough money to buy ten gross of hand-towels, and you can get them at a low price from the mills in Newburysport. Offer to give a towel away FREE with every purchase of two packages of soap powder. I'll bet you anything you like that any store in town will be glad to give you a window—it would draw the crowds and that is what every storekeeper wants."

The idea of a free hand-towel with every two-package purchase caught on like wildfire. The merchant who cooperated with the soap maker and put in the first window sold hundreds of packages. The manufacturer was soon being solicited by storekeepers who, only a week before, refused to have anything to do with his soap powder. They just could not stand by and see the women all going to their competitor to get the advantage of the special deal he was offering on soap powder.

Another way to promote a small business is by enlisting the aid of the school children. Just how this can be done, depends, of course, upon the nature of your business. But a live American youngster is just about the best press agent you can hire, and best of all, his services may be obtained at a trifling cost. An unusual shaped rubber balloon, offered on Saturdays with purchases of a certain amount, is almost certain to bring dozens of doting mothers into a store with their young hopefuls in tow. Simple puzzles, that can be bought for as little as two cents, draw the youngsters like magnets. Kites, "Fire Chief" hats, cross-word puzzles, stamp albums, magic sets, pop-out or cut-out sets, paper dolls, and clown hats are other premiums that have been used to attract children. About two years ago there was a "craze" for masks and their use as premiums stimulated the sale of many a slow-moving product. These masks included comic-strip characters, movie stars, clowns, etc.

Direct-Mail Advertising

One of the great wastes in promoting what might be called a "limited" appeal business is spending money to contact people who are not prospects. It might be all right to stand on a street corner and shout your wares to all who pass, if you have something to sell to the masses. But if you can sell only to people with a certain amount of money, or to owners of automobiles, or to farmers, or to some other specific class of people, then it is important in planning a promotional activity—whether it involves showmanship or advertising, or both—to pick those upon whom your effort is to be expended. The more you concentrate your promotional effort, the more resultful and effective it will be. That is where direct-mail advertising comes in. It enables you to hand-pick those with whom you wish to do business, and focus your entire sales promotional effort on them.

The first step in using direct-mail is to build a mailing list. A good mailing list is the backbone of a business, and that holds just as true of the large business as it does of the small business. It is not enough to take a telephone directory and call it a mailing list. That is just a list of names. A mailing list is something more. It is a list of people you definitely know to be prospects for what you have to sell. These names may be obtained through your own personal acquaintance, through friends, or by having a "survey" made by some person employed for the task. As a rule the money you invest in getting a good live mailing list is about the best investment you can make. Having compiled such a list, do not stop there. Spend a few dollars more for an addressing machine and make the most of the names. You can buy a small hand-addressing machine for as low as $25. You can use it not only to address advertisements to your mailing list, but also to print postcard announcements. You will find such equipment a big dividend producer.

Remember that a mailing list is no more valuable than the number of times it is used. Get something out regularly—the more often, the better. Keep the mailing list alive by adding steadily to the list of prospective customers. One of the best sources for obtaining names of desirable prospective customers—the store's own salespeople—has been overlooked or ignored by a majority of merchants.

Contest for Increasing a Store's List

By making the listing of possible new customers a game among their salespeople, the Tully-Abbott Company almost doubled the store's list within two weeks and impressed employees with the value of the names to the establishment. The contest also had a beneficial effect since its termination, all of the clerks continuing to turn in names to be added to the store's mailing list.

The contest was announced through a bulletin addressed to employees by the management. It was to run for two weeks. Employees were provided with special forms and asked to submit the names of people which they did not believe to be on the store's books or records at the time. It was expressly stated that "good names" were those who, because of some quality of standing, wealth, or social position, might be desirable prospects to buy merchandise of the establishment.

Three prizes were awarded. The employee submitting the greatest number of "accepted" names was given a $25 certificate entitling him or her to select merchandise of that value as a reward. The employee turning in the next greatest number was presented with a $10 certificate and the one contributing the third greatest number was rewarded with a $5.00 certificate.

To guard against employees turning in names of no value as prospects, one of the questions included on the form was, "Why do you feel this person is a desirable prospective customer?" A number of names were thrown out because the persons listed were unemployed or had no satisfactory business or family connections. Other names discarded included those already on the books or submitted during the contest by some other employee. Each entry declined for contest credit was turned back to the employee who submitted it with the reason for its refusal clearly stated.

At a time when waste in advertising is a particularly heavy tax on business, a great many retail executives may find the Tully-Abbott plan worth considering. When a list is top heavy with worthless names, a mailing has a hard time paying out. Inaccurate lists entail a great waste of postage, time and material. The plan reviewed here is one that any merchant, regardless of line, may convert to his use. The awards may be increased, decreased, or dispensed with altogether, without seriously affecting the success of the plan. Honorable mention and a daily list of the standings of contestants would probably prove almost as successful as the use of awards in cash.

How to Make Newspaper Advertising Pay

For the average small business depending mainly upon one locality for patronage, the accepted means of promotion is newspaper advertising. Just as direct-mail advertising has an advantage in selecting prospects, so newspaper advertising has an advantage in creating mass acceptance. It is the least expensive of all advertising, based on contacts made per dollar expended. It is particularly useful to those operating a retail business in a community served by a good newspaper.

Yet, like any other form of sales promotion, newspaper advertising must be rightly used or not at all. Too many business men regard advertising as something they can do when they feel flush, or they wait for some special occasion and then "take an advertisement in the newspaper."

Such hit-or-miss effort is not likely to do you, or the newspaper publisher, much good. The only effective way to make newspaper advertising pay is to have a plan—not a plan for a few weeks or a few months, *but a plan for three years*.

In setting up your plan, decide first of all just what you expect your newspaper advertising to do. You want it to attract new customers, of course. But more than that you want it to build up in your community certain definite impressions about your business and its ability to serve. You know, or should know, that it is going to take time to create such an impression. "Taking an advertisement" once in a while certainly will not do it. You have to advertise regularly, using a certain style of "copy" and building your advertising story around one dominating idea which the public will associate with your business. Keep repeating that dominant idea over and over and over again. There will come times when you weary of it. But remember that good advertising is repetition. To quote the motto of a famous advertising agency: "Keeping everlastingly at it brings success." New ideas and changes of copy are all right. Change your copy as frequently as you wish. But see to it that your advertising holds fast to two anchors—a distinctive style that gives it individuality and a dominant idea.

To illustrate these principles in action, and to show you what a tremendous force well-planned advertising can be in promoting a small business, a few examples follow showing how small beginnings grew into good-sized businesses through the untiring and intelligent use of good advertising backed by persistence.

■ ■

How Harding Built a Restaurant Business

WHEN John P. Harding opened his first Chicago restaurant, people paid little attention to it. It was just another addition to the hundreds of restaurants in Chicago. The general public and restaurant people expected him to have a fair business for a while, then the restaurant would settle down to a normal enterprise that would do well if it broke even. Some even said there were then too many restaurants in Chicago and Harding was foolish to start another. Harding had a different idea, however, and his amazing success in the Chicago restaurant field—he now has seven restaurants—proves he knows how to ring the bell so far as attracting trade is concerned.

There were several reasons why people came to Harding's. Good food was possibly most important. But the thousands upon thousands of first-time customers had to be sold on Harding's service before they bought their first meal. Harding recognized this fact. He got them to come by appealing to them through small advertisements in morning newspapers. The unique angle of the Harding advertising, the semi-humorous twist to the copy, and the cartoons illustrating these advertisements did the trick for him. But he didn't stop with just small copy. He planned his advertising in advance and when the copy appeared, one window of the restaurant was always trimmed effectively to tie up with the newspaper story. He began by featuring corned beef and cabbage in the advertising, and soon was known as the "Corned Beef King." Then he featured other special dishes. Soon he had many people calling at his restaurants to discover the secret of his good food—and they kept coming.

The windows frequently were trimmed with enlarged photographs of delectable food products, and the advertisements were planned to "tie in" with the seasonal eating habits of the public. Thus, just before Lent, and during Lent, the advertisements carried announcements of Lenten dishes. Shortly after the prohibition amendment was repealed, Harding ran an advertisement about ham, illustrated by a laughing little pig sitting in a glass of champagne. The copy follows:

HAM HAPPINESS!

"Years ago before prohibition became a fact, the old Righeimer bar at 131 N. Clark Street (now Harding's) was famous for its very unique treatment of ham. They didn't simply slice off a piece of ham and place it between two slices of bread. Oh no! First they dipped the ham into the most delectable concoction imaginable, champagne sauce. Ummmmm! Well, Harding's have resurrected the recipe and *now*—at all Harding restaurants the carver dips the slices of our perfectly baked sugar-cured ham into champagne sauce before making up the sandwich. Of course, if you prefer not to have the sauce just tell the carver. But it is good . . . The price is still 15c."

From the time these advertisements appeared in Chicago's morning papers, Harding's restaurants became crowded daily. The cost of the advertising each day was about seventy-five dollars. This expenditure, however, more than justified itself. In smaller communities, where the cost of advertising is not very great, this same advertising would run but three or four dollars, and the results would be proportionately greater. Harding's advertising ideas may be used to good advantage to tell people about your roadside stand or small restaurant. The same advertising appeal he uses would attract people from near and far.

Harding spent quite a lot of money in equipment and fixtures. By securing used equipment, however, you may start your restaurant with as small an amount as $300. Eye appeal may be enhanced in trimming windows by using enlarged photographs of the dishes you serve. Your local photographer will take these photographs for you and enlarge them to any size you wish for three or four dollars. By consulting your local newspaper publisher when planning your advertising, you may secure advance notice of special occasions which might connect up nicely with your advertising. There are a few more lucrative forms of business than a well-managed restaurant whose owner takes advantage of the many money-making opportunities advertising offers.

■ ■

A Change in Policy Started a Laundry on the Road to Leadership

LIKE a great many other men in the laundry business, B. C. McClellan never took advertising seriously. To him it was just one of "those things." He would buy an advertisement now and then just to be a good fellow and to make himself think he was advertising. Naturally, it never paid.

One day while having luncheon with a group of men, he voiced the old complaint that "advertising doesn't pay." A young advertising man in the group said: "You are wrong—advertising does pay. But perhaps *your* advertising doesn't pay. And I think I can tell you why—even without having any facts about your method of advertising. You have no plan, no campaign. Isn't that right? You just take an advertisement because you think you should advertise."

Mr. McClellan had to admit that the man was right. The result of that talk was a little conference with the advertising man and the preparation of a plan. When Mr. McClellan saw the plan, he was flabbergasted. It called for an expenditure of $5,000 over a period of one year. The idea of a laundry that was handling only 4,000 bundles a week, spending $5,000 for advertising, took his breath away. But the advertising man persisted, and finally Mr. McClellan agreed to try his plan.

As the advertisements began to appear and the bills began to come in, Mr. McClellan felt tempted to withdraw from the arrangement. But he didn't. Then the advertising began to "take hold." It wasn't long before the business grew from 4,000 to 18,000 bundles a week.

The advertising continued to pull. A dry cleaning business was started. The good-will which Mr. McClellan's advertising has built up assures its success. Methods were improved. Other laundries were opened. Within ten years it has grown to be the largest laundry in the world. Today there are McClellan establishments called the Laundry and Dry Cleaning Service, Inc., in fourteen cities. A $5,000 advertising acorn grew into a $10,000,000 business.

■ ■

Milo Jones Started His Sausage Business with a $30 Advertisement

ABOUT fifty years ago, the preacher in charge of the circuit of which Fort Atkinson, Wisconsin, was a part, took dinner at the farm of Brother Milo Jones. Instead of serving the regulation yellow-legged chicken, the main feature of the meal was farm sausage of Mrs. Jones's making.

The pastor complimented Mrs. Jones profusely on the delicious flavor of the sausage. As he traveled the circuit he praised Sister Jones's sausage to other members of his flock. Jones's farm sausage was soon in demand.

One day the thought came to Mr. Jones that if people in near-by cities knew about his good wife's sausage, it might be possible to sell more. So he decided to advertise. Being a conservative New Englander his first advertising was very modest, just a few inches in a Fort Atkinson newspaper. But it brought results.

Before Milo Jones knew it, his sausage had become famous throughout Wisconsin. Then he went after Chicago distribution, spending, of course, a little more on advertising. In spite of the fact that he charged ten cents a pound more for his sausage, it soon became nationally famous and was featured by leading hotels all over the country.

The Jones's business is not large compared to the great packing companies. It has purposely been held down by members of the family who were more concerned with their reputation than their fortune. Nevertheless, it is one of the romances of American business success—illustrating, as it does, the possibilities of building a national business by expanding a market one step at a time with advertising.

Restaurant Which Caters to Children

A RESTAURANT owner in a middle-western town has built up a lucrative side line in his business by catering to children. He has special menus made up listing wholesome dishes for children. Each dish, needless to say, is attractively prepared to entice the most fickle appetite. The preparation of this food does not entail any special labor as many of the dishes appear on the regular menu under different names. The children's menus have a border of children in silhouette—romping, jumping rope and playing marbles. The figures are stickers secured from a local novelty store and simply pasted on the daily menus. The portions listed on the children's menus are usually smaller than those on the usual bill of fare.

Another idea which has paid him well is preparing special parties for children. If you understand youngsters, you know that anyone of them would rather have a party in a restaurant than in his own home. A restaurant party makes a child feel so important and grown-up! Because his restaurant is in a neighborhood of homes and small apartment buildings, there is an opportunity to cater to quite a few children. He has also increased the number of his youthful patrons by contacting the churches and schools in the neighborhood, giving the youngsters special prices as inducements for holding their parties and suppers in his place.

■ ■

Bridge Prize Puts Over Home Library

IT IS easy to start a circulating library but it is not so easy to get customers. So when Mrs. Gertrude Murphy started a library in her home, she decided to do something spectacular and unusual to attract customers.

She had previously used a rental library operated in a neighborhood drug store in Chicago and found that the main reason the druggist lost "readers" was his unwillingness to add new books to the library. Three or four months would pass before the latest fiction was available.

"I'll start a library and specialize on 'best sellers,'" Mrs. Murphy decided. To get going quickly she adopted the "door-prize" idea, commonly used at bridge parties. Each time a member came in to rent a book, she was given a small piece of pasteboard on which the date was stamped. The member wrote her name and address on this card and dropped it into a box. On Wednesdays and Saturdays of each week, the names of three members were drawn from this box and prizes, usually inexpensive articles such as ash-trays, handkerchiefs, or dishes, were given the lucky winners.

Mrs. Murphy's plan for operating the library was similar to that of the drug store's. Books were rented at three cents a day and a dollar membership fee was required. This membership fee was used to buy additional books and in less than a month she had one hundred and ninety books on her shelves. Meanwhile eighty members were enrolled by the "door-prize" feature. Women frequently took out books for their husbands and daughters. At the end of this first month, Mrs. Murphy discovered that each member averaged two books a day. Her only investment was fifteen dollars spent at the outset for books, the membership and rental fees being sufficient to cover all other expenses.

You can start a rental library on a similar plan with twenty books. Order direct from publishers or wholesale booksellers who will give you a special discount. Well-selected books pay for themselves in rentals many times over before they lose their popularity. It is advisable to have two or three copies of "best sellers" on your shelves in order to meet the demand. The library can be conducted from your home or you may be able to make arrangements with some real estate office to give you desk space for a few dollars a month. You can pick up enough magazine subscriptions, if you are on your toes, to pay the rent. Obtain an agency from the American News Company, New York City, or one of the large subscription agencies such as the Franklin Square Agency of New York. These companies publish catalogs listing all the magazines and quoting a dealer's discount which is usually about 5 per cent.

■ ■

Returnable Containers Pep Up Sales

GREAT businesses have been built around a simple merchandising idea—Uneeda Biscuits, for instance. Before the National Biscuit Company hit upon the idea of putting up soda crackers in five-cent sealed cartons, people always bought them sparingly because they were hard to keep crisp. The soda crackers are probably no better than they were before the sealed package was introduced but that idea made the business. Today all sorts of things are sold in air-tight packages.

The same opportunity for clever packaging exists today in such products as cookies, butter, honey, and various specialties made in home kitchens. If you know how to bake good cookies, and offer them to a regular list of customers neatly packed in air-tight cookie tins, which you pick up when the next tin is delivered, you have a merchandising idea that will greatly simplify marketing your product. As a matter of fact one woman in Naperville, Illinois, built a profitable cookie business doing that very thing.

A farmer in Geneva, Wisconsin, had the idea of delivering butter in sealed three- and five-pound crocks instead of the usual bricks. The crocks were designed to fit into a small electrical refrigerator, and had a clamp to hold the cover on tight. In this way the butter was protected from odors that it would otherwise absorb. The customer made a deposit of twenty-five cents when she bought the first crock of butter, and the farmer picked up the "empties" very much as a milkman picks up his milk bottles. These returnable containers enabled him to increase his "unit of sale."

Another example: A woman in Ticonderoga, New York, who specialized in putting up strawberry jam, doubled her sales when she thought of putting up the jam in the very latest style beer glasses generally known as "Pilseners," instead of the usual preserve glass. They cost but very little more, and since prohibition had been repealed and every woman needed up-to-date glasses for serving guests, the utility value of the glass proved to be just the needed inducement.

■ ■

An Advertising Adventure Blazed the Path of Success for Weber's Bakery

IN LOS ANGELES everybody knows about Weber's bread. But that was not the case back in 1926. Dale Weber's bakery was then just one of the many bakeries that served that community.

One day Weber's bakery was singled out for an attack by organized labor. Mr. Weber decided to lay his case before the public through advertising. He not only won his case but found something even more valuable—faith in the power of advertising. That new-found faith proved to be the turning point in the growth of the Weber Baking Company.

When Weber began advertising, his bakery operated 18 trucks. A year after he had launched his program, which called for an investment of $2,000 a month, his business had grown to 42 trucks. He decided to plow back 3 ½ cents out of every dollar he took in, for advertising. By the end of the second year his fleet had grown to 65 trucks.

But he did not stop there. He pyramided his advertising. Business continued to grow. In another year the bakery was operating 84 trucks, and by the end of the fourth year of advertising, 110 trucks were required to service his steadily expanding trade. A growth, roughly, of 500 per cent in four years.

Of course, advertising alone did not accomplish this noteworthy result. But it did play an important part. Who can say that had not Dale Weber, fighting with his back to the wall, made that initial appropriation for advertising, what might have happened to his business. But he did make it.

■ ■

How $150 a Month Advertising Built a $10,000,000 Business

BACK in 1905, M. G. Gibbs opened a drug store in Washington, D. C. His friends told him he was foolish; that there were already too many drug stores in Washington, and that there was no money to be made in the drug business anyway.

But Gibbs figured that there was always room at the top regardless of how crowded the field might be. He believed that if a business had distinctive policies and kept telling people about them, day in and day out, it was bound to be successful.

So he took his capital of $9,000 and set $2,000 of it aside for an all-year advertising program. This gave him $150 a month for his advertising. Then he took the remainder and bought fixtures and stock with it. Perhaps the fact that Gibbs was the son of a small-town publisher had something to do with the faith he had in advertising. But he stuck to his plan in spite of all discouragements, and when the year closed his sales totaled $ 22,000. Not a bad first year's business back in 1905.

Today the Peoples Drug Stores are as well known in Washington as the White House. They do a volume in excess of $10,000,000 annually and their credit rating stands ace high in Dun & Bradstreet. Druggists from all over the country come to Washington to study the Gibbs methods. But the real secret of the success, according to an interview which Mr. Gibbs gave to *Printers' Ink,* is his year-in-and-year-out policy of plowing back 2 per cent of his sales into advertising. "It is inconceivable to me," he said, "that any retailer would attempt to operate without a consistent plan of advertising year in and year out."

Open-Air Market Brings Added Profits

A NUMBER of years ago, a grocer owning his own store in a Chicago suburb, purchased the adjoining lot on the corner because he had a chance to get it cheap and thought he might want to enlarge his store some day. One day on a trip out into the country, it occurred to him that the roadside stands were doing an excellent business on fruit and vegetables that were no better than his own. The prices, too, were about in line with his. He thought of the vacant lot alongside his store and decided to make an experiment. The next week, he had a carpenter build some stands and some uprights in the vacant space. A colorful striped awning was stretched from the side of the store to the uprights, and the stands were loaded with vegetables and fruits. There was plenty of parking space across the street.

Almost from the start, this addition to his store brought new customers. He kept it open from early spring until late fall and found that practically all of the new customers, attracted by the open-air market, continued to buy during the winter when the market was closed. The construction of the market required about $850, but through this outlay he cleared around $7,500 net and increased his business in staples considerably at the same time.

■ ■

Mixing a Good Time with Good Food

FOUR months ago Howard Stevens rented a vacant house on a ten-acre tract fifteen miles from Detroit, Michigan, along a much traveled highway, and here established a Wayside Inn. He stocked a few cases of beer, and some sandwich meats, but did very little business the first month. Then he decided to "doll up" the place. During the past two months, the result of his improvements has been to attract an increasingly large number of customers to his place, and his profits have climbed.

"I discovered that to draw people you must have something besides a few old tables and chairs and a couple bottles of beer," said Stevens. "So I paid $275 down on used bar fixtures and restaurant equipment, and agreed to payoff the balance of $640 in monthly payments. I got a couple of local carpenters and had them refinish the floor in the big room of the house for dancing, and along the sides of this room I then placed black and silver colored glass-top tables of a modern, though inexpensive, design. I was lucky getting a semi-circular bar, and some long panel mirrors to hang behind it. My initial investment, all told, came to $407, including the refrigerator and range for cooking. I had a couple of electric automatic fryers,

201

and a grill and roaster in which I was able to roast up to nine chickens, or four pork loins at one time.

"To let people know about what I had to offer them, I had seventeen signs painted and placed at strategic points along the road. Each sign featured a different type barbecued meat sandwich. I had the sandwich featured painted in colors and placed a price of fifteen cents on each. Then in large letters was the name of my stand, and the distance from the sign to the inn. That first night I opened was surprising to me. Between six and nine, 119 cars stopped and an average of three people came in from each car. My wife and I tried to take care of them, but we ran out of supplies at nine-thirty. We did volume enough to indicate future success, however. We spent all the next day roasting chickens, pork loins, and beef cuts and the business that night was unusual. Many stayed a little while to dance and the small dance floor was crowded. Music was furnished by a good radio picking up a hotel dance program from Detroit.

"People out in the country in their cars like to stop somewhere to rest and eat. If there's a little dancing, they'll stay longer. They don't like to feel they are paying excessive prices for food, however, and about fifteen cents is all they'll pay for a sandwich. This is a profitable price. The average check runs forty cents for each person. Inasmuch as there is a gross profit of 50 per cent on sales, we are doing nicely."

Each week since he added the new equipment, Stevens has served six hundred and three customers. He has two girls helping him take care of the business and pays them each $15.00 a week. His net profit for the week, after paying all expenses, averages $89.67. There are many such opportunities for opening wayside stands near big cities. Profits may be increased by placing a few pin games near the cash register, and by serving cold drinks.

■ ■

Using One Product to Sell Another

ONE enterprising hardware merchant had a stock of bird cages on hand which were moving very slowly. As considerable money was tied up in his stock he worried about ways and means of selling it. Finally he hit upon an idea. He purchased 400 canary birds and offered them at $3.87, or practically at cost. The sale was advertised in the newspaper. His idea sold the 400 birds, 150 bird cages priced from $2.98 to $35.00, as well as many hardware items.

CHAPTER NINE

SELLING THINGS BY MAIL

MANY great fortunes have been made in the mail-order business, even though it is one of the most exacting and difficult methods of making money. In addition to skill as a buyer, a successful mail-order merchandiser requires a keen sense of dramatic values and sound sales promotional judgment. Given these attributes it is possible for an energetic person, with a small amount of capital, to start a mail-order business on a modest scale and successfully develop it into a prosperous and worth-while business.

The mail-order business is essentially American in its conception and scope. It is a by-product of the development of the West, when impassable roads and great distances made it difficult for people living on farms or in small towns to get a satisfactory selection of merchandise. The industry is scarcely fifty years old, yet in that short time it has developed sales running well over $1,000,000,000 annually. This figure is interesting because it reflects a confidence on the part of the public in ordering by mail that is truly remarkable, when you consider that the method requires a person to buy "sight unseen." The buying impression is created by the printed word, and the buyer must send his money on faith, depending only upon the assurance of the seller that his money will be refunded if he is not entirely satisfied.

The first mail-order house to do a national, big-scale business was established in 1872 by A. Montgomery Ward and George R. Thorne in a small room at 825 North Clark Street, Chicago. The initial capital was slightly over $2,400. Ward conceived the idea of selling for cash, direct by mail, while employed as a clerk in St. Joseph, Michigan. Lack of capital prevented him from putting his idea into execution at the time. To make the needed money, he secured a position as a traveling salesman for a St. Louis house. That was in 1871. He finally accumulated $1,600, which was a sizable sum in those days, and persuaded his friend George Thorne, of Kalamazoo, Michigan, to go into partnership with him in Chicago. The firm's first catalog, a little pamphlet 3 x 5 inches in size, listing a few widely-used dry goods items, was issued in 1874. This was the forerunner of the giant mail-order catalog which is issued today.

While credit for the idea of selling by mail belongs to Montgomery Ward, the great strides which the industry made and public acceptance of the principle of buying by mail are due to the pioneering work of Richard W. Sears, who was a better promotion man than Ward. Sears had a flair for dressing up the "sales package"—one of the essential qualifications of a good mail-order man. For that reason the story of his rise to fame and fortune should be of particular interest to anyone contemplating going into the mail-order business. Much can be gained by studying his approach to the varied problems that the new business presented, and the development of some of his policies. The story of how Sears laid the foundation for the great Sears, Roebuck business is told elsewhere in this chapter.

Essentials of a Mail-Order Business

Contrary to general belief, it is not practical to sell everything and anything by mail. It must be remembered that conditions have changed a great deal since A. Montgomery Ward started his business. Good roads, the automobile and chain stores have narrowed the opportunities for general mail-order operations until mail-order selling has become too speculative for the man of small capital. But while the opportunities may be fewer for starting a general mail-order business, the door is wide open for starting a specialized business. National advertising, the radio and the movies have done one thing for the American merchant that is not always appreciated. They have created a multiplicity of new wants, they have sharpened tastes, they have made people dissatisfied with the garden variety of things bought in stores and have made them receptive to the specialized appeal. So we may set it down as principle number one in starting a mail-order business that there must be something distinctive either about what you are selling, or about the way you sell it.

People will buy most easily things which they are not able to buy in local stores, or because they feel that they are obtaining a definite price advantage. It is interesting to note, in this connection, that what gave Richard Sears his start on the road to success was not the kind of watches he sold but the way he sold them. When he became station agent at North Redwood, Minnesota, he had had some experience selling unclaimed merchandise. He found that people would pay top prices for such merchandise under the impression that they were profiting by another's misfortune. So he conceived the idea of buying watches at wholesale, and sending them to fictitious names in care of other ticket agents. When the ticket agent wrote him that the watch had not been called for, Sears wrote back to sell the watch at a certain price, and deduct a commission for making the sale. While this is hardly a method that would succeed in these days, the principle which Sears used, that is to say "staging the sale," is just as effective today as it was then. It is not enough merely to offer to sell a man; you must develop and present to him some reason why he should buy.

Since buying by mail requires complete confidence of the purchaser in the seller, the name of the company or business is important. Use Anglo-Saxon names, if possible. One of the big mail-order houses, which successfully sold women's wear by mail for a number of years before being merged with another company, was the Charles William Stores of New York. This was just a name. There was no Mr. Charles, nor was there any Mr. Williams. Had Morris Rosenbaum used his own name when he started the National Cloak & Suit Company, it is doubtful if it would have been so successful. Generally speaking, it is better to use an easily-remembered family name than a corporate name. People are funny about names. They like to do business with other individuals like themselves. They want to feel that if they are not satisfied with their purchase that they can write to the proprietor of the business and raise the dickens. It is less satisfactory to bawl out a corporation. Similarly there is a widespread notion that people with Anglo-Saxon names are more trustworthy than people with foreign names. It is only a feeling, of course, but when you are asking a man to send you his money solely on your guarantee of satisfaction, you cannot afford to disregard even such trifling details as public whims.

Importance of Repeat Orders

The backbone of a successful mail-order business is its list of regular customers. While it is possible to buy lists of people who buy by mail, and there are numerous directories from which names may be selected, it is a mistake to think that a profitable business can be built up entirely from such names. True, some business can be obtained in that way, but usually the cost of getting the business will absorb all the profit. With a good mailing list, the bulk of which consists of names of people who have expressed an interest in what you are selling, either by answering your advertisements or by having placed previous orders, selling costs can be controlled.

The following table, showing costs of sales by mail to the consumer, is taken from Wadsworth's Mail-Order Handbook:*

Auto Tires, 3 ½ per cent	Hardware, 8 per cent
Auto Supplies, 6 per cent	Jewelry, 12 per cent
Bicycles, 8 per cent	Lighting Fixtures, 10 per cent
Books, 20 per cent	Men's Clothing, 8 per cent
Fashions, 10 per cent	Pianos, 8 per cent
Furniture, 8 per cent	Redicut Houses, 3 per cent
Gas Engines, 9 per cent	Shoes, 5 per cent
Groceries, 5 per cent	Underwear, 6 per cent

It will be noted that most of the above items represent products for which a demand exists. When it comes to products for which a demand must be created, selling costs are much greater. For example, it costs almost 33 per cent to sell a home-training course by mail. Many publishers figure the cost of selling $2.00 subscriptions at 100 per cent. They must

*Published by the Dartnell Corporation, $3.75

depend entirely upon their renewals for a profit. A good rule to follow in selling products which are not in demand is to price them at three times their production cost. This formula applied, let us say, to an article priced to sell for $3.00, allows $1.00 for manufacturing cost, $1.00 for selling cost, and $1.00 for overhead and profit. The usual percentage of returns on mailings to new names is between 2 and 6 per cent, depending upon the acceptance which the product has and the manner in which it is presented. On the other hand, returns from a mailing directed to lists of known customers will run anywhere from 10 to 20 per cent. These figures will serve to illustrate the importance of the "repeat quality" of a product, if it is to be sold by mail successfully, and the necessity of building the whole business around a list of "known" buyers.

Too much emphasis cannot be laid on the importance of good "copy" in selling by mail. The difference between a well-written letter or catalog and one that is indifferently written and produced can make all the difference between a profit and a loss. There are no hard-and-fast rules which can be laid down for writing result-getting copy because very often success lies in breaking all the rules and striking out boldly along unblazed paths. The following suggestions by Ralph Wadsworth, well-known as a successful mail-order copy writer, may prove helpful however:

Writing "Copy" to Sell by Mail

If anyone thinks that mail-order copy is easy, let him try it. You will be surprised how many essential selling points you overlook. What they can mean to your sales is best illustrated by the following: In Illinois a certain farmer made up his mind to buy a cream separator. Unable to make a decision from Montgomery Ward's and Sears, Roebuck's catalogs, he hitched up his horse and buggy and drove around among his neighbors.

Those with Sears' separators acknowledged they were good; the ones using Ward's were just as sure that theirs were the best. So he returned home undecided, until his wife pointed out that Sears' copy read "Guaranteed 255 lbs." and Ward's just said, "190 lbs." Sears' got the sale. As a matter of fact, the lesser weight is an advantage, but the Ward advertising man had failed to capitalize on the fact in the advertising copy.

Because mail-order copy sells "sight unseen," you must be very careful to have it cover every selling point, especially the appeals to the five senses. Let us, for example, say that you are asked to write copy for a new velvet dress to sell at $25. You might say, in the usual copy style:

> What woman would not be delighted to appear in this beautiful velvet gown, $25?

From a mail-order standpoint you would have overlooked many vital features needed to close a sale. You have not said anything about the style, the use, the comparative value, the kind of velvet, its wearing qualities, the trimmings, whether suitable for misses or women, the colors, sizes, approximate length and perhaps use. To be complete your copy should run something like this:

> What woman would not be delighted to appear in this last-minute model of rich-looking silk chiffon velvet, smartly finished with three-quarter sleeves of good-quality silk satin? Just the thing for afternoon or informal party wear. The material will give you excellent wear and the price quoted represents unusual value. LENGTH: 40 to 44 inches, according to size. WOMEN'S SIZES: 34 to 44. COLORS: Navy blue, red and brown. Special Price, $25.

It does not appear difficult to write mail-order advertising for fashions, furniture, or cream separators, but until you have had plenty of practice you will be surprised how many essential features you will leave out of your copy. This training is a great help in handling general advertising copy, for it makes you careful to see that you do not overlook any points of selling value.

Your copy to retailers must naturally stress different points, but there are certain essential elements that must not be overlooked. You must emphasize the profits to be made, the big demand and the popularity of your article, the exceptional value it represents at the price you quote, as well as stating the material, sizes, weights or other information needed in order for your dealer to send in his order.

The above dress copy rewritten to the dealer should read somewhat like the following:

> This new Parisian model of good quality silk chiffon velvet is a fast seller in the New York market and should be very popular with your trade. Its satin sleeves are a feature in great demand. At our exceptionally low price this unusual number carries a good profit.
>
> WOMEN'S SIZES: 34 to 44. COLORS: Navy blue, red and dark brown. Prices: Each $16; in quantities of six or more, specially priced, each at $15.

You will note that copy to the retailer does not need to be so long as that to the consumer. Your dealer has a better conception of merchandise and does not require as much detail. Your terms, your guarantee and general reputation will have a great bearing on whether he sends you an order or not. The first and last thing he is interested in is profits. That's the angle you will emphasize the most.

What Can Be Profitably Sold by Mail

As stated at the beginning of this chapter, the building up of a demand for a product which is presented through the mails to a possible buyer, depends upon the way it is staged. It must have some distinctive quality, or there must be a distinctive plan for presenting it. For that reason it is desirable to build your mail-order business around products which lend themselves to dramatization. There should be an apparent reason for a mail purchase. To make this clear, you will find below a few suggestions for products which have been successfully sold by mail.

SPECIALIZED BOOKS:

There are many people who are always interested in books of a specialized nature. Some are men in technical lines of work who are prospects for valuable technical books out of print. Some are interested in collecting first editions. There is an opportunity to compile listings of books, both new and second-hand, along a hundred specialized lines. The catalog should be sent only to groups composed of people with known interests. A by-product of such an activity, particularly if you live in cities such as London, New York, Boston or Philadelphia, is to purchase, upon order, rare books from dealers. A fee is charged according to the time spent locating the book in the bookstalls.

MONOGRAMMED SPECIALTIES:

Most people have a weakness for monograms. A profitable mail-order business supplying monogrammed cigarettes, matches, playing cards, bridge scores, place cards, tallies, glassware, stationery, etc., can be built up by catering to this interest. The same groups can be sold monogrammed shirts and wearing apparel. It takes a little time and requires some capital to get a list of buyers together, since you have to depend largely on small advertisements in class publications, mailings to club members, etc. But once you have a list of buyers you have a business, because there is no end of things which can be sold through the personal monogram appeal. Arrangements can usually be made with manufacturers to fill your orders. You control the business through ownership of the monogram design.

HOMESPUN NECKWEAR AND BEDSPREADS:

In districts which are recognized as headquarters for certain kinds of craftsmanship, it is possible for a wide-awake person to make money marketing the local output by mail. At the present time there is a vogue for homespun neckties. In the same category come homespun bedspreads, hooked rugs, etc. While it is true, with the exception of neckwear, these products do not repeat, a person who buys her husband a tie can usually be sold a bedspread or a rug. In starting a business of this type it is important to price your merchandise to allow for a high selling expense. People buy handicraft work, not because of price, but because of certain distinctive qualities. The price, therefore, is not so important as the proper dramatization of the distinctive qualities of the product in your sales literature.

Distinctive Confections:

A young couple in New Mexico made considerable money selling "cactus candies" by mail. A wide-awake advertising man in San Francisco, who knew his way around the Chinese quarter of the city, built up a tidy business on rice candies, which he had made by the Chinese. A retired printing salesman in Florida took several hundred dollars out of the North every year selling candied citrus peel in glassine packages. In each of these instances the undertaking succeeded largely because the idea of having candy that was "different" appealed to certain types of people. Here again success depends upon the mailing list. Only a few out of every hundred people are prospects for mail-order candies. But once a list of buyers has been built up, a steady income is assured.

Indian Relishes:

It is also possible to make money by importing food delicacies from abroad and selling them by mail. In this case the secret of success is finding things which cannot be bought in food stores. An enterprising Englishman, who once lived in India, made a lot of money and established what is now a profitable business, by arranging with a manufacturer in Bombay, India, to ship him on consignment curries, relishes, and similar delicacies. He prepared an attractive catalog, illustrated to give it an East Indian atmosphere, which featured these novelties and explained how they were used in India. The appeal here was to natural human curiosity. People like to try things which they have never tasted, just so they can say they have tasted them. The catalog was advertised in magazines going to wealthy people, and from those inquiries he built up a good list of customers. By constantly changing his line, and adding food specialties from other countries, he got the needed volume of repeat business to make the undertaking profitable.

Making Your Letters Pull

There are few factors more important in building a mail-order business than the ability to write business-getting, good-will-building letters.

Fortunately this skill can be acquired. It is really more of a knack than anything else. It is simply the ability of being able to express yourself in writing, in a natural, friendly and effective way—by being able as one mail-order man expressed it, "to climb into the envelope and seal the flap behind you."

There are two primary things that make a sales letter pull. The first of these is an understanding of human nature, and the second, the ability to express yourself in a letter so that you can make quick contact with a problem of paramount importance to the prospect or customer. This is sometimes expressed as the ability to be able "to touch a live nerve."

Another essential is to be able to put personality into every letter you write. So many letters are cold and stilted. They read very much as though they are being ground out on some sort of nickel-in-the-slot machine. Other letters echo the personality of the writer, who literally stands out behind the letter extending his hand toward you.

To illustrate what is meant by a knowledge of human nature, a correspondent was assigned to draft a follow-up letter for an advertising record which a manufacturing concern had sent out to a list of concerns with the idea of getting them to place a trial order. The advertising record was a miniature affair and the card which accompanied the record requested that it should be taken home and played on the prospect's phonograph.

While this seemed to be a good advertising stunt, and caused lots of comment, it did not produce the number of replies which had been expected. So it was decided to follow it up with a letter.

The first letter which was drafted was purely and simply a reminder that the prospect had not replied. It asked if he had tried the record on his phonograph as requested. If he had, would he be good enough to answer it. This follow-up letter was not particularly successful, so another letter was written. The revised letter was written by the sales manager himself, and in it the prospect was asked to give his opinion of the advertising record as a selling idea. It was explained to the prospect that the plan was to use these records as a permanent part of the sales program, but before doing so the sales manager was anxious to find out what he thought of this method of advertising. The letter wound up with a paragraph asking authority from the prospect to send the order which was requested in the phonograph record.

The returns from the second follow-up letter exceeded the returns from the first letter three times over. The conditions were practically the same, but in the case of the second letter the sales manager had used his knowledge of human nature.

He knew what the first writer did not know, that everybody has decided opinions on the best way to advertise, and by asking their opinions you not only flatter them but they jump at the chance to air their opinions. This is exactly what happened in this case.

There are a great many ways where this knowledge of human nature can be brought into play when writing a sales letter. Nine-tenths of the sales letters which go out fail because the writer does not understand that point. The wording, the phraseology and the grammatical construction of the letter are very important it is true, but after all the plan is the thing, and it is much better to have a letter with a good plan and poor phraseology than it is to have a letter with no plan and the best grammar in the world.

So many letters ramble about and get nowhere. To read them is like watching an eight-ring circus. After you have read them you have no definite impression—just a mass of jumbled words. Make your letters paint a picture. All the words in the dictionary won't sell goods. Only ideas, indelibly impressed on the mind of a reader, will provoke action. Another reason some letters don't pay is that the writer forgets that the person he is writing to is not much interested in what he is writing about. On the contrary it has been demonstrated that seven times out of ten, the recipient of a letter, especially if he is a business man, will read only the opening paragraph, take a flying jump at the middle and then examine the last paragraph to see what it is all about and how much it costs.

The most successful sales letters are those which carry a complete selling message in the last paragraph. The practice of spending a lot of time in writing a letter and then enclosing a return card which gives the man the whole proposition in a nutshell without any sales setting is common. It has been found by many tests that when a return card is enclosed with a letter, or with a circular, that most business men will read the return card first because they have learned by long experience that they can get the whole proposition in a nutshell from the return card with a good deal less effort and a good deal less reading than they can from the circular itself. It is therefore fatal in planning a sales letter to tell too much in the return card. Some very effective letters have depended upon perfectly blank cards, on which the recipient jotted down his reply in his own way.

The Mechanics of a Good Sales Letter

When a sales letter is produced on the typewriter, and is a personally dictated letter, it is important that it be planned in such a way as to invite reading rather than repel reading. Many of the most prominent business concerns are very lax in the proper construction and technical arrangement of their business correspondence. Every concern should have a manual of style which can be turned over to a stenographer when she is first employed and which she can follow. Such a manual is the most practical way to build up standards in your correspondence. It not only saves the time of the stenographer, but it is good to fall back upon if some of the older stenographers become careless.

Such a manual of style should discuss, first of all, "Clearness." It should impress upon both the dictator and the stenographer the importance of making a letter clear. That is to say—in using short sentences and paragraphing it properly; also punctuating it correctly so that the meaning will be easily followed. The use of long words should be mentioned particularly. Language which is understood by the highly educated man is not always so easily understood by the man of average education.

It was said of Cyrus Curtis, of the Curtis Publishing Company, that a great deal of his success was due to his ability to edit letters. He was adept at wielding the blue pencil. One of his regular stunts was to take the last paragraph of a letter and put it up front.

It is a common fault of inexperienced writers to kill their story with a drawn-out introduction. Business men who wouldn't think of going into a prospect's office and opening a sales canvass with funny stories, think nothing at all of starting a letter with some grotesque yarn which they drag into the letter by the seat of the pants. There are even so-called letter experts who insist on beginning every letter they write with some far-fetched introduction which has no bearing at all on the product being sold.

These experts justify the practice from the standpoint that it gets attention. But if a letter writer has such a poor grasp of the problems of the man he is writing to, as to be unable to contact with him that way, he is not qualified for the work at hand. The American business man wants no long drawn out introductions. He wants you to come to the point quickly. Reading his morning's mail is a duty he wants to get over with just as soon as he can and get on with the business of the day. He has no time for jaunts out into fairyland.

Too Much "You" Is Worse Than Too Much "We"

Nearly all of the articles which have been written on the subject of letter writing lay emphasis on the "you" idea. They tell the reader that if his letters are to be successful he must talk to the prospect about his problems, about his troubles and his trials, and he must never for a minute talk about the desires or wishes of the man who is writing the letter or refer even in any way to his business. In fact, you would almost imagine it a sin or crime to use the word "we" in a letter. It is true that the closer a writer can get to his reader, the better results are going to be; and it is also true that nothing interests a man so much as himself. The salesman or the sales letter writer who can talk to him about himself is sure to have his interest. On the other hand, however, this "you" business can be and is being overdone. While the principle behind this idea is perfectly sound, the execution of it is too often abused by writers of sales letters.

TESTING CHART FOR LETTERS

Selling Qualities of the Letter

1. Is the Start Effective?

Be careful it does not challenge the reader and put him into an antagonistic frame of mind. When possible give it a new start, or embody it in the reason for writing. Don't start off from nowhere.

2. Does It Appeal to the Reader's Self-Interest?

The motives that make men act are: (1) Love; (2) Gain; (3) Pride; (4) Duty; (5) Fear; (6) Self-Indulgence. Unless your letter appeals to these motives in an irresistible way you will not get action.

3. Does It Make Him Want What You Are Selling?

You cannot sell a man something he does not want. If you are selling a chair make him think how nice it would feel to lounge in a big easy chair and smoke his after-dinner cigar.

4. Does It Create Confidence?

Are you asking him to take your word—a stranger whom he has never even met—that what you say is true? Why not use a testimonial paragraph and let someone else tell about your virtues? What provision have you made in case he is not satisfied?

5. Does It Ask for an Order?

Remember people are not mind readers. You may know perfectly well why you are writing them and what you want them to do—but do they?

Composition of the Letter

1. Does It Invite Reading?

Are paragraphs short and margins wide? Is it free from erasures? Is the signature legible?

2. Is It Easy to Understand?

Break up all involved sentences into several short ones. Use a sentence for each idea. Be careful about pronouns; be sure that the reference is clear in each case. Avoid parenthetical and explanatory clauses.

3. Is the Action Continuous?

Blue pencil all meaningless words and phrases. Get the message you want to convey clearly fixed in your mind and make each step in the letter a step to that end.

4. Does It Reflect Your Personality?

Tone down extravagant statements that will give the impression you are a braggart. Let it carry an atmosphere of sincerity and desire to serve. Be watchful for superlatives and the use of the word "very."

5. Is It Grammatically Correct?

Have you used "was" when you should have said "were"; "who" in place of "whom"; "differ with" instead of "differ from"; "shall" instead of "will," etc.

There is quite a difference between getting a "you" point of view into a letter and going over a letter and changing the "we's" to "you's" as so many writers seem to do. If the letter has a "you" point of view and is built up from that angle, it doesn't make any difference how many times you use "we" or how much you say about yourself, because what you do say about yourself will be of interest to the man you are writing to. How can he do business with you until he knows about you? For example, suppose you are selling soap. You are pardonably proud of the fact that your soap is nearly pure—purer, perhaps than any soap sold at the price. You work hard to acquire a reputation as a quality soap maker. You have made many sacrifices in order that your customers should know you as being fair and honorable. If you are guided wholly by instinct, you are inclined to harp on these points in your letters, but the man to whom you are writing doesn't care nearly as much about these things as he does about what your soap will do for him.

Let the Other Fellow Shout Your Praises

The tone of a letter makes or breaks it. The skilled salesman knows this and, consequently, strives in his letter to give it an atmosphere of restraint rather than of extravagance. There has been a lot of fun poked at such expressions as "we beg to state," "your obedient servant" and "with your permission." Perhaps these are a bit unnecessary, but they at least serve to give a letter a tone of humility which is pleasing.

Nothing influences the tone of a letter more than the fault of shouting your own praises, which so many letter writers seem to feel is necessary. In order to do this they overindulge in superlatives and make a lot of statements which may be perfectly true but which strengthen the doubts of a skeptical prospect. A master letter writer always tones statements down to a point where they will be accepted on their face, even if he has to understate the truth. He seldom, if ever, indulges in superlatives. Particularly is he careful not to overuse the word "very."

The letters of both Lincoln and Franklin, while not sales letters, are noteworthy for their tone of sincerity and deference to the opinion of others. Commenting on humility as a factor in dealing with men, Benjamin Franklin says in his autobiography: "I cannot boast of much success in acquiring the reality of this virtue, but I have learned a good deal with regard to the appearance of it. I made it a rule to forbear all direct contradiction to the sentiments of others, and all positive assertions of my own. I even forbid myself, agreeably to the old laws of Junto, the use of every word or expression in the language that imported a fixed opinion such as *certainly, undoubtedly*, etc., and I have adopted instead of them, *I conceive, I apprehend*, or *I imagine* a thing to be so and so, or *it appears to me at present* to be so and so. When another asserted something that

I thought an error, I denied myself the pleasure of contradicting him abruptly, and in answering I began by observing that in certain cases or circumstances his opinion would be right, but there seemed to me to be some difference. The modest way in which I proposed my opinions procured for them a readier reception."

There is a great deal of truth in Franklin's assertion, and in our letters to our customers and to our prospects we are wise if we avoid making assertions which challenge credulity, or in any way make it appear that we are trying to exaggerate the virtues of what we are selling.

If the virtues of our products must be expounded, let it be done by means of enclosures. Quite often we get letters from our customers which can be marked up in such a way that the heart of them is quickly found, and these letters can be used to bring out a point we want to get over.

Ask for the Order

You probably have had experience with the very friendly and agreeable young salesman who drops in on you every day and talks about the weather and everything else under the sun, but who never gets to the point of telling you what he wants or what he wants you to do. These salesmen are good-friend makers, but usually poor order-getters. The same thing holds true of writers of sales letters. There are many who can write a very human and interesting sales letter which will be read by the people to whom it is sent, but it fails to get the business. It brings back many favorable replies but comparatively few orders.

The trouble is the same in both instances. The salesman doesn't get the order because he doesn't ask for it, and the man who writes the letter doesn't get what he is after because he doesn't come out clearly in his letter and tell the prospect what he wants him to do.

No sales letter should be allowed to go out unless it ends up by telling the recipient just exactly what action you want him to take, and make it as easy as possible for him to take that action.

This does not mean that some hackneyed expression such as "Do It Now" or "Send Back the Card Today" is all that is needed. Neither does it mean that the letter should conclude with some domineering, arbitrary demand that the prospect do certain things without giving him any reason at all for doing them. But it does mean that a properly constructed sales letter will lead the prospect through the stages of attention, interest, desire, and conviction up to the final stage of action.

If the presentation is allowed to stop before the action stage is reached, all the work which has been done will have been in vain. So, be sure in your letters that in the last paragraph, or at least in the last few paragraphs, you make it clear that you are writing to the person for a definite purpose, and the reason why it is to his advantage to do what you want him to do. Then tell him what you want him to do so as to start the ball rolling. If you want him to sign an order, ask him to sign an order. If you want him to send back a reply card, ask him to send back a reply card.

■ ■

A Spare-Time Business Became the World's Largest Mail-Order House

RICHARD W. SEARS, founder of Sears, Roebuck & Co., made his first $1,000 in 1884, in a spare-time mail-order business under the name of the R. W. Sears Watch Company. He wrote his letters with pen and ink in his leisure hours. Later, when his correspondence demanded more time than he could spare, he enlisted the aid of a railroad man working on a near-by section. From this humble start grew the greatest mail-order house in the world. Soon Mr. Sears' spare-time work became so profitable that he resigned his position as telegraph operator, moved to Minneapolis, and started in the mail-order business in real earnest with $8,000 which he had managed to save.

In the late eighties he moved to Chicago. He continued to prosper. Then a Chicago firm made him an attractive offer for his business, which he accepted. A condition of the sale was that Mr. Sears should not engage in the mail-order business in Chicago for a period of five years. When the transfer was completed, Mr. Sears returned to Minneapolis. At this point the level-headedness of the man is shown in a striking manner. He was not yet twenty-four, yet he had over $100,000 in the bank, made entirely by his own efforts in the mail-order business. The possession of such a large sum of money by so young a man is often a signal for erratic actions. But it affected Mr. Sears not a particle. His first step was to buy his mother a home. Then he invested the major part of his capital in Minnesota 8 per cent farm mortgages. He never parted with this investment.

He started again in the mail-order business in Minneapolis. At this time, Mr. Roebuck worked for him as repairman. They later formed a partnership and the new business grew by leaps and bounds. The advantages of Chicago as a distributing center appealed strongly to Mr. Sears. So at the end of the specified five years, he moved again from Minneapolis to Chicago. This was in 1895. Mr. Roebuck stayed with Mr. Sears about four more years.

Mr. Sears was a prodigious worker. He would work eighteen hours a day for weeks at a stretch. In the early days he originated all the ideas and plans used in the business, and wrote his own copy. Once on the trail of an idea, he would forget all about time and would stick until it was developed, or at least in condition to turn over to an assistant.

Mrs. Sears often complained good naturedly about his devotion to business. When he left home in the morning she never knew just when he would return. Sometimes she would hear from him at his office in the early morning hours; other times the following day from one of his factories several hundred miles from Chicago, or from a train bound for New York. He never let up until the thing in hand was completed, even though it took him to distant parts of the country.

When building an advertisement or a catalog, thoughts of economy never entered Mr. Sears' mind. The main idea was to get it right. He was never really satisfied with his work and would take an advertisement or a catalog page which had just been printed, look it over carefully and suggest changes that would give the copy the right appeal or appearance. He would order pages that had been already set in type set up all over again.

The first advertisements were his famous "Send-no-money" series. When they appeared, the advertising world stood aghast. These advertisements violated every principle of good advertising. They were small sized, closely set in fine type, full of detailed description, hard to read, and without headings. They began "Send no money. Cut this advertisement out, return to us, and we will send you . . ." Nobody believed people would read such small type. But Mr. Sears felt that if the subject matter was interesting, people would not want to miss a single word. And he won his case.

Anywhere from five to twenty advertisements of this type appeared in each issue of a big list of publications, with from twenty to thirty million of circulation in the aggregate. Bills for advertising ran from $50,000 to $60,000 a month and the campaign distributed millions of dollars' worth of merchandising. At the same time he was building up his immense catalog mailing list.

During the 1907 panic, Mr. Sears showed his real mettle. Sales had dropped off on account of money being tight. However, he reasoned that people still wanted things even though they had no ready cash to buy them or feared to spend what money they did have. In order to overcome this attitude, Mr. Sears wrote on a slip of paper the following: "If you haven't the ready money to send us with your order, send us anything that looks like money. Your personal check or your clearing-house certificate will do, and will be accepted as cash." This advertisement was broadcast through the entire country. Millions of these slips of paper were printed and mailed each week. With every letter or package sent to a customer, one of these slips was enclosed.

The entire plan was startling, to say the least. When others were retrenching, Mr. Sears boosted and the result was such a flood of orders, resources of the company were taxed to the limit. By doing the unusual, Mr. Sears reaped unusual results.

Because he believed that merchandise should be thoroughly described in the advertisements, Mr. Sears went the limit on description. He wanted to be certain that the prospective buyer would know from the advertising just what he would receive for his money. In an advertisement for suits, for example, he would even go so far as to describe the linings of the coats and the buttons—even the buttonholes were mentioned.

One of his policies was that merchandise must be guaranteed. It was his contention that the customer was always right and no matter what it might cost to satisfy a customer that satisfaction had to be made. When a customer complained that the merchandise he received was not right, he was told to return the goods, even if he had used them, and his money would be refunded. There was never any backing out on this position—the money was instantly returned without question.

He insisted that his goods must always be as represented and he backed up this policy by offering to send goods C.O.D. Mr. Sears was probably the first merchant to send his goods subject to approval with transportation charges guaranteed both ways. He was always willing to take every risk himself—the customer had to be protected by every safeguard.

Another policy which probably originated with Mr. Sears was that of placing emphasis on the personal element in all his advertising. Letters were always phrased in a personal tone and every letter was signed by his name rather than by the name of the company. He wanted every customer to feel that he was dealing with a flesh-and-blood person rather than an institution. He addressed customers in their own language, in a simple, neighborly way that they could easily understand. Each letter breathed honesty and sincerity, and a genuine desire to serve.

He knew that country people were not used to writing and found it difficult to express themselves easily. He also knew that the mental inertia of people, generally, prevented them from sending for goods. He had to get these people, who did so little writing, to send him an order. To overcome all these obstacles he originated the "Do This" style of advertising. Advertisements read: "If you want this catalog, simply write us a letter or a postal, and say 'Send me your big catalog,' and it will go to you by return mail, postpaid." He also knew that there was usually a scarcity of writing material in the average country home, so he would say in his advertisement: "Write to us in your way, in any language; we will understand and will fill your order correctly. If you haven't an order blank handy, use any plain paper; use pencil or pen—it makes no difference. Don't be afraid of making a mistake. We will take all the risk and will return your money immediately, including whatever you paid for freight or express charges, if the goods are not perfectly satisfactory."

Mr. Sears believed that after a man had accumulated a fortune in business, he had earned the right to retire. With this idea in mind, he began early in his business career to build up an organization which would be able some day to carry on without his guidance and management. It was in 1908 that he withdrew from the active management of the business. He died in 1914.

■ ■

A One-Man Business with a Million Customers

BACK in the eighteen-nineties, the sight of a young man driving his horse and buggy along the lonely country roads became a familiar one to the farmers of southwestern Iowa. His name was Henry Field, and on the buggy seat beside him rested a basket of seed packets which he sold from farm to farm in the country and from house to house in the small towns and villages. He had planted, raised and prepared that seed in his own garden. He had even printed his own seed packets, and after he had filled them he went out himself to sell them. His was strictly a one-man business.

There weren't any large towns down in southwestern Iowa in those days. There weren't any surfaced roads, and sometimes there weren't any roads at all. He had to cut across fields to reach some of the farmers who bought his seed. But whether the temperature was 110 in the shade or down below zero, whether the roads were heavy with dust or hub-deep with mud, Henry Field was on the job. He brought more than seed to the isolated farms he called on; he brought helpful suggestions about planting, news about what other farmers were doing, information about the need for good seed in getting good crops. But most of all he brought friendliness and encouragement. The farmers and their families got to know him and to like him. They looked forward with eagerness to his visits. They talked about him with their neighbors.

Before long these customers wanted to buy more of Henry Field's seed than he alone could raise and deliver. He thought he was well enough acquainted with his customers to get their orders by mail just as well as in person. That would permit him to devote his full time to producing and shipping the seed. So he got hold of some second-hand printing equipment in Shenandoah, Iowa, printed a modest catalog, and started a mail-order business.

The Knack of Appealing to Farmers

Through years of personal dealings with them, he knew how to appeal to farmers as successfully by the written word as by the spoken word. First of all, he must make his story brief and to the point. As he himself once expressed it: "When you're driving along the road on a freezing day and meet a farmer taking a load of corn to market, you can't make him stop and shiver all day while you're talking to him. You have to tell him your business in just as few words as you can, get his order, and let him go on to town. Well, it's the same way when you write him a letter or send him a catalog. You've got to get down to cases right away."

That doesn't mean, though, that Henry Field's letters and catalogs didn't radiate the same friendliness and intimacy which had made him so successful as a salesman. He didn't make the mistake of writing in a literary or "bookish" way. He simply wrote the same way he would talk to a man if he met him face to face. He used the common, everyday colloquial expressions his customers used. He treated them as though they were his next-door neighbors. He even gossiped a little, but was careful not to be long-winded about it.

From the start, people liked his way of doing business. They got in the habit of sending in their orders by mail, and it wasn't long until orders began coming in from people he had never called on in person, from Nebraska, Missouri and Kansas. Year by year his catalogs grew larger and larger, but he continued to write them in the first person and he never deviated from the friendly, personal, informal style which established his early success.

Today the Henry Field Company in Shenandoah, Iowa, has over a million customers on its books. Its volume of business has grown from a few hundred dollars a year to $3,000,000. In addition to selling seeds and plants, Henry Field has branched out into the general merchandise field. He sells overalls, shoes, hats, prunes, oranges, tires and an endless variety of other products. In order to sell them successfully by mail, he developed many innovations in the established mail-order practices. Finding it unprofitable to sell a single pair of overalls, for example, he sells them in units of three. Since farmers buy potatoes, apples and corn by the bushel, he thought they'd also buy oranges by the bushel, so that's the way he sells them. Coffee is packaged in three-, five-, ten- and twenty-five-pound containers. Canned goods are offered only in units of twelve. Although stores sell prunes in one-, three- and five-pound packages, Henry Field sells them only in twenty- and twenty-five-pound units.

Using the Radio to Create Consumer Acceptances

Ten years ago he bought a run-down radio broadcasting station in Shenandoah, rehabilitated it, and has used it ever since to sell even more goods by radio than he ever sold strictly by mail. He is now known as a "radio-order" merchant as well as a mail-order merchant. He does most of his own broadcasting, and where once he called personally on hundreds of customers, then wrote letters and sent catalogs to thousands, now his voice is heard by literally millions throughout the whole Middle West. In the twenty-five years from 1899 to 1924 his mail-order sales grew to a $600,000 annual volume. Since he has been able to get closer than ever to his customers over the air, they have grown to $3,000,000.

But in spite of the huge plant which his business occupies, in spite of the acres of fields where his seeds, plants and bulbs are now grown, in spite of his broadcasting station and the huge department store which covers the ground floor of the building, all the million customers on the books of the company still feel that they are dealing directly with Henry Field. They may never have seen him in person, although each year close to half a million farmers and small-townspeople visit his plant, but through his letters and broadcasts and catalogs they feel that he is an old and trusted friend. That's why they continue sending in their orders by mail at a rate of a thousand every day.

■ ■

Reaching the Smoker by Mail

J. W. **ROBERTS** and Son sells its entire production of fine Havana cigars direct to the smoker by mail and has been selling them this way for over 30 years. The firm, of course, depends upon a carefully compiled mailing list to secure the right type of customer. This mailing list is made up from thousands and thousands of rated names every year. New mailing lists are continually purchased but rated names alone can be used as the company wants only names to which it can make shipments on open accounts. Many of the standing-order customers have been on the books for twenty years and a list of their names reads like pages from *Who's Who*.

Experience has proved that it pays to test a mailing list three times before sending out a mailing to the entire list. In no other way can the probable returns of a list be estimated; and in no other way can expenses be kept down to the point where mail selling is profitable. Test mailings on lists are made as quickly as possible, for if any appreciable time elapses between the test and the actual mailing entirely different results would be obtained. The men, whose rated names compose the lists, receive personal letters from J. W. Roberts and Son by first-class mail, offering to send them, strictly on open account (no cash and no C.O.D.) a box of Havana cigars. The smoker is invited to smoke ten or more free. He is billed in the usual manner if he is pleased with the quality and the price and indicates that he wants to keep the box.

Given a quality product, one which many people use, a product not too costly to ship, simple sincere sales letters, and a "quality" mailing list, and you have an excellent set-up for a fine mail-order business. That it can be done has been proved by this 30-year-old business, still going strong.

CHAPTER TEN

SELLING YOUR SERVICES

THE first thing to do is to take an inventory of yourself. What do you like to do? What can you do especially well? What can you do skillfully that most people do indifferently? What need exists which you could fill? These are just a few of the searching questions which you should ask yourself before attempting to sell your services. If you can find the right answers to these questions, you will have little difficulty in establishing yourself in a personal service business.

Now there is a difference between selling your services and getting a job. In one case you are what is called an *entrepreneur*, while in the other case you are an employee. Just what is an *entrepreneur*? He is a man who takes the risks that go with a business venture, and profits or loses in proportion to those risks. He derives his income from customers or clients, as the case may be, rather than from an employer. The *entrepreneur* may be, and usually does become, an employer. But he still assumes the risks and the possibilities for profit that go with them. It is from the *entrepreneur* class that most of our successful business men, merchants and manufacturers come. They usually got their start selling their own services. Then, as they acquired skill and knowledge, they branched out and sold the services of others on whom they in turn made a profit.

It is an axiom of success that to receive the applause of the multitude you must find out what your public wants and then do it better than anyone else in the world is doing it. The foregoing applies particularly to artists— those whose services take the form of entertaining or educating people. But it also applies to less colorful work. To achieve success in any human activity, you must excel others. When you have done that, your reputation will be made and your success will be assured.

The thing which you select to do need not be—in fact, it should not be—a broad activity. The more you concentrate your interest, the more quickly you will succeed. In Chicago, there is an advertising man who discovered twenty years ago that very few men knew how to write inspirational letters to salesmen. He further discovered that there was a need for interesting, practical, informative letters which would actually help salesmen to meet successfully the difficult problems they daily encountered. So he quit his job and offered his services to sales managers of companies which employed salesmen. In some cases these sales managers could have written just as good—perhaps better—letters than this advertising man offered to write for them, but they did not have time to do it. They were too engrossed in the activities of their jobs. So they were glad to pay the young advertising man $10 a month to write a weekly letter to their salesmen. Since salesmen's problems have much in common, the young man found that the same letter, with a few changes, would work equally well for any business, and within the year he was receiving $10 a month from more than 200 companies for his services, At the age of twenty-seven he was earning over $20,000 a year! Yet, had he been employed by any of these companies on a salary, he could not have made more than $7,000 at the most. What was the secret of his success? It was simple. He became expert at doing one thing better than any other person in the world was doing it. If he had set out to be a better advertising man than anyone else in the world, he would still be on the way up the ladder. But he lifted out of the selling field one little thing: A service for which a need existed, and then he concentrated all his efforts and thought on doing that one thing superlatively well. In other words, he was a specialist.

This principle of specialization is most important in our modern complex life. It applies not only to business, but to whatever we do. To be able to do many things well is an asset and a credit. And perhaps the world needs more versatile people. But when it comes to making a thousand dollars quickly by selling your services, *specialize*. We are living in an age of specialists. Doctors specialize because they know that the big opportunities in medicine go to the one who thoroughly masters one particular disease or concentrates on one certain part of the body. The general practitioner served a very useful role in our community life. It is too bad to see him pass. But the big money in medicine lies in specializing. The same is true in law and in educational activities. It is true in engineering. People will pay a premium to get the advice or the opinion of those who are recognized as knowing more about the particular thing in which they are interested than anyone else in town, or in the country or in the world.

■ ■

Training Gave Chapin a Start

GETTING the "first thousand" didn't worry Howard Chapin so much as preparing himself to get it. When he left high school, he considered technical courses offered by various schools, and decided to go in for mechanical engineering. He didn't have enough money to matriculate at a university, so he decided to do the next best thing—get a job, and take a correspondence course. That was five years ago. Today, Chapin is operating a successful engineering service of his own. It's small, but his profits for the past year have been a few times a thousand dollars.

"When I decided to study engineering, I went to the office of an engineering company here in Chicago, and explained that I wanted more than anything else an opportunity to get an education. I agreed to work for a small salary. I would be satisfied, I told them, if it would barely cover the cost of my correspondence course. The manager thought I had the right idea. 'That's how I got started myself,' he admitted, and arranged to take me into his office. Supplementing the correspondence work was class instruction which didn't interfere with my hours at the engineering company. With the practical suggestions I picked up in the office, plus the practice work and theories studied in class, I soon saw that I was getting somewhere.

"It took me two years to complete my correspondence studies. Meanwhile, I was advanced to a better position, and a raise in salary. I saved every cent of this raise, having accustomed myself to living economically during the period of my school work. Something went wrong with a big job my employers were handling during my third year with them, and they were forced out of business. Without a job, I analyzed my future. I had saved a hundred and ninety dollars and I was qualified to do specialized work. I wrote out a list of the places that had use for such work and called on them. I found many small factories where motors were being neglected because it didn't pay to keep a full-time electrician. This looked like a good opportunity to me and I began contracting to keep such equipment in good condition and service it monthly on a yearly contract. I called upon factories, laundries and such places where there are motor-driven shafts and machines, and charged a service fee ranging from five to fifty dollars a month, depending upon the amount of work. I agreed to furnish labor for repairing and installing equipment, and for maintaining it on this basis. In four days I had contracts from seven concerns, totaling $104 a month. I did the work myself and it kept me going seventeen hours a day for almost a month. Those motors certainly were in bad condition! After that, it was easier and since there were now only a few days' work to be done each month, I called on a number of other firms, and signed up five contracts totaling $120. Again I found that the equipment had been sadly neglected for a good many months, and that I had to work my head off. I was now assured of an income of $224 a month for a year. However, as I still had some idle time on my hands, I sallied forth for another batch of customers.

"At the end of four months, I had signed up twenty-one companies on contracts totaling $885 a month. This was too much work for me to do alone, so I hired two good electricians, paid them the full union wage, supervised their work, and got more contracts. Profits quickly mounted.

In less than a year, my contracts were paying me a profit of $490 a month, and I was paying full regular union wages to five good men."

Chapin offers a service much needed in every manufacturing community. Men trained and skilled as mechanics might do well to follow his example and offer a similar service to small manufacturers at a regular, reasonable, monthly fee.

They certainly will be welcomed by the smaller manufacturer who is at present worried about costs, and who may be permitting machinery to operate without the necessary repairs.

■ ■

A Flower-a-Day Service

G URNEY CHRYSLER, an alert young New York advertising woman, had a suspicion that florists could get more business if they went after it, instead of waiting for it to come to them. So she rented a loft in an old building and sent out announcements advertising her flower-a-day or bouquet-a-week "service." For one flower a day she charged 10 cents and for two a day, 15 cents. Those who wished this service contracted to pay her by the week or month. Within a short time she had 1,000 customers.

Mrs. Chrysler's work begins at four-thirty each morning, when she goes to market, buys her flowers, and starts her helpers making the boutonnieres. By eight o'clock, messenger boys have started to deliver the packages. Her customers may have their order varied any way they choose—a rosebud on Monday, a carnation on Tuesday, a gardenia on Wednesday, and so on through the week. Customers may also contract to have flowers sent daily to friends who are ill.

Another idea Mrs. Chrysler inaugurated was the anniversary service. You turn over to her a list of the anniversaries in your family and flowers are delivered automatically on those exact dates, the bill being sent to you once a month, according to contract. In addition to these regular services, she prepares special table decorations for parties and arranges for floral decorations for weddings, teas, bridal showers, coming-out parties and other social functions. She also makes up special floral designs, many of which are sent to Paris salons and London parties. The use of the cellophane box by florists today originated with Mrs. Chrysler.

Margaret Harper, of Cleveland, has somewhat the same idea but depended upon her own garden for her flowers. For years she had been an enthusiastic gardener, and the grounds about her old home bloomed with flowers of many varieties from spring through the early autumn. This was the one subject in which she was most interested and enthusiastic. Her beautiful arrangements of cut flowers within her home brought as many compliments as her garden did. Having the time, the flowers and the artistic ability to arrange them, all she needed was a list of customers. She knew nothing about advertising, but a friend who owned a letter shop prepared some clever little folders for her at cost and she addressed the envelopes on her son's portable typewriter. The list was made up of names of friends and acquaintances she knew who were in business; all the professional people she knew, such as her banker, lawyer, dentist, the principal of her son's school, some of the teachers of the school; the owners of several hotel apartment buildings near her section of town; the heads of small business firms within walking distance, and the managers of two tea rooms and a restaurant a few blocks away. Many of these announcements were followed by personal calls and with practically every call she sold the idea to the prospective customer. Her two young sons delivered the flowers each morning and once a month Mrs. Harper collected the money for them. This personal contact with her customers gave her a chance to handle any complaints and also the opportunity to sell her customers on other uses for her flowers. Through subtle suggestion, she secured many orders for table decorations, decorations for parties, weddings, bridal showers, "new baby" baskets, and holiday festivities. During the winter, she bought her flowers from the flower market and continued the service to her customers at a slightly higher cost.

Two young New Yorkers also found the establishment of a flower service a way out of their difficulties. They had been wearily trudging from employment office to employment office looking for jobs until one day they realized that the only way to get a job was to make one. They pooled their resources which amounted to the grand sum of $1.50 and started in business. With their "capital" they purchased a thousand business cards and distributed them on foot from office to office, hotel to hotel, restaurant to restaurant. A little sales talk went with the distribution of each card. Today, they have built up a nice little business. Having no capital left to buy the flowers would have made things difficult for them if a wholesale florist had not agreed to wait until the tenth of the month following their purchases to bill them. This arrangement gave them time to collect their money before the bills fell due. Since they have access to the wholesaler's stock at all times, there is no need for them to invest in stock of their own. The flowers are sold on a monthly fee basis and the bouquets are changed every third day. The fee depends, of course, upon the number of bouquets furnished.

Rug Washing Is a Quick-Profit Business

EDWARD ANDERSON washed his first thousand dollars out of other people's carpets. And he surprised himself at the ease with which he accumulated the money. He started in this unique way of earning a living when he lost his job as a manager of a department store in central Ohio, where a carpet-washing machine, specially made to wash carpets and rugs, was used in the store.

"I wrote the manufacturer of this machine and learned I could buy one on the easy payment plan," said Anderson. "So I hustled around the neighborhood and got a few orders for cleaning rugs without removing them from the floor at one dollar and fifty cents a rug. Then I mailed my initial payment to the manufacturer. Full instructions for operating came with the machine. When I started on the jobs ordered, though, I was surprised that I could clean rugs in about one-third the time I had figured. During one morning I cleaned seven rugs and pocketed ten dollars and fifty cents.

"That afternoon I went around the neighborhood looking for more rug-cleaning orders. I secured my first orders without any trouble. I experienced some difficulty getting more, however. Most housewives thought I might ruin an expensive rug, or wouldn't efficiently clean carpets for the price I quoted. One woman said: 'I can't see how you can do it so cheaply, if you do a good job.' I explained the way the machine operated in vain. She wouldn't believe it. Others said they didn't want their rugs cleaned, and then quizzed me about the kind of work I was doing.

"I asked each of these women to call up the people whose rugs I cleaned that morning, but they wouldn't bother. Going home, I listed the number of office buildings, offices, hotels, and apartment buildings in town. I called upon the managers of those places the following days but got only thirty dollars' worth of work during the balance of that week. This wasn't bad. The second week, however, was a disappointment and I wondered how I would ever get enough business to pay for the machine. I began to make desperate efforts. I argued and pleaded for orders, but it seemed that I always called just after rugs had been cleaned.

"One day it occurred to me that if people did not need rug cleaning at the moment I called, they might need it later, so I had some cards printed explaining the kind of service I was offering. These didn't bring me any immediate orders, however, and the time for the first payment on the machine was drawing near. I called back upon my first customers then, and asked them if they could send me to some friends. One woman said that she would see some of her friends the next day, and let me know. Two days later, she phoned that a friend on the other side of town wanted her rug cleaned, and promised if I did as good as claimed to get me additional business. I lost no time getting over to do the job, and was rewarded with three additional orders. Then I wrote the manufacturer and asked if there was a better way to get business than I was using. The company sent me a good deal of solid instruction in salesmanship, which I carefully digested. I found that my method of getting the business was too "high pressure." I was antagonistic when people didn't agree with me. I changed these tactics, and the difference in my reception was amazing. In two months, I was becoming known for my pleasant manner and uniform good nature. A courteous manner toward prospects made them listen to me.

"Politeness also smoothed a path for me in approaching the managers of office buildings and hotels. One hotel manager with whom I quarreled the first time I called on him gave me a job cleaning the carpets in the corridors of the hotel. This work brought me ninety-three dollars, and took thirteen hours to complete. I didn't get that order on the second or the fifth call, however. But I was as polite and courteous as I could be each time I called back on him. I had learned my lesson. In one office building, after many calls upon the manager, I was able to get orders from tenants totaling $107, besides twelve dollars' worth of work from the building owners."

Anderson's experience has convinced him that the value of courtesy and politeness in sales work cannot be overemphasized. He charges one dollar and fifty cents for cleaning a nine by twelve rug, and does the job in twelve minutes. Daily profits average about sixteen dollars. The machine operates from a light socket with electric current, on the rotary brush principle, and is fully guaranteed to do satisfactory work by the manufacturer. This machine washes the carpet with soap and water, which are fed into the brushes by a patented process. However, it is impossible for the machine to spill water or soap upon the floor, or injure the rugs in any way. Anderson's total investment, which included the price of the machine, was $317.

■ ■

Starting a Package Delivery System

TWO years ago, James Overhause took his last hundred dollars, bought a second-hand truck for thirty-five of them and spent several dollars fixing it up. He had a sign painted, and announced to the world that he was in the expressing and moving business. But nothing happened. He sat around the front room of his flat for several days, but no one seemed to want to express anything or move things about the city of Chicago. He then went out to stores, and sought odd jobs delivering heavy boxes to warehouses and picking up loads to be brought back to the stores. In this way, he managed to eke out a bare existence, but he thought he was progressing. A chain-store manager stopped him on the street one day, asked how business was with him, and said if Jimmy wanted to take over the delivery of groceries for the store, he could pick up a few dollars a day from making store deliveries. This was his start. Today he has seven new delivery wagons operating on the south side of Chicago, and more on the way.

"When that A & P store manager asked me to make deliveries of groceries for his customers, he explained that the store was a cash and carry store, and did not make deliveries," said Jimmy, "and then he pointed out that the fellow who was making deliveries up to that time gave poor service. 'There are a few dollars a day in it if you give service,' the manager told me. I thanked him. A charge of ten cents for each box delivered was added to the store customer's bill, and collected at the time the groceries were paid for. All I had to do was stop at the store, put the deliveries on the truck, and deliver them. But there weren't many boxes every day. That one store hardly paid for the gasoline. I lined up another chain store, two independent grocers and three butchers, however, and made the rounds of each, loaded up the truck and delivered. At the end of each day, the store managers or owners paid me the amount they had collected, and I was able to carry on.

"The most important thing about this type of service was to make frequent deliveries. Food is wanted quickly. I make four trips to the stores, one at ten, one at eleven-thirty, one at two and one at four. I pick up all the boxes and packages of meat and groceries for delivery that are ready, and carry them around. It takes about an hour to make all the deliveries, so that those who buy at any of the stores on this route have their groceries early enough to start supper.

"When store customers discovered they could depend upon my service, more of them had things delivered. Women hate to carry heavy parcels. Potatoes weigh fifteen pounds to the peck, and no woman wants to carry a peck of potatoes herself. She is glad to have the potatoes and her other groceries carried for her, and willing to pay a dime for it. In a month, my business had increased from 40 packages daily from that one neighborhood to 129. In two months, I was averaging 150 deliveries a day, and that was about the top. I arranged with stores in other communities, got a helper and another second-hand truck. Soon that was booming also."

There isn't a small or large town where a good delivery service from stores is not welcome. Most store people have either discontinued making deliveries, or would be willing to discontinue delivering if there were a local, dependable service such as Overhause offers. Furnishing this type of service is a quick way to get started in a business.

Sewing for the "Hard-to-Fit" Woman

ONE day a Chicago seamstress overheard an extremely stout woman telling a small shopkeeper that she experienced so much difficulty in finding suitable clothes in the stores that she had just about given up bothering about her appearance. With an apology, the dressmaker entered the conversation and made an appointment with the stout woman for a fitting. The stout woman had a sister of about the same build and she too became a customer. Both of them knew friends who found difficulty in getting suitable apparel because of their size and soon the dressmaker had built up a nice little business.

Being an ingenious person, this dressmaker sold her customers on having their lingerie as well as their dresses made to order. She also encouraged them to plan their needs for each season in advance, thus showing them how to be well-dressed with a minimum of expense and time. This plan not only helped her to organize her work, but also gave her extra work to do in fixing over last season's dresses for her customers.

She realized that unless she had ideas to offer her customers she would not be able to plan their wardrobe, and she knew that was the secret of success in this business. So she scanned the pattern books, looked at the new fabrics in the better department stores, and also looked over the dresses sold by the "stylish stout departments" in these stores. She brought samples of fabrics home from the stores and mounted them on cards with the prices listed beneath. Pictures of dresses made from patterns that she thought would make up well for stout figures were also mounted on cards. Customers came to rely more and more on her judgment as to style and good taste, which, of course, made the work much easier for her to handle.

While most of this dressmaker's work came to her through customers' recommendations, some of it also came through a corsetiere who had a number of stout women on her customer list. An agreement was made between the two women to recommend each other to their customers—a plan that worked to their mutual benefit.

Recently, she found another "market" making clothes for unusually tall women. These women, like stout women, find it hard to be fitted in ready-made things and to make it more difficult, there are no special departments in the stores which cater to their needs. Tall women need longer sleeves, longer skirts, and often longer waists than the average figure requires, so practically everything they buy has to be altered. This business was a little harder to build up but it is slowly increasing, mostly through "word-of-mouth" advertising by satisfied customers.

An Airplane Junk Yard

ARRIGO BALBONI, a young California pilot, finds little competition in his line of business, which is salvaging wrecked airplanes. His market for parts of wrecked planes includes movie directors who can use battered planes in filming crashes, owners of obsolete engines who need repair parts, aviation schools, amateur plane and glider builders, inventors and souvenir hunters.

The idea for his airplane junk yard, just outside of Los Angeles, was the result of an airplane crash. On a flight one day from San Francisco to Santa Monica, he crashed just north of Los Angeles. He escaped serious injury, but his plane was completely wrecked. With it went his savings which had been invested in the plane. He later salvaged what he could of the plane and sold the parts to aviators. By selling his wrecked plane in this way, he got together $930. It was then that he realized that an airplane junk yard might be a profitable business. And so it turned out to be. It was not long before he was known far and wide as a source of supply for airplane parts, and orders began coming from foreign countries as well as the United States. Aviation schools abroad use the old engines salvaged from the ships to teach the students the mechanics of flying. Inventors buy them and tear them down hoping to find a better way of building engines. The instruments and mechanical devices are also used for this purpose. In order to keep his supply complete, Mr. Balboni is on the alert for news of airplane crashes. Instantly, he takes steps to salvage the parts and buys them direct from the pilot or others interested.

■ ■

A Business in Organizing Archery Clubs

IN 1929, J. M. Deeds was a business man in the Northwest with seventy people on his pay roll. In 1931, he was a common laborer in Oakland, California. Digging ditches was arduous labor for an aging man in poor health; but when one has a wife and children . . .

The following year Mr. Deeds, without work or money, told a minister: "I'll either have to take up a hobby or go crazy." The minister replied: "Good idea—the hobby I mean."

Mr. Deeds chose archery because his son and daughter were Scouts and because half a century ago as a small boy in the wilds of northern

California, he had been taught by the Indians how to make bows and arrows from the native woods and how to shoot.

By autumn, 1932, he had become a committee man for the Scouts and had converted 60 per cent of the members over to the idea of archery as a project. The following spring saw his interest so intense that he had committed himself to the pastime as a lifework with the goal of making the East Bay District the archery center of America.

That summer, while conducting a Scout expedition, he came across some exceedingly tough grass which he thought had target possibilities. He mailed a sample to the Department of Agriculture, at Washington, and learned that it was the toughest grass in the United States. The owner of the property on which it grew gave Mr. Deeds permission to take all he wanted. He said it was called wild lyme grass and was useless for hay. Mr. Deeds made a trial target and found it more practical than any he had ever used. He cut and hauled away a ton of the grass and in his spare time made targets. These he traded to tackle makers for raw material which he made into tackle (bows and arrows).

In the meantime, he had organized a club called Berkeley Archers and was known as its guiding genius. There were sixty members—teachers and the tired-business-man element of the East Bay; also a junior section of thirty boys and girls. In addition, there were fifteen men calling themselves "The Rovers," whom he was training for big game hunting.

When the Federal Emergency Educational Program provided for recreational activities, Mr. Deeds visited the directors but was turned down; they considered archery unsafe. He kept on visiting them until they agreed to experiment if he could furnish tackle for the class. He could. Hadn't he been fashioning dozens of bows and hundreds of arrows for just such a contingency?

Five hundred enrolled during the next six months and in two thousand student hours not one accident has occurred. Of the group, seventy have joined archery clubs, many securing their tackle from Mr. Deeds.

He learned how to make tackle by trial and error and by winning the friendship of expert bow makers, one an Indian chief who winters in California, and the other a leading craftsman of the West. Today Mr. Deeds' bows combine beauty with sturdiness, and a fifteen-pound practice bow of his devising has proved far better for the novice than the customary twenty-five or thirty-pound bow.

Mr. Deeds attributes his enviable reputation as a teacher to the fact that he takes the mystery out of archery and puts it on a purely mechanical basis. It is his constant delight to see stooping, pallid men, women and children transformed into healthy individuals with sparkling eyes and erect carriage.

His hobby has meant the support of his family and the accumulation of tackle worth a thousand dollars. But, best of all, it has meant his personal rehabilitation.

■ ■

Ghost Writing Is a Business

BACK in February, 1933, when Fred E. Baer, of New York City, realized his publicity business was dying on its feet, he let it expire and he and Henry F. Woods organized the Ghost Writers' Bureau. What does a Ghost Writers' Bureau do? Well, if you are called upon to say something or to write a paper for your association you get in touch with the Bureau and presto! Your speech or paper is all prepared for you. Professional and business people use the service. Many general agents of insurance companies who must prepare inspirational material for salesmen, make constant use of the Bureau's services.

When the Bureau was first organized, the charges for the service ranged from four to eleven cents a word. This was too high, but it was some time before the owners realized it. The charge now is one and one-half to six cents. Part of the amount charged goes to the writer; the rest is the Bureau's compensation.

There are now more than 200 writing specialists on the staff—specialists in science, architecture, finance, engineering, merchandising, and several other fields. About 1,200 calls for help on speeches, books, articles, and reports come through the Bureau in a year.

As people don't like to admit they employ specialists to do their writing for them, there is little chance of "word of mouth" advertising. Consequently, the Bureau has been advertised almost every week from the start through a one-inch advertisement in the New York newspapers.

A bureau of this sort could be organized by any alert young business man or woman with an idea of the needs in his particular community. People active in trade associations, professional clubs, social clubs, women's clubs, literary clubs, scientific organizations—all need the help of a trained writer in the preparation of manuscripts for publication or the preparation of speeches. The backbone of an organization, such as this, is a good staff of associates who are experts in their particular fields. There are any number of able writers who would welcome the chance to make a few extra dollars in their spare time.

Snapshots Pay Vacation Bills

YEARS ago, Robert E. Hughes, a teacher in a high school in one of Chicago's suburbs, started taking pictures with a little, inexpensive Brownie. As time went on he became more and more interested in his hobby and invested in a better camera. During his long summer vacations, he carried his camera with him. One day after he had developed some pictures taken around a boys' camp, he showed them to the camp director. As a result, he got orders for 200 pictures. From that time on, he paid for his vacations with the sale of snapshots. Summer hotels, camps, railroads, tourist agencies, inns, dude ranches, clubs, all offered a market. He made the pictures sell themselves. He figured—and rightly—that if he asked if pictures were wanted, the response would be negative.

Mr. Hughes has found some unusual outlets for snapshots. During one vacation spent in the West and Southwest, he made pictures to order for a lecturer and then developed them for colored slides. Another time he was commissioned by a travel agency to "shoot" some pictures in Wisconsin. Out of this commission he grossed $2,500. From time to time he has prepared illustrations for advertising booklets. A furnace company not long ago had him shoot pictures of registers in floors and ceilings at unusual angles.

There is considerable fun to be had out of this hobby also. One picture he enjoyed doing was for a fisherman who had caught an average-sized fish. He made a picture of the fisherman holding the fish. Then Mr. Hughes was instructed to "blow up" the fish only—that is, to make the fish so large it would literally drag on the ground. At the same time, the figure of the fisherman was to be kept to its original size. Needless to say, the fisherman had plenty of fun over this picture with his fishing cronies. Most summer resorts are eager to obtain post cards of guests who have caught fish or game, and will order quantities of them to sell at the desk, or to use in their advertising.

Mr. Hughes develops and finishes all his pictures himself. Thus he can secure the effects he wants, and he can make various experiments with the negatives. He has also been able to learn considerably more about taking pictures than he would if they had been developed by someone else. He has acquired the knack of reproducing old pictures, such as daguerreotypes, and has saved many a valued old picture from oblivion. There is simply no end to ways of making money from snapshots once you have mastered the knack of taking pictures of people in action.

Style Scouting with a Camera

MANUFACTURERS in the textile field are constantly seeking ideas and "motifs" that can be used in new designs. They pay liberally for photographs—in some cases as much as $1,000—that suggest unusual style themes. Marion Stephenson, of New York, was aware of this but never suspected that style scouting had business possibilities until she sold her first photograph to a New York silk company. Inside of three months she was making good money, and was going all over the world with her camera looking for unusual "shots" which might suggest interesting or unusual style motifs to designers.

"I went to France, England, Germany and Italy," said Miss Stephenson, "where I hunted out gatherings of smart people, and snapped moving pictures and stills of them for style notes to help manufacturers plan new lines. It is interesting work, and there is an ever-widening field for it. I pay my own expenses, but there is enough profit from this specialized work to make it worth while. Style scouting isn't difficult. I don't know exactly how to tell anyone how to go about it because there are no definite rules to follow. However, I believe that any woman who loves clothes and is observant could do well as a style scout. In my work, I use photographs because I am not an artist and cannot make sketches. A woman with a sense of line and color, who can sketch a little, should be able to get more feeling in design than I am able to and could soon earn a nice income."

Any concern dependent upon style is a prospect for such pictures and is constantly on the alert for suggestions. As special training is not required for this type of work, the girl who is observant and anxious to get started in an interesting and profitable profession, might well consider style scouting.

■ ■

Walking the Dog

A PROFITABLE business has been developed in New York by a group of enterprising young men who call themselves the "dog-walkers." The only capital necessary consists of proper clothing for the season, good legs, and a love of dogs. The dog-walkers are to be seen on upper Fifth and Park Avenues and in Central Park, giving their pedigreed charges an airing.

This service is appreciated by elderly people who like the companionship of dogs but do not have the energy to give them long walks; by invalids, and by business people who cannot find time regularly for this duty.

In Chicago, another group has also developed a dog-walking, dog-washing and dog-clipping service for busy dog owners.

Another service for dogs, developed in New York, is what is called the "Puppy Club." The Park Lane Hotel inaugurated the "Puppy Club," which is located on the roof. Here dogs may lunch, snooze, play or be groomed while their owners have their luncheon in the hotel dining room. The pup's owner may leave him all afternoon, if he wishes, to sun himself. An expert veterinary prescribes diet and treatments. The space used for the purpose is so located that it is suitable for nothing else and the equipment and decorations are both inexpensive. The idea has not only brought in money for otherwise wasted space, but it keeps the canine pets of hotel guests and visitors out of the hotel proper.

■ ■

What One Man Did with an Old Truck

SEVERAL years ago the company that employed him failed and James Bradley was out of a job. In the small town of Ft. Atkinson, Wisconsin, there were none too many jobs and he found it more difficult every day to get something to do. From time to time, of course, he would pick up a little job here and there, but nothing that was permanent.

One day he was walking around his little place trying to decide what to do, when he happened to glance at an old truck chassis in his garage. Perhaps he could get some work trucking if he could fix the old machine up, was his thought. A junk yard a few blocks away furnished the material for a body and when it was put on the truck and painted, James Bradley was ready for work.

Business was hard to get at first. Both he and his wife kept eyes and ears open for any possible chances of trucking jobs. The first job was hauling the household goods of a local resident who was moving to Milwaukee. Another similar job in a near-by town turned up, and gradually he found himself picking up odd jobs here and there that the large trucking companies would not bother to handle. In a short time, James Bradley had a fleet of trucks, had the franchise for all the trucking on the route to Milwaukee, and had several special contracts to handle the hauling of various companies. One of these companies was Republic Steel of Milwaukee. Arrangements have also been made with other trucking companies all over the country to connect with their shipments at specific points in the territory which he covers.

Trader's Exchange Does a National Business

THE Trader's Exchange, an agency for national barter, only a few years old, became one of the largest swapping agencies in the country. Mr. Savino Morizzo, who runs it, claims that he handles $500,000 in goods annually and has taken in as many as 4,500 items in a month. Around 36,000 letters pass through his hands each month and he will handle the swapping of anything under the sun—merchandise, farm produce, livestock, pets, etc.

The story goes, that a student in Alabama who had a saxophone wanted a microscope; a widow living in Arizona had a microscope but wanted some pigs, and a farmer in Oklahoma, who had six baby pigs, wanted a saxophone. The Trader's Exchange put the farmer, the widow, and the student in touch with one another, the exchange was made all around, and everyone was satisfied. Some of the strangest trades have been six grey squirrels for a vacuum cleaner; 49 shaving brushes and a marble slab for a coupe; and a set of castanets, a Spanish comb and a fancy costume for a course of six beauty treatments.

While this exchange has a national set-up and is in a position to make considerable money through the large volume of business done, there is an excellent opportunity in many a small town for a similar exchange which could operate more or less locally. An inexpensive store, your own home, or space in another store, could be used for the purpose. Handbills and local newspaper advertising will bring you requests for items or will put you in touch with people who have things to sell. Once your store becomes known around the countryside, your clientele will naturally develop through word-of-mouth advertising. At a period like the present, when money is scarce, swapping is in high favor.

■ ■

Boys' Club Proves Profitable

JOHN BANCROFT had been quite an athlete in college. He found it difficult to get the sort of work he wanted after he left school, so he made a job for himself which not only paid him well but filled a community need. He started a club of boys interested in athletics. He calls it the "Springfield Boys' Club," and divides the boys into two groups. The first group is composed of boys eight years old or younger. It meets after school two days each week and on Saturday mornings. The second group of boys from nine to fourteen years of age meets three afternoons each week. The charge for each boy varies from $3.50 to $5.00 a month and with from twenty to twenty-five boys in each group, John Bancroft's income runs well over $1,000 a year. Out of this amount he pays such expenses as the fee for the use of a swimming pool, the salary of an assistant, the operation of a "caddy wagon," and other incidentals.

The club is a year-round affair and is divided into two semesters: the spring-summer term and the fall-winter term. The athletic activities vary according to the season and include baseball, football, swimming, boxing, hiking, rowing and gymnasium work. Special arrangements are made with one of the local hotels for the use of the swimming pool during periods when it is too cold for the lake. Of course, during the swimming season, the boys are taken to the beach for their swimming lessons. On rainy days, the boys are instructed in making such things as kites and toy airplanes which they are later taught to fly. From time to time, John Bancroft or his assistant takes the boys on all-night hikes or hikes over the week-end in order that they may learn something about woodcraft. A caddy wagon—a truck fitted with seats—is used to transport the boys to the various locations where they are to play.

At the end of the term he holds an athletic event at the hotel swimming pool and all the boys' parents and friends are invited to attend. Even the little fellows are entered in the boxing contests and their skill is always a surprise to the spectators. Naturally, this exhibit has a promotional value and results in added names to the roster of the Boys' Club.

This is an activity which any young man residing in a fairly prosperous community can undertake if he has had some athletic training and knows how to handle groups of boys. Young women can also handle similar groups of girls. In this case, the athletic training would be in such sports as swimming, diving, tennis, basket-ball, hiking and skating.

■ ■

Meals for Dogs Is a Business Now

A WIDE-AWAKE woman in New York has built up an unusual business preparing meals for dog owners who do not have the time or do not want to bother preparing food for their pets. This daily service to dog owners is operated under the name of the Canine Catering Company. The business has grown so rapidly that branches have been established in a half dozen near-by towns as well as offices in Philadelphia and Washington. Businesses of this nature have also thrived in Chicago and Los Angeles.

A business such as this can only be started in a community where there are plenty of pure-bred dogs, whose owners have money enough not only to purchase such dogs but to care for them properly. It naturally follows that you must know something about diets for dogs, the quantity necessary for daily feedings for the various breeds, and the costs of the foods that go into the preparation of the meals. However, this information can be secured from any good book on the care of dogs.

The only investment required is a light delivery truck which can be purchased second hand for a few hundred dollars, and paid for on time. The rate being charged for medium-sized breeds such as Airedales and Chows is 22 cents for one diet and 20 cents for a second. On Friday each dog is served a fish diet for which a charge of 14 cents is made. Meals for the smaller breeds such as Boston and Cairn Terriers are priced at 14 cents; Pekingese, 10 cents, and Scotties, Sealyhams and Wire Haired Terriers, 18 cents. A specimen meal for the day for an Airedale consists of raw or cooked lean beef which is cubed or ground, string beans, or other greens and zwieback.

■ ■

How to Start a Postal Card Advertising Service

A DAM K. ANDERSON, an accountant in Salt Lake City, happened to come into a certain modernly equipped butcher shop when one of the partners was greeting a customer.

"How do you do, Mrs. Smith," he said. "I haven't seen you for more than six months. Have you moved away?"

"No," she answered. "I still live at the same place, but it was a couple of blocks closer to go down the street the opposite direction and I just got into the habit of buying my meats there."

"I do hope you will come back and trade with us now," the butcher continued. "We certainly appreciate your business."

"Think I will," she said. "Everything seems to look so nice here and you always took good care of our meat requirements. We're having company tomorrow evening and I'll telephone you what I will need. Give me a small sirloin for tonight."

Thus an old customer was easily won back. It reminded Anderson that just a month ago he received a postal card from a local clothier which had caused him to buy an Easter suit at a store which he had not patronized for several years. The card was very simple. A little bar of music was reproduced roughly across the top. It was a couple of measures from the verse, "Should Auld Acquaintance Be Forgot." Brief wording on the card said the management had missed his patronage, that his business was appreciated, and that they hoped he would be in to buy an Easter suit. If winning back old customers was that easy, he thought, why didn't more merchants take steps to go after old customers?

Mr. Anderson talked it over with the butcher and explained about the postal card idea. He found out that the butcher had recently counted the old accounts on the books which had showed no entries for the past couple of months and the total, nearly six hundred, startled him. Anderson left the shop determined to find out how those postals were produced.

The next day he learned there were several different duplicating and addressing machines for handling postal card advertising and that these small machines were available for as low as thirty-five dollars. A salesman selling one of the machines became interested in the idea and gave him several samples of postal cards produced on his machine for advertising purposes.

Anderson was satisfied that here was a means for making money during his forced vacation of one month without pay in a dull season. He took the sample cards to the butcher. The butcher ordered a series of three to be sent to old customers at monthly intervals. Then, he went to the druggist who had a larger list, and secured an order for cards to old customers who had stopped buying and another lot to present customers featuring some new special items. Next, a dry cleaner saw the possibilities of using the card idea. Soon Anderson had sold small jobs totaling over $2,500, to the upholstering shop, music store, paint store, lumber yard, and many other types of merchants and small manufacturing plants all around the city. He paid for the machine the first two weeks. His ink and supplies amounted to comparatively little. His biggest cost was the postal cards costing a cent each at the post office, which, for the period, totaled less than $9.50. He was quick to offer ideas to the merchants and for that reason got a little higher price for the work which included writing up the cards for each case. The first month showed a nice profit; the second month with the aid of his son, who had just graduated from high school, he handled the remaining orders that had been obtained. By the time the third month had rolled around the total profit was sufficient to buy larger equipment and to set up his son in a small business.

■ ■

Bringing the Show to the Audience

WHEN the carnival to which he was attached disbanded, J. E. Cox found himself in a small town in Georgia. Forced to remain there for several days, he studied this town carefully. Its population was less than one hundred. It had no entertainment facilities. It was drab and colorless, yet as he looked it over, Cox hit upon an idea that since has brought him profits enough to cause the mouth of any big city theater man to water. Cox's idea was patterned after that which brought prosperity to owners of showboats in the old river days. He brought a show to people in the hinterland, miles from the railroads. But he didn't bring a troupe of players. He brought talking motion pictures instead.

He went down to Atlanta and bought a portable sound projecting unit, dipping into an old-fashioned money bag for the $300 to pay for it, and put the unit in his second-hand truck. With the equipment, he was given a portable screen and a 1,000-foot film, entitled the "Battle," which he used when he put on his first show the following night in a town one hundred miles from Atlanta. He rented a schoolroom for this first performance and invited the town to attend. They turned out in force, and many in this audience were listening to a talkie for the first time. He traveled to the next town the day following, and again rented a schoolroom, crowding in 175 customers to each of two performances. Cox charged an admission fee of 15 cents in both towns, and decided to maintain that fee as a fixed policy. At the end of the first week his profits were $104.50, so he decided to get a better film to show in a town of 1,600 population on his schedule for the following Saturday. This new film featuring a musical comedy was ordered shipped to that town and was there when he arrived. There was a larger attendance in this town than in the others. People came in from the hills to see it and he stayed there for four days. This proved so profitable that he abandoned one-night stands, and now makes two stops weekly. Before leaving one small town, he makes an early morning trip to the next town on his schedule, stopping along the way to post announcements on trees, fences, and barns telling where his next show will be given, thus assuring himself of a good audience. His average weekly expenses have been running about $62.00 and his profits generally a little better than $150.00 a week—a tidy little income.

Cox's idea may profitably be carried out in many parts of the country, where the towns and villages are some distance removed from railroads and cities. There are even communities of 2,000 population which do not have a motion picture theater. Cox does not rent first or second run films, but buys old numbers and uses them over and over again at a small cost for each performance.

Trucking Fruit from Florida

A TRUCK farmer living near Menominee, Michigan, found the going rather hard during the depression, and in trying to find ways and means of bolstering up the family income, hit upon the idea of trucking fruit. The truck he had been using to transport his garden produce was now standing idle most of the time. His eldest son was also idle, having been unable to find any work since he had finished high school. The truck and the boy were accordingly dispatched to Florida to buy citrus fruits, and when the truck returned loaded with fruit, he sold out all of it within a few days.

Until now, tropical fruits had been high in Menominee. Now that he could sell them a little cheaper, the public bought him out each time the truck returned from a trip. Before long he had four trucks running between Florida and Menominee to supply the demand for fresh fruits. In addition, he opened four stores to handle the produce brought in by his trucks. Two of these stores are in Menominee, and two in Marinette, Wisconsin, which is just across the river. His market, which takes in these two towns and the surrounding territory, includes about 35,000 population.

■ ■

How Money Can Be Made in Cemeteries

D URING an automobile trip from his home in Kansas City to a near-by town, Arthur T. Ruggles noticed several run-down cemeteries. "Here," thought Ruggles, "is an opportunity to make some money." So he went to see the key man on the board who had charge of one of the cemeteries.

This man was frank to admit the cemetery was in sad need of having the edges of the drives cleaned up, removing the ruts from the roadways, removing the brush from various spots where lots were unsold, leveling the land in locations where it was rough, planting grass seed, and similar work which the keeper was unable to do. He said it was difficult to keep lot owners satisfied and to sell additional lots with the cemetery in such a condition.

Then the real obstacle came to light. There is always some obstacle to be hurdled. The board member said they just did not have the money to get this extra work done. But Mr. Ruggles was not to be stopped by this hurdle. This alibi about not having the money is an ancient one. He thought for a moment. Then an idea came to him. He told the board member that he might take cemetery lots in payment for the job. The board member jumped at the opportunity.

So a deal was made. The arrangement was that Ruggles was to receive cemetery lots valued at $2,000 for the work specified. He hired a couple of gardeners to help him do the work. In the meantime, he employed a salesman on a commission arrangement to help him sell the lots.

Mr. Ruggles knew that the psychological time to sell the lots was when the work was progressing on the improvements. Before the job was finished, the lots had been sold. The labor and materials for the job actually came to less than $500. The salesman's commissions totaled $500. This left Ruggles with an actual profit of about $1,000 on the deal.

It was a deal that made everyone concerned satisfied and happy. Mr. Ruggles then started a more ambitious plan to make the same deal with cemetery companies in other localities, with the result that he is now at the head of a thriving and prosperous business, netting him several thousand dollars a year.

■ ■

Turning Ashes into Gold

JOHN TOWNS, assayer, owner of the Maryland Smelting & Refining Company, San Antonio, Texas, struck gold right in the heart of the city!

It was like this: One day, while Mr. Towns chanced to be watching the janitor of a local building, which housed a number of dentists, carting away ashes from the building's incinerator, a sudden idea came to him. "Give me a sample of those ashes," he remarked. He took the ashes to his office and assayed them. He discovered that the sample contained enough gold to average $140 worth of gold to the ton!

So his hunch was right. Dentists work with gold; filing, scraping and molding it. Naturally, tiny particles of gold fell to the floor and were swept up, finally ending up in the ashes of the incinerator. He contracted to buy the sweepings from this building.

Thus began one of America's strangest businesses, and one of the most profitable in consideration of the investment required. Beginning in San Antonio, Mr. Towns rapidly expanded his purchases. He bought sweepings from medical office buildings in Dallas, Fort Worth and Houston, one Dallas building's sweepings assaying $700 worth of gold to the ton.

Today Mr. Towns buys sweepings from medical office buildings in thirty different states. He receives about ten tons of ashes and sweepings per month, with the assay running all the way from a little better than $100 to

$2,000 per ton. Yet the famed Juneau gold mine of Alaska is being operated successfully with an assay of only fifty cents worth of gold per ton.

Naturally, this is a specialized business, requiring special skill and knowledge. Not everyone could do it, of course. It does show, however, the buried opportunities that lie all about you, if you will keep your eyes and mind open for them!

■ ■

A Club Truck Garden

A TRUCK farmer in New York State had been raising garden truck for several years and peddling it house to house. For some time he had been dissatisfied with the small returns on his labor but he didn't seem to be able to find a way out of his difficulties. One evening as he stood looking out over his farm pondering how his customers and his crops could be brought together in a more lucrative manner, he hit upon the idea of organizing a group of people and planting their gardens for them. His family at first thought the idea impossible, but he went ahead with building up his club and soon he had organized a group of one hundred members.

Each member may select the vegetables he wants—peas, sweet corn, carrots, radishes, lettuce, and other vegetables—and the truck farmer plants them on his place. The charge for planting, cultivating and fertilizing the vegetables is $1.00 a row. The members have the pleasure of driving out to the farm whenever they wish to select and gather their own vegetables. Nine times out of ten, when they depart with their cars filled with vegetables, they have some honey, butter, or eggs packed away in the car, too. The farmer is clever enough not only to get them to come to him for their vegetables, but while they are on the spot, he sells them some of the products from which he gets a good cash income.

■ ■

Planning "Little Dinners" for Restaurants

HELEN EWING, living in the city of Chicago, was just one of the many thousands of women rated as good cooks. Not long ago she became acquainted with the wife of a restaurant owner, who one day remarked about the difference in home and restaurant cooking. "If someone could only get my husband to make up a more varied menu," said this friend, "he would probably be able to keep his customers. So many people stop coming because they say that the menu is monotonous." Later, upon hearing about a successful restaurant operator in California, who attributed his success to the great variety of dishes he served, Miss Ewing decided to look into the subject of menus.

"After going around to many restaurants and examining the menus, I discovered that restaurant men wanted to be relieved from making up their own menus," stated Miss Ewing. "I also found that they needed variety in their menus—something fresh and different daily which would revive interest in their dinners. At the same time it occurred to me that the secret of keeping flavor and appeal in food was to cook it in smaller quantities. This is the only way that chefs can get that 'home-cooking' flavor. So I made up what I call a series of little dinners and submitted them to several restaurant proprietors. They considered them and then agreed to use them. That's how I got started on my present career."

Miss Ewing opened an office in a Chicago "Loop" office building and began selling little luncheon menus to Chicago restaurant proprietors. She called this unusual business a "Planning Service," and charged a flat rate of $5.00 a month for it. In less than a year, she secured subscriptions to this service from nearly two hundred restaurants, and her profits began to add up to a tidy sum. She did what thousands of women have the ability and qualifications to do: planned simple, inexpensive meals. A similar service might be profitably started in other cities, inasmuch as there are thousands of small restaurant proprietors who lack the imagination to plan a well-balanced and varied menu themselves. In making up the menu for a small luncheon which retails say, for 25 or 30 cents, it is well to bear in mind that the restaurant must secure a minimum of twice the retail cost of each food item served, in order to make a profit. Thus a 25-cent meal should cost the restaurant not more than 12½ cents. Recipes showing the proper amount of each food offered should be submitted daily with this service, the same recipes being sent to each chef using them. It is not necessary to invest much money in a service of this nature. Simply prepare the first menu, have it mimeographed, and mail copies to each subscriber. In preparing these menus always keep in mind the seasonal changes in foods.

■ ■

A "Fix-lt" Shop on Wheels

FOR fifty years, George Burley, of Des Moines, Iowa, who is now seventy-seven years old, has made a good living fixing things that others can't. His slogan is "If Burley can't fix it, throw it away." In his little shop which is at the back of his home he repairs furniture, picture frames, replaces broken glass in mirrors or pictures, re-silvers mirrors, paints old furniture with great skill, mends china, repairs broken dolls, re-canes broken seats or backs of chairs, restores the finish on old furniture, polishes silver and brass, cuts glass to any required size, repairs enameled signs, repairs pottery, cleans leather saddles and other leather goods, cleans rust from metal objects and instruments, cleans and mends ivory objects, sharpens knives and lawn mower blades, and repairs many other things the average person lacks skill to handle.

People have come to have perfect confidence in him and will entrust some of their most prized possessions to his skillful hands. It has taken time, of course, to build up this confidence and its resulting list of steady customers. He secured the needed formulas for use in this work by reference to standard books in the field such as *Henley's Twentieth Century Book of Recipes, Formulas & Processes*. Additional money is made by the preparation and sale to customers of an excellent furniture polish. In preparing this polish he did not try to compete with any of the cheaper polishes on the market, but made a high-priced product which brings him a good profit on each bottle.

Most of his work is done in his own shop where he has the proper equipment and tools to handle almost any kind of repair job. However, in some cases the work is of such a nature it has to be handled in the customer's home.

In Philadelphia the "fix-it" business has been developed by one man to a point where he requires a fleet of Ford trucks to "patrol" the city. If a housewife has a leaky faucet, or her electric iron goes on the "fritz," instead of sending for a plumber or an electrician who would probably charge two or three dollars to fix it, she calls "Mr. Fix-It." Within an hour the "Fix-It" truck rolls up to the door and in a few minutes the repair has been made. The success of this venture lies in the fact that each truck carries a complete assortment of repair parts for fixing almost anything that can go wrong in a house, and using the block system to speed up service. Truck drivers are required to keep in telephone communication with a "dispatcher" at headquarters. As each call comes in, it is put on file, and when the driver telephones he is given a list of all calls on file in his district. This makes it possible to give rapid-fire service and low prices to the customer. Since the needed repairs and tools are in the truck, and not in some plumber's or electrician's shop a mile or more away, the usual excessive charge for going back after tools and repair parts is avoided.

There is no reason why there should not be a "Fix-It" truck in every city. All that is needed to start such a business is some knowledge of home appliances and equipment, about $50 for an initial stock of miscellaneous repair parts, a few special tools such as a reamer for "seating" faucet valves, and a light truck which can be converted into a "Fix-It" shop on wheels.

■ ■

Starting an Art Academy on a "Shoestring"

HAVE you considered that in these days of leisure one of the surest ways to make money is to help people to use their leisure time to improve their minds? Americans are fast becoming "art conscious." Business men are organizing art clubs, and women, released from housekeeping drudgery by the advent of electrical appliances, are going in for music, drama and the other arts. Young people just out of school, finding jobs scarce, are studying drawing and design. All of which spells opportunity for those who know something about art. Best of all you can start an art school with no money whatever.

Eleanor Verande had no money at all when she decided to start the New York Academy of Arts. So she went to the owner of an office building and offered a course of instruction in art for his daughter in exchange for office rent. Then she discovered that she needed a stenographer and a clerk, so she arranged instruction in art and music for stenographic work.

A piano, two large mirrors, easels and a model stand were given to her by a woman in exchange for her daughter's painting lessons and the new art academy was soon on its way. The day it opened, the energetic Miss Verande enrolled several students, and soon had sufficient money to carry her along.

"I taught a carpenter how to dance in exchange for a neat job of installing partitions, and because a Polish cook wanted her daughter to be a dancer, I arranged to give lessons which were paid by supplying the faculty with meals," declared Miss Verande. "There wasn't a great deal of money in the first few months, but trading around as I did, enabled me to get by. About a hundred pupils were enrolled, most of them working out their tuition in one way or other, but a few paid real money. I started this school because I was tired of the stage, and though I had no money, I was determined to start anyway."

This determined little lady at fifteen was giving imitations of Spinelli, Mistingette, and Yvonne Printempts in Paris night clubs. At sixteen she was premiere danseuse of the Lyon Opera. She danced in Ziegfeld's "Three Musketeers," appeared in movies as a double for Vilma Banky, and studied dancing with Tarasoff, Kobeleff and Fokine. With this background, Eleanor was a competent instructress in art, and felt at the time, she needed nothing but a chance to start.

Young and ambitious people who are determined to do things, may find a way of getting started by applying the barter principle as Miss Verande applied it. If you have no money, start in a business for which you are qualified, using the barter-and-trade idea for capital.

■ ■

Catering to School Children

WHEN Mrs. Frank Hartman, who lived in a Chicago suburb, found it difficult to keep the family going comfortably on its diminished income she hit upon the idea of serving luncheons and dinners to school children. Once she had decided upon the plan it didn't take long for the news to get around the neighborhood. Her little girl of nine told the school children and Mrs. Hartman told her neighbors, friends, members of her church and club. She found getting luncheon for a group of youngsters was a lot of fun. The children said that the luncheons were like parties and they eagerly looked forward to a day that mother would be going to a bridge luncheon or into Chicago or visiting elsewhere so that they could have luncheon at Mrs. Hartman's with the other youngsters.

The fact that they were served nourishing food was a big point in favor of having the children eat at Mrs. Hartman's. Instead of the youngsters buying fifteen cents worth of candy and a ham sandwich or a bowl of soup at some school store, they paid their twenty-five cents for a well-balanced meal. Luncheons consisted of milk or cocoa, bread in some form, butter, fruit for dessert, homemade cookies or cake and a main course. In winter the main course was a hot dish such as baked eggs, baked rice with little pieces of meat in it, or a baked tomato stuffed with rice or meat. In summer she served a vegetable salad with graham bread, or a scooped out tomato filled with cottage cheese, or some other cool dish. The meals were served on a long refectory table and each dish was daintily prepared and served. Whenever possible, she served dishes in fancy forms such as individual molds of jello, individual iced cakes, cookies cut in fancy shapes, etc. These little touches did not mean any more expense but they did entail more work. However, it was such attention to detail that brought the same children back again and again. Whenever possible she catered to a child's particular liking for some one food, serving it in turn with some other dish that the other children liked. Her own little girl being at the table made the luncheon group seem like one big family.

Her figures on a meal run about fifteen cents for dessert, twelve to fifteen cents for milk, eight cents for a loaf of bread, twenty cents for the main course and about five or six cents for butter. Adding about ten cents to this amount for gas consumed, the cost of each meal runs around seventy or eighty cents. A group of ten at 25 cents each thus leaves a profit of about $1.50 to $1.75 and the work at the most takes only two hours. As she charges 50 cents for dinner, two or three little guests pay for the family dinner and leave a little for profit. Mr. Hartman is a kindly, genial man who enjoys having children around and he generally walks home with them after dinner to see that they reach there safely. If the mothers want them to stay for the entire evening until called for, Mrs. Hartman charges 50 cents additional for each child.

At one time she made a list of the names of children's parents and had her sister type each mother a letter in which she described the various menus served the children. She also emphasized the fact that the best ingredients were used in cooking and that the children were served only foods suitable for young, growing people. A few of these letters were also sent to others she thought might be prospects and resulted in a number of new faces around her luncheon table.

■ ■

"Nickel-in-the-Slot" Pool Tables

COIN-OPERATED machines have become a craze in this country. Marvin Owens, for instance, bought three tables, placed them in busy taverns and is well on the way to making his $1,000. These tables require no attention. They are standard, official billiard tables upon which a regulation pool game may be played. You simply drop a nickel in the slot, and are then ready to play a full game of pool. Counters, cues, chalk, and other necessary equipment are furnished with the table.

"I thought when I first saw the illustration of this table that it was another one of those pool table toys," Mr. Owens told our editor. "But investigation quickly dispelled this idea. The table is a regulation table on which you 'shoot' a regulation game. The beauty of it is that one or more persons can play for the same price. Many men have an idea they're pool sharks and, of course, when they see the pool table, they want to prove their skill. The result is a good play wherever a table is set up—especially in taverns.

"I started with three tables. Today I have ten in operation, and collect once every two weeks. The tables cost me seventy dollars each, and pay me a profit of about fourteen dollars weekly. I give the tavern owner a commission of 25 per cent. The novelty of a coin-operated pool game appeals to almost every man who has ever handled a cue. Even people who have not played a game of pool in years become enthusiasts. More play is given the coin-operated table, therefore, than a regular pool table. The one drawback to continued operation of these tables is that when the tavern owner sees how good a play he gets, he wants to buy the table outright. This has happened several times, and while I haven't as yet sold the tables, I'm figuring on letting the tavern owners have them since the re-sale price of $125 offers a good profit on each table."

Owens feels there is never a good reason for turning down profit. He declares his future policy will be to take the profit from operating the machines as long as possible, and then to sell them to the taverns, insuring himself of a two-way profit on his money. The idea is worth considering, if you want to make money operating this type of coin machine. There are many good locations in all parts of the country where this table ought to pay since no "gambling" objection may be raised to the machine.

■ ■

Turning a Natural Flair to Profit

A PRINCIPLE of business success too often overlooked is striving to do some one thing better than anybody else is doing it. This idea is well expressed in that old saw about the man who can build a better mouse-trap being sought out, however far he may be from the beaten path. Take guns, for instance. You would hardly think of "gun doctoring" as being a business that would make money. Guns are such incidental things. Yet Jack Roske, of San Francisco, has found it highly profitable.

In 1927 while still in high school, Jack Roske used to drop in on a gun-smith because he was curious about firearms. Some of his questions were too deep for the gunsmith (he was an artisan not an oracle) but he was deeply impressed. The boy was a "natural"! He let Jack help him after school, teaching him many things, and after graduation took him in as an apprentice and kept him until the business failed.

Roske then went to punching cattle, but his interest in firearms never flagged and he continued studying about guns past and present. There are few really authoritative books on the subject of firearms and these, having been printed in limited editions numbering a thousand or less, come high. Some cost five dollars, some twenty-five, but the gun student gladly sacrificed many pleasures in order to possess these books. He joined the

National Rifle Association and read magazines, catalogs—anything he could find about guns. Eventually he was able to look at any gun and tell you all about it, which means something when you consider that there are approximately 90,000 types, not counting minor variations.

When Jack returned to San Francisco, his gunsmith friend was back in business but could give him only part-time work. Anyway, repairing ordinary guns was no kind of job for one with his highly specialized capabilities. His talent had been molded into an art. But where could he make his services valuable?

Then came the proof that an artist in any line will inevitably find his right place. Two years ago there opened in San Francisco, a unique establishment known as the Far West Hobby Shop—a collector's Mecca. China, pioneer relics, costume books, and hundreds of things rare and curious are found there. Its most noteworthy collection, however, is firearms. The shop has the largest stock of guns on the Pacific Coast—over six hundred and principally collectors' items. There are little Derringers, like the one used to assassinate Lincoln, big 1836 Pattersons, and the first Colt model; there are ornate French dueling pistols in elaborate hand-carved cases, and plain, solid, purely American rifles such as Daniel Boone used to fight off the Indians.

The need was for a gun expert thoroughly familiar with the history and operation of firearms—one who could put into condition old models bought by the shop and tell visitors all about the various guns in stock. A man, in short, who could take charge of the firearms from the time they entered the shop until they went out. It is a difficult post but Jack Roske fills it to perfection. Being young, handsome and as physically fit as a Zane Grey hero is one more point in his favor.

His native talent, combined with his knowledge acquired through years of study and experience, gives him a sixth sense which enables him to take an ancient, incomplete model to pieces, fabricate the missing parts, and reassemble the whole with no guide or precedent.

He says it's like learning shorthand. "You keep on working and practicing until it becomes second nature." His four years of mechanical drawing and two years of woodworking crafts have, no doubt, helped him considerably.

■ ■

How to Get the Doctor

IF YOU will look in the classified section of your local telephone directory, you will probably see at least one "Telephone Secretarial Service" listed. These telephone services have developed during the last few years because of the demand by doctors and other professional men and women for a telephone arrangement which automatically takes incoming calls when the subscriber is out of his office.

For instance, if you should call Dr. Brown and he is out on an "emergency call" there may be no way to get in touch with him unless his family can manage to handle calls for him. However, if he has subscribed to a telephone secretarial service the call is automatically relayed to the office of the service and relayed to the doctor or given to him when he makes his check-up. Doctors may arrange to call the Service at certain intervals during the day to pick up incoming calls or they may arrange for a relay of calls during the day.

While the service is extensively used by doctors, other professional men and women or those in small shops have found the service valuable. Frequently the business of a contractor, an interior decorator, or a commercial photographer does not warrant a full-time secretary. By making use of a telephone service, he can leave his office or shop on business and know that any important calls coming in will be handled.

A number of people have started such a service in a small way and built it up to where it makes an excellent income. The Telephone Answering Service of New York City, for instance, now has about eleven branches in addition to the general office. This Service also has arrangements in other large cities whereby the same name is used for directory listing in order to facilitate the use of the service.

A number of young women are operating a telephone secretarial service from their own homes. Usually when the service is operated on a small scale, all the subscribers to it are located in one building. For instance, you may be able to secure 30 to 50 doctors in a near-by building as subscribers to your service.

The service for subscribers varies in accordance with the need for it. One man may want only a noon-hour service, another a day service, and another a 24-hour service. There are other variations, of course. Holidays and Sundays may or may not be included, according to the subscriber's requirements. In addition to handling incoming calls, the service may also relay calls to subscribers. Charges are based upon the type of service required.

Even the physically handicapped can find some measure of financial independence in this work. A young woman living in Marion, Indiana, who has been an invalid for a number of years makes her living by operating a physicians' telephone service from her home. Although she can get about only by means of a wheel chair, and is often confined to her bed, this courageous young woman manages a business of her own that any young person would be proud to own. She has arranged with the doctors of her community to keep her informed of their whereabouts and their patients may call her at any hour.

Arrangements can be made with the local telephone company to rent the necessary equipment. In view of the fact that the company invests considerable money in an undertaking of this sort, it must be assured as to the character and financial integrity of the lessee. Building up a service of this sort requires little but a sense of responsibility, initiative, and a willingness to work. If there is no such telephone service in your town, talk it over with the local telephone manager. Such a service may be just what your town needs and, incidentally, the answer to your problem of what to do to make some money.

■ ■

Specializing in Dog Sketches

THE name Diana Thorne immediately calls up a picture of a most successful artist. Yet Miss Thorne had a tremendously difficult time just earning enough to keep body and soul together until she found the way to capitalize her skill. Like many another person with a talent, many a man or woman with a clever business idea, she lacked the right slant on her work. She failed to specialize; she made no effort to stand out from the crowd.

Miss Thorne had all the advantages of study in Germany and England. But in London, when nineteen years old (this was at the beginning of the war), she sold and mended typewriters, worked as a reporter, as a typist, as a scenario writer—anything to make some sort of living. She could find no demand for her sketches and almost despaired of getting ahead. When she returned to New York, she turned to typing to earn a living for herself and younger sister and brother. She admits that today she might still be struggling along except for a dog. She found him in a pet shop, and while his antecedents were probably not to be checked too carefully, he made a marvelous model. She was amused by his puppy antics, the clumsiness of his pudgy body and the frequent expressions of bewilderment at the strange world about him. She sketched him and sketched him, and in 1926 Diana Thorne sold her first dog picture—a young girl skating at breakneck speed behind a terrier. She called it "Rollin' Home"—and it clicked. Just putting an appealing little pup in a picture made the difference between "sold" and "no sale."

She found that nine out of ten people like dogs—especially puppies. A picture of a puppy just "gets them." So with pencil and brush she pictured them in every conceivable mood, every sort of pose. The more Diana Thorne sketched dogs the better she sketched them. People stopped to look at her sketches because the puppies were appealing. Then they took a second look for these puppies were real dogs. Diana Thorne had made a hit with the great mass of dog lovers. Before long, dog owners were requesting her to do sketches of their own dogs. Today, pedigreed pets are brought to her from all over the world to have their portraits done. She has become a dog illustrator of renown both here and in Europe. You look at the pictures of her Scotties and think they are the best she has done. Then you see the Spaniels, and you think they are the most cunning. Yet the Boston Terriers may intrigue you even more. Diana Thorne has "arrived."

If you feel that you cannot make a success of the one good talent you possess, if your business for some reason does not succeed, look around for an idea that will put your work above that of your competitors. If you make things, there is a way to make them more attractive to the buyer; if you sell things, you can change your method of selling so it will mean the difference between success and failure. Whatever you do, you can find some new slant that will open up a market for you.

■ ■

A New Slant on the "Grab Bag" Idea

"**H**ERE is my recipe for making $1,000," said Chester Ryan. "Get some 'Gold Diggers.' This novelty machine which looks like a small traveling crane or excavator, operates for a penny or a nickel. Five or six dollars' worth of novelty merchandise, together with a quantity of candy, is placed in it and the little excavator picks out the candy or a novelty, depending upon your luck. The novelties include cameras, fancy cigarette lighters, wrist watches, fountain pens, celluloid dice and similar items. These novelties may be redeemed by the store owner or retained by the lucky player as desired. I buy good-looking cameras for three dollars a dozen, cigarette lighters for three-sixty a dozen, and fountain pens for twenty-nine cents. I can get cheaper articles but they do not have the looks. This is an important factor in your success, for the secret of getting people to 'go for' your cameras, lighters, watches, etc., is the appearance of quality in these items. They must look good and they must look easy for the 'digger' to pick up.

"While the retail selling price of any article in the case may be only a dollar or two, the fun of taking a chance seems to be sufficient to get most players to take a few chances. The machine needs little servicing and always works. When I started using them, however, I made the mistake of thinking I could get by with shoddy merchandise. I didn't know much about picking the best locations either.

"Realizing that one good location is worth ten poor ones, I studied ways of selecting choice spots. I learned quickly that the fellow who wants to make big money has to study locations as scientifically as the chain stores. He must check the number of persons entering a drug store, barber shop, cigar store, candy store or delicatessen. He should know just about when the big crowd comes in and if there ever is a big crowd. He will find that if a crowd hangs around a place for an hour and then moves on with practically no more patronage coming in that night, there is no chance of success with this machine. At best, a machine in such a place will take in only about ten dollars a week. A tavern, cafe, drug store, or candy store on a good neighborhood corner in any city, however, has people coming in and out all afternoon and evening. If more than five people are in the store all the time, you can bet that your average play on the excavator is going to be pretty good. A machine placed in a location of that kind will easily 'kick out' a profit of twenty-five or thirty dollars a week.

"I pay my store owners a 35 per cent commission on the amount in the cash box, less redemption pay-off. That's a liberal split, but then I have my machines in good spots and it's worth the difference. In one drug store where I placed a machine a year ago, the play runs twenty-nine dollars a day. It's a busy place all day long. A number of doctors drop in there off and on, and they never go out without putting from fifty cents to a dollar in the machine. Because of the heavy play in this place, I have to drop around every three or four days and put in new merchandise.

"One reason why the 'gold digger' is so popular is because of the average man's belief he can beat these machines. As a matter of fact no machine is made to be beaten. It's made to pay a profit, and always does. But the belief is strong enough to cause people to play them over and over again. They don't care what they win. Their objective is to beat the game. A few do beat it. But a majority don't. All play it for the fun of playing and for the sport of winning. That's the spirit that animates every player."

During his first five months operating these machines, Ryan's profit amounted to well over a thousand dollars. He bought the machines outright, paying eighty-nine dollars for each one. If you intend operating a machine of this kind, it might be well to start with one or more second-hand machines, which may be picked up at small cost. There is real money to be made in this enterprise.

Service to Mothers Becomes a Business

OVER two million babies are born in this country every year. That means a market for all sorts of clothing, equipment, toys, furniture, and other things. It also means a sizable market for equipment, clothing and supplies for the mothers. It remained for a woman to think up a service that would appeal to the majority of these two million mothers. She knew that they would like to find someone who would relieve them of the incessant laundry work connected with the baby's first year. She talked the idea over with her husband, Albert Lau. He was skeptical at first, but decided to give it a trial. The Dy-Dee Wash, Inc., Chicago, was the result.

The service appeals to practically every woman with a tiny baby. The company is developed somewhat on the towel supply service idea. It supplies the babies' napkins, calls for the soiled laundry and leaves the clean "necessaries." Naturally a business such as this must be built on the basis of absolute cleanliness and sanitation. A trip through the plant of the Dy-Dee Wash proves beyond a doubt that these two requisites are not just slogans, but absolute facts. So successfully has this idea taken hold that over a dozen branches of the Dy-Dee Wash are now in operation. These are not branches in the real meaning of the term as each plant is independent of the parent plant. The operators of the branches merely pay for the privilege of using the Dy-Dee license.

This money-making business is another proof that where there is a genuine need for a service in a community, the man or woman who undertakes to provide that service economically and efficiently will soon be on his way toward making his first thousand dollars and many more thousands.

■ ■

Put a Billiard Table in a Store

WHEN a tenant operating a cigar store in a building owned by H. L. Martin, Columbus, Ohio, renewed his lease for only one-fourth of the store, Martin was worried. It was almost impossible to get store tenants at that time. No one seemed willing to rent the rear of a store, and Martin soon gave up hope of finding a tenant. Then he considered the possibility of profitably using the space himself.

A study of the cigar store's operations revealed that the younger men were inclined to remain in the store where they could meet and talk with friends late afternoons and evenings. After four o'clock each afternoon there were always several men grouped about the cigar stand, who seemed to have nothing much to do. Catering to these men, reasoned Martin, providing them with wholesome amusement that would help his tenant's cigar sales, would be profitable.

There was space in the store for two or three pocket billiard tables. There were enough men in the store most of the time to justify expectation of a fair play on the tables. So Martin decided to put in two tables. His tenant liked the idea, appreciating that the more people who entered the store, the more cigars and cigarettes he would sell. Tables and equipment were secured, and Martin opened the billiard room. He charged five cents a cue, or rented the tables to players at fifty cents an hour. Few rented the table by the hour, however. Two, three or four men usually played and paid for each game when they finished. The play on the tables was heaviest in the afternoons and evenings, and his profit for the first month was one hundred and fifty-six dollars.

Martin's total investment in tables and equipment was $198. The tables, bought from the manufacturer, had been reconditioned and were in good playing condition when he placed them in his store. He bought them on deferred payments, so that very little cash investment was necessary.

Opportunities for opening pocket billiard rooms exist in many cities, and reconditioned equipment may be picked up from manufacturers everywhere. Store space in good locations is readily obtainable. By making arrangements with a barber or cigar dealer for use of space in barber shop or store, your rent is reduced and profit assured.

In time, as your business prospers, and you have accumulated a few thousand dollars in profits from it, you can spread out into a store of your own, with more tables. It is a business that requires no special training, and does not tie you down. It offers many opportunities for money-making "side lines."

A Coca-Cola cooler in the corner, for instance, will make almost enough to pay the rent, and a few pin games or similar attractions are sure-fire money-makers. In these days of leisure there is a real opportunity to start a business which offers wholesome recreational facilities to the people in the community. It's almost a "natural." There are few easier ways to make $1,000.

■ ■

A Profitable Auto Travel Business

SOME years ago, A. A. Preciado planned to make a trip to the West Coast by automobile. In order to reduce his expenses and, at the same time, make the trip more pleasant, he advertised for a traveling companion on the share-the-expense basis. His advertisement in the newspaper brought over a hundred replies and a similar advertisement inserted when he was ready to make his return trip brought twice as many replies. When he reached home he realized there was an opportunity for a business catering to tourists, so he opened a travel agency which he called the "Auto Travel Bureau."

Most of the "traveling companions" on his list are students, summer-school teachers, college professors, and business girls. However, even doctors, lawyers and movie stars have made trips as extra passengers through the Bureau. "Women especially hate to go on long trips alone," he remarked, "and part of my job is to locate responsible young college men to drive their cars for them."

Because he filled a long-felt need and because of good business management the business grew and prospered. Today, Mr. Preciado has several assistants and representatives in various key cities. He also has many competitors, but he lays claim to having been the first in the field. His cars now go all over the country, of course, but there is a certain demand for transportation to such cities as San Francisco, Chicago, St. Louis, etc., which has made it possible for him to arrange for regular transportation to such points. All rates are figured on a mileage basis—the greater the distance, the greater the cost. The Bureau gets a standard commission from the extra passenger, the balance going to the car owner.

■ ■

A New Slant Made This Circulating Library a Success

WHEN J. J. and R. M. Sullivan, of Chicago, investigated the circulating library business they discovered larger profits were in store for the library which delivered its books regularly to readers, rather than waited for readers to drop in for books when they felt inclined. Making no provision for drop-in business they rented room space only in an office building on the north side of town, and stocked a few volumes of standard authors. With a dozen of these volumes in a shopping sack each began making the rounds of the large office buildings on Michigan Avenue and in the central business district of the city. Secretaries, stenographers and clerks were, for the most part, the clientele at which they aimed. When a secretary on whom they called was not interested in the standard author they offered, one of the Sullivan brothers would inquire her taste in books and ask what book she would like him to bring her the following week.

Making up their lists in this way from the preferences and requests of the office people on whom they called, they eventually built up a library of several thousand volumes and a clientele of twenty-eight hundred customers. The charge for membership in this perambulating library was one dollar and the rental fifty cents per week on books costing three dollars and over, thirty-five cents on books from two dollars and a half to three dollars, and twenty-five cents per week on books under two dollars and a half. The Sullivan brothers each had regular days for calling on specified buildings, and they made the rounds of their entire clientele once a week.

In order not to overload themselves unnecessarily with books in their daily rounds, each night preceding their morning call, they went over the file cards of the clients on whom they would call the following day, noting the books they had already read and making a selection from their new stock which would suit their customers' tastes. If, for instance, a client had started to read *Jalna* or *The Whiteoaks of Jalna*, he was sure to want *Finch's Fortune* next and then *The Master of Jalna*, also by the same author. A client who liked Hugh Walpole would be glad to get *Vanessa*; and a client who liked William Faulkner would probably like Erskine Caldwell.

When *Well of Loneliness* was published, the brothers made a killing, buying four hundred copies of this book, charging fifty cents per week rental and allowing members to hold it for one week only. For two years the four hundred volumes were in constant circulation. Another big renter was Mrs. Mitchell's *Gone with the Wind*. Four hundred copies of this book were bought and kept in steady circulation.

Books like these bring in tidy profits to the Sullivans. They guessed wrong, however, on *Ulysses* and, in this case, were overloaded with a book the public did not want. They buy their books wholesale for 30 per cent off, or from the publishers for 40 per cent off. This latter arrangement seldom represents any saving, however, because of the cost of expressage.

When books are finished as renters and stop moving entirely, they are sold to hospitals or other institutions and also to second-hand bookstores.

Getting personally acquainted with their clientele, knowing their tastes, and having the patience and the time to come back if a girl is busy taking dictation when they call (so that she can always depend upon the arrival of her new book and the collection of her old one) have been chiefly responsible for the many steady and well-satisfied customers which these two Sullivans have accumulated. A satisfied customer in any business is the best advertising it can have.

A Clipping Service for Artists

WHILE Carl Jackson was selling magazine subscriptions to artists and their friends, he learned that they frequently were at a loss for authentic illustrations to follow in making drawings. In the larger cities, the public libraries have files of illustrations but it takes a great deal of valuable time to locate what is needed—and time to an artist is money. So he started a clipping service for artists. During the past two years, he has made better than fifteen hundred a year at practically no expense from this enterprise.

"The good artist, the leader in the field, uses my service as much as the poor man who can't afford to hire models," Jackson pointed out. "Here in Chicago several hundred men and women make their living from art work of one kind or another. They can't buy all the magazines that are published (especially the higher priced foreign publications) because it would take every cent they earn to do it. And they might never get an idea out of the publications they do buy. But there is art work in every magazine. I clip the well-drawn illustrations from a group of picked magazines and index them. I am able to supply almost any type of illustration that an artist wants whenever he wants it, for making a sketch. For example, an artist is told to make a drawing that calls for an archer of the Robin Hood period. He could make the long trip to the library, secure the pictures needed and make several sketches. Instead of wasting so much time, he calls me on the phone. I go to my file, pick out two or three, and send them to him. My fee is three dollars.

"You see forty-seven steel filing cabinets here. I started with one, and about three dozen magazines, which I had been carrying as samples when I was with the magazine subscription agency. I clipped every illustration and told a few artists about it. They had some special work such as illustrating a school textbook or making a drawing of old Mexico for a magazine and they needed certain kinds of clippings. I happened to have them. The fees I got out of the illustrations from magazines enabled me to buy other magazines. I picked some up for a song at second-hand book stores and I subscribed to the leading periodicals. One artist told another, and it wasn't long before I was doing a highly profitable business. Then I wrote a letter to several film companies, and explained the type of service I was offering artists, and mentioned that some of them had requested photographs of film stars to be used for magazine purposes. I was given a break by two studios, with the understanding that under no circumstances were the photographs sent me to be used for advertising in any way. The movie people have a remarkable facility for artistically posing their subjects and the artists were hungry for those photographs. They bought them outright, at good prices, and for one lot, I received seventy-five dollars.

"In many cases the clippings are returned by the artist. When an artist returns the clippings in good condition, I allow him a discount of 50 per cent. On an average, I have nine calls for clippings, daily. Since most of the clippings are returned to my files, I average a dollar and eighty cents an order. I deliver and make the collections myself."

Frequently meeting a problem of a group of persons, such as artists, provides a service which is invaluable to the group, and at the same time, is highly profitable to you. A similar service for artists may be started in any town where there are enough artists to make a clipping service pay. However, the service need not be restricted to one locality. It may be expanded by mail to include near-by cities or towns, where such a service is certain to be highly appreciated. Practically no investment is required.

■ ■

Starts Printing Business at Sixty-Five

HALF a century ago, in the little town of Rossville, Illinois, Frank Frailey decided to learn the printer's trade. His stepfather owned the hotel in that village, and until he became a "printer's devil," Frank had spent most of his time making beds, waiting on tables, stoking the old-fashioned stoves, and doing the many other odd jobs that turn up around the small town inn. But in those days, the printer was the aristocrat of the trades, going to work with a long frock coat and high silk hat. To a young man, the idea of becoming such a grand fellow was fascinating.

So a printer he became, and a good one. In turn, he drifted from Rossville to Danville, to Bloomington, to Springfield, and finally to the twin cities of Champaign-Urbana, where he has spent the most of his life. For a while, he worked as foreman of several of the local shops, and with the *Urbana-Courier Herald*. "Dad" Frailey became known as a printer who planned each job with as much feeling for craftsmanship as the painter who does a picture, or the musician who writes a symphony. There are few printers today who can equal "Dad" as a typographer. Soon he had his own shop in Urbana, and leading business men went to him for their printing jobs, and the students at the University of Illinois for their dance programs.

But the life of the owner of a printing shop is strenuous. "Dad" Frailey's boy had finished college, and there seemed no reason why his father should continue to work so hard. He sold his business, and became the shop superintendent for the Twin City Printing Company. He owned his home and had accumulated enough money to live comfortably. But he did not want ever to forsake the smell of printer's ink or the clang of the Gordon presses, as strong a lure to the printer as the odor of the sawdust and the clop of horses' hoofs, to the circus performer. He meant to go on working until his time on earth had ended.

But there came a day when the owner of the business decided that he could reduce expenses by putting a younger man in charge of the shop. "Dad" Frailey was more than sixty. It was time for him to retire. "Too old to work any longer, you ought to take things easier," said the proprietor—words that begin to haunt all men and women who have passed fifty, and words that many thousands heard during the depression. So they were spoken to "Dad" seven years ago in the front office of the Twin City Printing Company, and he left that night, branded "too old to work."

But there was something different between "Dad" Frailey and the majority of men who face the same problem. He didn't agree that he was too old, and he didn't intend to take things easy. He knew that the quickest way for him to die would be to sit around doing nothing. That night there occurred a directors' meeting in the Frailey homestead. Mr. and Mrs. Frank L. Frailey were the members present. "I'm going to start a little shop of my own right here in this house," said the president of the corporation. "I'll buy some type, a press, a cutter, and the other things I need—there are a lot of folks in these two towns who know my work and like it. They'll be glad to give me as many jobs as I can handle. Now down in the basement—"

But that was when the meeting got warm. No woman wants a printing plant in her basement—too much noise and confusion. So they finally compromised on the little one-car garage which up to that moment had done nothing more eventful than house several cars made and sold by another elderly man who seems destined to keep on working—Henry Ford. And in that brick garage—no bigger than a tourist's cabin—"Dad" Frailey established a new business—one with very little overhead and soon quite profitable. It was only a year or so until every inch of floor space was crowded with the tools and machinery of the master printer. The news got around somehow that "Dad" was still turning out superior printing, and he has never had a dull minute, or had to solicit a single job. With only a young man to kick the press, and a girl occasionally for bindery work, this man who was "too old to work any longer" has often averaged $100 a week clear profit in his little brick printing shop.

Why? Well, perhaps, "Dad" himself has explained the secret of his success by quoting from Emerson on one of his folders: "If a man write a better book, preach a better sermon, or build a better mouse trap than his neighbor, though he build his house in the woods, the world will make a beaten path to his door." Mouse traps or printing—it is all the same. The man who has achieved distinction in any kind of craftsmanship, who is still strong in body and young in spirit, need not fear the specter of old age.

■ ■

Be a "Free Lance" Photographer

BIG money can be made taking "human interest" photographs. That has been proved by Lee Clarke, who has averaged $15 daily by snapping his camera around Chicago during the past several months.

Clarke started "shooting" human interest photographs when he entered a contest conducted by an out-of-town newspaper. The paper promised to pay five dollars for each photograph published. Clarke decided he could pay for a camera with money accruing to him from photographing unusual subjects for the contest, and bought a second-hand camera for which he paid $73. Included were two packs of films. He made "close-up" photographs of points of interest in and around Chicago which he mailed to the newspaper. A week later he received a check for $80 in payment for sixteen of the twenty-four pictures. He did not win the prize, but in the next three weeks received checks totaling $70 for photographs from various newspaper syndicates and advertising agencies throughout the country. That you will agree, was mighty good money.

"Many photographs are not salable," Clarke pointed out, "because they have poor composition, or lack human interest. You can take a photograph one way, and it doesn't mean anything. Take the photograph from a 'sharp' angle, however, and it stands out. Photographs of kittens, puppies, babies and prominent people sell best. Snap a good photograph of a small kitten poking its head above the rim of a shoe, and you have something that will bring five dollars or more from a newspaper syndicate. I put three little brown, curly-haired puppies in a wire paper basket, took a fast close-up of them, and got $20 for it from a New York advertising agency. They used it sometime later to advertise a client's canned dog food. Another reason why Lee Clarke's pictures sell is that he analyzes the pictures being used today in national advertising, watches the trend, and then keys his output accordingly.

Because developing and printing negatives and prints has a great deal to do with the salability of a photograph, Clarke has it done by professionals who know best how to get results. Some photographers prefer to develop their films themselves. It costs him twenty cents to have a film-pack developed, and he pays five cents for each print. Not every photograph he takes sells, of course, but his average is about one in nine. He takes between thirty-five and forty photographs every day and his costs, including films, printing and developing run close to six dollars daily.

You can readily discover the best angle from which to take a photograph by studying the subject through the camera ground glass. The image shown in the ground glass is exactly the same as that which will appear in the finished photograph. Making camera studies in spare time will prove lucrative and enjoyable. Newspaper syndicates, magazine publishers, advertising agencies, big corporations, department stores, dress shops, men's stores, and schools furnish a ready market for the proper type of photograph. Striking photographs are hard to find but there are many opportunities for snapping them right in your own community. If you have good "camera sense" and develop the necessary skill, you will find a good market for out-of-the-ordinary photographs among companies which produce calendars for syndicating the retail stores, such as, the Gerlach Barklow Company of Joliet, or Brown & Bigelow of St. Paul. There are men like John Kabel, of Dayton, who earn upward of $10,000 a year just traveling about taking "calendar" photographs. Can you imagine any business more pleasant?

■ ■

Selling Sales Information

IN EVERY city there are usually four or five dealers, in various household products. There is an electrical dealer who sells washing machines and similar devices. There is usually a utility company selling gas stoves. There is a store which sells radios. Another sells oil burners. And in the last few years stores are being established to sell air-conditioning equipment. All of these business men work on "leads"—that is to say they need to know the names of people in town who are contemplating buying equipment such as they sell, so that they can call on these "prospects" and interest them in their particular appliances.

To get "leads" by a door-to-door canvass is expensive. It costs a lot of money, and takes too many salesmen, although it is being done. If these dealers can be shown how they could get such "leads" for less money, so that they could keep all their salesmen busy calling on *known* prospects, they would jump at the opportunity. An advertising man who was out of work, figured that by making a personal canvass of every house in town, he could find out from one call what these five dealers make five calls to learn, thus meeting the first requirement of a successful business-rendering a definite and needed service.

So he had some blanks printed, on which he listed various questions designed to secure from the housewife such information as: (1) Do you use a vacuum cleaner? (2) How old is it? (3) When will you be ready to trade your present vacuum cleaner for a new one? (4) What make of vacuum cleaner will you probably buy? He headed up these blanks with the imposing title: "Rockford Home Equipment Survey." With about 50 of these blanks in a loose-leaf binder he started out making his calls. He introduced himself in the following manner:

"My name is Stamm. I am making a survey of household appliances being used in Rockford homes for an article in the *Rockford Star and Register.*" (He previously had approached the publisher of the newspaper who said he would be glad to publish the summary of his investigations in his news columns. It helped his advertisers.) "Would you be good enough to answer a few questions about the gas and electrical appliances which you are using in your home?"

Next he went to the leading dealers, showed them the sort of information he was obtaining as a result of his calls, and asked them if they would be willing to pay him 25 cents for every lead he obtained for equipment such as they were selling. He admitted frankly that some of the leads would be names of people with whom the dealer was already in contact, but demonstrated that there would be such a small percentage of these that it would not represent much of a waste. In many such cases he obtained data that the dealer did not have, but which were helpful to him such as, for example, the home-owner's preference for equipment sold by his competitor. This proposition, of course, was made to only one dealer in each line of business, first come first served.

In nearly every case where Stamm called he got a lead for at least one of his "clients" and in many cases for all five. He found he was able to canvass about forty home-owners in a day, working evenings as well as during the daytime. Since it was all profit, except for the cost of printing up the questionnaires, you can figure out how long it took him to make $1,000.

This same idea, in a slightly different form, was used by the Women's Guild of St. Luke's Episcopal Church in Evanston, Illinois, to raise funds for the church budget. Each woman in the church was given a page from the Evanston telephone directory, and required to call up these names within a month. She was furnished with blanks printed for the purpose. In this case, however, a wide range of needs was covered by the survey, including automobiles, tires, radios, water heaters, incinerators, etc. Hundreds of dollars were raised as a result of the plan.

Making Money with a Portable Duplicator

WHEN Mildred Connery graduated from business college, she intended to start out on a secretarial career. She soon discovered it was impossible to find a job, so she became a public stenographer. Business didn't rush into her office, though, and there were days when she had no work to do.

"The way to get business is to go after it," thought Mildred. "But how am I to go after it?" She considered various ways, and tried a few without success. She left cards in offices. She called on business men in the building where she rented space. But her business didn't increase. One day a small boy entered her office with a magazine in his hand. Holding the magazine out to her, he said: "Ten cents." She paid him, saying she wished she could make sales as quickly as he did. "All you have to do is show the thing you're selling, and name the price," said the boy.

"That boy didn't know it but he gave me an idea," declared Mildred. "I thought if I could find some way to show the kind of work I did for people, I could make money. Up to that time I had practically no stencil business. I knew small business men were using form letters, and got them somewhere. Later I recalled using a portable duplicating machine in school, and I decided to get one, carry it from office to office, and leave a sample of the kind of work it did in each office I visited."

The success of this plan was immediate. Mildred did not say a word to anyone when she entered an office. She opened the duplicator, ran off a sample letter, handed it to the business man, and smiling, waited for him to remark about it. This sample letter was illustrated with a tracing of a girl's head, and read: "This is a sample of the duplicating work I will do for you. Note the perfect typewriter ribbon 'match.' You can fill in the names and addresses on these letters on your typewriter if you wish. Glance over the following low prices, and give me a trial order." Detailed list of prices followed. Her entire investment, including the portable duplicator and other incidentals, was thirty dollars. Mildred secured eighteen small orders the first day and her net profit was sixty dollars for the week. The demonstration required but a few seconds, since this machine is ready to operate the moment it is opened. The sample letter was short enough to be read quickly, and the prices quoted were reasonable. In addition, the illustration which was a tracing from a magazine drawing, gave the business man an idea of the possible uses for this type of letter.

Anyone securing one of those portable duplicators can build a good income in the same way Mildred did if the business is there. Small business concerns, lawyers, sales agents and real estate men are the best prospects since they regularly use small quantities of letters and price lists. Restaurants and drug stores with lunch counters often have a number of menus run off for circulation in the vicinity of their stores. As many as three thousand copies may be run off from one stencil.

■ ■

Hunting Rare Coins

A NEWSPAPER story about a woman who sold a half dollar to a coin collector for $400 prompted W. F. Williams to devote his spare time to a search for rare coins. He got a list of "wanted" pennies, nickels, quarters, and half dollars and memorized the dates and mint marks of all coins for which big premiums were offered. Each night he examined every small coin he had received during the day when changing paper money in restaurants, cigar stores, and gasoline stations, and this spare time effort paid handsome profits. Williams declares that many coins are worth more than one thousand times their face value, and that there are thousands of wanted American coins circulating throughout the country every day, their value unknown to their owners.

"The first coin I sold was a 1913 Liberty Head nickel. This brought me $50 and encouraged me to search for other rare coins," said Williams. From a street car conductor a few days later, he received an American half-dime in change, a silver piece minted in 1803. "That conductor believed he was giving me a dime when he handed me that small silver piece. I was glad to get it, however, for I sold it a few days later for $30. One day, about a week later, I was stepping up to pay my check in a lunch room. The man ahead of me was arguing with the cashier about a coin handed out in change for a dollar bill. It was a half dollar minted in 1853, and the cashier said it was good as any. 'I'll take it,' I said as carelessly as possible. I got $165 for it two weeks later."

Williams didn't get all of his rare coins that way. He purchased some at nominal prices from friends and neighbors, and resold them at a handsome profit. A friend of his dug up an old tin can in his backyard which contained among other coins, seven dimes dated 1894, and knowing Williams was searching for 1894 dimes, he brought them all over to Williams. Williams carefully examined them, selected one, and offered a dollar for it. His friend sold it willingly. "You see," Williams explained, "he thought all those dimes had the same value. The one I selected was the only one of the seven, however, that was worth more than ten cents. That coin had an 'S' mint mark on it which made it valuable. A little later I was paid $100 for it."

Among the American coins for which premiums have been offered are: half-cent piece, dated 1796 for which up to $75 is offered; a one-cent piece dated 1799 commands up to $80; up to $150 will be paid for an 1802 half-dime; up to $300 for an 1827 quarter-dollar; up to $500 for an 1838 half-dollar New Orleans mint, marked with an "O" between bust and date; up to $250 for an 1853 half-dollar; up to $2,500 for an 1804 silver dollar; up to $250 for an 1885 trade dollar; up to $250 for an 1863 "S" mint two-dollar-and-a-half gold piece; up to $500 for a gold dollar (North Carolina) letter "C" below the wreath; up to $1,000 for an 1873 three-dollar gold piece; and up to $5,000 for an 1822 U. S. five-dollar gold piece. Hundreds of other coins are listed at values ranging between $15 and $70.

Anyone may turn his spare time into a profitable search for wanted American coins. A complete list of wanted coins may be obtained from a reliable coin collector. These lists show the dates, marks, and other specifications which will enable you to identify wanted coins, and the prices collectors will pay for them. By examining them through a magnifying glass (which you may buy at any novelty store for twenty-five or fifty cents), coins worn smooth by handling, special mint letters and marks become clear which cannot be detected with the naked eye.

When a rare coin comes into your possession mail it to a coin dealer, and he will send you his check promptly. Be sure that the coin collector is reliable and can show references for fair dealing. There are a lot of fakers among coin dealers just as there are among stamp dealers.

■ ■

A Handy Shop in Your Home

MRS. LINDSTROM, of Wilmette, Illinois, has always been a very energetic and busy woman. When her husband's business, which was sanding and refinishing floors, began to slip she decided to give a lift and add to the family income.

Her forte was sewing, so she conceived the idea of starting a "Handy Shop" right in her own home. She inserted a small advertisement in the local paper announcing that the "Handy Shop" was ready to mend, quilt, make over clothes, and in general do any of the little odd jobs that so many women neglect, just because they don't like to do them or haven't the time.

Not long after the advertisement appeared, many small repair jobs started coming in. Then later, as her reputation grew, not only repair jobs but orders for work on new materials were received. Soon the business outgrew the corner in the dining room of their big old-fashioned house and it was necessary to turn the whole dining room with its cheerful bay window into a workshop that fairly hums with activity from early morning hours until night. Shelves for storage and wardrobe space for hanging the finished garments line the walls.

Mrs. Lindstrom soon outgrew the repair and overhauling jobs, and for the past four years has been busily engaged in making draperies, fine satin comforters, appliqued and patch work quilts, as well as regular dressmaking. Lately she has had to hire extra help to meet her delivery dates.

For some time the "Handy Shop" was the sole support of the entire family of six, her husband's business having just gradually died out. The husband is now engaged in another line of work, her two grown sons are also employed, and the daughters are off to school, but the shop hums on busier than ever. This idea has always been a "pet dream" of Mrs. Lindstrom's, but it took a real need to develop it. Today she counts among her clientele some of Chicago's best North Shore families and several large interior decorating shops.

When you ask her if she is going to retire, since the family is now able to get along without her help, she quickly answers, "Oh no! This is my business, and I intend to carry on full steam just so long as the orders come in." So far each year has shown a substantial gain in profits over the previous year.

■ ■

A Country Store on Wheels

INSTEAD of sitting in their crossroads country store waiting for business to pick up, Rea & Moore, storekeepers near Logansport, Indiana, went out after their customers. They built a body, lined with shelving, on their old truck and started out to sell the farmers. A sufficient stock of groceries is put in the truck for a day's trade. Four and one-half days each week this traveling store is on the road covering a seven-mile radius. About 200 farmhouses are visited. When the truck drives into the dooryard, a flight of steps is put down and the housewife steps up into the "store." Here she can select the groceries she needs, paying in cash or eggs.

In addition to saving the farmer's wife the trip to town to buy her necessities, it saves her the trip to market her eggs. The overhead is not more than $1.25 a day for gas and oil as the truck travels only about 15 miles a day. The cost of building the new body on the old truck ran about $65, but as the first four months of the experiment quadrupled their business, Rea & Moore feel that it was a good investment.

■ ■

"Penny-Weight" Scales Lure Pennies

"**HOW** much do you weigh?" When that question was asked Harry Larson in a drug store, back in 1933, he looked around for a scale. He dropped a penny in the slot of the coin-operated machine. A moment later he stepped off and sauntered over to the counter to buy a package of cigarettes. As he stood at the cigar counter seven others stepped up and weighed themselves. Curious, Harry asked the druggist how much money the scale made each month.

"He told me that it averaged about $20 a month, but that he didn't own the machine. An operator had placed it there and his 'cut' was 25 per cent of the amount taken from the machine each month. The scale itself was a beauty. I could see that people were attracted to it because of its appearance, and that they wondered what it cost. I noted the name of the manufacturer and wrote for full details about becoming an operator. That was how I got started in the scale business.

"I bought 70 machines altogether. The first three I paid for out of my savings. The other 67 were paid out of the pennies taken from the first three. These first three machines cost me $175 and paid me a profit every month of $98. That was a pretty good return on the investment. I found that there is no servicing needed for these machines and nothing to adjust. You just pick a good location, set them up, and there they are all ready to lure pennies from the curious. It's a clean, simple proposition, and you can't hit upon a surer or better way of making money easily. After buying the first three scales, I established a line of credit with the manufacturer, and got five more on the time-payment plan. The machines vary a little in their monthly earnings. The first three locations average $33 each, the next three run $19.85 each, and there are two that pay under $17 monthly. My monthly income for the 70 machines amounts to $768, a little better than $10 each. In nine months, I've earned enough to pay for the scales, and made a good living besides.

"The stores where my machines are placed, are usually drug, candy, and grocery stores. I've found that a live grocery and meat market, where a number of women shop every day, is as good a location as you can get. Women are always worried about their weight. They want to know whether they've gained or lost, and to make sure, like to weigh themselves on the same scale all the time. Since they make a practice of doing most of their shopping for meat and groceries in a neighborhood store, they patronize the penny scale set up there."

There are several manufacturers of coin-operated scales. They all furnish detailed plans to help you interest merchants in keeping your scales in the front of the store, or in a spot near the cash register, where people standing around to be served may step on the scale. These instructions make it easy for anyone who is a hustler, and can make a convincing sales talk, to be successful from the start.

■ ■

A Shrimp Fisherwoman

AFTER the real estate bubble burst in Florida, Sadie Miller, like many others, was broke. In looking around for ways and means of getting back on her feet, she discovered "shrimping." When she first opened her shrimp dock, she had a man running it, but after he failed to come back from a vacation up North, she decided to manage it herself.

"Shrimping" is hard work for anyone, but particularly hard for a woman. During the busy season, the work goes on night and day. In rubber overalls and hip boots, Sadie Miller and her helpers search for the elusive shrimp so much in demand as bait by fishermen. As shrimps vary their habitat from day to day, they must be hunted. Small or large—the size matters little. The fisherman just wants fresh live bait. Because they are harder to find in winter, they are worth more. In January, February and March, when they are scarce, they bring 50 or 75 cents a dozen. In summer, the price runs as low as 25 cents a hundred. However, Sadie Miller never sells her catch for less than a dollar a hundred.

From a small start, this business has grown to the point where a number of helpers are needed during the busy season. While "shrimping" hasn't made Sadie Miller wealthy by any means, she has made several times a thousand dollars at it.

■ ■

Specializing in Social Printing

MANY a successful publisher or printer today started his career with an old Kelsey printing press in his basement. There is an old saying that once you get printers' ink in your system you can never get it out. Frank Doubleday, Don Sietz, Tim Thrift, Joe Mitchell, and Rudyard Kipling are just a few of the many who began their careers putting in their spare time "kicking" a printing press. Today, with a used printing press, there is still an opportunity, not only to make money, but to get a start toward a fascinating career in one of the three allied fields: publishing, advertising, or writing.

Several years ago a young chap, who was a clerk in the offices of a large Chicago packing plant, started an agency for the sale of social stationery. He secured samples and a price list from a local engraver. It happened to be near graduation time so he called at the schools near by and secured orders from the students for their first engraved cards which they needed to enclose with their graduation invitations. When the orders were ready to pack, he placed a sticker in the bottom of each box giving the registration number for the copper plate from which the cards were made, his name and address, and a simple form for reordering in quantities when the present supply of cards was entirely used.

His success with these cards encouraged him to look around for further business. By watching the neighborhood newspaper, he learned of many engagements and coming marriages. He noted the addresses, immediately called on the mothers of the brides-to-be and solicited orders for wedding announcements and calling cards. Between working out ideas of his own and making use of the sales suggestions the engraver gave him, he managed to build up a rather nice little business. During this time he continued with his regular job, and handled the engraving agency at night and on Saturday afternoons.

Before long, he decided that a small printing press might be of help to him, so he purchased a used press on the time-payment plan, installed it in the rear of a store and began to look around for printing orders. He found that professional men were particularly good prospects as they were likely to put off ordering their supplies until the last moment. They were glad to be able to get prompt service in a hurry, and soon he had developed a good business among professional men for bill heads, letterheads and envelopes. Before long, his space proved to be too small, so he selected a larger office in a modern building at a nominal rental. Here he established himself as the "Society Specialty Shop." About this time the reorders were beginning to come in for calling cards and he was also receiving many orders for engraved Christmas and New Year cards.

In order to get repeat business wherever possible, he made every effort to sell his customers on the idea of leaving their copper plates with him under a registered number. His sales argument was built around the importance of having the plate kept in perfect condition so that there would be no scratches or dents to mar the engraved work later. When his competitors found that he had built up a good-sized file of registered plates, he began receiving offers for his business, including the file of plates, monogram dies, etc. Within a few weeks after his competitors started to bid for his business, an opportunity came along for him to better his regular position, so he accepted the best offer of the lot and sold his establishment for $1,500.

■ ■

Servicing Beer Coils a New Industry

THE return of legal beer opened taverns in almost every state. While in one such tavern, Jimmy Coyle heard the bartender curse under his breath. "What's the matter?" Jimmy asked. "This blasted coil is giving trouble again. The coil cleaner fellow who ought to service it hasn't been around for several weeks." Jimmy wondered at that. Later, he investigated and found out that the coils in every tavern should be cleaned thoroughly every few days, and that the tavern owners were glad to pay a regular service fee for this type of service. So he got in touch with the manufacturer of a coil cleaner and established himself in a business of his own, servicing the beer coils in taverns, restaurants, lunch rooms, hotels, soda fountains, cafes, road houses, clubs, and amusement places. As his income from this service is better than $100 a week, it didn't take him long to corral that first thousand dollars.

"The beauty of this coil-cleaning device," said Jimmy, "is that anybody can operate it, and no one needs experience to work it. Yet there's a good income in owning one and working up service accounts. I charge a small fee of $1.00 for each bar I service, and I am now servicing 112 beer-selling bars. However, I didn't build up this business overnight. No sir! It took a lot of real work to build it, but I figured at the time that no matter what line of business you go into, you've got to work hard or you won't make a nickel. As a matter of fact, there was practically no one servicing these bars, when I started. Naturally, the coils were in bad shape, and it took longer to do each job. The fellow in town who had been servicing them was too busy to take care of all the business. When I started, he called me up and gave me some of his customers' names, and told me to be sure and call on them. I did. But the way he had handled their service had left a bad taste in their mouths, and it took me a couple of months to overcome this."

Jimmy carries his coil cleaner in a handy case when he makes the rounds of the taverns he services. He simply connects the cleaner to the coil, turns on the little handles and the machine does the rest. This device, which is operated by electricity, leaves the coils thoroughly cleaned and scoured, without the use of chemicals, acids or steam. It can be carried anywhere, is compact and handy, and can be operated from a light socket in any taproom.

The total investment Jimmy made in this equipment was $107. He owned a roadster at the time he made his purchase, and was therefore ready to make calls in any emergency. The fact that the coils must be cleaned and kept clean to give good tasting beer, makes the beer coil-cleaning service a permanent business which can be built up as big as you want to make it.

This business, in its infancy now, is ideal for anyone anxious to start a business on small capital, with promises of good returns. There is no doubt that once established, any person who gives quick service in this industry will enjoy a good business for many years to come. Jimmy was furnished everything complete by the company when he bought his equipment.

■ ■

Renting Tires Solves Sales Problem

WHEN you think of a tire station, you think of a fellow who bought a few hundred tires, procured a license, rented a store and went into business. That was the way that Harold Holt started. His investment in equipment and stock was under $300, but he didn't set the world afire. It wasn't until a friend advised him to learn something about business management, that he began to realize the reason he was not making enough to cover expenses was because of his inexperience. So he inquired about a business management course and enrolled with a well-rated correspondence school. After he had been studying for three months, be began to change things. He completed the course in eighteen months, but long before that, he had placed his business on a sound, profitable basis, and was well on his way to his second thousand dollars.

"At first I had the notion that all the business management course would teach me was bookkeeping methods, and other things like that, which would produce no revenue. My bookkeeping didn't have to be systematized. What I really needed was ideas for creating new business, and holding the business I had. I was surprised, early in the course, to discover that many of my lessons were devoted to exactly the type of business-building ideas I needed. There was one example cited, showing how a man had taken an idea, worked it into his business and, finally, made a lot of money. That was the Hertz Drive-It-Yourself idea, and I got to thinking it over. I decided to try a similar one, applying the principle to auto tires. I figured out the wholesale cost of a tire, and the number of days it would take to pay for one on the rent-a-tire principle. I was surprised at the amount of profit there would be in it. But I had no conviction that any man would want to rent an auto tire. It might be good advertising, I thought, and put up a sign, offering to rent motorists a new tire for 25 cents a day.

"The next morning, two men came in and rented four tires each for their cars. I took their license numbers, and changed the tires. They said they needed new tires, but hadn't money to buy them yet, and I assured them that half the rental would apply to the purchase of new tires. This pleased them. When they went out, I decided I should have collected a minimum charge for daily rentals, but didn't. Later that day, I rented six more tires, made a minimum charge of 75 cents for changing tires and 50 cents for two days' rental. That gave me a little guarantee on the tires, and cut the probable risk down a great deal. I learned before the week was out, however, that there was no risk. Of the 26 tires I had rented that week, 24 were bought by the renters. The other two were returned, and the full rental fee paid.

"I was surprised, moreover, to discover that in a short period, I had doubled my tire sales to non-renters, many new customers being attracted to my store by the sign."

Business management training certainly is of great value, and materially helps not only to reduce expenses, but to keep you from making dangerous decisions due to lack of experience. Such courses of instruction vary greatly in price. All of them, however, are available on deferred payment of a few dollars a month.

■ ■

Fifty-Two Money-Making Ideas for Women

ONE versatile woman, who has done part-time work for over eight years, claims that any woman can make money in her spare time if she is really willing to work, will not scorn the smallest sort of job, and is prompt and dependable.

She emphasizes the importance of letting everybody in the community in which you live, know that you are available for all the varieties of work you can do. "Visit every place of business that you might serve; do not ask for work, but leave your name and address, with telephone number, and suggest that in an emergency they might be glad to know that you would work for them. Ask the president of the woman's club, the church societies, and other organizations to announce that you are available. Contact the doctors and the Red Cross nurse and the local Red Cross head. Ask other women, who are doing what you are doing, to pass opportunities on to you when they are too busy to accept the work. In turn, you must remember to pass work on to them whenever possible. Have a telephone number, even if you have to pay a neighbor to take calls for you. Many a hurry-up job has been lost because a woman could not be reached by telephone. Don't refuse small jobs—if it is only for one hour's work, take it; many such short periods of work add up at the end of a month."

The best way to discover how you can make money in your spare time is to make a list of the things you can do. When you start to make this list you will be surprised at the number of accomplishments you have acquired through the years. The following list contains a number of activities that most women can follow—in fact, you may be able to handle a half-dozen or more of these jobs without the difficulty of their conflicting one with the other:

BOOK REVIEW GROUPS—Any woman who is "well read" will find an enjoyable and profitable diversion in getting a group of fifteen to twenty women to organize a reading club, and let her review current books. A club of this type meets at the members' homes about once a week, and a nominal membership fee is charged from which the reviewer is compensated. One such reading club in the Chicago suburban area has thirty members who pay $10 for a series of twelve lectures or reviews. In this case, the woman who does the reviewing arranges with a local woman to call up friends and get them to join the club. In return for her cooperation her dues are canceled.

SHOP FOR OUT-OF-TOWN CUSTOMERS—The professional shopper in the small town saves time and railroad fare for her customers. She need not charge them a fee because the shopper's discount given by city stores runs as high as 10 or 15 per cent. The shopper who makes a weekly trip to the city may earn as much anywhere from $15 to $40 for the trip, and even more.

DELIVER BOOKS FOR A CIRCULATING LIBRARY—A library can increase its circulation by delivering books to customers. If you have a car, you can make two or three trips a day. By making deliveries for several shops at one time, you can increase the amount of your earnings.

TEACH BALLROOM DANCING TO A GROUP OF MEN AND WOMEN; ALSO CHILDREN—Small classes can be taught in your own home. The radio or phonograph records will provide the music. If there is no large academy in your town, you may be successful in starting such a school. The admission fee may be paid at the door, or season tickets may be sold. Include a refreshment bar (this can be leased to someone) and get as good an orchestra as you can afford.

TELL FORTUNES—Tea rooms have found today that the addition of a fortune teller has stimulated business. The fortunes may be told with cards, the palm, or a crystal. Astrology is also popular. If you are a fair judge of human nature you can become rather adept. There are any number of books on fortune-telling methods and a little application is all that is needed. This is also a lucrative business at summer and winter resorts.

SING IN A CHURCH CHOIR—Many churches pay for this service—naturally you must have a fair voice.

WAIT ON TABLES—Tea rooms which serve only luncheons and dinners need extra help during the rush hours. Caterers, hotel restaurants, and inns also employ extra help. Leave your name and telephone number with the managers of these places.

TEACH BRIDGE—Many a woman who is an expert bridge player, has found, when the family income started to decline, a way to make a good income. Bridge may be taught in private lessons (the charge is usually higher) or in groups. If the group meets at your home, twenty-five cents an hour for each person is a reasonable charge.

TAKE COMPLETE CHARGE OF A HOME DURING ILLNESS—When a mother is in a hospital or convalescing at home, and no child is old enough to assume responsibility, someone is needed to take care of the household and the children. Often this is an emergency job and pays well.

COUNSELOR FOR A GIRLS' CAMP—If you understand children and can handle them easily, this work offers not only an income but a pleasant summer.

IF YOU HAVE A CAR—Arrange to drive four or five neighbors to work each morning and pick them up in the evening. Give instructions in driving—a course of lessons should bring you about $1.00 or $1.50. Take a group of children to and from school. Leave your name and number with the local hotels and travel agencies and offer your services to tourists who want to see the town. If there is a summer resort near by, meet the trains or boats and drive visitors to their hotels.

MEND LINENS AND FINE LACES—With a little practice you can become an expert in this work. One of the best ways to mend linens is to weave linen threads in the worn or torn places. These may be secured from the inside of the hems. Laces are more difficult. However, there are books on laces which will give you this instruction.

LAUNDER CURTAINS AND FINE LINENS—Most women are fussy about their curtains and fine linens and dislike turning them over to the average laundry. By doing excellent work, it is a simple matter to establish a reputation in this field. In larger cities, where it is smoky and dusty, contract to launder the curtains a certain number of times a year for a stipulated sum to be paid each time the curtains are laundered.

TEACH GOLF—Many women play a good game of golf but have never tried to teach it. There are always men and women interested in learning how to play the game. The charge varies from $2.00 to $4.50 an hour.

ORGANIZE A COURSE IN PUBLIC SPEAKING—Build your class around the idea that training in public speaking develops poise and diction. Women who belong to clubs and many business men can be sold on this idea. If you were good as a debater in school, you can probably handle such classes. Study the books that have been published on public speaking.

COACH BACKWARD STUDENTS DURING THEIR VACATIONS—If you have done any teaching, or if you have kept up with school work by helping your children with their lessons, you can qualify for this work.

BOARD CHILDREN IN YOUR HOME DURING THE SUMMER—If your home is spacious and in the country or at the seashore, you can handle a few children as summer boarders. A comfortable, modern farm, where the children will get exercise and good food is an ideal place.

CLEANING AND DYEING AGENCY—It is not enough to open up an agency and wait for the work to come to you. You must go out and solicit orders. One of the advantages of this business is the opportunity to repeat orders.

REAL ESTATE RENTING AGENCY—This business can be handled in your own home. Contact the owners of property in your neighborhood and adjoining sections. Do not neglect any chance of selling a piece of real estate if such a chance should come your way. In fact, after you have established yourself as a renting agent, you can expand into selling real estate. Study the books on real estate law and contracts—you cannot acquire too much knowledge on this point.

PREPARE PAPERS AND SPEECHES FOR CLUB WOMEN—The charges for this service depend upon the time spent in preparation and the amount of research work done. The library will furnish you with material on any subject. The speech or paper should be carefully typed in duplicate and delivered several days before it is needed. Secure this type of work by contacting clubs and literary societies. Also watch the papers for announcements of meetings.

INVALID COOKING—The care of many invalids is not so much a matter of nursing as the preparation of the right food. One who has had little training in nursing, but who is a good cook, is able to make food look appetizing, can earn many a dollar catering to the finicky appetites of invalids. Contact the doctors in your neighborhood to secure appointments.

DEVELOP A\AN ENTERTAINMENT BUREAU IN YOUR TOWN—Book talent in your community and then contact churches, fraternal organizations, clubs. A percentage of what the entertainers are paid is your commission. Sometimes it will be necessary to contact the larger booking agencies in near-by cities for better talent than your community affords. Establish a reputation for preparing programs and outlining entertainment projects.

SOLICIT ACCOUNTS FOR YOUR LOCAL BANK—Establish a connection with your local bank and offer to turn in names of prospective accounts for a nominal fee. Interesting work for the woman who knows her community well and likes meeting people.

COACH AMATEUR THEATRICAL GROUPS—If you have had any experience with dramatics, organize a theatrical group in your town, offer to coach benefit theatrical performances given by church groups, or handle skits and one-act plays given by clubs. A moderate fee is charged for this service.

HANDLE A SWITCHBOARD—Some hotels and apartment hotels are willing to provide living quarters for switchboard services. If you do not know how to operate a switchboard now, get someone to show you how and pay her by relieving her at her work for an hour or so. You can also fill in during vacation absences at various hotels and offices.

BOOKKEEPING—Many small retailers, manufacturing firms, hotels, and shops cannot afford to hire a full-time bookkeeper. If you have had experience in this work at any time, you can work up a clientele by calling on these firms and offering to handle their books once a month for a small sum.

ADDRESS ENVELOPES—This may be done in your own home if you have a typewriter. Nearly every business house, letter and multigraphing shop is a prospect. Register with these concerns, with the employment agencies in your city, and also with clubs, associations, etc. Some firms prefer addressing done in your own handwriting. The rate for three-line addresses varies from $2.00 to $3.00 a thousand. A good typist can address a thousand envelopes in a day.

TEACH MUSIC—If your parents once spent considerable money for your music lessons and you have a piano in your home, get out your old music books and brush up on technique. You will be surprised to find how easy it is to get into the swing of this again. Remember you do not have to be an accomplished musician to teach the piano. A few piano students will pay many a bill or buy new shoes or other necessities.

MANICURES—In every community there are women who dislike coming into town to a beauty shop. If you have a car you can give them manicures in their own homes. All you need to carry with you is a kit with your instruments. Manicuring is easy to learn and should be well done to insure repeat business. The charge should, of course, be a little higher than in the beauty shop.

MANAGE CHARITY BAZAARS—Often the reason a charity bazaar or other charitable enterprise does not make more money, is lack of good management. If you have a flair for this sort of thing, you can earn from 10 to 15 per cent of the receipts. After you have made a success of one or two affairs it is easy to secure the management of others.

TELEPHONING—Many retailers have commissioned women to call their customers and tell them about special sales or to make appointments for special salesmen selling electric appliances, etc. The retailer pays for the telephone and adds a fee for your work. Some also pay a commission on all orders received.

TOWN INVESTIGATOR—Investigations for collection firms, food manufacturers, mail-order concerns, and advertising agencies are frequently made by women. Write to these concerns and tell them you can handle this sort of work. The public library will be able to tell you where to get lists of names.

CARE OF CHILDREN—Take charge of children while their parents go to the movies, bridge parties, etc., in the evenings. From 75 cents to $1.25 is the usual charge. Arrange to take care of children while their parents are on summer vacations. The charge for this service will depend upon the length of time the parents are away, and other factors.

ENTERTAIN INVALIDS—Shut-ins and invalids find their days long and boring. If you are good natured, have a pleasing voice, can read well or tell stories, entertaining invalids, both young and old, will prove a profitable job. Contact the doctors, ministers, and nurses in your neighborhood.

TAKE CARE OF GRAVES—Check over the cemeteries in your town, look for neglected graves, find the nearest relatives and sell them on the idea of keeping the graves planted with flowers and the grass cut. Many women have found this a lucrative line of work.

BOARDING DOGS, CATS AND BIRDS—When people go away on their summer vacations, Rover, Peter, and Dickie have to be boarded as it is usually inconvenient to take them along. If you have a large place on the outskirts of town where a pup can run about and be happy, advertise your "boarding kennels." Get in touch with local veterinary doctors, pet departments in the stores, and pet shops. Watch the vacation notices in your neighborhood paper and check up to see if the people who are leaving town have pets to board.

EMBROIDER MONOGRAMS ON LINENS—Open a monogram shop in your own home. Sell brides on the idea of letting you monogram their fine, new linens. You might add a hemstitching service and also a hosiery mending service. The hemstitching is easily done by an inexpensive attachment which can be placed on your sewing machine.

TEACH SWIMMING—If you are a good swimmer and have done a lot of swimming, make arrangements with one of the hotel swimming pools and organize classes. There should be a junior class for children and two adult classes—one for beginners and one for advanced students. An exhibit of fancy diving and swimming at the end of each term will maintain interest in the classes. If your funds are low in the beginning, offer to teach the hotel guests free in return for the use of the pool.

WITH YOUR CAMERA—If you possess a good camera and have some skill in taking pictures, specialize on taking snaps of children, pets, and people's homes. Parents are proud of their children and will nearly always buy your snaps. People like pictures of their pets and their homes—snap them and then when they are developed, show them. Nine times out of ten they will buy your snaps. Take pictures at summer camps of the children, of picnic crowds. Watch for the unusual—freaks of nature, a sudden storm over a valley, a dramatic occurrence. The trade papers, newspapers, and magazines will buy these snaps. The Eastman Kodak Company has published several inexpensive booklets which will give you a number of ideas about making money with a camera. These booklets are to be found in camera shops and the public libraries.

TRAINING ANIMALS AND BIRDS—Many women are successful in this field because they have the patience of Job and they are naturally kind to their pets. One woman has been unable to supply the demand for her trained cats. The cats are trained when they are little kittens and are so droll and amusing, her entire supply is always in demand. Another woman has had considerable success training canaries to sing special songs such as "Yankee Doodle." She also is unable to supply the demand. Still another woman stands out in her field as a trainer of dogs to lead the blind. Now she is training others to train dogs.

RENTING EQUIPMENT—If you own a vacuum cleaner, an electric washing machine or ironer, an electric sewing machine, a sun lamp, a moving picture machine, rent them for a small fee to your neighbors, when you are not using them. Be sure to check your equipment carefully before you hand it over to anyone and check it again when it is returned.

COMPILE LISTS FOR MAILING HOUSES—Most of the companies which compile mailing lists are interested in specific lists, such as well-to-do residents, farmers, prospective brides, fruit growers, poultry raisers, newborn infants, etc. The same lists of names and addresses may be sold to several firms. General lists are also of interest to these concerns from time to time.

CLIPPING SERVICE—Undoubtedly, there are individuals and companies in your locality which are more or less in the limelight. People like to know what is being said about them. To operate a clipping service, notify these people or companies that an item has appeared in such and such a newspaper recently. Explain to them that they may have a copy by sending you twenty-five cents. Give your clipping bureau a name that is dignified. Subscribe to some of the better-known newspapers and secure others from the second-hand magazine shops, from the editor of your local paper, or buy the unsold newspapers from your news dealer.

PLAN GARDENS—If you know how to grow plants and flowers, and have an eye for arrangement of color and form, help people plan their gardens. If you will look about at your neighbors' gardens you will see that many of them are hit-or-miss propositions. Draw up a plan on paper, indicating the most attractive arrangements for shrubs, flowers, trees, etc. Show how the garden will grow in beauty from year to year and the future changes to be made in it. When your plan is complete, call on the garden owner and show him the plans. Be careful not to belittle his present planting; sell him on the idea of making his garden even more beautiful than it is. Your plans should sell for about $1.00. If you are to superintend the plantings, then your charge should be higher. Consult the garden magazines for planting ideas.

HOSTESS—If you have had a good social background, capitalize on it by becoming a hostess or an assistant to a hostess. Help arrange dinners, bridge parties, literary or musical evenings. Plan decorations, menus, and entertainment. Hotels, dude ranches, resorts, clubs, associations, steamship lines, and others often need this sort of help. Individuals who entertain a great deal but lack a flair for this sort of thing are also prospects.

PACKING ASSISTANT—Some people have a natural ability to pack things well. If you have this knack, have some cards printed and leave them with real estate offices, storage warehouses, managers of apartment buildings, and mail them to wealthy people that you know make many trips. Some families are more than willing to turn over to you the entire job of packing when they leave on summer vacations, when they move to another city, or when they go abroad. Another job that ties up with this work is to close and open summer homes, to close and open homes in the city for those on trips abroad. This may include storing valuable silver, pictures, or china and preventing moth damages to furs and woolen garments.

ESTABLISH A LAUNDRY AGENCY—Many women have developed a good business handling an agency for a laundry. Often the laundry company furnishes living quarters behind the laundry office and pays in addition a flat salary each month. If the agent is aggressive and endeavors to secure additional business, he can make arrangements for a commission on all new business. Some agents also handle the ironing of fine table linens or silk wearing apparel which cannot be ironed by machines.

MULTIGRAPH OPERATORS—If you have ever done any multigraphing work or it is easy for you to learn simple operations such as this, get a second-hand multigraphing machine and advertise your service. There are any number of offices, clubs, and institutions, which use multigraph work from time to time during the year. Make a canvass of your town and you will soon have enough work to keep you busy several hours a day.

FOOD DEMONSTRATOR—Many manufacturers in the food field hire women to demonstrate their foods in retail stores. This work pays well and is easy for the woman who likes to meet people, can talk well and is neat and healthy looking.

FREE LANCE SECRETARY—Often small business firms cannot afford a full-time stenographer or secretary. Build up your list by calling on the small firms located in office buildings in your town. Doctors and dentists and sometimes ministers also have a need of such services. You may also secure work from society women in your town. A social secretary is rather rare in small towns, so there should be considerable work for an enterprising woman who can devote a few hours a day to such clients. A portable typewriter is a necessity in this work. By selling a line of business stationery, in your spare time, you can earn enough to pay for a typewriter. Or, if you prefer, you can rent a typewriter.

NURSING—As the average home finds it too expensive to engage the services of a trained nurse, practical nurses are in great demand. Nearly any woman can learn to perform the duties of a practical nurse. These duties include massaging, bathing, preparing the food of the patient, and following the usual orders of the doctor. You should register with doctors in your neighborhood, nurses' registries, clinics, and hospitals. It is well to let the merchants in your neighborhood know that you can handle cases—frequently they are asked to recommend someone. Your town may have a branch of the Red Cross which offers training. It is a good idea to take this training, as it may be of help to you in securing work.

KNITTING INSTRUCTION—The proprietor of many a neighborhood knitting shop often finds herself with too much work for one pair of hands. Every beginner, of course, wants immediate attention. The woman who is an expert at knitting can sell her services to the proprietors of these little shops in and around her neighborhood. While the owner of a shop may not need a full-time assistant, she may be glad to have an expert come in for two or three hours a day to help her. Go around to the shops in your neighborhood and find out when they have their busiest hours. Then suggest to the proprietor that she pay you so much an hour for instruction work during the busy period. Some shops are open certain evenings in the week and you can supplement your afternoon work in one shop with evening work in another. Some shops may require your services two or three afternoons a week; some two or three evenings.

Charge for your services by the hour and then if you are needed for an extra hour or half hour over your usual time, your remuneration can be easily figured.

TELEPHONE SERVICE—Professional men, especially doctors, require someone to answer the telephone when they are out on calls. This type of service is often referred to as a Doctors' Telephone Service. Through arrangements with the local telephone company calls for those on your service list are transferred to you and you take the messages for your clients. The client arranges to call you at certain intervals to pick up the messages if any have been received. There may be a service of this type in your town, but like many such specialized services, there is usually room for another one. The telephone company will give you the necessary information regarding costs of operation and method of operation.

CHAPTER ELEVEN

PAYING FOR A COLLEGE EDUCATION

THE lives of many of today's business leaders were shaped by what they did in college to pay for their education. The interest thus developed by a student often became the foundation for his future career. Sometimes young people, faced with the necessity of paying their own way through school, have uncovered latent ability as salesmen and have stepped out of college into sales positions with large corporations. Others have worked on college papers and thus become interested in editorial work and journalism. Still others have shown marked ability as promoters, managing the affairs of their college football or baseball teams.

For that reason it is highly desirable that every opportunity be given students to develop their money-making tendencies. No matter what work a person may do after leaving college, this experience in dealing with human nature and persuading people to act on sales suggestions will prove invaluable. The knack of meeting people on an equal basis and the ability to express oneself clearly and concisely, thus acquired, remain long after school days are forgotten.

More important is the fact that a boy or girl, who has to earn money while getting the advantages of an education, acquires an appreciation of the value of money that is most important in the building of character. It is a credit to our American social system that the young man or woman who works his way through school is respected and admired. It is generally true, also, that those who do work to pay for their schooling get more out of college than the rich man's son or daughter who is provided with all the money needed for expenses.

There are, of course, the conventional ways of earning money to pay expenses, such as waiting on tables, coaching backward students, helping in the school library or office, clerking in a local store, doing a column for the local newspaper, etc. It is possible to make sufficient money doing any one of these things to pay expenses during the school years. However, the greatest opportunities to make money lie in the unusual type of work. What this work may be depends, of course, upon the community in which the school is located, the natural aptitude of the student, and the opportunities which the versatile student can develop.

For example, one young man paid his way through Purdue University by selling jewelry. He was so successful that after graduating he was given a sales position with the manufacturer and is now on his way to becoming sales manager of the company. Another student in the same college hit upon the idea of publishing a school calendar. This calendar was similar to a poster, with space in the center for listing the school events of the month. The advertising space around this central portion was sold to the local merchants in the community. The placards were posted in every place frequented by students. The revenue from the advertising paid for the printing of the posters and yielded a profit large enough to pay the greater part of the student's tuition and living expenses.

Several years ago at Ames, two engineering students, faced with the necessity of earning money to pay their expenses, organized a boarding club. Many students were renting rooms where meals were not available and consequently were eating around at little lunchrooms. These two students saw the possibility of providing meals and looked about for a place suitable for the enterprise.

A woman in town who rented rooms in her home to students, but who provided no meals, was willing to rent her large dining-room to the club and also to provide space in her basement for food supplies. Each Friday, the two boys figured up their expenses for the week, added their charges for administration, and then assessed each member of the club his proportionate share of the expense. Included in the expenses were the wages of two women who prepared the meals. Two students waited on the tables for their meals. The total cost was kept down by buying all groceries wholesale and watching for special bargains. About thirty students were served at each meal—all the room would accommodate.

The meals were simple, but good, and as the cost was less than at other boarding places, the club always had its full quota of members. Both boys were on their toes and never missed an opportunity to sell the club idea to new students. Of course, the student rooming houses in the vicinity were solicited for members.

In order to promote interest in the club, the boys ran a lottery for a season ticket to the home football games and a separate lottery for the most important out-of-town game of the season.

■ ■

Taking Pictures in the Street
Pays College Expenses

AN AMATEUR interest in photography—a hobby with Harold Walker for several years—became the means of making enough money during vacations to pay expenses during his last two years in college. The new type camera Walker uses operates on the motion picture principle taking clear, sharp photographs at high speed. Walker straps on this camera so that it is held rigidly against his chest, leaving both hands free. Its focus is fixed for any distance, and its exposure limited to 1/250 of a second, eliminating the danger of bad photographs from lack of exposure or wrong focus adjustment. Thus any amateur can secure good results.

Getting some cards printed and numbered, Walker took his camera to a busy street corner and snapped photographs of everyone entering the range of his lens. To each he handed a coin card on which was printed: "Your photograph has just been taken. Send this card and twenty-five cents to Harold Walker and prints will be mailed to you." Between ten o'clock in the morning and four in the afternoon, Walker photographed about three hundred persons, and within a few days received one hundred and fourteen cards with silver quarters from these people. His average cost for each person photographed was slightly over two cents. There is no reason why you could not do as well.

A simple system is used for determining the right photograph for each card. The first three numbers of the card indicate the week of the month, the day of the week, and the month in which the exposure was made. The last numbers indicate the number of the photograph itself. The lowest number for each day is the number for the first exposure; the next number represents the second exposure, and so on. Thus, number 15637 would be the number of the thirty-seventh person photographed on the fifth day of the first week in June. It is easy to keep the exposures in rotation when cutting the film after the film is developed.

The total investment Walker made to get started, including the cost of the camera, was $135. He does his own printing, but has the negatives developed under an inexpensive arrangement at a local studio. There are few days, he declares, when he does not make ten dollars or more with his camera.

You can use a camera of this type anywhere, on the street, at beaches, summer camps, fairs, carnivals and even along highways, and make a good profit from a few hours' work. It is not necessary to have experience handling a camera to get good results, since the entire operation consists of pushing a button.

■ ■

Venetian Blinds Provide School Money

PERHAPS you have noticed that Venetian blinds are quite the thing these days and that they are being widely used in private homes, as well as in public institutions and business offices. This type of window shade has a big advantage over the usual roll blind, in that it admits the light and air while keeping out the sun. Robert Peterson, who had taken a manual training course in the Nicholas Senn High School, Chicago, wanted to make enough money during his summer vacation to finance his first year in college. Observing this growing demand for Venetian blinds, which it seemed to him could be easily made, he decided to go into the business. He bought a scroll saw, drill press, spray gun and a few other tools, purchased a supply of wooden slats from a mill that specialized in them and did some experimenting. The only difficulty he had was getting a cord that would operate properly in the shade. He tried several different kinds of cord until he found that Italian hemp gave the desired results. He also had trouble at first getting a suitable tape, but an uncle in the furniture manufacturing business made inquiry, and finding that the best tape came from England, arranged to get him a supply. While the tape was coming over, Robert made a canvass of the homes in his locality and succeeded in booking enough orders for shades to keep him busy all summer. He found that small factories were especially good prospects, as most of them needed blinds which would keep out the sun but let in the light and air.

■ ■

Martha Hopkins' Exchange Helps Pay Tuition

ALTHOUGH fifty-five years old, Martha Hopkins was a youthful, active person—one who had never lost her zest for adventure. She figured she might have a chance to make enough money to help pay her niece's college tuition by starting a woman's exchange in the "second best" parlor. As she belonged to the Woman's Club, was active in church work, attended lectures, community meetings, and was well known in her community, it wasn't long before everyone in that part of town knew about her "Exchange."

For the sale of her neighbors' antiques, she received a commission of 25 per cent. In some cases when a customer lacked the ready cash, Martha Hopkins would accept a piece of furniture, a picture or something else of value, which together with a small sum of money, would pay for the coveted item. There was much bargaining, but Mrs. Hopkins was a "born" trader. The "Exchange" soon began to pay and if you asked her why she succeeded she would answer: "Well, I guess I just like to sell—and I like to buy, too. Then, of course, I know so many people; my father, you know, was a pioneer in this section of town. He was a doctor, so we came to know about every old family around these parts. But I believe the real reason is that everyone has something he doesn't want which someone else would like to have. This is really just swapping—and swapping is as much fun for grown-ups as for youngsters."

■ ■

Five Dollars a Day Stenciling House Numbers on Curbstones

BACK in 1937 it looked as if two students, Ralph and George, at Northwestern University (Evanston, Illinois), would be unable to return for their fourth year unless some unknown source of revenue could be tapped—and, as they agreed, "the sooner the better." It was Ralph who got the bright idea for making money one evening when calling on his latest "big moment." Two people in a car stopped in front of the house where he was calling and inquired whether it was such and such a number. After he had directed them, he realized that you simply could not see the house number from the curb. That night when he got back to the room he shared with George, they put their heads together and after some plain and fancy figuring found they could make a tidy sum of money by painting house numbers on the curbstones in front of the houses of Evanstonians, with a set of marking stencils.

Each boy took one side of the street. In front of a house one of the boys would brush a square of white paint on the curb and then ring the doorbell. When the householder appeared the white space was pointed out, and he was asked if he wouldn't like to see his house number painted in black on the white space. It is surprising how many were actually eager to have the job done. In fact, about three-quarters of the householders of Evanston had house numbers painted on their curbstones before the boys had finished.

The white spaces were painted first along the street and then the boys came back and stenciled the black numbers thus allowing time for the white paint to dry. A charge of twenty-five cents was made for any combination of numbers and the first morning in four hours they completed twenty-two orders each, making a total of $5.50 for the morning's work a piece.

Every Saturday and as many hours before and after classes as they could manage these two enterprising "business men" worked at their jobs. Before long they found that they had about exhausted the market in Evanston. They then moved on to the section just south of Evanston which is Chicago proper and worked that territory. When that was worked out they moved on to other suburbs north and "numbered" the residents as Ralph termed it. During the spring vacation they finished the sections north and west of Evanston and when the summer vacation came around they decided to take their paint and brushes and "number the natives" along the route to Ralph's home where George was spending the summer. In the farm sections along the way they painted rural mail boxes with aluminum paint and stenciled the name, post office, R.F.D. route, and box number. For this work a charge of fifty cents was made. During the summer they worked the territory, in and around Ralph's home town of 150,000 people and the fall term saw them with more than enough money to finish their fourth year's tuition.

■ ■

There's a Good Market for Sports Pictures

"GUESS I'm lucky," replied Aaron Rubino, San Mateo (California) Junior College "frosh" when asked how he had succeeded so well with the side line to his premedical course. A smiling, black-haired giant of nineteen, Rube, as he is known, takes pictures with a Graflex plate camera—pictures that sell.

Photography always interested him but it became his hobby in 1935 when he was given a photo finishing outfit. He went to football games and snapped highlight plays. One Saturday on the field he asked a photographer for help in getting a picture. The man was star camera man for the *San Francisco Chronicle*. He not only gave the advice but told Rube to come to the office any time he needed information. Rube did, a friendship developed, and today that newspaper man is a friend of the Rubino family.

The boy spent every spare moment taking and developing pictures. He was getting orders. He specialized in athletic subjects because he was so "keen" about sports.

One day he showed some pictures to the sports editor of the *Chronicle* who accepted them and offered to buy others as good. Rube submitted them by the dozen, gaining the liking of the editorial staff by his perseverance and enthusiasm. He was given use of the dark room and the benefit of expert advice. At first he supplied his own films and paid his way to photographed events—many times wasted effort when his photos didn't sell. But today he rarely has a failure and the newspaper gives him assignments and pays for films in addition to pictures used. He has a press badge, gets free passes to all athletic events, and knows practically every newspaper-man in town.

Being "with the staff but not of it" is an advantage, he points out. The free lance can sell prints and retain his negative, something a staff photographer cannot do. Rube sells to the United Press, Associated Press, Wide World, and other good markets. Here are his suggestions to prospective free lance camera men:

Always be on time. He learned this when, after watching a school fire from twelve until three in the morning, he rushed home to develop his pictures and got them to the *Chronicle* by four o'clock only to be told "Too late; we've gone to press."

Don't be afraid to talk to people. He often hitch-hikes the nineteen miles home from college because he likes to contact people and has had "lifts" in everything from a Ford to a Packard. "It's a swell way to learn human nature," he declares.

Be resourceful. Resourcefulness brought him his biggest thrill and a scoop. At college one morning he heard that a "red" demonstration was to be staged on the campus at high noon. What a chance for pictures! But, alas, his camera was at home. Attending morning classes he wrestled with the problem of getting those pictures and when the demonstration came off there was Rube in the thick of it clicking away. He had borrowed the school camera. He recorded the wild scene with eggs and tomatoes by the bushel flying through the air hitting policemen and college dignitaries who were trying to quell the disorder. Rube was the only photographer present and the rioters tried to smash him and his camera but he got away and rushed down to the *Chronicle* office. Other newspapers tried to buy his pictures but he wouldn't sell and the *Chronicle* was the only paper carrying photographs to accompany the big headlined story.

Said Rube: "I just fought my way through the mob. Guess it was luck." Luck? Sounds more like pluck.

■ ■

Making College Expenses with an Ice Cream Machine

WHEN Lucy Manners discovered that no arrangement had been made for supplying ice cream to the girls in a camp where she was spending her summer vacation from college, she bought a hand-operated ice cream machine. Her investment in this machine was a little under fifty dollars. This included cost of transportation and incidental equipment. It was large enough to make ten gallons of ice cream at one time. With the machine she received detailed instructions on operating it and on making various kinds of cream. She set the machine up in a tent. Then she visited a near-by town and ordered the required amount of ice and supplies. She bought milk from a farmer and made up the first ten gallons of ice cream.

"I thought the girls would like a rich vanilla cream best," said Lucy, "but I was surprised to learn most of them preferred chocolate flavor. So I made ten gallons of the vanilla and ten gallons of the chocolate that first day. There were two hundred and sixty girls in the camp, all between the ages of fifteen and twenty-two. And all wanted ice cream. But twenty gallons were more than they seemed willing to consume in one day. It took two days to sell it."

Lucy sold her cream in cones at five cents each, getting five hundred and fifty cones for the ten gallons of ice cream. Each girl in the camp bought an average of two cones daily. Her profits from ice cream sales averaged thirteen dollars and sixty cents daily and during the hundred days she spent at the summer camp she made a profit well over a thousand dollars—a welcome contribution toward her college expenses.

"One really hot day I had to make thirty gallons of cream. I had to work rather hard, but I was thrilled at the money I made. That was my biggest day. It was a visiting day in the camp, and some boys came over from a boys' camp about twenty miles away during the afternoon. Many of the girls' parents had come up there too, so I did quite a good business." The cost of making a gallon of cream, including the ice, milk, extracts, and other ingredients, Lucy found to be sixty-four cents. Cones cost one dollar for each three hundred.

A machine such as Lucy used may be operated by anyone, and there are almost unlimited opportunities for making money with it. In small towns an ice-cream machine may be made to pay for itself many times over if placed in a store, or near a school, or on a business street.

■ ■

Students Earn Money as Proxy Parents

ABOUT two years ago, Miss G. Alison Raymond, a graduate of Bryn Mawr, found it impossible to locate anything other than a temporary job. After weeks of unsuccessful scouting she realized that she would have to make her own job. Making a job is, of course, much more difficult than finding one. However, Miss Raymond's special aptitude for organization has enabled her to make an unusual success in an out-of-the-ordinary enterprise she calls Proxy Parents.

"Proxy Parents" provides employment for young students who find it necessary to make money during odd hours. These "proxy parents" are on call any time during the day and evening. For instance, if Mrs. Jones' little daughter is coming home from school or camp and the mother cannot meet the train, she calls Proxy Parents and a student is called to take over the job of seeing that Priscilla reaches home safely. Or, if a mother has a convalescent child and wants someone to amuse him, read to him or play games with him, she calls "Proxy Parents."

Besides meeting trains, amusing convalescent children in their homes or in hospitals, Proxy Parents will take charge of play hours during rainy days, take children singly or in groups to museums, the moving pictures, beaches, playgrounds, parks, or other specified places. Students are also on call for an hour or two to stay with a child while the mother shops, or they will take charge of a child during the evenings when the parents are away.

A clever girl whose course of study is not too heavy could develop such an enterprise during her third and fourth college years with the idea of continuing it after graduation. A card file of students names, free hours, and special abilities, and a list of families in town having children, form the basis for a "proxy parent" business.

■ ■

Collar Specialty Pays Profits

WHEN Al Handler, a student at Northwestern University, Evanston, decided to make some extra money on his vacation, he elected to sell a device that makes soft collars set properly. In his vacation period he earned well over $1,000 selling them. That's a remarkable achievement when you consider he was selling a 25-cent item.

"This specialty certainly appealed to me," declared Handler. "Wearing soft-collard shirts myself, I recognized the disadvantage of the soft collar. It didn't look as neat and snappy as the starched collar. Often the soft collars on my own shirts were messy, uneven in appearance, and in hot weather, wrinkled very easily. So when I found out about this little wire device that makes soft collars behave, I fell for it hard. I got a gross of them. I called upon men of my own age at first, made a quick demonstration, and usually got their money. Still, it took quite a while to sell the gross. Sometimes I wouldn't make more than two sales in an hour, and that wasn't much, for on a 50-cent sale my commission amounted to only 35 cents. It was plain that I had to increase the number of sales, and increase them quickly, to make the money I needed.

"I tried calling on pool rooms, barber shops, and similar places, often to find but one or two men inside—not enough to step up sales appreciably. Where could I go and do a better business? That became my dominating idea. I went to a baseball park one afternoon, an hour before the game started. Here were thousands of men. If I could sell only a few of them, I thought I could get somewhere. So I talked with a couple of men in the grandstand, made a few sales, then I moved to another part of the grandstand, and made a few more sales. In that one afternoon, I sold a hundred and fourteen of these wire gadgets to make soft collars set right, and pocketed $19.95 in commissions. I called back at the ball park the next day, and made better than ninety sales. The following day, I didn't do so well. I next tried the bathing beaches, where I was sure to find a number of men sitting around in their shirt sleeves. In two hours I sold thirty-five, and left the beach highly elated. I was convinced. I was getting somewhere. My problem, however, was to find some place every day where there would be a crowd of men. Once in the crowd, I would be able to do a brisk business. This brought me to all parts of the city. I sold lay-right devices even in hotel lobbies.

"Some men asked me for my card. Some took two or three of the devices at one time. Many turned me down, of course. But out of every forty men I spoke to, I was able to sell ten. It was easy to talk to a great many men who remained in a place like a ball park or at the beach for several hours, and get their yes or no answer. I was careful to avoid any kind of group demonstration, however. I didn't want to give the impression that I was making a soap box demonstration. I wasn't a hawker, crying out my wares. I spoke to men in a quiet way, told them to look at the way my collar lay, and made a quick demonstration. That was all."

Handler received some business from men who asked for his card. One such prospect, a big-league catcher at that time for the New York Giants. He took half a dozen of Handler's devices and told the other men on the team about them. Several sent their orders on to Handler from New York later.

■ ■

Mrs. Fenton's Canned Vegetable Business

BY THE time her daughter was almost ready to enter college, Mrs. R. W. Fenton, of Lynn County, Texas, began to realize that with the low prices for farm crops there might not be enough money for the four years at school. But, as the old saying goes, where there's a will there's a way, and, when the time came, the money was there each year of the four to pay the expenses.

Mrs. Fenton made that money by canning vegetables. Experience in home demonstration club work had enabled her to produce a high-grade product and she had gained the privilege of using official demonstration labels on her canned goods. One of her big orders came from the Texas A & M College to which she had submitted samples of canned peas. This order was for use in the college dining halls and consisted of 1,000 No. 3 cans. Another order from the school was for 300 No. 2 cans of peas and a dormitory at Texas Technological College purchased 100 No. 3 and 200 No. 2 cans of black-eyed peas. Another of her regular customers was a large hotel in Lubbock which bought her canned products for banquets and other special occasions.

All the members of the family took a hand in preparing the goods for market by helping to gather, clean and prepare the vegetables for canning. Two large pressure cookers were used in canning, one accommodating nine No. 3 cans and the other fifteen No. 3's. In one day, with the aid of the family, Mrs. Fenton put up 150 No. 3 and 200 No. 2 cans of vegetables. The canning season lasts about eight weeks and while the Fenton kitchen was a busy place during that time, careful planning of the work and kitchen arrangement has simplified the job considerably. By planting the vegetables at two-week intervals, sufficient time elapsed between the maturing of each crop to allow for a smooth flow of work in the kitchen.

While many of the vegetables were raised under field conditions, most of them were grown in a subirrigated home garden. The subirrigation was necessary because of a mineral deposit in the soil which made it impossible to farm after several years of surface irrigation. The simple subirrigation method consisted of three lines of homemade concrete tiles which cost one cent a foot, exclusive of labor, a windmill and water tank, and a hose. The windmill pumped the water into the overhead tank and gravitation forced it down through the hose where it enters the intakes of the tiles. Watering for two or three hours once a week was sufficient to moisten the soil unless the weather became extremely hot.

As the market for Mrs. Fenton's products grew, the money earned was more than sufficient for her daughter's use. There was even enough left over to buy some of the labor-saving devices most women want in their homes.

"Pinch Hitting" for Housewives Solves College Problem

JEANNETTE HARDY had her heart set on going to college. Before she entered high school, she had her plans all made to study home economics with the idea of teaching the subject when she finished college. But her aunt, while able to see her through high school, could not afford to send Jeannette to college.

When Jeannette was still in grade school she was saving the money she made running errands and doing small household tasks. However, her specialty was cooking and she decided to become a past master of this art. By the time she entered high school she was able to prepare excellent meals. She found a field for her talent in preparing dinners for the "cliff dwellers" in her neighborhood who liked to play bridge or golf in the afternoons. The night before her engagement, she would call her "client" on the telephone and get a list of the things needed for dinner the next night. On her way home from school at three-thirty, she would do the marketing.

When she arrived at her employer's home and got the key from the janitor, she would wash up the luncheon or breakfast dishes, prepare the vegetables and the dessert, and set the table. While the dinner was cooking she would straighten up the dining and living rooms, picking up the scattered newspapers and books, emptying the ash trays, plumping up the cushions, setting the window shades straight, and giving the rooms the attention that every good housekeeper knows makes a place look right. If a roast had been selected for the evening meal it would be in the oven, but if steak or chops, she would have them ready to pop into the broiler as soon as she heard her employer's key in the door. In twenty minutes or so, she would be ready to serve the dinner. Then after dinner, she washed the dishes and tidied up the kitchen. Her charge for this service was $1.25. When she didn't have to do the marketing, the charge was $1.00.

She started out with one "customer" a week. Then she added two more to her list. In the meantime, she helped prepare food and serve it at several big parties. During the school year she averaged about four engagements a week. In the second summer vacation from school she spent one month taking complete charge of an invalid who needed to have her food carefully prepared. The family in this case paid the girl $15 a week. Whereas the first year in high school she had made only $150, the second year she made $200. These sums added to the $150 she had in her college fund made a total of $500 when she entered her third year in high school. In the next two years she was able to set aside $400. At Christmas time and other holidays, she earned some extra money by preparing and selling coffee cakes, plum puddings, fruit cake, and similar delicacies. Upon her graduation, her savings made it possible for her to be certain of at least two years in college without scrimping or missing any of the social activities. At the end of her first two college years, an insurance policy her aunt had taken out when Jeannette was a little girl, fell due and provided a sufficient sum to pay for the two remaining years.

■ ■

A College Education from Walnuts

O N A FARM just outside a small town in Missouri, lived Mrs. Harris, a widow, with one daughter in college. Money was scarce as it usually is on farms. One day Mrs. Harris noticed that the walnut trees were loaded with nuts. Perhaps, she thought, they could be sold. The next day she had the boy who did odd jobs around the farm gather a couple of bushels of the walnuts and they were spread out to dry in the sun. Later when they were dry, he cracked them and she picked out the nut meats and carefully separated them from the shells.

In the meantime she had written a sister in Chicago and asked her whether there was any demand for black walnuts in Chicago. The sister replied at once that she could sell about ten pounds to two candy firms located not far from her immediate neighborhood and quoted the price the firms wanted to pay. She also suggested another ten pounds which she believed could be sold to friends and acquaintances. The thirty pounds were mailed by parcel post and the two ten-pound lots delivered to the candy factories. At her bridge club the sister served a cake baked with some of the walnuts and mentioned the fact that the walnuts came from her sister's farm. That was the start of a nice little business. The walnuts were also put up in little cellophane bags and sold somewhat higher than the general market price. The daughter at college also helped. She induced a local store catering to the fudge-loving college students to try a ten-pound package and she secured an order from an ice cream manufacturer. A candy shop that made a variety of candy known as "black walnut kisses" also ordered a ten-pound package. Word got around the college town and soon orders came to the girl from the mothers of some of the local college students. The walnuts were mailed from home in ten-pound packages and she put them up in cellophane bags as her aunt in Chicago had done.

The sister in Chicago was a "live wire." She called upon bakeries and upon confectioners, upon local specialty food shops, and soon had worked up a good list of customers. Many of these firms ordered direct because they wanted to secure larger quantities and correspondingly lower prices. Others continued to purchase their needs locally from the sister.

Why do not more farm families do this sort of thing? And why do not more city folks who would like to make a thousand dollars, arrange with people living on farms to market the particularly fine things they grow? A young man in Winnetka, Illinois, made a tidy sum of money taking orders for California figs which he cleared through a fig grower in the Santa Clara Valley. A chap in Atlanta earned well over a thousand dollars last year by selling Florida Key limes to local soda fountains and fancy grocery stores. He secured limes grown on Captiva Island just off Fort Myers. Any number of fancy food products, such as these, can be sold at a nice profit by anyone who is not afraid of work.

■ ■

Earns Tuition by Polishing Cars

ONE Saturday afternoon, E. A. Huntley was busily washing his car in "gasoline alley," when a young chap came up to him and said: "I believe that car would look better if it were simonized." Huntley agreed. "It certainly would, but it costs about $5.00 or $6.00 and I don't feel like spending that much right now." The young man produced an inexpensive card on which was printed in the center the one word "Simonizing." In the lower left-hand corner was his name, address and telephone number.

"I will simonize your car for you for only $3.00, and I will do a real good job. Right now I'm working on your neighbor's car just down the alley a bit. I am a student in Washington University and have Saturdays and Sundays free, of course. Would next Saturday morning be O.K. to work on your car?"

There was no question that the car did need polishing and the chap was so engaging in his manners—so Huntley told him to come around next Saturday morning and he could have the job. Then he became curious about the boy's work. "Do you have many jobs such as this?" he asked. "Yes, I do," the student replied. "Every Saturday and Sunday I have jobs and also throughout the week, during my free time. I would say that I average at least a car a day. Right now I am in my junior year at Washington and I have paid my way so far, with the exception of the first term, by cleaning and polishing cars. I have my regular customers and they are always recommending me to their friends. That's because I do such a good job," he ingenuously added.

"But how did you build up your 'clientele'?" asked Huntley. "Just the way I got the job to simonize your car," answered the student, grinning. "I had these cards printed, went along the alleys and wherever I found a man cleaning up his car, I would present my card and offer to do a good job on his car. Whenever I sold one man on the idea, I went to his neighbors and sold them. I also went around to the offices and factories. Whenever I saw a man getting into a car that looked like it needed polishing, I would step up and give him one of my cards and a little talk about the kind of job I can do. It seems to work all right because I always have enough work to keep me busy and, as a general rule, several jobs booked ahead.

"Well, I'll have to get back to my job down the alley—I promised to have it finished by 4:30. I'll leave a couple of my cards with you and if you have any friends who want their cars cleaned and polished, I'd appreciate it if you would let them know about my work. I'll be around bright and early Saturday morning to do your car. Thank you sir, for the job. You'll be surprised when you see how nice your car will look Saturday after it gets one of my good 'rub-downs.' "

As Huntley said to his wife later, "How could you turn down a polite, ambitious boy such as that and especially one with so much initiative?"

■ ■

Wooden Dogs Pay Student's Expenses

A YOUNG college student living in Webster Groves, Missouri, was, unlike most girls, interested in woodworking, and much of her spare time was spent at her Dad's work bench in the basement of her home. One day while experimenting with some thin pieces of wood and a scroll saw, she turned out the figure of a little Scottie. By attaching a pin to it she had a dress ornament. When the girls at school saw it, they too, wanted one. So she made several for her friends and gave them away. However, the first thing she knew, almost everybody in her sorority wanted one of the cunning little wooden dogs for a hat or scarf pin. She began to make all sorts of dogs, but the Scotties were the favorites. And she began to charge a small price for the pins. As the fad grew, she found that the shops wanted quantities of the pins, so dad and brother and sister got together and began turning out dozens of the ornaments. Before long, the basement workshop was a regular little factory and all hands were busily engaged.

The fad grew and spread, and it wasn't long before every girl on the campus was wearing a little wooden dog pin. And, incidentally, where before there was hardly enough money to pay for four years' college expenses, now there was plenty and to spare. The fad for wooden ornaments, buttons, belt buckles, clip pins and even earrings, as well as for match holders, trays, candle holders and similar items, is still going strong and looks like it will last at least another season or two.

■ ■

A Hundred and One Ways to Earn College Expenses

SPORTS AND GAMES—Besides teaching swimming, tennis, golf, skiing, and other sports, there is an opportunity for the student proficient in athletics to secure work coaching high school teams, to act as referee or umpire, to give gymnastic instruction in clubs in the community, to manage a summer golf club, act as assistant to a playground instructor, manage a skating rink, be an athletic counselor at a summer camp, work as a life guard during the summer months, organize athletic activities in clubs or churches. Naturally, those students on football or other teams cannot accept such work for they would lose their amateur standings and be barred from college athletics. Teaching bridge offers another means of earning money.

TUTORING AND TEACHING—Tutoring pays from 50 cents to around $1.50 an hour, and if the student can find a sufficient number of jobs, he can make a nice little income. Many students enter college who need tutoring in special subjects in order to fulfill the entrance requirements. The subjects in which most of them need help are: mathematics, foreign languages, physics, and English.

MUSIC—Students with a musical education can often help to pay their expenses by giving music lessons to children and adults in the community. They may also be able to find part-time work in the local school of music teaching voice, the violin, the piano and other instruments. Teaching hours can usually be arranged so that they do not interfere with the student's regular class work. If you are a good organist, you may be able to secure the job of chapel organist. Organize a college orchestra and sell your services to a summer resort, hotel, or other place of amusement. Many students find an opportunity to play in a dance band over the week-ends. A few dollars can also be made by singing in a church choir.

Assistant Instructors—Students can arrange with the dean to secure work in the laboratories or the libraries. There is also an opportunity in work such as the correction of class papers, checking student attendance, the supervision of music practice, etc. While this work does not pay much, it is worth securing because it is right on the campus thus making it possible to sandwich in the work at odd moments.

TEACHING—Positions are often available in the local schools for advanced students. These jobs usually pay well, but they are exacting and take more of the student's time than some of the other activities by which he can earn money. Some of the colleges employ student instructors in various departments and the positions pay fairly well.

CLERICAL WORK—This type of work may be secured in the school itself, in local business houses, and in local retail stores. The student who has learned typewriting and shorthand is in a position to take advantage of such part-time jobs available. In addition to secretarial work, these jobs may include billing, filing, stencil cutting, mimeographing, addressing and mailing. The compensation ranges from 15 to 40 cents an hour, depending upon the labor market, the community, and the importance of the work.

SELLING YOUR SERVICES—Reading to invalids; taking care of children; giving patients massage; cleaning and pressing garments; mending; housework; gardening; tending furnaces; window washing; waiting on tables; delivery service for stores; washing dishes; catering; janitor service in clubs, college dormitories, and churches; shoveling snow; beating rugs; typewriting term papers; chauffering; cutting grass; cleaning and polishing automobiles; caddying; delivering books from the libraries, and distributing circulars for merchants, all offer means of making money to pay expenses. In many colleges, student agencies have been organized to handle much of this sort of work. There are laundry agencies, boarding clubs, pressing and cleaning agencies, travel agencies, news agencies, etc. When these agencies are well organized and managed, they yield their promoters sufficient profit to pay tuition as well as other expenses during the college years.

ODD JOBS—Students are frequently able to secure part-time jobs with the local ice company, banks, lumber and coal yards, trucking companies, manufacturing plants, hotels, summer resorts, steamboat companies, garages, etc. Jobs with such concerns will include all sorts of work—food checkers, truck drivers, pursers, icemen, bell hops, freight handlers, auto mechanics, timekeepers, bank runners. In addition to being a means of earning expenses, work such as this often leads to full-time jobs with the company after graduation.

HANDICRAFTS—Those who are skillful with the needle, the saw, the paint brush, or scissors, can often make quite a bit of money during the holidays by catering to the demand for handmade articles. Some of the articles that can be made and sold during the holiday season include: hand-knitted scarfs, ties, and novelty gloves such as are worn for winter sports; cut-out silhouettes which can be likenesses of students, historical figures, or pet dogs, cats, squirrels, etc.; hand-painted greeting cards; handmade handkerchiefs; collar and cuff sets; monogram work; dolls; laundry and shoe bags; boutonnieres; cloth or paper-covered scrapbooks; dress bags; bookstands; folding screens; ship or airplane models; photographs of points of interest on the campus; hanging bookshelves, and cretonne or chintz cushions. These articles can be sold direct to the students for their own use or as gifts for their families and friends; they may also be sold through the gift shops, the woman's exchange, or the student's exchange.

CONFECTIONERY—If someone in the family makes excellent candies, you can sell pounds of them to your fellow students. During the holidays, there is always a good demand. Butterscotch, molasses kisses, taffy, fudge, caramels, maple candy, peanut clusters made with a syrup coating, old-fashioned peppermint sticks, candied fruits, stuffed dates or figs, "seafoam," and coconut kisses, are all popular.

PROMOTIONS AND CONCESSIONS—Student agencies mentioned above come under this classification. There is also an opportunity to earn money by handling the sale of souvenirs, jewelry, novelties, food, fruits, engraved cards and other merchandise on the campus. Student exchanges handling the sale of handicrafts and art work offer a good return for the time invested. These and other unusual promotions are generally operated by upper classmen and require both initiative and executive ability.

FARM AND GARDEN WORK—Students attending college in agricultural sections often secure their room and board as well as wages during the summer months by helping with the milking, care of poultry or live stock, picking fruit, threshing, stacking wheat, shucking corn, and other farm activities. Agricultural colleges also offer students work in the truck gardens and the greenhouses on the campus. Agricultural experiment stations pay students for special technical work.

TRADES AND PROFESSIONS—The man who is proficient in some trade can often secure work in his particular line which pays well. Radio repair work, barbering, automobile repair work, making blue prints, typesetting, electrical appliance repairs, finishing photographs, woodturning, carpentry, watch repairing, and other work of this type is often available. Girls frequently earn money enough for board and room rent by giving shampoos, cutting hair, giving facials and manicures.

SELLING—Many companies are glad to secure the sale of their products through college students and many a boy or girl has secured a college education through the money earned by selling. Among the dozens of items that have been sold by students—and are still being sold—are: hosiery, jewelry, magazines, candy, greeting cards, books, electrical appliances, aluminum cooking utensils, nursery stock, insurance, coal, notions, novelties, fire extinguishers, eggs and poultry, advertising, calendars, cosmetics, disinfectants, pen and pencil sets, Neon signs, gas savers, auto club memberships, lubricants, clocks, brushes, lingerie, men's suits, shirts, etc.

JOURNALISM—Students of journalism find a field for their activities and a way to earn money by reporting for local and metropolitan newspapers. This work is paid for by the inch. Generally the student does not have to write his material, but telephones it in to the paper. Gifted students can often write special articles well enough for publication. The college publications also offer an opportunity to earn money. The student interested in advertising can sometimes secure a part-time job writing retail store advertising or preparing copy for the newspapers. The college print shop is another source for earning money. Typesetting, linotype work, and proofreading jobs can frequently be secured on local publications. This may be part-time work or the student may find it possible to get work during a rush period when extra help is needed.

If the student is an expert with the camera, he can often make extra money by snapping pictures of the big football games, track meets, or interesting scenes in his locality. These pictures may be sold to the local papers, to magazines or newspaper syndicates. Pictures should be taken with a sharp angle in mind, that is, they should emphasize some point or idea. They should be different enough from the average picture of the same sort to at least warrant a second look. The amateur camera addict can learn a great deal about the market for pictures by looking over the current magazine and newspaper picture sections with a critical eye.

CHAPTER TWELVE

RAISING MONEY FOR CHARITY

DURING the depression there were so many demands upon people to give to charity that most of the time-honored methods of raising money proved inadequate. Churches, which had always been able to depend upon an annual bazaar for funds, found that the decline in spendable income reduced the net proceeds from such undertakings very substantially. Carnivals, once the main source of funds for American Legion posts and similar community enterprises, failed to draw nickels and dimes in the needed volume. Even the "Charity Ball" lost its pull. Yet the need for money was greater than ever, and those responsible for raising the funds had to resort to new innovations.

One outstanding development was the so-called Goodwin plan, which had quite a vogue for a time. The Goodwin Corporation of Chicago arranged with a group of manufacturers to list their products in a special catalog. These catalogs were distributed in quantities to church workers and others with the understanding that a commission would be paid by the Goodwin Corporation on all orders sent in for products listed in the catalog. Thousands of charitable institutions took up the plan, but it met with opposition on the part of local merchants. They looked upon it as a competitive activity which was taking business away from their stores. Naturally the merchants boycotted the products of the manufacturers who went into the plan, and soon the opposition became so pronounced that many discontinued using it.

This experience serves to illustrate one important point that should be given consideration in any kind of money-raising activity for charity. Is it going to interfere with the business of local merchants and business men to whom the community owes allegiance? For example, one of the first things most churches decide to do when they put on an affair is to get out a souvenir program and sell advertising to the local merchants at "all the traffic will bear." Little or no thought is given to the value of the advertising to the merchant. The common attitude of the promoters is that they have been doing business with these merchants for years, and this will be a good way for them to reciprocate. They overlook the fact that in most cases such advertising is a waste of money, and that the merchants in order to cover their cost of doing business, must add the money thus spent to their prices. Since the big chain stores have a very definite rule that they will not do this kind of advertising, the "tax" falls upon the independent merchants and tends to make their difficulty of competing with the chain store even more acute. Thus, unwittingly, these well-intentioned people, in their effort to raise money for a worthy charitable undertaking, help to drive the independent merchants out of their communities.

For this reason it is wise in planning a money-raising activity to be careful that it is tuned to a sound community policy, and that it does not "rob Peter to pay Paul." Fortunately, there are any number of ways for raising money that are not competitive to local business enterprises as the examples which follow demonstrate.

■ ■

Baby Shows Go Over Big

EVERYBODY loves a baby, and there is probably nothing which has so much interest to the mothers in a community as a baby show and contest. Since the very nature of such a show is to stimulate interest in better babies, it not only serves as a means of raising money, but it indirectly promotes the sale of many things sold in the local stores, which babies need. In fact, it is easy to get local merchants to tie in with such a contest, and give good display to posters and advertising.

There are a dozen different plans for holding baby shows. The most popular plan is to have the mothers of the babies bring them in to be shown and judged. Arrange with local merchants to have displays of baby goods in the church hall or wherever the contest is held, and charge them a percentage of their total sales for the concession. If the community is large enough, the contest can last several days, a different age group being judged each day. A committee of local doctors will gladly serve as judges, and if accommodations permit lectures can be held every hour on some phase of baby care. Admission is charged, and door prizes awarded. While the amount of money that can be raised from a baby show is limited, it has compensating advantages from a publicity standpoint. The newspapers will give it a good play because it offers an opportunity for a human interest story of wide reader interest.

■ ■

White Elephant Sales Are Exciting

THE idea here is to give everybody interested in a charity an opportunity to unload "a white elephant." This is something one owns but does

not need, which he is willing to give to charity to raise money. These dona-
tions, which should be of a gift nature, are then brought to the place where
the sale is to be held, and each "prize" is put in a box or wrapped separately.
Tickets are sold for the sale, usually at 25 cents each. The purchasers of
the tickets are arranged in groups of twenty, and required to sit around
in a circle. When they are so seated each one in the circle is given one
of the "blind" packages containing some one's "white elephant." A leader
then asks everyone to pass his package to the person on his left, and to
keep passing it until a bell is rung. When the bell sounds, everybody opens
the lid on his package or peeks into the wrapper to see what it contains.
He must not let his neighbors see it however. Three minutes are allowed
for examination. Those who want to keep their packages drop out of the
circle. The bell rings again, and the packages are started rotating. Another
bell, another period of inspection and decision, and so on until everyone in
the circle has a "white elephant." A time limit is set and when it is up, those
remaining have to take what they hold at the final bell. This stunt never fails
to get a good crowd, and interest runs high. It is simply the old grab bag
idea in a new suit of clothes. It is not unusual to sell 200 tickets to a single
sale, which means ten circles and $50 clear profit. Ten such sales a year will
net your charity $500. In some communities, of course, tickets can be sold
for thirty-five or fifty cents which will make the net amount correspondingly higher. As there is little or no expense attached to the enterprise, all
the money paid for the tickets is clear gain.

■ ■

Home Furnishing Lecture Series

THESE lectures are arranged in cooperation with the local furniture
store, the china store, rug dealer, jeweler, etc. From five to seven
women give their homes for the lectures.

The first lecture might be on period furniture, and the merchant who
cooperated would have a display of furniture at the home where the lecture was to be held, which he would decorate in connection with his talk.
The second lecture might be on crystal, and an exhibition table displaying various glasses would be arranged before the talk by the lecturer. The
third lecture might be on oriental rugs, always a subject of great interest to
women. The local rug dealer will be glad to arrange a display of rugs at the
home where the lecture is to be given. The fourth lecture could deal with
china. There is an unlimited number of subjects which lend themselves to
a series of lectures of this sort: linens, laces, silverware, pictures, lamps—

anything and everything that goes to make a home livable. To realize the most out of such a series of lectures, tickets should be sold in advance for the entire series. The price may be nominal—$1.50 for a series of five lectures, or $2.00 for a series of seven. The advantage of selling a series ticket, rather than permitting the guests to pay for each lecture at the door is that it insures attendance. Because such lectures are good advertising for the local merchants they are usually willing to furnish a door prize. Posters announcing the lectures should be prepared and put up in the stores of those merchants who cooperate in the plan. Organizations such as women's clubs, churches, etc., which have an auditorium, will find this plan particularly profitable, since such facilities permit a much larger sale of tickets than when the lectures are given at private homes in the community.

■ ■

Sample Night for Local Merchants

THIS is another idea which is designed to support the independent local merchants in their fight against chain competition. To stage the affair successfully a large hall is needed. Display space is sold for a nominal amount, five to ten dollars, to local merchants. The merchant puts in a display of select merchandise and arranges with as many sources of supply as possible for samples to be distributed from his booth. There is no limit to the number of samples that one exhibitor may distribute. Thus the food shop may pass out samples of breakfast food, coffee, etc. The druggist may sample such items as toilet soaps, tooth paste, and medicines. The tobacconist may sample cigarettes, smoking tobacco, etc. The confectioner may pass out samples of gum and candies. These samples will be furnished in most cases without cost to the local merchant by the manufacturer whose advertising budget carries a provision for this kind of sampling. Some manufacturers will be glad to send demonstrators to prepare foods, or to demonstrate their products, if invited. To get out the crowd, a major attraction should be arranged. Door prizes are usually given. These sample nights are quite popular, and it is an easy matter to sell tickets at 25 cents each. In fact, a reasonable charge is desirable to hold down the number of children attending. Arrangements should be made with a paper house to furnish everyone who attends, a large paper bag with handles to carry home the samples. Additional revenue may be raised by permitting the exhibitors to sell the products they have on display, paying the organization sponsoring the "Sample Night" a small percentage of their sales in addition to the rental of the space.

Christmas Pudding Sale

IT IS hard to beat a food sale as a means of raising money, especially if arrangements can be made with a centrally located store to hold it there. A hardware merchant in Eagle River, Wisconsin, gives one of the churches the use of his store for one morning each year to hold a bake sale, a feature of which is a baking demonstration in the store while the sale is in progress. An electric range, for which the merchant is the local agent, is used for the demonstration, and the church gets 10 per cent on all ranges which are sold as a result of leads secured during the bake sale. Another charitable organization in New England makes upward of a thousand dollars annually from its Christmas pudding and mince meat sale held a few days before Thanksgiving. An old-fashioned English plum pudding will bring as high as $1.00 a pound at such sales. The usual plan is for the organization to buy the materials, and then everyone helps to make the puddings under the direction of someone who is especially good at this sort of thing. The same procedure applies to making the mince meat.

■ ■

Chain Luncheons and Card Parties

THIS is a particularly good idea for a suburban community. Each member of the organization invites four people, and each one attending in turn invites four others to a luncheon at her home the following week. The process is repeated until the entire community has been covered.

Each hostess plans what shall be done after lunch. Some invite their guests to bring their sewing or knitting, others play cards, and others have readings. The advantage of the plan is that it does not place too much of a burden on any one hostess. The money is raised by each guest paying fifty cents or a dollar for the luncheon. In order to insure the success of the undertaking, a committee is appointed to follow up the guests at each luncheon to make sure that the chain is not broken. The same idea can be adapted to evening card parties. In that case, however, four couples, rather than four people, comprise a chain unit. To add interest to these card parties, rules are set up, and a certain number of hands are played each evening. At the conclusion of the series a grand prize is given to the person turning in the highest score. This eliminates the necessity of having a prize for each party, which would make a big hole in the profits.

Florentine Fair

ONE of the old, dependable methods of raising money for a church or charity is to hold a bazaar; but, because bazaars have become commonplace, they need to be dramatized in order to attract the crowds.

A suburban church did this very successfully by calling its bazaar a Florentine Fair. The auditorium in which the bazaar was held was decorated to resemble a street scene in Florence, Italy. Colorful hangings were used over the booths and elsewhere around the room, and those who took part in the bazaar were dressed in the picturesque Italian costumes. A high spot of the fair was an "open air" restaurant, with bunches of garlic and all the other things which give atmosphere to a Florence street cafe prominently displayed. Street singers strumming Italian melodies added the final touch of color to the scene.

As a further attraction, arrangements were made with an importer of Italian delicacies to have a booth at the fair. Those members of the organization who had Italian hangings or furniture were asked to lend them for the occasion. The most popular attractions were the flower booth, with its bevy of dark-haired flower girls, and the Italian handicrafts booth.

The fair was a great success. Whereas the ordinary bazaar held by this church would net $1,000, the bazaar with this Florentine setting netted better than $3,000. One of the reasons for this was that the local newspapers gave the fair unusually good publicity because of its human-interest value.

■ ■

A Mile of Pennies

THE idea here is to induce all the members of an organization and their friends to save their pennies in small cloth bags. Each bag holds sixteen pennies, which laid side by side make one foot of pennies. A tag explaining the plan is attached to the bags when they are given out. Since there are sixteen pennies to a foot, and 5,280 feet to a mile, if all the bags are filled and turned in, it will net an organization $844.80.

A Year 'Round Thrift Shop

A NUMBER of women's clubs have been able to obtain a steady income by fixing up a vacant store as a place for selling things various members have discarded or wish to dispose of on a commission. The usual plan is to ask each member to give one day a month to looking after the shop. When the shop becomes sufficiently profitable, a permanent attendant may be employed. The revenue from a store of this kind can be augmented by including a circulating library, the books being donated by members of the organization. Because the library is run for charity, no set rental rate is charged. Those taking out the books are expected to give what they can toward the work of the organization. They deposit their contribution in a small envelope which is pasted inside the front cover of the book, when they return the book. An explanation of the plan and the purpose of the charity is printed on the envelope.

Another good source of revenue for such a shop is selling knitting yarns. One shop of this kind has one of the members of the organization, who is an expert at knitting, come in one afternoon a week to give instruction in knitting. The yarn is purchased at wholesale as required, so the amount invested in stock is relatively small.

■ ■

Put on a Dog and Pet Show

THERE are usually people in every community who are very proud of their pet dogs. They may be lap dogs, hunting dogs, watch dogs, or "just dogs." But whatever type of dog it may be, the owner thinks his dog is better than his neighbor's dog. Capitalize on this dog-loving instinct in your community by putting on a local dog show. Prizes in the form of ribbons should be awarded. Because of the many breeds entered, and perhaps the lack of pedigrees, prizes are usually awarded for the smallest dog entered, the largest, the prettiest, the funniest, the smartest, the dog with the longest tail, the dog knowing the most tricks, the dog with the largest ears, etc.

■ ■

Country Fairs Are Always Good

THIS is another form of bazaar which is particularly popular in cities. A barn is usually rented for the fair, and everyone who participates wears a suitable costume such as overalls and denim shirts or gingham dresses. The feature of the fair is an old-fashioned barn dance. Various side attractions characteristic of country fairs are used to obtain added interest and revenue.

■ ■

A Prune and Apricot Drive

A BOYS' Scout troop raised enough money to buy all their necessary equipment and had some money left over toward their outdoor activities by canvassing the community and securing orders for boxes of Santa Clara Valley prunes and apricots. Prizes were offered to the scouts who sold the greatest number of boxes. Arrangements were made with a packing company in the Santa Clara Valley, California, to ship the prunes in season. The same idea can be used with pecan nuts or other specialties, but since prunes are a staple article and are usually consumed in quantities, most housewives are willing to buy them by the box or boxes, at the same time helping the boys.

■ ■

Progressive Luncheon and Style Show

O NE objection to holding luncheons as a means of raising money for charitable purposes is the difficulty of handling the crowd. A way to overcome this difficulty is to get four or five people in a neighborhood each to serve one course of a luncheon. Thus the appetizers will be served at one home, the entree at another, the salad at another, and the dessert at still another. The guests, of course, may come in relays if the homes are small and the number to be served large.

In order to add interest to the luncheon, a style show or some similar attraction is held at the same time. At the first home there might be a showing of house dresses by a local dress shop which specializes in garments of that kind. At the next home sports wear and millinery might be shown, afternoon dresses at the next, and evening dresses and wraps at another home. In each case the models are offered for sale, and the organization receives a commission on the sales made.

Spring Garden Carnival

THE open-air flower and garden sale which has become an institution in Evanston, Illinois, is sponsored by the Garden Club of Evanston. The city square is used for the event which lasts two or three days. Club members save their seeds and bulbs from the preceding season and place them in envelopes for sale. Each envelope bears the name of the person who grew the seeds. Other club members contribute potted flowers from their greenhouses or hotbeds. Concessions are sold to pottery manufacturers on a commission basis, and local merchants are invited to take part and sell all sorts of garden tools and supplies, paying a small commission for the privilege. In addition to the spring flowers and garden accessories, there is a food booth that does a land office business, and the usual concessions that go to make a street fair a real event for a youngster.

■ ■

"Days of Forty-Nine" Celebration

ANOTHER variation of the charity bazaar is to hold it in a setting which has the atmosphere of the California gold rush. The principal money-making attraction for such a bazaar is the dance hall with its various gambling devices and tables. In cities where gambling is prohibited, those attending are "sold" a package of stage money at the door, which is used at the various tables in place of currency. At the end of the evening, prizes are given to those holding the most greenbacks. One organization built up attendance by parading an old covered wagon and a team of oxen through the streets for several days before the fair opened.

■ ■

Spring Garden Tours

IN COMMUNITIES where there are unusually fine gardens, charitable organizations are able to raise considerable money by getting the owners of these gardens to set aside one day each spring for visitors. Books of tickets entitle the holder to admission to the various gardens, a ticket for each garden to be torn out as used. The usual price is fifty cents for a book of ten tickets.

"Double-Your-Dollar" Contest

A T THE beginning of the season each member of an organization is given one dollar from the treasury. With that money he is supposed to buy something to make or sell, and turn back at least $2.00 at the end of the season. There is, however, no limit to the amount of money which can be made from the dollar. Prizes are offered to those who "turn" their dollars the greatest number of times.

■ ■

"Most Treasured Possession" Exhibit

I N LOCALITIES made up of well-to-do families, each family usually has a museum piece of some kind—work of art, a book, shawls, an ornament, a stamp or coin collection, a piece of lace, or some other "treasured possession." These people are invited by the committee in charge of the affair to place such things on exhibition in one of the larger homes in the community on a specified day. Cards are typewritten giving interesting particulars about each exhibit and the name of the person who loaned it. Invitations are then sent to everybody in the neighborhood, who might be interested, to bring their friends. Admission may be charged or, if tea is served, contributions may be made as they are at a silver tea.

■ ■

Hostesses, Incorporated

T HE New York League of Girls' Clubs needed money. The League was the pet project of Mrs. Courtlandt D. Barnes and it was up to her to find a way to get some money. From time to time she had helped friends with various problems by calling upon the League for assistance. Someone in the League always knew someone else who could handle the particular job to be done.

With this experience to work on, Mrs. Barnes did not see why an organization could not be built up that would make money for the League. After talking it over with several friends, it was decided that the idea was a sound one, so "Hostesses, Incorporated" was organized. Miss Louise Evans was placed in charge and given one assistant. These two were the only ones on the staff who were paid full-time salaries. In reserve is a large staff of part-time employees. All profits, of course, go to the League.

Over the period of years it has been in existence, the organization has built up a staff which is capable of covering any emergency call. The call may be for a flying instructor, someone to close or open an apartment, someone to entertain out-of-town clients, a chaperon, a nurse, advice on a travel wardrobe, a plumber, a correspondence course in etiquette, someone to take care of the baby, secure transportation to any part of the world—Miss Evans will handle the problem without batting an eyelash. She will also arrange to have someone move your office over the week-end, someone to buy your old clothes and sell them for you, someone to prepare papers and speeches for you, to write letters, to take your child to school or home for the holidays. Nothing is too simple or too difficult for her to handle. Since the organization of "Hostesses, Incorporated," hundreds of dollars have found their way into the treasury of the League, work has been provided for many who needed it, and not a few business men or householders have had their problems neatly and quickly solved.

CHAPTER THIRTEEN

BEYOND THE FIRST THOUSAND

THERE is a saying, the wisdom of which was impressed upon many during the recent depression, to the effect that *it is easier to make money than it is to keep it.* The man who is out to make his first thousand dollars has but to seize an opportunity, and if he applies himself intelligently he is reasonably sure of a measure of success—certainly under normal conditions he should easily make a thousand dollars. In the preceding chapters you have read how hundreds of men and women have accomplished that objective. But after all, this first thousand dollars is only the first rung of the ladder. Having one foot on the ladder you are now faced with temptations which did not bother you when your major concern was making that first thousand.

First, there will come the temptation to rest on your oars and take it easy now that you are "in the money." You fought a good fight and won. Being a normal human being you feel that your efforts have entitled you to the rewards of victory. So you buy a new automobile, take a trip or do any one of a dozen things that you have been planning to do when you made some money. But one swallow does not make a summer. If you squander your money for a good time now, you will have nobody but yourself to blame if you must spend your old age dependent upon the State or relatives.

The real test of your business ability and your capacity for success is not behind you. It lies directly ahead of you. Are you going to take that first thousand dollars and use it as a seedling for a real fortune, and a place in the sun? Or are you going to treat it as a small boy treats a dime given him for a Saturday night lark? You may think, as thousands of others have thought, "Now that I have the secret of making money, nothing can stop me." There is danger in that philosophy, for you are now in a position where you are more likely to attract the attention of men who are looking for "suckers" with a thousand dollars in the bank. Soon it will be noised about town that you are making money, that you are prosperous, that you are even wealthy. Men will begin to "proposition" you. One of these men will have a sure-fire way of making money without working. All you have to do is to buy some stock in a company that is being formed. Another has inside information about an oil lease and there is a million dollars waiting for those who are smart enough to get in on the ground floor.

Make no mistake, for every person who has made a thousand dollars speculating, a thousand have lost. If there is a substitute for patient application and hard work, so far as making a permanent place for yourself in this world is concerned, no one has yet found it.

Generally speaking, you cannot make money playing the other fellow's game. However plausible his reasons may be for putting money into his business, remember that nine out of ten new ventures fail. There is only one chance in ten of your getting your money back. There are many successful business men who have an ironclad rule never to put money into any kind of business enterprise that they do not control. That does not mean that they would not invest in the common stocks of established companies with a long earning record, which is more in the nature of an investment than a speculation, but they will not put money in any new enterprise unless they control it.

Good Advice from a Veteran Financier

Former Secretary of the Treasury, Andrew Mellon, in a notable interview to the press just before the 1929 crash, pointed out that most common stocks were overpriced and by implication advised people who were "in the market" to put their money into bonds. He laid down eleven principles on handling money, which are well worth keeping in mind when that first thousand dollars begins to burn a hole in your pocket and you are considering how you can pyramid it into a fortune without work! Mr. Mellon's eleven points follow:

"Never buy stocks in mines you know nothing about. Shun alluring promises about mines in a faraway land.

"None but the rich can afford to trifle with oil wells.

"A patent may be only the right to a lawsuit. Schemers take advantage of every important discovery and invention, and some have nothing but promises to sell.

"Do you want to buy a swamp? There are real estate promoters who will sell you swamps as 'shore frontage.' If you buy property, buy near home.

"Look out for new companies that are going to sell by mail. They may never earn more than salary money, and that is paid out.

"New manufacturing methods should always be personally checked and investigated.

"'Invest quick or it may be too late' is the favorite urge of wild cat stock salesmen. That should make you suspicious.

"Look with suspicion on offers with special inducements in cash discounts or stock bonuses.

"Your banker will tell you that 'tips' on the stock market are worthless. Do not think you will be let in 'on the ground floor.'

"The rich man can afford to speculate. If he loses he has other money in the bank. Not so the small investor. Never play the stock market on 'margin.'

"Stock in companies being organized on the success of others, rarely turns out well. Do not put your money into another man's dreams."

You say that is good advice, yet look at the fortunes that have been made by the men who put money into Ford's business, and Standard Oil and other now well-known enterprises. Where would they have been if they had invested only in properties?

You Can't Beat the "Kitty"

There are exceptions to every rule. There are men who have played the stock market all their lives and made money at it. There are men who have played the races and made money doing it. There are men who have bought tickets in the Louisiana Lottery and have drawn winning numbers which paid them thousands. *But always remember that you can't beat the "kitty."* If you play the stock market, the horse races, and poker long enough, the broker and the bookmaker and the "kitty" will get it all. You hear of a great many rich bankers who are satisfied with 6 per cent. But how many times can you remember hearing of a speculator or a gambler dying wealthy? They make money, but they usually lose it equally fast. Most of them die in poverty.

According to an analysis made by one of the large insurance companies, the average earnings on a lifetime investment are less than 4 ½ per cent. This, it will be noted, is less than the income from a gilt-edge bond. One would naturally think that during a man's lifetime he would make a number of investments which would pay him large returns, in addition to his investments in bonds and mortgages yielding a conventional return. But on the contrary, the yield from speculative investments is shown to be less than their yield from gilt-edged securities over a period of time.

This is not hard to understand. Suppose you do make 10 or 15 per cent on some "long shot" investment. The next time you are likely to lose everything you put into the investment, and this loss would more than neutralize your previous winnings. The worthless stocks which a man usually acquires before attaining mature judgment, not only represent a loss of principal, but *a loss of four or five times as much again in compound interest.*

A Concrete Illustration

To make this last point clear, let us assume that two business men, yourself and one of your friends, had $1,000 in the bank at the time the Commonwealth Hotel stock was being sold, and that you were each thirty years of age at that time.

Your friend, carried away by the promise of handsome dividends, put his thousand into the stock of the hotel company and lost it. The idea of putting money into another man's dream did not appeal to you, so you bought a 6 per cent bond in a well-seasoned business.

We will suppose further that you had promptly reinvested the interest from your bond, in other approved 6 per cent securities, as the interest was paid to you every six months.

Fifty years have passed. You are now eighty years old, and ready to retire. Let us see what has happened. The thousand dollars which you had invested in a gilt-edge bond grew to $1,806 when you were forty. By fifty it had climbed to $3,262. At sixty it had reached $5,891 and by seventy the $5,891 had grown to $10,640. Today, at eighty, your original $1,000, with a little nourishing and watching, amounts to nearly $20,000 which, invested at 5 per cent, will give you an annual income of $1,000 a year for the rest of your life.

By playing safe and exercising banker's caution you *made* $19,000 on your original investment. By looking for big returns, rather than safety, your friend *lost* $20,000. That is the difference between investing money, and speculating with it. It is not so much the loss of your original investment which should worry you but the loss of the compound interest on that investment. Get acquainted with compound interest. It is a wonderful discovery.

The Best Investment for a Business Man

There are many ways of investing money safely. Some think that building and loan associations are the best. Others favor first mortgages on good property. Others cannot see anything but listed bonds. Still others prefer seasoned preferred stocks. The plain truth of the matter is that there is no "best" investment. The best investment for one man, may easily be the worst investment for another. It depends on a great many conditions besides the value of the proposition itself.

The depression has proved the wisdom of the old advice to diversify your investments, and not put all your eggs in one basket. After you have accumulated a working reserve, it may also be advisable to set aside a part of your savings for the purchase of *listed* stocks with a long dividend record, which you think should enhance in value. Speculation in even listed stocks, should never be attempted unless one can afford to lose, and does not need the additional income.

Buy old issues at the bottom. Select an industry, closely allied to national prosperity, which is temporarily depressed.

Buy bonds with a high collateral value—meaning bonds on which a bank will loan you up to 80 per cent. You can never tell when unforeseen conditions may make it necessary for you to raise money quickly. The sum needed may be just a little more than the collateral value of your bond, in which case you would have to sell it perhaps at a time when values were depressed. Bonds on high collateral value are usually "listed"—an additional advantage.

Buy bonds in as large denominations as possible, as the banker or broker charges a minimum fee for selling your bond. As a rule this fee is based on $1,000 units. It is easier to keep track of a few bonds of higher denominations, than it is a lot of baby bonds. The only advantage in having five $100's instead of one $500 is in case you wish to dispose of one of the bonds. For a business man, however, it is better to borrow on a bond than to sell it.

Few outside investments, however, are as good for a business man as his own business. You may not want to put all your money into expanding your business, but beware of those who tell you that you are foolish to plow back the earnings of your business into buildings and equipment. They will tell you that it is better to put your surplus in the stock market where it can make 10 or 20 per cent, whereas the best you could earn would be 5 or 10.

An Anchor to Windward

There is more to making money than merely allowing for a return on your capital. When you put your money back into your business you are buying protection against the next downward swing of the business cycle, and don't ever forget that it will come down some day, just as it may be going up today. If you have a business of your own, with the plant and equipment paid for, and you are free and clear of debt, you have nothing to fear, however hard the winds of depression blow. You have in effect built yourself a cyclone cellar. And no matter what you may be told, a cyclone cellar is mighty handy in a country where business is one long series of ups and downs. Most of those who make money when the tide is coming in, lose it when the tide runs out. That is why, if you are wise, you will take advantage of good times to put out a shore anchor against the day when the tide ebbs.

Never be stampeded by crowd movements. All the great fortunes that have been made in the financial world have been made by "playing the market against the crowd." In other words, never buy when there are more buyers than sellers, and never sell when there are more sellers than buyers. Buy when it is the fashion to sell, and sell when it is the fashion to buy. To quote Herbert N. Casson, a well-known financial writer: "Most people are optimists during a boom, and pessimists during a depression. It is the natural way. But the man who makes money is the man who is a pessimist during a boom, and an optimist during a depression. *Always buy from pessimists.* Always sell to optimists." You can make a lot of money by following this advice when investing your first thousand.

APPENDICES

APPENDIX A

Retail and Wholesale Operating Budgets

Operating Budgets for Retail Businesses

SOURCES OF INFORMATION: Bureau of Business Research, Harvard University, International Association of Electragists, Florists' Telegraph Delivery Association, National Retail Furniture Association, The National Haberdasher and Consolidated Press, Ltd., Cinchona Club and St. Louis Retail Druggists Association, "National Hairdresser," National Shoe Retailers Association, National Retail Hardware Association, National Association of Retail Clothiers and Furnishers, Interstate Merchants' Council, "The Progressive Grocer," "Meat Merchandising," "National Petroleum News," Druggists' Research Bureau, U. S. Department of Commerce.

Items of Expense	Auto Tires and Accessories	Drug Stores								Grocery Stores (Independent)			
		Eastern	Central	North Central	Western	Southern	Middlewest Group	Electrical	Florist	Service	Cash	Complete Food Market	General Store
Total Salaries	15.2	19.5	17.8	15.8	17.6	16.4	18.9	12.71	18.0	7.2	6.8	9.8	8.3
Direct and General Selling ¶	.....	10.0	10.1	7.1	11.1	....	11.2	8.48	....	....	....	7.9	....
Buying, Management, etc. ¶	.....	9.5	7.7	8.7	6.5	....	7.7	4.23	....	....	....	1.9	....
Rent	2.5	4.0	3.8	3.4	3.8	3.1	5.1	1.51	4.0	1.33	1.0	1.0	1.2
Advertising	1.1	0.6	0.8	1.0	1.1	0.3	1.1	1.01	5.0	0.50	0.8	0.7	0.4
Wrappings and Supplies	0.4	....	....	....	....	....	....	0.41	....	0.34	0.6	0.6	0.3
Delivery	0.9	0.1	....	....	....	....	....	0.88	3.0	1.64	....	1.8	0.5
Heat, Light, Power, Water	0.9	1.1	1.0	1.2	1.0	0.8	1.5	0.34	....	0.41	0.3	0.6	0.6
Insurance	0.5	0.2	0.5	0.5	0.4	1.4	0.6	0.62	1.0	0.41	0.3	0.5	1.0
Taxes	0.3	0.2	0.4	0.7	0.9	†	0.4	0.43	....	†	†	†	†
Telephone and Telegraph	0.3	....	....	....	....	....	....	0.43	....	0.08	....	0.2	0.1
Repairs	0.4	0.2	0.2	....	0.3	....	0.1	0.68	....	0.48	0.5	0.8	0.6
Depreciation (Total)	1.0	1.4	1.2	0.6	0.7	0.4	1.4	0.65	....	‡	‡	‡	‡
Interest	1.3	....	....	....	0.4	....	....	0.56	....	0.16	....	0.1	0.3
Donations	....	....	....	....	....	....	....	....	....	0.12	....	0.1	0.1
Losses from Bad Debts	0.8	....	....	....	0.3	0.4	....	0.72	1.0	0.62	....	0.5	0.6
Unclassified	1.2	0.5	1.4	2.3	2.6	5.4	2.0	2.10	6.0	0.51	0.4	0.5	0.6
TOTAL EXPENSE	26.8	27.8	27.1	25.5	29.1	28.2	31.1	23.05	38.0	13.8	10.7	17.2	14.6
MARGIN	28.8	36.0	32.0	32.9	35.2	35.1	32.3	.....	45.6	17.8	14.7	20.6	17.8
NET PROFIT	2.0	8.2	4.9	7.4	6.1	6.9	1.2	.....	7.6	4.0	4.0	3.4	3.2
Stock-turn (times a year)	5.7	2.6	3.6	2.2	2.8	3.3	3.1	.....	.....	11.5	13.0	18.5	4.5

¶—The sum of these equals total salaries. †—Taxes included with insurance.
‡—Depreciation included with repairs.

Operating Budgets for Retail Businesses

Items of Expense	Haberdashery	Jewelry	Meat Stores Under $50,000	Meat Stores Over $50,000	Men's Clothing	Millinery	Shoe Stores Under $35,000	Shoe Stores $35,000 to $75,000	Shoe Stores Over $75,000
Total Salaries..................	16.5	25.6	14.7	14.6	13.4	18.7	16.0	17.3	18.8
Direct and General Selling ¶.....	12.1	......	......	......	......	......	......	......	......
Buying, Management, etc. ¶.....	4.4	......	......	......	......	......	......	......	......
Rent...........................	3.4	6.0	3.9	2.2	3.94	3.9	5.0	5.8	6.9
Advertising....................	3.3	3.9	......	......	3.79	2.2	2.5	2.9	3.7
Wrappings and Supplies...........	0.8	1.8	0.9	1.1	......	......	......	......	......
Delivery.....................	0.4	......	......	......	......	......	......	......	......
Heat, Light, Power, Water........	0.55	0.8	1.4	0.9	......	1.5	1.0	0.9	0.8
Insurance......................	1.13	0.8	0.4	0.3	0.56	0.6	0.6	0.5	0.5
Taxes..........................	0.11	1.2	......	......	0.66	0.4	0.7	0.6	0.5
Repairs........................	0.5	1.1	......	......	......	......	......	......	......
Depreciation (Total).............	1.7	‡	1.7	1.3	......	......	0.5	0.7	0.9
Interest.......................	......	......	......	......	......	......	0.4	0.7	0.3
Losses from Bad Debts...........	0.34	......	......	......	......	......	0.4	0.4	0.3
Unclassified....................	1.7	4.5	2.3	2.4	*9.88	2.1	2.8	3.2	2.4
TOTAL EXPENSE...........	30.43	45.0x	25.3	22.8	32.23	29.4	29.9	33.0	35.1
MARGIN.....................	35 88	43.2	29.3	27.6	......	34.7	27.0	29.9	30.7
NET PROFIT...............	5.45	Loss 1.8	4.0	4.8	......	5.3	Loss 2.9	Loss 3.1	Loss 4.4
Stock-turn (times a year)..........	3.6	0.9	58.7	57.0	2.8	3.1	1.6	1 8	2.2
Sales per Employee................	......	......	$16,328	$17,576	......	......	......	......	......

¶—The sum of these equals total salaries.   ‡Depreciation included with repairs.
*—Includes 2.56% for busheling. x—This total is not the exact sum of the separate expense items, because item figures were arrived at independently and with a varying number of stores.

Operating Budgets for Retail Businesses

Department Stores

Items of Expense	Less than $150,000	$150,000 to $300,000	$300,000 to $500,000	$500,000 to $750,000	$750,000 to $1,000,000	$1,000,000 to $2,000,000	$2,000,000 to $4,000,000	$4,000,000 to $10,000,000	$10,000,000 or More
Total Salaries..................	18.2	18.5	17.9	18.5	18.7	18.1	18.0	17.6	17.9
Real Estate Costs..............	4.0	4.0	4.5	3.6	4.7	4.2	5.0	5.0	5.5
Advertising.....................	2.6	2.8	2.85	3.4	3.9	3.8	3.75	4.25	3.65
Wrappings and Supplies...........	0.8	1.0	1.05	1.25	1.45	1.45	1.6	1.65	1.75
Service Purchased	1.15	1.05	1.05	1.25	1.15	1.0	0.9	0.85	0.7
Insurance......................	0.65	0.55	0.55	0.45	0.45	0.35	0.3	0.25	0.25
Taxes..........................	0.75	0.6	0.6	0.65	0.5	0.4	0.4	0.4	0.25
Telephone and Telegraph.........	0.3	0.45	0.45	0.45	0.55	0.45	0.45	0.45	0.45
Repairs........................	0.2	0.25	0.3	0.3	0.3	0.3	0.3	0.3	0.3
Depreciation (Total).............	0.75	0.85	0.9	0.9	1.2	0.85	1.0	0.85	1.0
Traveling......................	0.3	0.4	0.4	0.45	0.55	0.45	0.45	0.45	0.35
Professional Services.............	0.2	0.25	0.35	0.45	0.65	0.5	0.5	0.55	0.45
Interest.......................	3.1	3.0	2.75	2.6	2.6	2.35	2.35	2.3	1.95
Losses from Bad Debts...........	0.35	0.4	0.4	0.4	0.4	0.6	0.5	0.4	0.45
Unclassified....................	0.65	0.6	0.65	0.65	0.9	0.7	0.7	0.7	0.85
TOTAL EXPENSE...........	34.0	34.7	34.7	35.3	38.0	35.5	36.2	36.0	35.8
MARGIN....................	26.0	28.1	29.5	30.8	32.2	31.6	32.7	33.4	33.9
NET PROFIT...............	Loss 8.0	Loss 6.6	Loss 5.2	Loss 4.5	Loss 5.8	Loss 3.9	Loss 3.5	Loss 2.6	Loss 1.9
Stock-turn (times a year).........	2.2	2.5	3.0	3.5	3.8	3.6	4.1	4.5	5.0
Sales per Employee..............	$7,300	$7,300	$6,700	$6,000	$6,400	$6,200	$6,550	$7,000	$7,800

331

Operating Budgets for Retail Businesses

Items of Expense	*Specialty Stores			Hardware Stores (Classified by Volume of Sales and Population) Under 1,000 Population			
	Less than $500,000	$500,000 to $2,000,000	$2,000,000 or More	Under $25,000	$25,000 to $40,000	$40,000 to $60,000	$60,000 to $100,000
Total Salaries (a)	17.9	17.4	16.9	16.78	13.88	12.24	8.78
Direct and General Selling ¶	....	....	....	12.38	9.53	8.80	5.92
Buying, Management, etc. ¶	....	....	....	2.53	2.50	1.72	1.52
Office ¶	....	....	....	1.87	1.85	1.72	1.34
Real Estate Costs	5.8	5.2	5.4	....	....	....	....
Rent (b)	....	....	....	4.17	2.98	2.21	1.66
Advertising	3.5	4.5	4.5	0.74	0.57	0.69	0.60
Wrappings and Supplies	1.05	1.2	1.6	0.54	0.50	0.41	0.37
Service Purchased	1.2	1.05	0.95	....	....	....	....
Delivery (c)	....	....	....	0.92	1.29	1.20	1.43
Heat, Light, Power, Water	....	....	....	0.95	0.67	0.47	0.41
Insurance (d)	0.4	0.5	0.3	0.81	0.82	0.70	0.60
Taxes (d)	0.45	0.35	0.25	1.29	0.97	0.80	0.65
Telephone and Telegraph	0.45	0.6	0.6	0.33	0.26	0.21	0.19
Repairs	0.2	0.25	0.3	0.25	0.23	0.08	0.13
Depreciation (Total)	1.0	0.85	1.1	1.30	1.11	0.89	0.55
On Delivery Equipment	....	....	....	0.48	0.49	0.51	0 31
On Furniture, Fixtures, Tools	....	....	....	0.82	0.62	0.38	0.24
Traveling	0.55	0.65	0.65	....	....	....	....
Professional Services	0.35	0.8	0.7	....	....	....	....
Interest	2.4	2.1	1.8	1.09	0.89	0.55	0.31
Donations	....	....	....	0.14	0.14	0.10	0.06
Losses from Bad Debts (e)	0.3	0.6	0.35	0.70	0.96	0.69	0.78
Unclassified	0.85	0.65	0.8	0.55	0.62	0.25	0.64
TOTAL EXPENSE	36.4	36.7	36.2	30.56	25.89	21.49	17.16
MARGIN	32.4	32.2	34.5	22.80	20.76	20.97	19.37
NET PROFIT	Loss 4.0	Loss 4.5	Loss 1.7	Loss 7.76	Loss 5.13	Loss 0.52	2.21
Stock-turn (times a year)	4.2	6.0	6.8	1.44	1.68	1.88	2.43
Sales per Actual Salesperson	....	....	....	$10,657	$15,662	$17,105	$29,192
Sales per Employee (a)	$7,700	$7,800	$8,300	$7,791	$10,751	$12,126	$18,227

¶—The sum of these equals total salaries. *—By "Specialty" is meant those stores specializing in women's wearing apparel, and not handling either yard goods or home furnishings.

(*Notations below for Hardware Stores only*)

a—Except deliverymen and shopmen. b—Includes taxes, insurance, and depreciation on buildings when owned and interest on real estate indebtedness. c—Includes wages of deliverymen. d—Insurance and taxes on real estate are included in rent. e—Includes legal expense in making collections and fees for collection agencies.

Operating Budgets for Retail Businesses

Items of Expense	Hardware Stores (Classified by Volume of Sales and Population)									
	1,000 to 3,500 Population					3,500 to 10,000 Population				
	Under $25,000	$25,000 to $40,000	$40,000 to $60,000	$60,000 to $100,000	$100,000 and Over	Under $25,000	$25,000 to $40,000	$40,000 to $60,000	$60,000 to $100,000	$100,000 and Over
Total Salaries (a)...........	17.77	15.56	13.97	14.02	13.79	20.57	16.57	15.01	13.90	12.95
Direct and General Selling ¶	12.99	10.66	9.46	9.06	9.27	14.87	11.55	10.17	9.27	8.44
Buying, Management, etc. ¶	2.82	2.66	2.47	3.02	2.66	3.17	2.67	2.66	2.67	2.23
Office ¶................	1.96	2.24	2.04	1.94	1.86	2.53	2.35	2.18	1.96	2.28
Rent (b).................	4.80	3.73	2.87	2.52	2.47	5.87	4.32	3.73	3.12	2.32
Advertising..............	1.09	0.97	0.77	0.88	0.86	1.58	1.20	1.37	1.12	0.98
Wrappings and Supplies.....	0.61	0.61	0.54	0.56	0.48	0.63	0.66	0.67	0.68	0.60
Delivery (c)..............	0.91	1.36	1.31	1.19	1.74	1.50	1.37	1.71	1.71	1.56
Heat, Light, Power, Water..	0.99	0.79	0.59	0.61	0.51	1.06	0.86	0.75	0.65	0.41
Insurance (d).............	0.72	0.76	0.64	0.72	0.53	0.67	0.67	0.58	0.65	0.86
Taxes (d).................	1.24	1.09	0.83	0.70	0.57	1.22	1.03	0.99	0.85	0.85
Telephone and Telegraph....	0.35	0.30	0.23	0.23	0.20	0.40	0.27	0.25	0.25	0.26
Repairs..................	0.16	0.13	0.13	0.24	......	0.28	0.14	0.13	0.23	0.28
Depreciation (Total)........	1.29	0.94	0.82	0.72	0.74	1.14	0.87	1.03	0.76	0.78
On Delivery Equipment...	0.43	0.39	0.32	0.34	0.44	0.38	0.36	0.39	0.32	0.42
On Furniture, Fixtures, Tools	0.86	0.55	0.50	0.38	0.30	0.76	0.51	0.64	0.44	0.36
Interest..................	0.99	0.83	0.69	0.51	0.61	1.16	0.99	1.24	0.59	0.60
Donations................	0.14	0.11	0.10	0.05	......	0.18	0.14	0.15	0.07	0.07
Losses from Bad Debts (e)...	0.83	0.93	0.78	1.14	1.09	0.58	0.80	0.71	0.88	1.13
Unclassified..............	0.42	0.56	0.47	0.86	0.90	0.60	0.49	0.61	0.67	1.31
TOTAL EXPENSE......	32.31	28.67	24.72	24.95	24.49	37.44	30.38	29.93	26.13	24.96
MARGIN..............	25.66	25.05	21.70	21.92	20.99	30.33	27.31	26.91	24.49	24.13
NET PROFIT..........	Loss 6.65	Loss 3.62	Loss 3.02	Loss 3.03	Loss 3.50	Loss 7.11	Loss 3.07	Loss 2.02	Loss 1.64	Loss 0.83
Stock-turn (times a year)....	1.42	1.68	2.20	2.11	3.11	1.41	1.61	1.84	1.91	2.37
Sales per Actual Salesperson.	10,466	14,597	17,532	20,657	23,326	10,307	13,242	16,229	19,876	24,935
Sales per Employee (a)......	7,556	9,832	11,720	12,755	16,177	6,939	9,344	10,768	13,080	16,088

¶—The sum of these equals total salaries. a—Except deliverymen and shopmen. b—Includes taxes, insurance, and depreciation on buildings when owned and interest on real estate indebtedness. c—Includes wages of deliverymen. d—Insurance and taxes on real estate are included in rent. e—Includes legal expense in making collections and fees for collection agencies.

Operating Budgets for Retail Businesses

Items of Expense	Hardware Stores (Classified by Volume of Sales and Population)									
	10,000 to 50,000 Population					Over 50,000 Population				
	Under $25,000	$25,000 to $40,000	$40,000 to $60,000	$60,000 to $100,000	$100,000 and Over	Under $25,000	$25,000 to $40,000	$40,000 to $60,000	$60,000 to $100,000	$100,000 and Over
Total Salaries (a).........	19.63	18.80	17.39	15.97	15.67	21.47	18.16	16.29	17.32	16.97
Direct and General Selling ¶	13.98	12.68	12.07	9.87	10.25	15.48	13.04	10.89	11.14	10.92
Buying, Management, etc. ¶	2.97	3.11	2.78	3.23	2.96	3.81	3.09	3.18	3.68	3.25
Office ¶................	2.68	3.01	2.54	2.87	2.46	2.18	3.03	2.22	2.50	2.80
Rent (b)..................	6.90	6.09	5.76	4.26	3.48	6.79	5.59	5.11	5.45	4.75
Advertising..............	1.43	1.35	1.44	1.24	1.33	1.01	1.10	1.40	1.39	1.22
Wrappings and Supplies.....	0.76	0.65	0.72	0.81	0.74	0.62	0.76	0.80	0.76	0.80
Delivery (c)..............	1.63	2.09	2.02	1.95	1.61	2.06	2.07	2.55	2.05	1.98
Heat, Light, Power, Water..	1.34	0.98	0.78	0.61	0.61	1.19	1.02	0.74	0.73	0.64
Insurance (d).............	0.72	0.69	0.63	0.80	0.62	0.70	0.74	0.72	0.64	0 57
Taxes (d)..................	1.16	0.82	0.69	0.88	0.64	0.72	0.65	0.64	0.72	0.63
Telephone and Telegraph....	0.42	0.35	0.27	0.25	0.29	0.70	0.43	0.37	0.35	0.38
Repairs...................	0.09	0.07	0.12	0.11	0 09	0.21	0.09	0.18	0.08	0.08
Depreciation (Total)........	1.35	0.99	0.82	0.75	0.74	1.51	1.08	0.99	0.79	0.61
On Delivery Equipment...	0.36	0.38	0.30	0.26	0.30	0.45	0.40	0.40	0.28	0.28
OnFurniture,Fixtures,Tools	0 99	0.61	0.52	0.49	0 44	1.06	0.68	0.59	0.51	0.33
Interest..................	0.95	0.86	0.90	0 79	0.60	0.51	0.50	0.63	0.64	0.54
Donations.................	0.15	0.16	0.11	0.12	0.09	0.18	0.10	0.16	0.17	0.11
Losses from Bad Debts (e)...	0 75	0.99	0.73	1.01	1.12	0.60	0.88	1.16	0.85	0.92
Unclassified..............	0.70	0.68	0.54	0.55	1.14	0 55	0.44	0.57	1.13	1.07
TOTAL EXPENSE......	37.98	35.57	32.92	30.10	28.77	38.82	33.61	32.31	33.07	31.27
MARGIN..............	30.70	29.20	30.22	25.77	26.21	31.55	30.62	28.42	29.54	28.93
NET PROFIT..........	Loss 7.28	Loss 6.37	Loss 2.70	Loss 4.33	Loss 2.56	Loss 7.27	Loss 2.99	Loss 3.89	Loss 3.53	Loss 2.34
Stock-turn (times a year)....	1.37	1.64	1.81	1.73	2.01	1.53	1.75	1.95	2.00	2.19
Sales per Actual Salesperson.	11,558	13,919	15,170	17,732	18,903	10,857	13,648	15,221	18,447	18,294
Sales per Employee (a)......	7,578	8,860	10,454	11,234	12,464	7,729	9,463	10,285	11,762	12,558

¶—The sum of these equals total salaries. a—Except deliverymen and shopmen. b—Includes taxes, insurance, and depreciation on buildings when owned and interest on real estate indebtedness. c—Includes wages of deliverymen. d—Insurance and taxes on real estate are included in rent. e—Includes legal expense in making collections and fees for collection agencies.

Operating Budgets for Retail Businesses

Beauty Shops

Items of Expense	
Salaries and Commissions	51.49
Rent	11.83
Supplies	5.93
Advertising	5.30
Depreciation	2.62
Laundry	1.87
Cleaning	1.56
Light, Heat and Power	1.42
Repairs	1.37
Insurance	.88
Telephone	.58
Various Other Expenses	1.04
TOTAL EXPENSES	85.89%
NET PROFIT	14.11%

Furniture Stores

Items of Expense	Below $100,000	$100,000 to $250,000	$250,000 to $500,000	$500,000 to $1,000,000
Administrative—Salaries, etc.	12.4%	14.0%	16.0%	18.2%
Occupancy—Rent, etc.	11.2	10.8	10 5	11.3
Publicity—Advertising and Display	6.8	7.0	7.6	8.2
Selling—Salaries, Commissions, etc.	7.3	7.0	7.8	6.8
Handling—Receiving, Shipping, Repair Service	3.5	3.0	3.0	3.4
Delivery	4.0	3.5	3.0	3.3
TOTAL EXPENSE	45.2%	45.3%	47.9%	51.2%
Stock-turn (times a year) 2.75	....	....	....	....

Operating Budgets for Retail Businesses

Building Material

Items of Expense	Lumber	Mason Material	Lumber and Mason Material	Lumber and Coal	Mason Material and Coal
Wages of Yard and Warehouse Force..............	3.3	2.5	2.8	3.2	2.5
Total Outward Transportation and Delivery..........	3.6	6.0	3.9	6.0	7.8
Executive Salaries (Including Buying)	4.0	3.3	3.3	5.1	3.1
Salesforce Salaries, Commission and Bonuses........	2.2	1.9	1.3	2.3	1.5
Office Salaries and Wages.........................	1.9	1.6	1.9		1.4
Total Buying, Selling, and Administration Salaries.....	8.1	6.8	6.5	7.4	6.0
Traveling Expense................................	0.35	0.55	0.3	0.15	0.35
Advertising..	0.65	0.3	0.55	0.5	0.65
Office Supplies, Postage and Stationery..............	0.35	0.25	0.3	0.35	0 35
Telephone and Telegraph..........................	0.2	0.2	0.2	0.1	0 2
Legal, Collection, and Other Buying and Administration	0.25	0.2	0.2	0.15	0.2
Losses from Bad Debts.............................	0.9	0.75	1.1	0.65	1 0
Dues, Subscriptions and Contributions..............	0.2	0.15	0.2	0.2	0.25
Net Rental Expense...............................	1.9	1.6	1.8	1.8	2.5
Heat, Light, Power and Water.....................	0.15	0.15	0.1	0.1	0.15
Taxes..	0.45	0.2	0.45	0.45	0.3
Insurance..	0.45	0.3	0.45	0.5	0.25
Repairs and Depreciation..........................	0.35	0.3	0.4	0.35	0.45
Miscellaneous....................................	0.5	0.45	0.45	0 4	0.45
Total Expense before Interest......................	21.7	20.7	19.7	22.3	23.4
Total Interest....................................	3.3	2.0	3.1	2.8	1.7
TOTAL EXPENSE.............................	25.0	22.7	22.8	25.1	25.1
MARGIN......................................	25.8	23.2	24.4	26.7	25.7
NET PROFIT..................................	0.8	0.5	1.6	1.6	0.6
Stock-turn (times a year).........................	3.1	+	3.5	3.0	+

+Impracticable to determine.

Operating Budgets for Retail Businesses

Stationery Stores

Items of Expense	General	Commercial	Commercial and Printing
Salaries of Proprietors	6.2	6.2	5.2
Sales Salaries and Commissions	8.6	8.7	9.7
Office Salaries and Wages	2.4	2.5	3.2
Wages, Porters and Stock Clerks	1.1	1.5	1.4
Total Salaries and Wages (Except Delivery)	18.3	18.9	19.5
Salesmen's Traveling and Other Direct Selling	0.5	0.9	1.1
Advertising	1.4	1.3	1.3
Delivery Expense	1.4	1.95	2.1
Office Supplies and Postage	0.7	0.8	0.8
Telephone and Telegraph	0.3	0.4	0.4
Net Store Rent	4.5	3.8	2.7
Heat, Light, Power, Water	0.6	0.5	0.4
Taxes	0.5	0.4	0.35
Insurance	0.5	0.45	0.4
Repairs of Store and Office Fixtures	0.2	0.15	0.2
Depreciation of Store and Office Fixtures	0.5	0.3	0.3
Losses from Bad Debts	0.3	0.45	0.4
Dues, Subscriptions and Contributions	0.3	0.2	0.25
Miscellaneous	1.1	0.9	1.1
Total Expenses before Interest	31.1	31.4	31.3
Total Interest	2.4	2.2	2.0
TOTAL EXPENSE	33.5	33.6	33.3
MARGIN	34.5	36.0	34.9
NET PROFIT	1.0	2.4	1.6
Stock-turn (times a year)	2.5	2.8	+

+ Impracticable to determine.

Typical Operating Expenses in Wholesale Businesses
(*Classified by Volume of Annual Business*)

Gross Sales	No. of Concerns Represented	Sales Force Expense	Advertising	Total Selling Expense	Warehousing Expense	Executive and Office Salaries	Losses from Bad Debts	Rent, Light, Heat, Power, Insurance	Total Administrative and General Expense	Repairs, Depreciation, Taxes, Interest	Total Expense	Margin	Profit	Stock Turns—times per year
DRUGS														
Under $750,000	35	3.80	0.06	3.94	3.12	3.60	0.30	2.19	6.09	2.85	16.00	16.90	0.9	3.1
750,000 to 1,500,000	37	3.70	0.15	3.95	3.47	3.30	0.30	1.91	5.51	2.47	15.40	16.80	1.4	3.8
1,500,000 and over	45	3.50	0.18	3.76	3.69	3.40	0.30	2.10	5.80	2.25	15.50	17.20	1.7	4.7
GROCERIES														
Under 500,000	29	2.60	0.05	2.72	2.07	2.10	0.40	1.51	4.01	1.82	10.60	11.30	0.7	5.9
500,000 to 1,000,000	173	2.70	0.06	2.86	2.14	1.90	0.40	1.34	3.64	1.91	10.60	11.30	0.7	6.0
1,000,000 to 2,000,000	122	2.60	0.06	2.75	2.15	1.90	0.30	1.30	3.50	1.91	10.30	11.00	0.7	5.8
2,000,000 and over	77	2.70	1.10	2.90	2.29	2.00	0.40	1.35	3.75	1.81	10.80	11.60	0.8	6.0
DRY GOODS														
Under 1,000,000	40	6.00	0.09	6.20	1.11	3.30	1.10	2.42	6.82	3.57	17.70	18.00	0 3	3.1
1,000,000 and over	31	5.30	0.16	5.63	1.06	2.20	0.90	2.17	5.27	3.33	15.30	17.10	1.8	3.7
AUTOMOTIVE EQUIP.														
Under 250,000	24	8.50	0.90	9.80	2.90	4.60	0.70	4.60	9.90	2.64	25.00	25.20	0.2	2.8
250,000 to 750,000	71	7.70	0.70	8.65	2.20	4.80	0.70	3.55	9.05	2.76	22.70	24.60	1.9	3.4
750,000 and over	33	7.60	0.80	8.55	3.20	4.90	0.70	3.55	9.15	2.50	23.50	25.50	2.0	3.7
SHOES														
Under 600,000	6	4.01	0.16	4.17	*4.15	x2.63	1.07	3.85	7.55	2.24	17.98	....	....	....
600,000 to 1,000,000	3	4.28	0.27	4.55	*4.81	x4.61	1.58	3.79	9.98	3.83	22.69	....	....	....
1,000,000 and over	4	4.43	0.39	4.82	*3.28	x1.75	1.21	3.33	6.29	3.62	18.01	....	....	....
HARDWARE														
Under 500,000	11	4.97	0.64	5.61	2.72	3.94	0.35	3.10	7.39	4.77	20.03	....	....	....
500,000 to 1,000,000	32	4.72	0.33	5.05	2.67	4.23	0.74	2.88	7.85	4.08	19.19	....	....	....
1,000,000 and over	83	4.44	0.55	4.99	3.14	3.99	0.63	2.43	7.05	3.88	18.91	....	....	....

*Including office salaries.   x Excluding office salarie

APPENDIX B

Sources of Supply

Sources of Supply

THE accompanying list has been compiled to help you to get in touch with manufacturers of equipment which you may require to start your business, as well as the supplies and merchandise that you need to operate it. The list is not intended to be complete. For additional sources of supply consult Thomas' Register of American Manufacturers, or the trade publications listed in this book.

Addressing Machines

ADDRESSOGRAPH-MULTIGRAPH CORP.
Euclid Station
Cleveland, Ohio

ELLIOTT ADDRESSING MACHINE CO.
143 Albany Ave.
Cambridge, Mass.

Addressing Machines (Rebuilt)

PRUITT CO.
172 N. La Salle St.
Chicago, Ill.

Advertising Displays. Novelties and Specialties

AMERICAN ART WORKS
Coshocton, Ohio

AMERICAN NOVELTY CO.
Buffalo, N. Y.

BASTIAN BROS. CO.
Woolworth Bldg.
New York, N. Y.

CHANEY MFG. CO.
Springfield, Ohio

CRUVER MFG. CO.
2470 W. Jackson Blvd.
Chicago, Ill.

DORFMANN BROS.
Corona, N. Y.

THE EASTMAN CO.
226 S. Church St.
Rockford, Ill.

G. FELSENTHAL & SONS
4110 W. Grand Ave.
Chicago, Ill.

C. F. HERBESTREITH & CO.
Nutley, N. J.

THE MEEKER CO.
Joplin, Mo.

OHIO THERMOMETER COMPANY
116 W. Main St.
Springfield, Ohio

PALMEN MFG. CO.
Muncie, Ind.

PATENT NOVELTY CO., INC.
Fulton, Ill.

PARISIAN NOVELTY CO.
3502 S. Western Ave.
Chicago, Ill.

SANDERS MANUFACTURING COMPANY
Nashville, Tenn.

Automobile Tires

THE COFFIELD PROTECTOR CO.
Dayton, Ohio

ECONOMY RUBBER PRODUCTS CO.
Dayton, Ohio

MUSSELMAN DOENUT TIRES
Cleveland, Ohio

ROSE REBUILT TIRE CO.
Los Angeles, Calif.

Automotive Accessories

ADVANCE PRODUCTS COMPANY
Swetland Bldg.
Cleveland, Ohio

AUTOSCOPE MFG. CO.
Delta, Ohio

FRANK ROSE MFG. CO.
Hastings, Neb.

SERAN SALES COMPANY
Los Angeles, Calif.

SNAP-UP GAS CAP CO.
Ashland, N. C.

WHIRLWIND MFG. CO.
2621 N. Third St.
Milwaukee, Wis.

Band Instruments

BUESCHER BAND INSTRUMENT CO.
Elkhart, Ind.

C. G. CONN, LTD.
Elkhart, Ind.

Bee Keepers' Supplies

CARL F. BUCK CO.
College Pl.
Washington, D. C.

G. B. LEWIS CO.
Dept. T. R., 37
Watertown, Wis.

MARSHFIELD MFG. CO.
Marshfield, Wis.

FRED W. MUTH CO.
229 Walnut
Cincinnati, Ohio

A. I. ROOT
Medina, Ohio

Billiard Tables

BRUNSWICK-BALKE-COLLENDER CO.
623 S. Wabash Ave.
Chicago, Ill.

Birds, Ornamental and Game

W. P. ALLEN
Box 506
Paducah, Ky.

BADGER STATE GAME FARM
Lodi, Wis.

FLORIDA QUAIL FARM
Green Cove Springs, Fla.

GLENWOOD FARMS
South Caire, N. Y.

HENLOPEN GAME FARMS, INC.
Milton, Del.

HUNTSWELL GAME FARMS, INC.
Simsbury, Conn.

LAKE WHITTEMORE GAME FARM
Box 8 F
Spencer, Mass.

MRS. A. R. MOFFIT
Poughkeepsie, N. Y.

NICKERSON GAME FARM
Redding, Conn.

RAINBOW FARM PHEASANTRY
Barrington, Ill.

SCHAFT PHEASANTRY
Berea, Ohio

SILVER LAKE GAME FARM
New Albany, Ind.

TURKEYFOOT AVIARY
Wauseon, Ohio

Boats

CLEVELAND BOAT BLUEPRINT CO.
Station A-118
Cleveland, Ohio

FELLOWCRAFTERS, INC.
64 Stanhope
Boston, Mass.

L. W. FERDINAND & CO., INC.
599 Albany St.
Boston, Mass.

KAYAK BOAT COMPANY
152 E. 129th St.
New York, N. Y.

MEAD GLIDERS
15 S. Market St.
Chicago, Ill.

Bottle Stoppers

GORDON MFG. CO.
110 E. 23rd St.
New York, N. Y.

Brooders

BELLE CITY INCUBATOR CO.
1411 Wisconsin
Racine, Wis.

Brushes

BETTER BRUSHES, INC.
Palmer, Mass.

DONALD BRUSH COMPANY
Camden, N. J.

NEWAY BRUSH CO.
Hartford, Conn.

NORTH RIDGE BRUSH CO.
Freeport, Ill.

WIRE-GRIP SANITARY BRUSH COMPANY
2300 Fifth Ave.
New York, N. Y.

Building Materials

CELOTEX CORPORATION
919 N. Michigan Ave.
Chicago, Ill.

COLORCRETE INDUSTRIES
570 Ottawa Ave.
Holland, Mich.

MASONITE CORPORATION
111 W. Washington St.
Chicago, Ill.

Cameras
Dealers

BASS CAMERA CO., INC.
179 W. Madison St.
Chicago, Ill.

BURKE & JAMES
225 W. Madison St.
Chicago, Ill.

BURLEIGH BROOKS
127 W. 42nd St.
New York, N. Y.

CENTRAL CAMERA COMPANY
230 S. Wabash Ave.
Chicago, Ill.

ABE COHEN'S EXCHANGE
142 Fulton St.
New York, N. Y.

EASTMAN KODAK STORES CO.
133 N. Wabash Ave.
Chicago, Ill.

WILLOUGHBY'S
110 W. 32nd St.
New York, N. Y.

Manufacturers

AGFA ANSCO CORPORATION
Binghamton, N. Y.

EASTMAN KODAK CO.
343 State St.
Rochester, N. Y.

FOLMER GRAFLEX CORP.
154 Clarissa St.
Rochester, N. Y.

INTERNATIONAL RESEARCH CORP.
Ann Arbor, Mich.

E. LEITZ, INC.
730 Fifth Ave.
New York, N. Y.

CARL ZEISS, INC.
485 Fifth Ave.
New York, N. Y.

Movie Cameras

BELL & HOWELL CO.
1801 Larchmont Ave.
Chicago, Ill.

DEVRY CORPORATION
111 Armitage Ave.
Chicago, Ill.

EASTMAN KODAK CO.
343 State St.
Rochester, N. Y.

Chemicals

ENDO-CHEMICAL COMPANY
Columbia, S. C.

LUX-VISEL, INC.
Elkhart, Ind.

NORD CHEMICAL CO.
Duluth, Minn.

NOX-ODOR MFG. CO.
Blandinsville, Ill.

PILGRIM UTILITIES, LTD.
Hollywood, Calif.

THE PURO CO., INC.
3107 Pine St.
St. Louis, Mo.

ZENITH FACTORIES CO.
Minneapolis, Minn.

Chickens

ATZ'S MAMMOTH HATCHERIES
Huntingburg, Ind.

BAGBY POULTRY FARM
Sedalia, Mo.

BOOTH FARMS
Clinton, Mo.

CAPPER HATCHERY
Elgin, Ia.

CHESTNUT HATCHERY
Chestnut, Ill.

CLOVER VALLEY POULTRY FARM &
HATCHERY
Ramsey, Ind.

COLONIAL POULTRY FARMS
Pleasant Hill, Mo.

GOLDEN RULE HATCHERY
Bucyrus, Ohio

GRANDVIEW POULTRY FARM
Zeeland, Mich.

HALL BROS. HATCHERY, INC.
Wallingford, Conn.

HAYES BROS. HATCHERY
Hayes Bldg.
Decatur, Ill.

HUBBARD FARMS
Walpole, N. H.

ILLINOIS HATCHERY
Metropolis, Ill.

S. W. KLINE
Middlecreek, Pa.

W. A. LAUVER
McAlisterville, Pa.

MISSOURI STATE HATCHERY
Butler, Mo.

RICE LEGHORN FARMS
Green Ridge, Mo.

RUSK FARM
Windsor, Mo.

SUNSHINE HATCHERY
Corydon, Ind.

SUPERIOR HATCHERY
Windsor, Mo.

THORNWOOD, INC.
Louisville, Ky.

Cleaning Fluid

KOTOFOM CORPORATION OF AMERICA
South Bend, Ind.

Coin-Operated Machines

CHAS. A. BREWER & SONS
6320 Harvard Ave.
Chicago, Ill.

BUCKLEY MFG. CO.
2156 W. Washington St.
Chicago, Ill.

DAVAL MFG. CO.
200 S. Peoria St.
Chicago, Ill.

H. C. EVANS & CO.
1528 W. Adams St.
Chicago, Ill.

D. GOTTLIEB & CO.
2736 N. Paulina St.
Chicago, Ill.

HAMILTON SCALE CO.
1910 Vermont Ave.
Toledo, Ohio

INTERNATIONAL MUTOSCOPE REEL CO.,
INC.
516-22 W. 34th St.
New York, N. Y.

O. D. JENNINGS COMPANY
4309 W. Lake St.
Chicago, Ill.

MILLS NOVELTY CO.
4110 W. Fullerton Ave.
Chicago, Ill.

J. P. SEEBURG CORP.
1510 N. Dayton St.
Chicago, Ill.

SICKING MFG. CO., INC.
1922 Freeman Ave.
Cincinnati, Ohio

VIKING SPECIALTY CO.
530 Golden Gate Ave.
San Francisco, Calif.

Confectionery Equipment

ADOLPH SEIDEL & SONS
1245 W. Dickens
Chicago, Ill.

Cooking Utensils

ADVANCE ALUMINUM CASTINGS CORP.
2742 W. 36th St.
Chicago, Ill.

FAGLEY & HALPEN
37 N. Second St.
Philadelphia, Pa.

THE KITCHENCRAFTERS
1124 N. Orianna
Philadelphia, Pa.

STAR PRODUCTS, INC.
15109 Darwin Ave.
Cleveland, Ohio

SUPER MAID COOK-WARE CORPORATION
2742 W. 36th Place
Chicago, Ill.

THE TYLER MFG. CO.
901 S. Mulberry
Muncie, Ind.

WEST BEND ALUMINUM CO.
West Bend, Wis.

Correspondence Schools

AMERICAN LANDSCAPE SCHOOL
Plymouth Bldg.
Des Moines, Ia.

AMERICAN SCHOOL
58th and Drexel
Chicago, Ill.

AMERICAN SCHOOL OF PHOTOGRAPHY
3601 S. Michigan Ave.
Chicago, Ill.

AMERICAN TECHNICAL SOCIETY
58th and Drexel
Chicago, Ill.

CHARLES ATLAS, LTD.
115 E. 23rd St.
New York, N. Y.

DOBE ENGINEERING SCHOOL
Libertyville, Ill.

FASHION ACADEMY
30 Rockefeller Pl.
New York, N. Y.

FRANKLIN INSTITUTE
Rochester, N. Y.

FUNK & WAGNALLS CO.
360 Fourth Ave.
New York, N. Y.

ALEXANDER HAMILTON INSTITUTE
Astor Place
New York, N. Y.

INTERNATIONAL CORRESPONDENCE
  SCHOOLS
Scranton, Pa.

LASALLE EXTENSION UNIVERSITY
Chicago, Ill.

LEWIS HOTEL TRAINING SCHOOLS
2301 Pennsylvania Av., N.W.
Washington, D. C.

LIBERTY CANDY & SUPPLY CO.
355 S. Broadway
Los Angeles, Calif.

ARTHUR MURRAY SCHOOL OF DANCING
7 E. 43rd St.
New York, N. Y.

NATIONAL RADIO INSTITUTE
16th and U Sts., N.W.
Washington, D. C.

NATIONAL SALESMEN'S TRAINING
  ASSOCIATION
53 W. Jackson
Chicago, Ill.

NEW YORK DIESEL INSTITUTION
Albany, N. Y.

NEW YORK INSTITUTE OF PHOTOGRAPHY
10 W. 33rd St.
New York, N. Y.

NEW YORK SCHOOL OF INTERIOR
  DECORATION
515 Madison Ave.
New York, N. Y.

NORTH AMERICAN INSTITUTE
3601 Michigan Ave.
Chicago, Ill.

NORTHWESTERN SCHOOL OF TAXIDERMY
Elwood Bldg.
Omaha, Neb.

PAGE-DAVIS SCHOOL OF ADVERTISING
3601 Michigan Ave.
Chicago, Ill.

PATTERSON SCHOOL
Mercantile Bldg.
Rochester, N. Y.

RADIO & TELEVISION INSTITUTE
2130 Lawrence Ave.
Chicago, Ill.

Correspondence Schools (Cont,)

RCA INSTITUTES, INC.
75 Varick St.
New York, N. Y.

SHERWIN CODY SCHOOL OF ENGLISH
183 St. Paul St.
Rochester, N. Y.

TOWERTOWN STUDIOS
520 N. Michigan Ave.
Chicago, Ill.

U. S. SCHOOL OF MUSIC
225 Fifth Ave.
New York, N. Y.

UNITED STATES DIESEL ENGINEERING
SCHOOL
89 Brighton
Boston, Mass.

WALTON SCHOOL OF COMMERCE
332 S. Michigan Ave.
Chicago, Ill.

**Developing and Printing Outfits
(Photographic)**

AGFA ANSCO CORPORATION
Binghamton, N. Y.

EASTMAN KODAK Co.
Rochester, N. Y.

J. H. WINN MFG. Co.
124 W. 23rd St.
New York, N. Y.

Dogs

Address the "Dog World"
3323 Michigan Ave.
Chicago, Ill.

Dog Supplies and Equipment

AMERICAN PET SUPPLY Co.
4044 Elston Ave.
Chicago, Ill.

A. BACKUS, JR., & SONS
1340 Lafayette Blvd.
Detroit, Mich.

BUFFALO WIRE WORKS, INC.
1957 Clifton Ave.
Chicago, Ill.

BUSSEY PEN PRODUCTS Co.
1500 S. Western Ave.
Chicago, Ill.

GEORGE W. CLAYTON Co.
1810 S. Wabash Ave.
Chicago, Ill.

WILLIAM COOPER & NEPHEWS, Inc.
1957 Clifton Ave.
Chicago, Ill.

CROWN IRON WORKS Co.
Minneapolis, Minn.

CYCLONE FENCE Co.
Waukegan, Ill.

FIBRE CASE & NOVELTY Co., INC.
46 E. 20th St.
New York, N. Y.

FORD FENCE Co.
Indianapolis, Ind.

GLOVER'S
462 Fifth Ave.
New York, N. Y.

KENTUCKY BOX & CRATE Co., INC.
Henderson, Ky.

MASON KENNEL FENCE Co.
Leesburg, Ohio

SERGENT'S
Richmond, Va.

SPRATTS PATENT (AMERICA) LTD.
18 Congress
Newark, N. Y.

WARNER'S DOG SUPPLIES
Norwich, Conn.

Drafting Instruments and Materials

EUGENE DIETZGEN Co.
2435 N. Sheffield Ave.
Chicago, Ill.

Duplicating Machines

A. B. DICK Co.
720 W. Jackson Blvd.
Chicago, Ill.

DITTO, INC.
Harrison at Oakley
Chicago, Ill.

GENERAL DUPLICATOR COMPANY
148 Lafayette St.
New York, N. Y.

THE HEYER CORPORATION
911 W. Jackson Blvd.
Chicago, Ill.

THE ROTOSPEED CO.
5th and Wilkinson
Dayton, Ohio

SPEEDOGRAPH DUPLICATOR CO.
18 W. 18th St.
New York, N. Y.

Electrical Appliances

AMERICAN STOVE CO.
St. Louis, Mo.

McGRAW ELECTRIC CO.
Elgin, Ill.

Fire Protection

FIREX CORPORATION
516 S. Broadway
St. Louis, Mo.

THE FYR-FYTER COMPANY
221 Crane St.
Dayton, Ohio

RED COMET, INC.
Red Comet Bldg.
Littleton, Colo.

D. B. SMITH & CO.
Utica, N. Y.

Flavoring Extracts

AMERICAN CHEMICAL CO.
1930 Anthony Ave.
St. Paul, Minn.

AMERICAN PRODUCTS CORP.
Cincinnati, Ohio

C. FOSTER CHEMICAL CO.
Decatur, Ill.

KOHNSTAMM & CO., INC.
83 Park Pl.
New York, N. Y.

Floor Mats

FABRIX, INC.
620 N. Michigan Ave.
Chicago, Ill.

KOWELL
5372 St. Clair
Detroit, Mich.

Food Machines

H. ADAMS
620 N. Michigan Ave.
Chicago, Ill.

DICKERSON MANUFACTURING
Springfield, Mo.

FOOD DISPLAY MACHINERY CORP.
620 N. Michigan Ave.
Chicago, Ill.

GENERAL EQUIPMENT CO.
626 Tower Grove
St. Louis, Mo.

G. H. HART
620 N. Michigan Ave.
Chicago, Ill.

LONG-EAKINS CO.
27 Primrose
Springfield, Ohio

STAR MFG. CO., INC.
6300 St. Louis
St. Louis, Mo.

VITA SEALD POTATO CHIP CO.
500 N. Michigan Ave.
Chicago, Ill.

WIENIE-CHIEF
2301 W. Hubbard
Chicago, Ill.

Food Specialties

BATTLE CREEK SCIENTIFIC FOODS
Battle Creek, Mich.

FEDERAL PURE FOOD COMPANY
2944 W. Lake St.
Chicago, Ill.

GREAT EASTERN COFFEE & TEA CO.
914 Broadway
St. Louis, Mo.

F. GUNTRATH LORENZEN
5203 Lake Park Ave.
Chicago, Ill.

SWIFT MFG. CO.
4016 Nebraska Ave.
St. Louis, Mo.

Frogs

BRYAN BLEVINS
Combs, Ark.

GUY BRASHEARS
Combs, Ark.

J. LESTER MORRISON
Florence, Ala.

Fur-Bearing Animals

Fitch

STAHL'S OUTDOOR ENTERPRISE CO., INC.
New City, N. Y.

LESTER WILLIAMS
Jamaica, Vt.

Foxes

FRED G. BECKENBAUGH
Fort Dodge, Ia.

HERBERT A. NIEMAN & CO.
Thiensville, Wis.

ARTHUR QUIST
Two Harbors, Minn.

Mink

BLACKSTONE FUR FARM
Pilot Grove, Ia.

BLUE STOCK FUR RANCH, INC.
Woodstock, N. Y.

DAVIS FUR FARMS
St. Johnsbury, Vt.

KANE MINK RANCH
113 S. 42nd Ave., E.
Duluth, Minn.

LAKE SUPERIOR MINK FARM
Superior, Wis.

HARRY SAXTON'S MINK RANCH
Bemus Point, N. Y.

SCHETTL'S MINKERY
Two Rivers, Wis.

VALLEYWOOD MINK FARM
Swanton, Ohio

WILLIAMS & ALLEN MINK RANCH
Ontario, N. Y.

WILSON MINK RANCH
Somers, Conn.

Rabbits

FRED. E. BATCHELLER ASSOCIATES
De Land, Fla.

KLA FARMS
Sharon, Wash.

LAUREL RABBITRY
Cincinnati, Ohio

OUTDOOR ENTERPRISE CO.
New City, N. Y.

PET FARM
Holland Patent, N. Y.

MAURICE B. SIXBY
94 Melrose St.
Buffalo, N. Y.

Garden Equipment

MODERN WOODCRAFT
3316 Wadsworth Rd.
Saginaw, Mich.

CHANDLER MURPHY
Minneapolis, Minn.

NATIONAL POTTERIES COMPANY
424 Second Ave., S.
Minneapolis, Minn.

ROWE MFG. CO.
Adams St.
Galesburg, Ill.

WETZEL MFG. CO.
Cedarburg, Wis.

J. WISE & SONS CO.
33 Littleton Ave.
Newark, N. J.

Garden Tractors

AMERICAN FARM MACHINERY CO.
Como Ave. and W. City Limits
St. Paul, Minn.

GILSON-BOLENS MFG. CO.
Port Washington, Wis.

SHAW MFG. CO.
Galesburg, Kans.

STANDARD ENGINE CO.
St. Paul, Minn.

Gems (Cut)

GEM SHOP
Helena, Mont.

STEPHEN VARNI
580 Fifth Ave.
New York, N. Y.

Goats

Address the
AMERICAN GOAT SOCIETY. INC.
Herkimer, N. Y.
for list of breeders.

348

"Grandfather" Clock Plans

AMERICAN CHIME CLOCK CO.
1669 Rufner St.
Philadelphia, Pa.

KUEMPEL CHIME CLOCK CO.
Guttenberg, Ia.

Gymnasium Apparatus

J. B. HELLENBERG CO., INC.
Coldwater, Mich.

LIND HENDRICKSON CO.
321 Broadway
New York, N. Y.

FRED MEDART MFG. CO.
3548 De Kalb St.
St. Louis, Mo.

W. W. STANLEY CO., INC.
399 Broadway
New York, N. Y.

Homecraft

ABRASIVE PRODUCTS, INC.
100 Pearl St.
So. Braintree, Mass.

AMERICAN REEDCRAFT CORP.
130 Beekman St.
New York, N. Y.

ART INLAYERS
Blocksburg, Calif.

ARTWOODS
P. O. Box 255
New Albany, Ind.

BILD-UR-OWN DEVICES
5237 Lake St.
Chicago, Ill.

W. R. BROWN CO.
2014 N. Major Ave.
Chicago, Ill.

ALBERT CONSTANTINE & SON, INC.
799 E. 135th St.
New York, N. Y.

CRAFTSMAN WOOD SERVICE CO.
2727 S. Mary St.
Chicago, Ill.

CRAFTSMAN'S MODEL COMPANY
2030 N. 41st St.
Milwaukee, Wis.

THE CRESCENT MACHINE CO.
614 Cherry St.
Leetonia, Ohio

FELLOWCRAFTERS, INC.
64 Stanhope St.
Boston, Mass.

FIRESIDE INDUSTRIES
Adrian, Mich.

GENE'S
510 E. 11th St.
New York, N. Y.

HAMMER BLOW TOOL CO.
606 Third St.
Wausau, Wis.

HOBBY GUILD OF AMERICA
11 W. 42nd St.
New York, N. Y.

HOMECRAFT BOOK SHOP
919 N. Michigan Ave.
Chicago, Ill.

JAMESTOWN SPECIALTY CO.
Titusville, Pa.

KLOK FURNITURE RESEARCH INSTITUTE
Grand Rapids, Mich.

METAL CAST PRODUCTS CO.
1696 Boston Post Road
New York, N. Y.

NATIONAL POTTERIES CO.
Minneapolis, Minn.

NATIONAL SEWING MACHINE CO.
Belvidere, Ill.

ORNAMENTAL PRODUCTS CO.
3450 Wright
Detroit, Mich.

THE PARKS WOODWORKING MACHINE CO.
1546 Knowlton St.
Cincinnati, Ohio

PARTINGTON, INC.
Station H.
Cincinnati, Ohio

FRANK PAXTON LUMBER CO.
Kansas City, Kans.

H. H. PERKINS CO.
256 Shelton Ave.
New Haven, Conn.

PLAN SHOP
Palmolive Bldg.
Chicago, Ill.

Homecraft (Continued)

PLASTIC INDUSTRIES
1085 Washington
New York, N. Y.

E. A. SWEET Co.
Binghamton, N. Y.

STEWART'S STUDIO
2927 Wilcox St.
Chicago, Ill.

UNITED CRAFTSMEN
Sparta, Mich.

UNIVERSAL HANDICRAFTS SERVICE
Rockefeller Center
New York, N. Y.

WARNER NU-WAY ELECTROPLATER CO.
360 N. Michigan Ave.
Chicago, Ill.

H. L. WILD
510 E. 11th St.
New York, N. Y.

WOODCRAFT SERVICE
Plainview, Minn.

WOODCRAFT SUPPLY Co.
407 N. Hoyne Ave.
Chicago, Ill.

Household Specialties

BLEECKER COMPANY
253 E. 4th St.
St. Paul, Minn.

BRUSH POTTERY Co.
Janesville, Ohio

CELLULOSE SANITARY PRODUCTS
Hardwick, Mass.

CENTRAL STATES MFG. Co.
4500 Mary Ave.
St. Louis, Mo.

CHRISTY, INC.
Newark, N. Y.

H. C. COOK Co.
Ansonia, Conn.

CARTER PRODUCTS CORP.
938 Front Ave.
Cleveland, Ohio

G. N. COUGHLAN COMPANY
Orange, N. J.

DIAMOND MOP Co.
New Orleans, La.

FAMILY SUPPLY Co.
505 Elm St.
Cincinnati, Ohio

FORT MASSAC CHAIR Co.
750 Prospect Ave.
Cleveland, Ohio

FOSTER BROTHERS COMPANY
Decatur, Ill.

ARTHUR HERTZBERG & CRAFTSMEN
3325 Lincoln Ave.
Chicago, Ill.

S. LOWE & SONS
Fairfield, Conn.

MASTER METAL PRODUCTS Co.
291 Chicago St.
Buffalo, N. Y.

E. J. MILLS
7562 Monmouth Ave.
Cincinnati, Ohio

MOP PRODUCTION DEPT.
Box 4036
New Orleans, La.

PARISIAN NOVELTY Co.
3510 S. Western Ave.
Chicago, Ill.

THE W. T. RAWLEIGH COMPANY
Freeport, Ill.

RELIABLE MERCHANDISE Co.
657 W. Madison St.
Chicago, Ill.

RETRACTO MFG. Co.
3163 Cottage Grove Ave.
Chicago, Ill.

SPECIALTY MANUFACTURERS
5202 S. Humboldt
Minneapolis, Minn.

STAR NOVELTY UTILITIES
107 S. Wells St.
Chicago, Ill.

U-ZIT MFG. Co.
2848 Seminary Ave.
Chicago, Ill.

VAC-M-MOP SALES Co.
1600 N. Western Ave.
Los Angeles, Calif.

Insurance

NATIONAL AID ASSOCIATION
Springfield, Ill.

Jewelry

MISSION BEAD CO.
Los Angeles, Calif.

Key-Making Machines

BEISSER MANUFACTURING CO.
409 E. Fort St.
Detroit, Mich.

Laboratory Supplies

BIOLOGICAL SUPPLY COMPANY
1176 Mt. Hope Ave.
Rochester, N. Y.

KEMKIT CHEMICAL CORPORATION
397 Bridge St.
Brooklyn, N. Y.

J. C. WINN
124 W. 23rd St.
New York, N. Y.

Lamps and Lanterns

THE AKRON LAMP MFG. CO.
Akron, Ohio

Language Courses

LINGUAPHONE INSTITUTE
Rockefeller Center
New York, N. Y.

Leathercraft

OSBORN BROS.
223 Jackson Blvd.
Chicago, Ill.

WILDER & CO.
1038 Crosby St.
Chicago, Ill.

Letter Brokers

GUILD CO.
76 9th Ave.
New York, N. Y.

R. B. LEFFINGWELL CO., INC.
1916 Sunnyside Ave.
Chicago, Ill.

Marking Devices

ARKOGRAPH PEN CO.
3921 S. E. Stark St.
Portland, Ore.

LAKE CHEMICAL CO.
6 E. Lake St.
Chicago, Ill.

NATIONAL LABORATORIES
Portland, Ore.

Mending Materials

THE CASEIN MFG. CO. OF AMERICA, INC.
350 Madison Ave.
New York, N. Y.

KEYSTONE GLUE COMPANY
Williamsport, Pa.

MONITE WATERPROOF GLUE COMPANY
Minneapolis, Minn.

ROGERS GLUE CO.
Gloucester, Mass.

RUSSIA CEMENT CO.
Gloucester, Mass.

SEW-NO-MORE CO.
Cincinnati, Ohio

SMOOTH-ON MFG. CO.
574 Communipaw Ave.
Jersey City, N. J.

Men's Wear

BOSTONIAN MFG. CO.
89 Bickford St.
Boston, Mass.

BOULEVARD CRAVATS
22 W. 21st St.
New York, N. Y.

BROHARD-RAINER SHIRTS
3306 Fourth St.
Cincinnati, Ohio

CENTURY TIE CO.
2335 W. Grand Blvd.
Detroit, Mich.

CONTINENTAL TAILORING CO.
Throop and Congress Sts.
Chicago, Ill.

THE P. H. DAVIS TAILORING CO.
3079 Iowa Ave.
Cincinnati, Ohio

Men's Wear (Cont,)

BEN DOVE GARMENT CO.
Kankakee, Ill.

THE DOUBLE-KUFF SHIRT CO., INC.
Denver, Colo.

FAIRBANKS TAILORING CO.
2302 Wabansia Ave.
Chicago, Ill.

J. C. FIELD & SON
Harrison and Throop Sts.
Chicago, Ill.

"JIM" FOSTER CLOTHES
2250 S. Spaulding Ave.
Chicago, Ill.

C. O. GOODING, INC.
Indianapolis, Ind.

THE HAMILTON TAILORING CO.
404 Pike St.
Cincinnati, Ohio

HENLEIN BROS. CO., LTD.
4th and Elm Sts.
Cincinnati, Ohio

KING OUTFITTERS
831 W. Roosevelt Rd.
Chicago, Ill.

THE LEONARD CUSTOM TAILORS CO.
205 W. 4th St.
Cincinnati, Ohio

LEOPOLD TAILORING CO.
319 W. Van Buren St.
Chicago, Ill.

MICHAEL CRAVAT CO.
41 Union Sq.
New York, N. Y.

MISSION HAND WEAVERS
Santa Fe, N. M.

THE A. NASH CO.
1916 Elm St.
Cincinnati, Ohio

NIMROD CO.
4922 Lincoln Ave.
Chicago, Ill.

PACKARD SHIRT MFG. CORP.
Terre Haute, Ind.

PIONEER TAILORING CO.
Congress and Throop Sts.
Chicago, Ill.

PROGRESS CLOTHING
500 Throop St.
Chicago, Ill.

QUAKER SHIRT CORPORATION
1239 Broadway
New York, N. Y.

ROBERT TAILORING CO.
Power Bldg.
Cincinnati, Ohio

ROSECLIFF-QUAKER CORP.
1239 Broadway
New York, N. Y.

J. B. SIMPSON, INC.
Simpson Bldg.
Chicago, Ill.

ROBERT STRONG GARMENT CO.
2352 W. Cermak
Chicago, Ill.

SUPERIOR TEXTILE MILLS
20 E. 12th St.
New York, N. Y.

TAYLOR HAT & CAP MFRS.
15 W. 6th St.
Cincinnati, Ohio

LOUIS A. WALTON CO.
403 S. Market St.
Chicago, Ill.

THE WARD-STILSON CO.
Anderson, Ind.

THE WHISNANT CO.
Summerville, Ga.

WILTON SHIRT COMPANY
Milan, Tenn.

Merchandise Displays

WORLD'S PRODUCTS CO.
Spencer, Ind.

Microscopes

BAUSCH & LOMB OPTICAL CO.
635 St. Paul
Rochester, N. Y.

Moth Proofing

HOME SERVICE COMPANY
843 Waukegan
Deerfield, Ill.

Mushrooms

INTERSTATE MUSHROOM INDUSTRIES
7357 Cottage Grove Ave.
Chicago, Ill.

UNITED MUSHROOM CO.
3848 Lincoln Ave.
Chicago, Ill.

Nurseries

BRISTOL NURSERIES, INC.
Bristol, Conn.

BURGESS SEED & PLANT CO.
Galesburg, Mich.

W. ATLEE BURPEE CO.
Burpee Bldg.
Philadelphia, Pa.

CHAMPLAIN VIEW GARDENS
Burlington, Vt.

THE ALBERT DICKINSON CO.
2750 W. 35th St.
Chicago, Ill.

THE DINGEE & CONRAD CO.
West Grove, Pa.

FERRY-MORSE SEED CO.
P. O. Box 648
Detroit, Mich.

HENRY FIELD SEED CO.
Shenandoah, Ia.

ADOLPH FISCHER NURSERIES
Easton, Pa.

HELLER BROTHERS CO.
New Castle, Ind.

PETER HENDERSON & CO.
35 Courtlandt St.
New York, N. Y.

INTER-STATE NURSERIES
Hamburg, Ia.

J. W. JUNG SEED COMPANY
Randolph, Wis.

MANDEVILLE & KING CO.
1040 University Ave.
Rochester, N. Y.

PORTLAND SEED CO.
109 S. E. Alder
Portland, Ore.

MAX SCHLING SEEDSMEN, INC.
Savoy Plaza
New York, N. Y.

SOUTH MICHIGAN NURSERY
New Buffalo, Mich.

STARK BROS. NURSERIES & ORCHARDS CO.
Louisiana, Mo.

STUMPP & WALTER CO.
132 Church St.
New York, N. Y.

CHARLES H. TOTTY CO.
Madison, N. J.

VAUGHAN'S SEED STORE
601 W. Jackson Blvd.
Chicago, Ill.

WAYSIDE GARDENS
Mentor, Ohio

WELCH NURSERY
Shenandoah, Ia.

Oil Burners

UNITED FACTORIES
1302 McGee
Kansas City, Mo.

Oils, Lubricating

CENTRAL PETROLEUM COMPANY
542 Standard Bldg.
Cleveland, Ohio

SOCONY-VACUUM OIL CO., INC.
26 Broadway
New York, N. Y.

PYROIL COMPANY
Pyroil Bldg.
LaCrosse, Wis.

3-IN-ONE OIL COMPANY
Jersey City, N. J.

Paints and Varnishes

DAVIS PAINT CO., INC.
14th and Iron Sts.
Kansas City, Mo.

LOWE BROTHERS COMPANY
Dayton, Ohio

SAVOGRAN COMPANY
28 India Wharf
Boston, Mass.

Pants Pressers

EMPIRE ELECTRIC CO.
Cincinnati, Ohio

Pens and Pencils

AUTOPOINT PENCIL COMPANY
1801 Foster Ave.
Chicago, Ill.

DUR-O-LITE PENCIL COMPANY
Melrose Park
Chicago, Ill.

EVERLAST PEN & PENCIL CO.
303 4th Ave.
New York, N. Y.

THE WAHL COMPANY
1800 Roscoe St.
Chicago, Ill.

Perfumes and Toilet Articles

CALIFORNIA PERFUME CO.
30 Rockefeller Plaza
New York, N. Y.

MADAM WHITE COSMETICS, INC.
2528 Nicollet Ave.
Minneapolis, Minn.

ALLEN B. WRISLEY CO.
6801 W. 65th St.
Chicago, Ill.

Plastic Wood

THE A. S. BOYLE CO., INC.
267 Cornelison Ave.
Jersey City, N. J.

LIGNUM CHEMICAL WORKS
Brooklyn, N. Y.

ORNAMENTAL PRODUCTS CO.
3450 Wright
Detroit, Mich.

Portable Stores

FURST McNESS COMPANY
Freeport, Ill.

Premium Merchandise

AMERICAN NOVELTY CO.
32 W. Randolph St.
Chicago, Ill.

BANNER NOVELTY CO.
729 W. Madison St.
Chicago, Ill.

BOSTON NOVELTY CO.
402 S. Market St.
Chicago, Ill.

BROWN & WILLIAMSON
22 S. Michigan Ave.
Chicago, Ill.

MILLS SALES COMPANY
901 Broadway
New York, N. Y.

THE ROBBINS CO.
222 W. North Bank Drive
Chicago, Ill.

SALES STIMULATORS, INC.
337 W. Madison St.
Chicago, Ill.

N. SHURE & CO.
200 W. Adams St.
Chicago, Ill.

SPORS COMPANY
Lane St.
LeCenter, Minn.

Printed Specialties

ARROW PRESS, INC.
Produce Exchange Bldg.
Minneapolis, Minn.

FORT WAYNE PRINTING CO.
Fort Wayne, Ind.

KAESER & BLAIR
Cincinnati, Ohio

MERCHANTS INDUSTRIES, INC.
Merchants Bldg.
Bellefontaine, Ohio

THE SHELBY SALESBOOK CO.
Shelby, Ohio

UNITED STATES SAMPLE CO.
1445 Jackson Blvd.
Chicago, Ill.

WILLENS & COMPANY, INC.
2132 W. Gladys Ave.
Chicago, Ill.

Punch Cards

DeLUXE MFG. CO.
175 W. Madison St.
Chicago, Ill.

WORTHMORE SALES PROMOTION SERVICE, INC.
221 E. Cullerton
Chicago, Ill.

Radios

AMERICAN NOVELTY CO.
32 W. Randolph St.
Chicago, Ill.

AMERICAN RADIO
32 W. Randolph St.
Chicago, Ill.

Razors and Stroppers

BEARDSLEY & WOLCOTT MFG. CO.
Waterbury, Conn.

RHODES MFG. CO.
1418 Pendleton St.
St. Louis, Mo.

Restaurant Equipment

BASTIAN-BLESSING CO.
284 E. Ontario St.
Chicago, Ill.

BARTH EQUIPMENT CO., INC.
390 4th Ave.
New York, N. Y.

ALBERT PICK CO., INC.
2159 Pershing Rd.
Chicago, Ill.

TRAUB-ESTABROOK CO.
940 N. Clark St.
Chicago, Ill.

VITROLITE COMPANY
222 W. North Bank Drive
Chicago, Ill.

Rug Renovators

HAMILTON BEACH COMPANY
Racine, Wis.

HOME SERVICE CO.
Deerfield, Ill.

Rugs, Hand-Woven

THE BLIND WEAVERS
2309 S. Keeler
Chicago, Ill.

Schools (Resident Courses)

COYNE ELECTRICAL SCHOOL, INC.
500 S. Paulina St.
Chicago, Ill.

NATIONAL RADIO, ELECTRICAL & AUTOMOTIVE SCHOOL
4406 Figueroa St.
Los Angeles, Calif.

Scrubbing Machinery

THE FAY CORP.
130 Madison Ave.
New York, N. Y.

FINNELL SYSTEM, INC.
Elkhart, Ind.

GENERAL FLOOR-CRAFT, INC.
337 6th Ave.
New York, N. Y.

HILD FLOOR MACHINE CO.
Randolph and Elizabeth Sts.
Chicago, Ill.

THE KENT COMPANY
Rome, N. Y.

PONSELL FLOOR MACHINE CO.
224 W. 19th St.
New York, N. Y.

Sharpening Devices

BEHR-MANNING CORP.
Troy, N. Y.

THE CARBORUNDUM CO.
Niagara Falls, N. Y.

FATE-ROOT-HEATH CO.
435 Bell St.
Plymouth, Ohio

FOLEY MFG. CO.
42 Main St., N. E.
Minneapolis, Minn.

Shoes and Findings

BRONSON SHOE COMPANY
716 W. Lake St.
Minneapolis, Minn.

CONSOLIDATED SHOE SYSTEM
Chippewa Falls, Wis.

DAULEC SHOES
923 Washington
St. Louis, Mo.

DOUBLE WEAR SHOE COMPANY
315 E. Lake St.
Minneapolis, Minn.

KNAPP BROTHERS
70 Bellvue Ave.
Brockton, Mass.

Shoes and Findings (Cont,)

LANDAU SHOE COMPANY
1099 Massachusetts Ave.
Cambridge, Mass.

MARTIN SHOE CO.
Milwaukee, Wis.

GEORGE MERRITT SHOE CO.
202 Court St.
Brockton, Mass.

J. C. MOENCH SHOE CO.
Boston, Mass.

PERFECT MFG. CO.
Daylight Bldg.
Cincinnati, Ohio

TANNERS CUT SOLE CO.
321 Summer St.
Boston, Mass.

Slicing Machines

CURRIER MFG. CO., INC.
Minneapolis, Minn.

GENERAL SLICING MACHINE CO.
100 S. Third St.
Brooklyn, N. Y.

Smokers' Specialties

M. P. HEINZE MACHINE CO., INC.
341 W. Superior St.
Chicago, Ill.

STEEL PRODUCTS MFG. CO.
St. Louis, Mo.

Sporting Goods

BACKUS NOVELTY CO.
Smethport, Pa.

L. L. BEAN, INC.
Freeport, Me.

EATON SPORTING GOODS CO.
Waterville, Me.

WILLMARTH TACKLE CO.
90 Clinton Ave.
Roosevelt, N. Y.

BENJAMIN AIR RIFLE CO.
1525 Eighth
St. Louis, Mo.

BRUNSWICK-BALKE-COLLENDER CO.
623-633 S. Wabash Ave.
Chicago, Ill.

DAYTON RACQUET CO., INC.
Arcanum, Ohio

HARVARD SPECIALTY MFG. CORP.
Cambridge, Mass.

INDIAN ARCHERY & TOY CORP.
Evansville, Ind.

JAMESTOWN SPECIALTY CO.
Titusville, Pa.

NORTH & JUDD MFG. CO.
New Britain, Conn.

THE REDDY TEE
Norway, Me.

H. E. WILLS CO.
1047 W. 47th St.
Chicago, Ill.

Squabs

RICE FARM
Melrose, Mass.

P. R. SQUAB CO.
Melrose, Mass.

Stamps and Coins

ACE INTERNATIONAL POSTAGE STAMP CO.
328 S. Dearborn St.
Chicago, Ill.

BEN'S STAMP & COIN CO.
72 W. Washington
Chicago, Ill.

CLASSIC STAMP SHOP
30 N. La Salle St.
Chicago, Ill.

COIN EXCHANGE
Box 38
Le Roy, N. Y.

THE ELDER COIN & CURIO CORPORATION
8 W. 37th St.
New York, N. Y.

GLOBUS STAMP CO., INC.
268 4th Ave.
New York, N. Y.

H. E. HARRIS & CO.
108 Massachusetts Ave.
Boston, Mass.

B. MAX MEHL
Mehl Bldg.
Fort Worth, Tex.

SCOTT STAMP & COIN CO., INC.
1 W. 47th St.
New York, N. Y.

Textile Supply Houses

ACOMA TEXTILE MILLS
113 Ingrahm St.
Brooklyn, N. Y.

Tires

THE MUSSELMAN PRODUCTS CO.
6227 St. Clair Ave.
Cleveland, Ohio

Tools, Hand and Power

ACKERMANN STEFFAN & CO.
4532 W. Palmer St.
Chicago, Ill.

ADJUSTABLE CLAMP CO.
417 N. Ashland Ave.
Chicago, Ill.

ARCADE MFG. CO.
1217 Shawnee St.
Freeport, Ill.

ATLAS PRESS CO.
1860 N. Pitcher St.
Kalamazoo, Mich.

BALKO ELECTRIC TOOL & SUPPLY CO.
605 W. Washington St.
Chicago, Ill.

BARBER-COLMAN CO.
229 Loomis St.
Chicago, Ill.

BOICE-CRANE CO.
Dept. 1791
Toledo, Ohio

BRASS PRODUCTS CO.
228 N. Clinton St.
Chicago, Ill.

CHICAGO TOOL & ENGINEERING CO.
8389 Chicago Ave.
Chicago, Ill.

CHICAGO WHEEL & MFG. CO.
1101 W. Monroe St.
Chicago, Ill.

DELTA MFG. CO.
600 Vienna
Milwaukee, Wis.

HENRY DISSTON & SONS, INC.
Unruh and Delaware Aves.
Philadelphia, Pa.

DURO METAL PRODUCTS CO.
2657 N. Kildare Ave.
Chicago, Ill.

GISHOLT MACHINE CO.
Madison, Wis.

ALFRED FIELD & CO., INC.
93 Chambers St.
New York, N. Y.

HAMMER BLOW TOOL CO.
606 Third St.
Wausau, Wis.

HERBERTS MACHINERY CO.
2929 Santa Fe Ave.
Los Angeles, Calif.

INDUSTRIAL PLANTS CORP.
92 W. Broadway
New York, N. Y.

J. & H. METAL PRODUCTS CO.
2-4 Commercial
Rochester, N. Y.

JUSTRITE MFG. CO.
2061 Southport Ave.
Chicago, Ill.

THE OTTO KONIGSLOW MFG. CO.
3602 Perkins Ave.
Cleveland, Ohio

MILLERS FALLS CO.
57 Wells St.
Greenfield, Mass.

NATIONAL ELECTRIC TOOL CO.
558 W. Washington St.
Chicago, Ill.

NICHOLSON FILE CO.
23 Acorn St.
Providence, R. I.

NORTH BROS. MFG. CO.
Philadelphia, Pa.

OUTBOARD MOTORS CORPORATION
4143 N. 27th St.
Milwaukee, Wis.

PATTERSON BROTHERS
27 Park Row
New York, N. Y.

FAYETTE R. PLUMB, INC.
4837 James St.
Philadelphia, Pa.

PORTER-CABLE MACHINE CO.
100 Wolf St.
Syracuse, N. Y.

PREMIER COIL CLEANER MFG. CO.
459 W. St. James
Chicago, Ill.

SEARS, ROEBUCK & CO.
Homan and Arthington Aves.
Chicago, Ill.

SKILSAW, INC.
5033 N. Elston Ave.
Chicago, Ill.

SOUTH BEND LATHE WORKS
107 E. Madison St.
South Bend, Ind.

Tools, Hand and Power (Cont.)

STANLEY ELECTRIC TOOL DIVISION
THE STANLEY WORKS
105 Elm St.
New Britain, Conn.

L. S. STARRETT CO.
Athol, Mass.

WALKER-TURNER, INC.
639 South Ave.
Plainfield, N. J.

J. D. WALLACE & CO.
134 S. California
Chicago, Ill.

WATSON MFG. CO.
470 Watson Bldg.
Toledo, Ohio

J. H. WILLIAMS & COMPANY
73 Spring St.
New York, N. Y.

YATES-AMERICAN MACHINE CO.
415 N. La Salle St.
Chicago, Ill.

Traps

ANIMAL TRAP CO. OF AMERICA
Lititz, Pa.

Tropical Fish and Aquarium Supplies

AUBURNDALE GOLDFISH CO.
112 N. Halsted St.
Chicago, Ill.

BREWER'S TROPICAL FISH FARM
828 N. W. 22nd Ave.
Miami, Fla.

EVERGLADES AQUATIC NURSERIES, INC.
712 Plaza Place
Tampa, Fla.

NATURALIST'S SUPPLY COMPANY
P. O. Box 1024
New Orleans, La.

PEACOCK'S TROPICARIUM
620 N. E. 3rd St.
Fort Lauderdale, Fla.

SUWANEE WATER GARDENS
810 W. Congress St.
Chicago, Ill.

VINELAND TROPICAL FISH HATCHERY
Vineland, N. J.

WEBER'S AQUARIUM
2963 N. Lincoln Ave.
Chicago, Ill.

Turkeys

PINE CREEK TURKEY ROOST
Holland, Mich.

PETERS HATCHERY
Esko, Minn.

Typewriters

INTERNATIONAL TYPEWRITER EXCHANGE
231 W. Monroe St.
Chicago, Ill.

REGAL TYPEWRITER CO., INC.
75 Varick St.
New York, N. Y.

REMINGTON-RAND, INC.
315 Fourth Ave.
Buffalo, N. Y.

ROYAL TYPEWRITER CO., INC.
2 Park Ave.
New York, N. Y.

SHIPMAN-WARD
325 N. Wells St.
Chicago, Ill.

L C SMITH & CORONA TYPEWRITERS, INC.
701 E. Washington St.
Syracuse, N. Y.

Uniforms

FRED M. BATCHELDER CO., INC.
120 Harrison Ave.
Boston, Mass.

BRILL'S HOUSE OF UNIFORMS
908 N. Water St.
Milwaukee, Wis.

CROWN GARMENT MFG. CO.
Indianapolis, Ind.

HOOVER
251 W. 19th St.
New York, N. Y.

MASTER GARMENT CO.
Ligonier, Ind.

SCHOLASTIC CLOTHING CO.
Webster and Howard Sts.
Allentown, Pa.

VIKING APPAREL MFG. CO.
711 W. Lake St.
Chicago, Ill.

Vending Machines

THE AD-LEE CO., INC.
825 S. Wabash Ave.
Chicago, Ill.

ADVANCE MACHINERY CO.
4645 N. Ravenswood Ave.
Chicago, Ill.

BUCKLEY MFG. CO., INC.
2156 W. Washington
Chicago, Ill.

EXHIBIT SUPPLY CO.
4222 W. Lake St.
Chicago, Ill.

INTERNATIONAL MUTUOSCOPE REEL CO.
516 W. 34th St.
New York, N. Y.

O. D. JENNINGS & CO.
4309 W. Lake St.
Chicago, Ill.

KEYSTONE NOVELTY & MFG. CO., INC.
Philadelphia, Pa.

MILLS NOVELTY COMPANY
4110 W. Fullerton Ave.
Chicago, Ill.

QUARTERMATIC PHOTOS, INC.
371 Andrews
Rochester, N. Y.

REPEATOSCOPE
Grand Central Terminal
New York, N. Y.

GUSTAV W. RISTAU
Kaukauna, Wis.

ROCK-OLA MFG. CORP.
816 N. Kedzie Ave.
Chicago, Ill.

J. P. SEEBURG CORP.
1510 N. Dayton Ave.
Chicago, Ill.

SNAX AUTOMATIC STORES, INC.
2832 E. Grand Blvd.
Detroit, Mich.

VIKING SPECIALTY CO.
530 Golden Gate Ave.
San Francisco, Calif.

Women's Wear

ALLSTON MODEL FIGURE FORM CO.
383 Fifth Ave.
New York, N. Y.

BARCLAY CORSET COMPANY
155 Summit St.
Newark, N. J.

BERGER BROS. CO.
135 Derby Ave.
New Haven, Conn.

BERTH ROBERT-GROSS, INC.
846 Broadway
New York, N. Y.

THE C. & D. CO.
31 Ionia Ave.
Grand Rapids, Mich.

CHARIS CORPORATION
730 Linden St.
Allentown, Pa.

DURA-STYLE APRON & UNIFORM CO.
308 N. 15th St.
St. Louis, Mo.

FASHION FROCKS, INC.
3301 Coleman Ave.
Cincinnati, Ohio

HOOVER MFG. SALES CO.
251 W. 19th St.
New York, N. Y.

INITIAL-IT, INC.
500 N. Dearborn St.
Chicago, Ill.

LOCKWOVEN HOSIERY CO.
900 Hodiamont Ave.
St. Louis, Mo.

MOSS COMPANY
Hartford, Conn.

REAL SILK HOSIERY MILLS, INC.
Indianapolis, Ind.

SCHOLASTIC CLOTHING CO.
Webster and Howard Sts.
Allentown, Pa.

THE SPRIELLA COMPANY
Niagara Falls, N. Y.

THE STAYFORM COMPANY
4325 Ravenswood Ave.
Chicago, Ill.

THE WARD-STILSON CO.
Anderson, Ind.

WINGET KICKERNICK CO.
2843 26th Ave., South
Minneapolis, Minn.

WILKNIT HOSIERY CO.
Greenfield, Ohio

APPENDIX C

Sources of Information

Sources of Information

THE list of magazines which follows completely covers the various fields of endeavor described in this book. The list of books, pamphlets and government bulletins, however, is intended to be suggestive rather than complete, and offers the reader a choice of books in each field which should help him in his search for practical information.

Additional suggestions may be obtained from the various government departments, both state and federal; from public libraries; from the readers' service bureaus of the magazines; publishers' catalogs; the U. S. Catalog (on file in most public libraries); book dealers, and the series of booklets published by the American Library Association under the title of, "Reading with a Purpose," also available through the public libraries. The prices listed are, of course, subject to change.

BEE CULTURE

Periodicals:

American Bee Journal. Hamilton, Ill. $1.00 a year. (Mo.)
Country Life. 1270 6th Ave., N. Y. $5.00 a year. (Mo.)
Gleanings in Bee Culture. Medina, Ohio. $1.00 a year. (Mo.)

Government Publications:

Outdoor Wintering of Bees. Farmers' Bulletin No. 695. 5 cents.
Preparation of Bees for Outdoor Wintering. Farmers' Bulletin No. 1012. 5 cents.
Swarm Control. Farmers' Bulletin No. 1198. 5 cents.
Wintering Bees in Cellars. Farmers' Bulletin No. 1014. 5 cents.

Books and Pamphlets:

A B C and X Y Z of Bee Culture, by A. I. Root and E. R. Root, new rev. ed. A. I. Root, Medina, Ohio, 1935. $2.50.
Bee Primer, by C. P. Dodant. rev. ed. American Bee Journal, Hamilton, Ill., 1937.
Bee-Keeping for All, by T. Edwards. 5th rev. ed. Methuen, 1939.
Beekeeping, by E. F. Phillips. rev. ed. Macmillan, 1928. $4.00.
Bees in the Garden and Honey in the Larder, by M. L. Coleman. Doubleday, 1939. $1.75.

Better Beekeeping, by D. F. Rankin. Walter H. Ball printing corp., Huntington, Ind., 1937. 50 cents.

First Lessons in Beekeeping, by C. P. Dodant. American Bee Journal, 1938.

Starting Right with Bees, by H. G. Rowe, 4th ed. A. I. Root, Medina, Ohio, 1936. 50 cents.

BIRDS AND FISH
(Publications of interest to the pet shop dealer)

Periodicals:

American Canary and Cage Bird Life. 5014 N. Kedvale Ave., Chicago, Ill. $1.00 a year. Partly controlled free distribution. (Mo.)

American Canary Magazine. 508 S. Dearborn St., Chicago, Ill. $1.00 a year. (Mo.)

Aquarium. 129 N. 12th St., Philadelphia, Pa. $2.00 a year. (Mo.)

Aquatic Life. 614 N. Chester St., Baltimore, Md. $1.50 a year. (Mo.)

Pet Dealer. 63 Beekman St., New York, N. Y. $2.00 a year. (Mo.)

Pet Shop News. 614 N. Chester St., Baltimore, Md. $1.00 a year.

Roller Canary Journal and Bird World. Central Exchange Bldg., Kansas City, Mo. $2.00 a year. (Mo.)

Government Publications:

Canaries, Their Care and Management. Farmers' Bulletin No. 1327. 5 cents.

Goldfish, Their Care in Small Aquaria. U.S. Fisheries Bureau, Document No. 980.

Books and Pamphlets:

Aquaria and Garden Ponds, by W. H. Cotton. Macmillan, 1935. $1.50.

Aquariums and Fishponds, by A. L. Wells. Warne, 1936. 60 cents.

Bob Becker's Pet Book, by Robert Becker. McClurg, 1938. $1.50.

Breeder Secrets. (Cage birds) By W. C. Daustin. 3rd ed. Pub. by the author, Redlands, Calif. 1934. $1.00.

Canaries and Cage Birds, by G. H. Holden. Pub. by Holden, New York, N. Y. 1930. 50 cents.

Canaries and Other Cage Birds, by J. N. Albright. Campbell Printing Co., Des Moines, Ia., 1927. 50 cents.

Canary, by G. Eckstein. Harper, 1936. $2.50.

Canary Birds, by D. L. Burkett. rev. ed. Orange Judd, 1929. 80 cents.

Fundamentals of Raising Canaries, by W. C. Daustin. 2nd ed. Pub. by the author, Redlands, Calif., 1934. 35 cents.

Tropical Aquarium Fishes, by A. E. Hodge. Stokes, 1927. $2.50.

Tropical Fish, by L. Q. Mann. Leisure League. 25 cents.

Tropical Fish and Their Care, by Norbert Lederer. Knopf, 1934. $2.50.

Tropical Fish for the Home; Their Care and Propagation, by F. H. Stoye. Empire Tropical Fish Import Co., 37 Murray St., New York, N. Y., 1931. $4.00.

Tropical Fish Handbook, by L. D. Sauer. 4th ed. Pub. by the author, 601 Winters Bank Bldg., Dayton, Ohio. 25 cents.

Tropical Fishes and Home Aquaria, by Alfred Morgan. Scribner, 1935. $2.50.

BOOK REVIEWS AND LISTINGS
(Publications of interest to rental libraries)

Periodicals:

American News Trade Journal. American News Company, Inc., 131 Varick St., New York, N. Y. Free to dealers. (Mo.)

Booklist, The. American Library Association, 520 N. Michigan Ave., Chicago, Ill. $2.50 a year. (Mo.)

Book Review Digest. 950 University Ave., New York, N. Y. (Mo.)

Herald Tribune "Books" (A part of the Sunday Herald Tribune). 230 W. 41st St., New York, N. Y. $2.00 a year. (Wkly.)

Publishers' Weekly. 62 W. 45th St., New York, N. Y. $5.00 a year. (Wkly)

Retail Bookseller. 55 Fifth Ave., New York, N. Y. $1.50 a year. Controlled free distribution. (Mo.)

Saturday Review of Literatures. 25 W. 45th St., New York, N.Y. $3.50 a year. (Wkly)

Times Book Review (A part of the New York Sunday Times). 229 W. 43rd St., New York, N. Y. $2.00 a year. (Wkly)

Books and Pamphlets:

Book Shops: How to Run Them, by R. B. Park. Doubleday, 1929. $2.OO.

How to Run a Rental Library, by G. Conklin. Bowker. $1.25.

COOKERY, CANNING AND PRESERVING

Periodicals:

American Cookery. 221 Columbus Ave., Boston, Mass. (Mo.)

American Home. 444 Madison, New York, N. Y. $1.00 a year. (Mo.)

Better Homes and Gardens. 17th and Locust Sts., Des Moines, Ia. $1.00 a year. (Mo.)

Farm Journal and Farmer's Wife. Washington Sq., Philadelphia, Pa. 50 cents a year. (Mo.)

Good Housekeeping. 57th St. at Eighth Ave., New York, N. Y. $2.50 a year. (Mo.)

Ladies' Home Journal. Independence Sq., Philadelphia, Pa, $1.00 a year. (Mo.)

McCall's Magazine. 230 Park Ave., New York, N. Y. $1.00 a year. (Mo.)

Woman's Home Companion. 250 Park Ave., New York, N. Y. $1.00 a year. (Mo.)

Woman's World. 461 Eighth Ave., New York, N. Y. 50 cents a year. (Mo.)

Government Publications:

Canning and Preserving Citron. Agriculture Circular No. 13. 5 cents.

Canning Fruits and Vegetables at Home. Farmers' Bulletin No. 1471. 5 cents.

Diets at Four Levels of Nutritive Content and Cost. 1933. 59 pages. Agriculture Circular No. 296. 5 cents.

Farm and Home Drying of Fruits and Vegetables. Farmers' Bulletin, No. 984. 5 cents.

Food for Children. Farmers' Bulletin No. 1674. 5 cents.

Good Proportions in Diet. Farmers' Bulletin No. 1313. 5 cents.

Home Baking. Farmers' Bulletin No. 1450. 5 cents.

Making and Using Cottage Cheese in the Home. Farmers' Bulletin No. 1451. 5 cents.

Making Fermented Pickles. Farmers' Bulletin No. 1438. 5 cents.

Meat Dishes at Low Cost. 1934. 14 pages. Agriculture Misc. Publication No. 216. 5 cents.

Midday Meals for Pre-School Children in Day Nurseries and Nursery Schools. 1932. 45 pages. Agriculture Circular No. 203. 10 cents.

Practical Fish Cookery. 1935. 26 pages. Fishery Circular No. 19. 5 cents.

Rabbit Recipes. Agriculture Leaflet No. 66. 5 cents.

School Lunches. Farmers' Bulletin No. 712. 5 cents.

Unfermented Grape Juice, How to Make It in the Home. Farmers' Bulletin No. 1075. 5 cents.

Books and Pamphlets:

Alice Bradley Menu-Cook-Book, by Alice Bradley. Macmillan, 1934. $1.50.

Automatic Menu Maker for Quantity Cookery. The Dahls, Stamford, Conn., 1938. $2.00.

Boston Cooking School Cook Book, by Fannie M. Farmer. Little, Brown, 1933. $2.50.

Camp Catering, by L. Hildebrand. Daye, 1938. $1.25.

Candy and Candy Making, by M. B. Bookmeyer. Manual Arts, 1929. $2.00.

Century Cook Book, by Mary Ronald. Appleton. $2.50.

Choice Candy Recipes, by L. G. Allen. Little, Brown, 1930. $2.00.

Cooking for Profit, by A. Bradley. rev. 3rd ed. American School of Home Economics, 850 E. 58th St., Chicago, Ill., 1933. $2.50.

French Home Cooking, by Claire dePratz. Dutton. $2.50.

Good Cooking Made Easy and Economical, by Marjorie Heseltine and U. M. Dow. Houghton Mifflin. $2.50.

How to Prepare Food for Children, by P. P. Holt. Parker, Stone & Baird Co., 241 E. 4th St., Los Angeles, Calif., 1932. $1.25.

Party Menus and Recipes, by M. Hewett. Holt, 1939. $1.50.

Plain Sailing Cook Book, by S. S. Browne. Scribner. $1.50.

Practical Candy Making; Delicious Candies for Home or Shop. Stokes, 1929. $2.00.

Quantity Cookery, by L. Richards and N. Treat. rev. ed. Little, Brown, 1939. $2.50.

Recipes and Menus for Fifty. rev. ed. Barrows, 1937. $2.00.

Savarin Cook Book, by B. Allevi. Harper. $4.00.

Science and Practice of Confectionery, by D. Ellis and D. Campbell. Longmans, 1928. $2.00.

Settlement Cook Book, by Mrs. Simon Kander. 20th ed. Settlement Cook Book Co., 715 N. Van Buren St., Milwaukee, Wis., 1934. $2.50.

Seven Hundred Sandwiches, by F. A. Cowles. Little, Brown, 1928. $1.75.

Successful Canning and Preserving, by O. M. P. Malcolm. Lippincott, 1930. $3.00.

Three Hundred "American Home" Recipes and Menus. "The American Home." New York, N. Y. 40 cents.

Yankee Cook Book, by Imogene Wolcott. Coward, McCann, 1939. $2.50.

DAIRYING METHODS AND DAIRY PRODUCTS
(Publications for the cattle or goat dairyman)

Periodicals:

Ayrshire Digest. Brandon, Vt. $1.50 a year. (Mo.)

Dairy Goat Journal. Fairbury, Neb. $1.00 a year. (Mo.)

Dairyland News. Power & Light Bldg., Madison, Wis. $1.00 a year. (S-Mo.)

Dairyman's Journal. Broadview Bldg., E. St. Louis, Ill. 35 cents a year. (Mo.)

Dairymen's League News. 11 W. 42nd St., New York, N. Y. $1.00 a year. (Wkly)

Dairymen's Price Reporter. 450 Century Bldg., Pittsburgh, Pa. $1.00 a year. (Mo.)

Farm and Dairy. 185-189 E. State St., Salem, Ohio. $1.00 a year. (Wkly)

Goat World. P. O. Box 196, Vincennes, Ind. $2.00 a year. (Mo.)

Hoard's Dairyman. Ft. Atkinson, Wis. 50 cents a year. (S-Mo.)

Holstein Friesian World. Lacona, N. Y. $1.00 a year. (Ftntly)

Jersey Bulletin and Dairy World. 602 Majestic Bldg., Indianapolis, Ind. $1.50 a year. (Wkly)

Michigan Milk Messenger. 406 Stephenson Bldg., Detroit, Mich. 50 cents a year. (Mo.)

Stock and Dairy Farmer. Christie Bldg., Duluth, Minn. 50 cents a year. (Mo.)

Government Publications:

Dairy Barn Construction. Farmers' Bulletin No. 1342. 5 cents.

Farm Dairy Houses. Farmers' Bulletin No. 1214. 5 cents.

Making American Cheese on the Farm for Home Consumption. 1934. Farmers' Bulletin No. 1734. 5 cents.

Making Butter on the Farm. Farmers' Bulletin No. 876. 5 cents.

Manufacture of Cow's-Milk Roquefort Cheese. Agriculture Bulletin No. 970. 10 cents.

Milk Goats. rev. 1935. 33 pages. Farmers' Bulletin No. 920. 5 cents.

Neufchatel and Cream Cheese, Farm Manufacture and Use. rev. 1934. Farmers' Bulletin No. 960. 5 cents.

Operation and Management of Milk Plants. Agriculture Circular No. 260. 5 cents.

Principles of Dairy Barn Ventilation. Farmers' Bulletin No. 1393. 5 cents.

Production of Clean Milk. Farmers' Bulletin No. 602. 5 cents.

(For additional titles write the Department of Agriculture, Washington, D.C., for price list No. 38 entitled "Animal Industry." published May, 1935.)

Books and Pamphlets:

Aids to Goatkeeping. "The Dairy Goat Journal," 1936. $1.00.

Care and Handling of Milk. rev. ed. Orange Judd, 1939. $3.50.

Cheese, by L. L. Van Slyke and W. V. Price. rev. ed. Orange Judd, 1982. $3.25.

Cheese Making, by J. L. Sammis. 9th rev. ed. Cheese Maker Book Co., Madison, Wis., 1937. $2.75.

Dairy Accounts, by R. F. Daley. Pitman, 1937. $4.20.

Dairy Enterprises, by J. C. McDowell and A. M. Field. 3rd ed. Lippincott, 1936. $2.00.

Elements of Dairying, by T. M. Olson. Macmillan, 1938. $3.50.

Fundamentals of Dairy Science. 2nd ed. Reinhold Pub. Corp., 330 W. 42nd St., New York, N. Y., 1935. $6.00.

Goat Milk, by A. H. Lewis. Pub. by the author, Herkimer, N. Y., 1933. 50 cents.

Goatkeeping for Amateurs, by H. S. Holmes Pegler. "The Dairy Goat Journal." 75 cents.

Making Goat Milk Cheeses. "The Dairy Goat Journal," 1935. 25 cents.

Management of Dairy Plants, by M. Mortensen. rev. ed. Macmillan, 1938. $3.00.

Principles of Dairying, by H. F. Judkins. Wiley. $3.00.

When You Buy A Goat. "The Dairy Goat Journal." 10 cents.

Practical Manufacture of Cultured Milk and Kindred Products, by A. D. Burke. Olsen, 1938. $2.50.

DOG BREEDING, KENNELS AND SHOW NEWS
(Publications for the breeder or the pet shop dealer)

Periodicals:

American Field. 222 W. Adams St., Chicago, Ill. $5.00 a year. (Wkly)

American Kennel Gazette. 221 Fourth Ave., New York, N. Y. $4.00 a year. (Mo.)

Country Life. 1270 6th Ave., New York, N. Y. $5.00 a year. (Mo.)

Dog News. Third and Walnut Sts., Cincinnati, Ohio. $2.00 a year. (Mo.)

Dog World. 3223 S. Michigan Ave., Chicago, Ill. $2.00 a year. (Mo.)

Dogdom. John W. Bailey Bldg., Battle Creek, Mich. $2.00 a year. (Mo.)

Fur-Fish-Game. 174 E. Long St., Columbus, Ohio. $1.50 a year. (Mo.)

Game Breeder and Sportsman. 205 E. 42nd St., New York, N. Y. $1.50 a year. (Mo.)

Harper's Bazaar. 572 Madison Ave., New York, N. Y. $5.00 a year. (Mo.)

Hunting and Fishing Magazine. 275 Newbury St., Boston, Mass. 50 cents a year. (Mo.)

Outdoorsman. 386 S. Fourth St., Columbus, Ohio. $1.50 a year. (Mo.)

Sports Afield. Phoenix Bldg., Minneapolis, Minn. $1.00 a year. (Mo.)

Spur, The. 515 Madison Ave., New York, N. Y. $4.00 a year. (Mo.)

Town and Country. 572 Madison Ave., New York, N. Y. $5.00 a year. (Mo.)

Government Publications:

Breeds of Dogs. Farmers' Bulletin No. 1491. 5 cents.

Parasites and Parasitic Diseases of Dogs. rev. 1934. 35 pages. Agriculture Department Circular No. 338. 5 cents.

Books and Pamphlets:

Bob Becker's Pet Book, by Robert Becker. McClurg, 1938. $1.50.

Care and Handling Of Dogs, by J. L. Leonard. Garden City Pub. Co., 14 W. 49th St., New York, N. Y., 1933. $1.00.

Complete Dog Book, by the American Kennel Club. rev. ed. Blue Ribbon Books, 1938. $1.89.

Dr. Little's Dog Book, by G. W. Little. rev. ed. McBride, 1934. $3.00.

Dog Encyclopedia, by W. L. Judy. 2nd ed. Judy, 1936. $5.00.

Dog in Training, by Joseph Weber. McGraw-Hill, 1939. $2.75.

Dog Shows and Rules, by W. L. Judy. Judy. 25 cents.

Dog, The, by James Dickie. Lippincott, 1935. $2.50.

Dogs; Their Care and Training, by A. W. Meyer. McGraw-Hill, 1936. $2.50.

Dogs and Their Management, by E. Mayhew and A. J. Sewell. rev. ed. Scribner, 1935. $3.00.

Dogs' Medical Dictionary, by A. J. Sewell and F. W. Cousens. Scribner, 1935. $2.75.

Feeding the Dog, by W. L. Judy. 2nd rev. ed. Judy, 1934. $1.50.

How to Breed Dogs, by L. F. Whitney. Orange Judd, 1937. $3.50.

How to Sell Dogs, by W. L. Judy. Judy, 1936. 25 cents.

Kennel Building and Plans, by W. L. Judy. 3rd ed. Judy, 1934. $1.50.

New Book of the Dog, by E. C. Ash. Macmillan, 1939. $5.00.

Principles of Dog Breeding, by W. L. Judy. 2nd ed. Judy, 1934. $2.00.

Training the Dog, by W. L. Judy. 4th ed. Judy, 1932. $1.50.

Your Puppy and How to Train Him, by H. V. Beamish. Lee Furman, Inc., 886 4th Ave., New York, N. Y., 1938. $2.00.

FASHIONS AND NEEDLEWORK
(Publications for the woman who sews, knits and embroiders)

Periodicals:

Brides Magazine. 527 Fifth Ave., New York, N. Y. $1.50 a year. (Qr.)

Butterick Fashion Magazine. 10 E. 43rd St., New York, N. Y. $1.00 a year. (Qr.)

Butterick Fashion News. 10 E. 43rd St., New York, N. Y. (Mo.)

Glamour. 420 Lexington Ave., New York, N. Y. $1.50 a year. (Mo.)

Good Housekeeping. 57th at Eighth Ave., New York, N. Y. $2.50 a year. (Mo.)

Harper's Bazaar. 572 Madison Ave., New York, N. Y. $4.00 a year. (Mo.)

Ladies' Home Journal. Independence Sq., Philadelphia, Pa. $1.00 a year. (Mo.)

Mademoiselle. 79 7th Ave., New York, N. Y. $2.50 a year. (Mo.)

Mccall Fashion Book. 230 Park Ave., New York, N. Y. $1.25 a year. (5 times a year.)

Mccall Needlework. 230 Park Ave., New York, N. Y. (Twice a year.)

Mccall Style News. 230 Park Ave., New York, N. Y. Free distribution (Mo.)

Mccall's Magazine. 280 Park Ave., New York, N. Y. $1.00 a year. (Mo.)

New Yorker, The. 25 W. 45th St, New York, N. Y. $5.00 a year. (Wkly)

Vogue. 420 Lexington Ave., New York, N. Y. $5.00 a year. (S-Mo.)

Vogue Pattern Book. 420 Lexington Ave., New York, N. Y. $1.50 a year. (B-Mo.)

Woman's Home Companion. 250 Park Ave., New York, N. Y. $1.00 a year. (Mo.)

Woman's World. 461 Eighth Ave., New York, N. Y. 50 cents a year. (Mo.)

Books and Pamphlets:

American Needlework, by G. B. Harbeson. Coward McCann, 1939. $15.00.

Embroidery and Needlework, by G. W. Fry. Pitman, 1935. $5.00.

Fashion Careers; American Style, by C. Oglesby. 2nd ed. Funk, 1937. $2.00.

Fashion Drawing, by H. Doten and C. Boulard. Harper, 1939. $4.00.

Fashion For A Living, by Gertrude Warburton and Jane Maxwell. McGraw-Hill, 1939. $3.00.

Fashion Illustration, by Christine Schmuck and Virginia Jewel. Harper, 1937. $5.00.

How the Fashion World Works, by Margaretta Stevenson. Harper, 1938. $~2.50.

Various Needlecrafts, by V. C. Alexander. Pitman, 1932. $1.00.

FUR TRADE, FUR FARMS AND TRAPPING

Periodicals:

American Fur Breeder. Manhattan Bldg., Duluth, Minn. $1.00 a year. (Mo.)

American Rabbit Journal. Warrenton, Mo. $1.00 a year. (Mo.)

Black Fox Magazine. 425 Fourth Ave., New York, N. Y. $2.00 a year. (Mo.)

Field and Stream. 515 Madison Ave., New York, N. Y. $1.50 a year. (Mo.)

Fur-Fish-Game. 174 E. Long St., Columbus, Ohio. $1.50 a year. (Mo.)
Fur Trade Review. 370 Seventh Ave., New York, N. Y. $3.00 a year. (Wkly)
Game Breeder and Sportsman. 205 E.42nd St., New York, N. Y. $2.00 a
    year. (Mo.)
Hunting and Fishing Magazine. 275 Newbury St., Boston, Mass. 50 cents
    a year. (Mo.)
National Fur News. 444 17th St., Denver, Colo. $1.00 a year. (Mo.)
Rod and Gun in Canada. Sun Life Bldg., Montreal, Quebec, Canada. $1.00
    a year. (Mo.)
Small Stock Magazine. Lamont, Ia. $1.00 a year. (Mo.)

Government Publications:

Home Tanning of Leather and Small Fur Skins. Farmers' Bulletin No.
    1334. 5 cents.
Hygiene in Fox Farming. Agriculture Leaflet No. 47. 5 cents.
Mink Raising. Agriculture Leaflet No.8. 5 cents.
Rabbit Production. Farmers' Bulletin No. 1730. 5 cents.
Rabbit Parasites and Diseases. Farmers' Bulletin No. 1568. 5 cents.
Recommendations for Beginners in Fur Farming. Agriculture Leaflet
    No. 27. 5 cents.

Books and Pamphlets:

*American National Fox Breeders' Association Year Book of the Silver
    Fox and Fur Farming Industries.* Pub. by the assoc. 424 McKnight
    Bldg., Minneapolis, Minn. 25 cents.
Angora Wool Rabbit, by E. B. Carhart. Pub. by the author, Bellingham,
    Wash., 1930. $1.25.
Fur Farming for Profit, by F. G. Ashbrook. rev. ed. Orange Judd. $3.00.
Fur Rabbits, by M. W. Meek, 2nd ed. Southland Pub. House, Inc., 308
    Crocker St., Los Angeles, Calif., 1927. $2.00.
Hunter and Trapper, by H. Trasher. Orange Judd. $1.00.
Making a Living with Rabbits, by E. H. Stahl. Stahl's Outdoor Enterprise
    Co., Inc., Holmes Park, Mo., 1929. 50 cents.
Mink Book, by R. G. Hodgson. "Fur Trade Journal," 1937. $4.00.
Mink Farming, by J. L. Edwards. 3rd ed. Fur Farms Pub. Co., Utica, N. Y.,
    1938.
Mink Raising, by L. D. McClintock. 2nd ed. "Fur Trade Journal," 1927.
    $2.00.
Rabbit Book, by F. L. Washburn. 2nd rev. ed. Lippincott, 1933. $2.00.
Selling Furs Successfully. Prentice-Hall, 1938. $3.00.
Silver Fox Ranching, by R. G. Hodgson. "Fur Trade Journal." $2.00.

Successful Muskrat Farming, by R. G. Hodgson. 6th ed. "Fur Trade Journal," 1930. $5.00.

GAMES
**(Publications of interest to those teaching games
and handling boys' or girls' clubs, etc,)**

Government Publications:

Backyard Playgrounds. Children's Bureau Folder No. 2. 5 cents.
Brief Manual of Games for Organized Play. Children's Bureau Publication No. 113. 10 cents.

Books and Pamphlets:

Backgammon Tactics, by H. Thorne. Dutton, 1931. $1.00.
Better Badminton, by C. H. Jackson and L. A. Swan. Barnes, 1939. $1.00.
Contract Bridge Blue Book, by Ely Culbertson. Bridge World, 30 Rockefeller Plaza, New York, N. Y., 1934. $2.00.
Boys' and Girls' Book of Indoor Games, by A. F. Collins. Appleton, 1934.
Complete Book of Games, by C. Wood and G. Goddard. Blue Ribbon Books, 1938. $1.89.
88 Successful Play Activities, by the National Recreation Association, 315 4th Ave., New York, N. Y., 1936. new ed. 60 cents.
Games, by J. H. Bancroft. Macmillan, 1937. $4.00.
Games for the Playground, Home, School and Gymnasiums, by J. H. Bancroft. Macmillan, 1934. $2.40.
Girls' Guide to Games, Sports, Hobbies and Other Interests, by P. J. Langland. Thomas Nelson & Sons, 381 4th Ave., New York, N. Y., 1933. $1.50
Indoor and Community Games, by S. G. Hodges. Lippincott, 1935. $1.25.
Official Summary of the New Standardized Official System of Contract Bridge, by M. C. Work. Winston, 1933. $1.00.
Pastimes and Diversions, by R. M. Abraham. Dutton, 1934. $2.00.
Recreational Games, by E. N. Hebbert. Putnam,1929. $1.50.
Recreational Games and Programs, by J. A. Martin, comp. National Recreation Association, 315 4th Ave., New York, N. Y. 50 cents.
Recreational Programs for Summer Camps, by H. W. Gibson. Greenberg, 1938. $3.50.
Table Games, How to Make and How to Play Them, by R. J. Marran. Barnes. $1.50.
Work-Peterson Accurate Valuation System of Contract Bridge. Winston, 1934. $1.50.

GIFTS, NOVELTIES AND TOYS
(Publications for the gift, antique, art or toy shop owner)

Periodicals:

Antiques. 40 E. 49th St., New York, N. Y. $5.00 a year. (Mo.)

Art Digest. 116 E. 59th St., New York, N. Y. $3.00 a year. (S-Mo.)

Art News. 136 E. 57th St., New York, N. Y. $7.00 a year. (Wkly)

Arts and Antiques. 630 St. Ann St., New Orleans, La. $3.00 a year. (Mo.)

Arts and Decoration. 116 E. 16th St., New York, N. Y. $3.00 a year. (Mo.)

Crockery and Glass Journal. 1170 Broadway, New York, N. Y. $2.00 a year. (Mo.)

Fine Arts. 405 Lexington Ave., New York, N. Y. $7.00 a year. (Mo.)

Gift and Art Buyer. 260 Fifth Ave., New York, N. Y. $3.00 a year. (Mo.)

Gifts and Housewares West. 1355 Market St., San Francisco, Calif. $1.00 a year. (Mo.)

Hobbies. 2810 S. Michigan Ave., Chicago, Ill. $1.00 a year. (Mo.)

Magazine of Art. Barr Bldg., Farragut Sq., Washington, D. C. $5.00 a year. (Mo.)

Notion and Novelty Review. 1170 Broadway, New York, N.Y. $2.00 a year. (Mo)

Picture and Gift Journal. 537 S. Dearborn, Chicago, Ill. $2.00 a year. (Mo.)

Playthings. 381 Fourth Ave., New York, N. Y. $1.00 a year. (Mo.)

Toys And Bicycles. 307 N. Michigan Ave., Chicago, Ill. $1.00 a year. (Mo.)

HANDICRAFTS
(Publications for the man or woman interested
in making things for sale)

Periodicals:

Hobbies. 2810 S. Michigan Ave., Chicago, Ill., $1.00 a year. (Mo.)

Home Craftsman. 115 Worth St., New York, N. Y. 80 cents a year. (B-Mo.)

Model Airplane News. 551 Fifth Ave., New York, N. Y. $1.65 a year. (Mo.)

Model Craftsman. 110 W. 42nd St., New York, N. Y. $2.50 a year. (Mo.)

Modern Plastics. 122 E. 42nd St., New York, N. Y. $5.00 a year. (Mo.)

Popular Homecraft. 919 N. Michigan Ave., Chicago, Ill. $2.00 a year. (B-Mo.)

Popular Mechanics Magazine. 200 E. Ontario St., Chicago, Ill. $2.50 a year. (Mo.)

Popular Science Monthly. 353 Fourth Ave., New York, N. Y. $1.50 a year. (Mo.)

Upholstering. 373 Fourth Ave., New York, N. Y. $2.00 a year. (Mo.)

Veneers and Plywood. 2232 N. Meridian St., Indianapolis, Ind. $1.00 a year. (Mo.)

Woodworker. 2232 N. Meridian St., Indianapolis, Ind. $1.00 a year. (Mo.)

Government Publications:

Gluing of Wood. 78 pages. Agriculture Bulletin No. 1500. 25 cents.

Gourds for Bird Houses and Other Purposes. Agriculture Leaflet No. 36. 5 cents.

Home Tanning of Leather and Small Fur Skins. Farmers' Bulletin No. 1334. 5 cents.

Homes for Birds. Farmers' Bulletin No. 1456. 5 cents.

Materials for the Household. 259 pages. Standards Circular No. 70. 50 cents.

Pain Concrete for Farm Use. Farmers' Bulletin No. 1279. 5 cents.

Shellac. Standards Technologic Papers. No. 232. 5 cents.

Small Concrete Construction on the Farm. Farmers' Bulletin No. 1480. 5 cents.

Sundials. Standards Circular No. 402. 5 cents.

You Can Make It Series. Prepared by the National Committee on Wood Utilization.

Vol. I Practical Uses for Second-hand Boxes and Odd Pieces of Lumber. 52 pages. Report No. 11. 5 cents.

Vol. 2-Practical Uses for Second-hand Containers and Odd Pieces of Lumber. 49 pages. Report No. 16. 5 cents.

Vol. 3-You Can Make It for Profit. Report No. 20. 5 cents.

(For additional titles write the Department of Agriculture, Washington, D. C.)

Books and Pamphlets:

Applied Design in Precious Metals, by F. W. Davidson. Longmans, 1929. $3.00.

Art Metalwork, by A. F. Payne. Manual Arts. $3.25.

Art of the Potter, by H. Barnard. Macmillan, 1932. $1.00.

Art of Whittling, by W. L. Faurot. Manual Arts, 1930. $1.35.

Basketry and Weaving, by P. Orman. Pitman, 1931. $1.00.

Beaten Metal Work, by A. C. Horth. Pitman. $1.00.

Bench Metalwork, by J. W. Gischins. Manual Arts. 56 cents.

Boats, Airplanes and Kites, by A. J. LaBerge. Manual Arts, 1935. $2.00.

Book of Craftsmen, by M. Bruce. Dodd, Mead, 1937. $2.75.

Book of Weaving, by A. N. Shook. John Day, 1930. $3.00.

Book Of Indoor Hobbies, by E. Stieri. McGraw-Hill, 1939. $3.00.

Bookbinding, by F. R. Smith. Pitman, $1.00.

Cabinet Making, by A. L. Keeble. Longmans, 1930. $1.50.

Chip Carving, by H. W. Moore. Manual Arts, 1922. 75 cents.

Cold Metal Working, by E. P. Van Leuven. McGraw-Hill, 1931. $2.25.

Color, Finishing and Painting Wood, by A. C. Newell. Manual Arts. $3.50.

Complete Book of Modern Crafts, by H. A. Reynolds. Greenberg, 1938. $2.50.

Constructive and Decorative Woodwork, by A. C. Horth. Pitman. $1.00.

Craft Work, by E. S. Cave. Appleton, 1929. $3.00.

Creative Handicrafts, by M. R. Hutchins. Leisure League, 1938. $1.00.

Cut Woolly Toys, by E. Mochrie and I. P. Roseaman. Manual Arts. $1.55.

Decorative Handicrafts. Manual Arts. $2.00.

Decorative Leather Work, by P. W. Davidson. Longmans. $3.00.

Design, by F. R. Smith. Pitman. $1.00.

Design. Book Department, Leisure. 5 cents.

Design in Woodwork, by P. A. Wells. Lippincott, 1935. $2.00.

Educational Metalcraft, by P. W. Davidson. Longmans. $3.00.

Felt Toys, by E. Mochrie and I. P. Roseaman. 2nd rev. ed. Manual Arts, 1933 $1.25.

Furniture Upholstery, by E. A. Johnson. Manual Arts. $1.25.

Group of Small Crafts, by R. W. Holliday. Pitman. $1.00.

Handicraft as a Hobby, by R. E. Dodds. Harper, 1939. $2.00.

Handicraft Pottery for Workshop and School, by H. D. Wren and D. K. I. Wren. Pitman, 1928. $3.75.

Handloom Weaving, by P. Orman. Pitman, 1930. $1.00.

Handy Man's Book. "The American Home." 35 cents.

Handy Man's Handbook, by C. T. Schaefer. Harper, 1931. $2.50.

Hobbies for Everybody, by Ruth Lampland. Harper. $3.00.

Home Craftsmanship, by Emanuele Stieri. McGraw-Hill, 1935. $2.50.

Home Upholstery, by M. Dane. Pitman. $1.00.

Homecraft Rugs, by L. L. Walker. Stokes, 1929. $4.00.

Homespun Handicrafts, by E. S. Bowles. Lippincott. $3.00.

Hooked Rugs and How to Make Them, by M. L. Phillips. 2nd ed. Macmillan, 1930. $2.00.

How to Make Electric Toys, by R. F. Yates. Appleton. $2.00.

Jewelry, Gem Cutting and Metalcraft, by W. T. Baxter. McGraw-Hill, 1983. $2.50.

Leather Work, by Adelaide Mickel. Manual Arts. 85 cents.

Make It Yourself, by Julian Starr. McGraw-Hill, 1938. $2.50.

Make It Yourself. new ed. Popular Mechanics Press, 1935. $3.00.

Making of Soft Toys, by C. E. Endlmann. Manual Arts. $1.60.

Metal Craft and Jewelry, by E. F. Kronquist. Manual Arts. $2.00.

Modern Boat Building, by Edwin Monk. Scribner, 1939. $3.00.

Money-Making Hobbies, by A. F. Collins. Appleton, 1938. $2.00.

Naturecraft Creatures. (The art of woodland and sea beach modeling.) By L. W. Lippincott and G. J. Roberts. Lippincott. $1.50.

Old Furniture Restored, by F. E. Wright. Webb Book Pub. Co., 55 E. 10th St., St. Paul, Minn.

101 Things for a Boy to Make, by A. C. Horth. Lippincott, 1933. $2.00.

101 Things for the Handyman to Do, by A. C. Horth. Lippincott, 1938. $2.00.

Outdoor Handicraft For Boys, by A. N. Hall. Lippincott, 1938. $2.OO

Painting And Enameling, by C. S. Johnson. Pitman. $1.00.

Pewter Work, by F. R. Smith. Pitman. $1.00.

Plastic Wood; Two Hundred Things You Can Do with Plastic Wood. Book Department, Leisure.

Plywood, by W. B. Little. Pitman. $1.00.

Pottery In The Making, by Dora Lunn. Manual Arts. $2.75.

Pottery, The Finger Built Methods, by Henry and Denise Wren. Pitman, 1932. $1.50.

Practical Craftwork Design, by W. M. Clarke. Scribner, 1938. $3.00.

Quilting, by Elizabeth King. Leisure League. 25 cents.

Raffia, Methods and Suggestions for Work, by A. L. Begg. Pitman. $1.00.

Rug Making, by Dorothy Drage. Pitman. $1.00.

Rush-Work, by Mabel Roffey and C. S. Cross. Pitman. $1.00.

Seat Weaving, by L. D. Perry. Manual Arts. $1.25.

Selected Furniture Drawings, by W. W. Klenke. Manual Arts. $2.50.

Shuttle Craft Book of American Hand-Weaving, by M. M. Atwater. Macmillan. $3.00.

Simple Basketry, by Mabel Roffey. Pitman. $1.00.

Small Jewelry, by F. R. Smith. Pitman. $1.00.

Soft Toy Making, by Ovida Pearce. Pitman. $1.00.

Stenciling, by F. R. Smith. Pitman. $1.00.

Things to Make and How to Make Them, by W. W. Klenke. Manual Arts, 1938. 2 vol. $3.00 ea.

Things To Make Yourself. "The American Home." 35 cents.

Tin Can Craft, by E. T. Hamilton. Dodd, Mead. $3.50.

Various Needlecrafts, by V. C. Alexander. Pitman. $1.00.

Weaver's Craft, by L. E. Simpson and M. Weir. Manual Arts. $5.00.

Whittling and Woodcarving, by E. J. Tangerman. McGraw-Hill, 1936. $3.00.

Wood-Carving as a Hobby, by H. W. Faulkner. Harper. $2.00.

Wood Pattern-Making. 2nd ed. McGraw-Hill, 1932. $2.25.

Wood Working as a Hobby, by Emanuel Stieri. Harper, 1939. $2.50.

Woodcut Manual, by J. J. Lankes. Holt, 1932. $3.50.

Working with Tools for Fun and Profit, by A. F. Collins. Appleton, 1937. $2.00.

Working Drawings Of Colonial Furniture, by F. J. Bryant. Manual Arts. 85 cents.

HORTICULTURE AND LANDSCAPING
(Publications for those raising flowers, fruits and vegetables for sale)

Periodicals:

American Fruit Grower. 1370 Ontario St., Cleveland, Ohio. 50 cents a year. (Mo.)

American Home. 444 Madison Ave., New York, N. Y. $1.00 a year. (Mo.)

American Landscape Architect. 45 W. 45th St., New York, N.Y. $5.00 a year. (Mo.)

American Nurseryman. 508 S. Dearborn St., Chicago, Ill. $1.00 a year. (S-Mo.)

Better Fruit Magazine. 225 S. W. Broadway, Portland, Ore. $1.00 a year.

Better Homes and Gardens. 17th and Locust Sts., Des Moines, Ia. $1.00 a year. (Mo.)

Bulletin of the American Dahlia Society. 251 Court St., West Haven, Conn. $2.50 a year. (Qr.)

California Citograph. 1118 Story Bldg., Los Angeles, Calif. $1.00 a year. (Mo.)

Country Home. 250 Park Ave., New York, N. Y. 25 cents a year. (Mo.)

Country Life. 1260 Sixth Ave., New York, N. Y. $5.00 a year. (Mo.)

Florida Grower. 305 Morgan St., Tampa, Fla. $1.00 a year. (Mo.)

Florist Exchange and Horticultural Trade World. 448 W. 37th St., New York, N. Y. $2.50 a year. (Wkly)

Florist's Review. 508 S. Dearborn St., Chicago, Ill. $2.50 a year. (Wkly)

Flower Grower. 99 N. Broadway, Albany, N. Y. $2.00 a year. (Mo.)

Garden Digest. Great Oak Lane, Pleasantville, N. Y. $1.50 a year. (Mo.)

Garden Gossip. 1406 E. Franklin St., Richmond, Va. $1.00 a year. (Mo.)

Garden Landscape and Architecture. 565 Fifth Ave., New York, N. Y. $3.00 a year. (Mo.)

Garden Quarterly. 560 Howard St., San Francisco, Calif. $1.50 a year. (Qr.)

Gardeners' Chronicle of America. 1270 Sixth Ave., New York, N. Y. $2.50 a year. (Mo.)

Homes and Gardens of Tomorrow. 186 Buffalo St., Buffalo, N. Y. $1.00 a year

Horticulture. 300 Massachusetts Ave., Boston, Mass. $1.00 a year. (S-Mo.)

House and Garden. Greenwich, Conn. $3.00 a year. (Mo.)

House Beautiful. 572 Madison Ave., New York, N. Y. $3.00 a year. (Mo.)

Landscape Architecture. 9 Park St., Boston, Mass. $3.00 a year. (Qr.)

Leisure. 683 Atlantic Ave., Boston, Mass. $1.00 a year. (Mo.)

National Horticulture Magazine. 116 Chestnut St., Washington, D. C. $3.00 a year. (Qr.)

National Seedsman. 211 W. Wacker Drive, Chicago, Ill. $4.00 a year. (Mo.)

Seed Merchant. 1230 W. Washington Blvd., Chicago, Ill. Controlled free distribution. (Mo.)

Seed Trade News. 109 N. Dearborn St., Chicago, Ill. $2.00 a year. (Wkly)

Seed World. 223 W. Jackson St., Chicago, Ill. $2.00 a year. (Ftntly)

Southern Florist and Nurseryman. 120 St. Louis Ave., Fort Worth, Tex. $1.50 a year. (Wkly)

Your Garden and Home. 6523 Euclid Ave., Cleveland, Ohio. $1.00 a year. (Mo.)

Government Publications:

American Bulbs Under Glass. Agriculture Bulletin No. 1462. 15 cents.

Apple Orchard Renovation. Farmers' Bulletin No. 1284. 5 cents.

Citrus Fruit Growing in the Southwest. Farmers' Bulletin No. 1447. 5 cents.

City Home Garden. Farmers' Bulletin No. 1044. 5 cents.

Commercial Cabbage Culture. Agriculture Circular No. 252. 10 cents.

Culture of Citrus Fruits in Gulf States. Farmers' Bulletin No. 1343. 5 cents.

Daffodils. rev. 1934. 74 pages. Agriculture Circular No. 122. 10 cents.

Dahlias. Farmers' Bulletin No. 1370. 5 cents.

Diseases and Insects of Garden Vegetables. Farmers' Bulletin No. 1371. 5 cents.

Farm Garden. Farmers' Bulletin No. 1673. 5 cents.

Garden Irises. Farmers' Bulletin No. 1406. 5 cents.

Grape Propagation, Pruning and Training. Farmers' Bulletin No. 471. 5 cents.

Greenhouse Construction and Heating. Farmers' Bulletin No. 1318. 5 cents.

Growing Annual Flowering Plants. Farmers' Bulletin No. 1171. 5 cents.

Growing Christmas Holly on the Farm. Farmers' Bulletin No. 1693. 5 cents.

Growing Fruit for Home Use. rev. 1938. Farmers' Bulletin No. 1001. 10 cents.

Growing Sweet Corn for Cannery. Farmers' Bulletin No. 1634. 5 cents.

Handling and Transportation of Cantaloupes. Farmers' Bulletin No. 1145. 5 cents.

Herbaceous Perennials. Farmers' Bulletin No. 1381. 10 cents.

Insect Enemies of Flower Garden. Farmers' Bulletin No. 1495. 5 cents.

Marketing Cantaloupes and Other Muskmelons. 1934. 51 pages. Agriculture

Technical Bulletin No. 425. 5 cents.

Mushroom Culture for Amateurs. Farmers' Bulletin No. 1587. 5 cents.

Onion Culture. Farmers' Bulletin No. 354. 5 cents.

Orchard Irrigation. Farmers' Bulletin No. 1518. 5 cents.

Packing Apples in Boxes. Farmers' Bulletin No. 1457. 5 cents.

Permanent Fruit and Vegetable Gardens. Farmers' Bulletin No. 1242. 5 cents.

Planting and Care of Lawns. Farmers' Bulletin No. 1677. 5 cents.

Planting the Roadside. Farmers' Bulletin No. 1481. 5 cents.

Preparation of Cabbage for Market. Farmers' Bulletin No. 1320. 5 cents.

Preparation of Eastern Grapes for Market. Farmers' Bulletin No. 1558. 5 cents.

Preparing Apples for Market in Barrels and Baskets. Farmers' Bulletin No. 1687. 5 cents.

Preparing Strawberries for Market. Farmers' Bulletin No. 1560. 5 cents.

Seed Potatoes and How to Produce Them. Farmers' Bulletin No. 1332. 5 cents.

Sweet Potato Growing. Farmers' Bulletin No. 999. 5 cents.

Tomatoes as a Truck Crop. Farmers' Bulletin No. 1338. 5 cents.

Transplanting Trees and Shrubs. Farmers' Bulletin No. 1591. 5 cents.

Trees for Roadside Planting. Farmers' Bulletin No. 1482. 5 cents.

(For additional titles write the Department of Agriculture, Washington, D.C., for price list No. 44 entitled, "Plants," published January, 1935.)

Books and Pamphlets:

Adventures In Backyard Farming, by Gove Hambidge. McGraw-Hill, 1935. $2.50.

All About Flowering Bulbs, by T. A. Weston. De La Mare, 1931. $2.00.

American Greenhouse Construction, by Richard T. Muller. De La Mare. $1.50.

Annuals in the Garden, by H. S. Ortloff. Macmillan, 1932. $1.25.

Art of Floral Designing, by William Harry. De La Mare. $2.50.

Backyard Garden, by E. I. Farrington. Stratford, 1934. $1.50.

Book of Annuals, by A. C. Hottes. De La Mare, 1928. $1.50.

Book of Perennials, by A. C. Hottes. De La Mare, 1930. $1.50.

Bulbs for American Gardens, by J. C. Wister. Stratford, 1934. $6.50.

Commercial Floriculture, by Fritz Bahr. De La Mare. $5.50.

Commercial Rose Culture, by Eber Holmes. 4th rev. ed. De La Mare, 1937. $5.50.

Floral Designs De Luxe. De La Mare. $5.50.

Fruits and Vegetables Under Glass, by William Turner. De La Mare. $5.00.

Fundamentals Of Fruit Production, by V. R. Gardner and Others. 2nd ed. McGraw-Hill, 1939. $5.00.

Garden Maintenance, by H. S. Ortloff and H. B. Raymore. Macmillan. $2.50.

Garden Planning and Building, by H. S. Ortloff and H. B. Raymore. McGraw-Hill, 1939. $3.00.

Gardener's Handbook, by L. H. Bailey. Macmillan. $3.00.

Gardening for Fun, Health and Money, by A. F. Collins. Appleton. $2.00.

Gardening Under Glass, by F. F. Rockwell. De La Mare. $2.50.

Gardening With Herbs for Flavor and Fragrance, by H. M. Fox. Macmillan, 1933. $3.50.

Gardens: A Guide to Modern Landscape Design and Gardening. Book Department, Leisure. 15 cents.

Gardens in Glass, by M. N. Andrews. De La Mare. $1.50.

How to Grow Vegetables and Berries, by Adolph Kruhm. Doubleday, 1935. 50 cents.

How to Make Garden Pools, by William Longyear. Doubleday, 1935. 50 cents.

How to Plan the Home Landscape, by A. H. Carhart. Doubleday, 1935. 50 cents.

Informal Gardens, by H. S. Ortloff. Macmillan. $1.60.

Landscaping the Small Home, by E. W. Olver. De La Mare. $2.00.

Making Lily Pools and Rock Gardens. "The American Home." 25 cents.

Natural Rock Gardening, by H. B. Symons-Jeune. Scribner. $3.50.

New Album of Floral Designs, by Robert Kift. De La Mare. $2.50.

New Illustrated Garden Encyclopedia, by R. Sudell. Scribner. 1933, $3.75.

Nursery Sales and Management, by Nelson Coon. De La Mare. $1.50.

Orchard and Small Fruit Culture, by E. C. Auchter and H. B. Knapp.
Wiley, 1937, 3rd ed.

Perennial Gardens, by H. S. Ortloff. Macmillan. $1.25.

Plant Culture, by G. W. Oliver and A. C. Hottes. De La Mare. $3.50.

Practical Book of Garden Structure and Design, by H. D. Eberlein and
C. V. Hubbard. Lippincott, 1937. $5.00.

Practical Landscape Gardening, by R. B. Cridland. De La Mare. $2.50.

Practical Tomato Culture, by F. C. and M. A. Pellett. De La Mare. $1.50.

Practical Vegetable Culture, by A. E. Wilkinson. De La Mare. $2.00.

Principles of Tree and Small Fruit Culture, by V. W. Kelley. Burgess
Pub. Co., Minneapolis, Minn., 1937. $2.00.

Rock Garden Primer, by Archie Thornton. De La Mare. $2.00.

Water Gardens and Goldfish, by R. V. Sawyer and E. H. Perkins. De La
Mare. $2.00

Wayside Marketing. (Marketing flowers and plants, vegetables, etc.) By
Schuyler Arnold. De La Mare. $1.50.

INTERIOR DECORATION AND FURNISHINGS

Periodicals:

American Home. 444 Madison Ave., New York, N. Y. $1.00 a year. (Mo.)

Arts and Decoration. 116 E. 16th St., New York, N. Y. $3.00 a year. (Mo.)

Better Homes and Gardens. 17th and Locust Sts., Des Moines, Ia. $1.00
a year. (Mo.)

Country Home. 250 Park Ave., New York, N. Y. 25 cents a year. (Mo.)

Decorative Furnisher. 381 Fourth Ave., New York, N. Y. $3.00 a year.
(Mo.)

Fine Arts. 405 Lexington Ave., New York, N. Y. $7.00 a year. (Mo.)

Good Housekeeping. 57th St. at 8th Ave., New York, N. Y. $2.50 a year.
(Mo.)

House and Garden. Greenwich, Conn. $3.00 a year. (Mo.)

House Beautiful. 572 Madison Ave., New York, N. Y. $3.00 a year. (Mo.)

Interior Decorator. 373 Fourth Ave., New York, N. Y. $1.00 a year. (Mo.)

Interior Design and Decoration. 30 Rockefeller Plaza, New York, N. Y.
$2.00 a year. (Mo.)

Ladies' Home Journal. Independence Sq., Philadelphia, Pa. $1.00 a year.
(Mo.)

McCall's Magazine. 230 Park Ave., New York, N. Y. $1.00 a year. (Mo.)

Woman's Home Companion. 250 Park Ave., New York, N. Y. $1.00 a year.
(Mo.)

Woman's World. *461 Eighth Ave.*, New York, N. Y. 50 cents a year.
(Mo.)

Your Garden and Home. 6523 Euclid Ave., Cleveland, Ohio. $1.00 a year. (Mo.)

Government Publications:

Furniture, Its Selection and Use. National Committee on Wood Utilization. Report No. 18. 10 cents.
Slip Covers. 8 pages. Agriculture Leaflet No. 76. 5 cents.
Window Curtaining. Farmers' Bulletin No. 1633. 5 cents.

Books and Pamphlets:

American Furniture and Decoration, Colonial and Federal, by E. S. Holloway. Lippincott, 1928. $5.00.
"American Home" Portfolio of Period Furniture. "The American Home." 50 cents.
Color Charts and Color Schemes. "Better Homes and Gardens." 25 cents.
Colour in Everyday Rooms, by Basil Ionides. Scribner, 1935. $2.75.
Decorating Livable Homes, by E. Burris-Meyer, Prentice-Hall, 1937. $5.00.
Furniture Arrangement and Balance. "Better Homes and Gardens," 1935. 25 cents.
How to Make Your Own Slip Covers and Draperies. "The American Home." 20 cents.
Ideas for Successful Interiors, by M. F. Roberts. McBride, 1939. $3.50.
Inside 100 Homes, by M. F. Roberts. McBride, 1936. $3.50.
Interior Decorating, by H. M. Doggett. Leisure League, 1935. 25 cents.
Period Furniture Handbook, by G. G. and F. H. Gould. Dodd, Mead. $2.50.
Period Influences in Interior Decoration, by W. R. Storey. Harper, 1937. $3.00.
Personality of a House. Funk, 1933. $7.50.
Practical Book of American Antiques, by H. D. Eberlein and Abbot McClure. Lippincott. $8.50.
Practical Book of Furnishing the Small House and Apartment, by E. S. Holloway. Lippincott. $7.50.
Practical Book of Interior Decoration, by H. D. Eberlein and Others. new rev. ed. Lippincott, 1937. $2.95.
Practical Book of Learning Decoration and Furniture, by E. S. Holloway. Lippincott. $4.50.
Practical Book of Period Furniture, by H. D. Eberlein and Abbot McClure. Lippincott. $5.00.
Refurbishing the Home, by C. G. B. Knauff. ,McGraw-Hill, 1938. $2.75.

Ross Crane Book of Home Furnishing And Decoration, by Ross Crane. Drake. $2.00.

Selling Home Furnishings Successfully, by S. W. Reyburn. Prentice-Hall, 1938. $3.00.

Smart Interiors. "The American Home." 50 cents.

Story of American Furniture, by T. H. Ormsbee. Macmillan. $1.39.

Study of Interior Decoration, by A. F. and B. Jackson. Doubleday, 1934. $2.50.

Well-Dressed Windows. "Better Homes and Gardens," 1935. 25 cents.

INVENTIONS AND EVERYDAY SCIENCE

Periodicals:

Diesel. 307 Fifth Ave., New York, N. Y. $2.00 a year. (Mo.)

Diesel Progress. 2 W. 45th St., New York, N. Y. $3.00 a year. (Mo.)

Everyday Science and Mechanics. 99 Hudson St, New York, N. Y. $1.00 a year.

Illustrated Mechanics. 1411 Wyandotte St., Kansas City, Mo.

Invention. 635 F. St., N.W., Washington, D. C. $3.00 a year. (Mo.)

Patent and Trade Mark Review. 230 Park Ave., New York, N. Y. $5.00 a year. (Mo.)

Popular Mechanics Magazine. 200 E. Ontario St., Chicago, Ill. $2.50 a year.

Popular Science Monthly. 353 Fourth Ave., New York, N. Y. $1.50 a year.

Science and Mechanics. 800 N. Clark St., Chicago, Ill. 50 cents a year. (B-Mo.)

Scientific American. 24 W. 40th St., New York, N. Y. $4.00 a year. (Mo.)

Trade Mark Reporter. 32 Nassau St., New York, N. Y. $6.00 a year. (Mo.)

Books and Pamphlets:

Art Of Inventing And What To Invent, by R. F. Yates. Appleton, 1935. $3.00.

Can It Be Done? by R. Gross. Simon & Schuster, 1933. $1.25.

1,500 Needed Inventions, by R. F. Yates. Donley Pub. Co., 509 Fifth Ave., New York, N. Y. 1936. $2.50.

HowTo Patent and Commercialize Your Inventions, by D. B. Miller. Pitman, 1937. $1.00.

If You Want to Invent, by H. D. Carter. Vanguard Press, 424 Madison Ave., New York, N. Y., 1939. $2.75.

Invention and the Law, by H. A. Toulmin. Prentice-Hall, 1936. $5.00.

Inventions and Their Protection. Penton, 1938. $5.00.

Inventions, Patents and Trade-Marks, Their Protection and Promotion. 2nd ed. McGraw-Hill, 1933. $2.50.

Making Inventions Pay. Crescent Tool Company, 2nd and Elm Sts., Cincinnati, Ohio. 3rd ed. 1932. Gratis.

What to Do About your Invention, by E. Thomas. Leisure League, 1934. $1.00.

Your Invention; How to Protect and Merchandise It, by E. B. Lyford. Radio & Technical Pub. Co., 45 Astor Pl., New York, N. Y., 1935. $1.50.

MODEL MAKING

Periodicals:

Hobbies. 2810 S. Michigan Ave., Chicago, Ill. $1.00 a year. (Mo.)

Model Airplane News. 551 Fifth Ave., New York, N. Y. $1.65 a year. (Mo.)

Model Craftsman. 110 W. 42nd St., New York, N. Y. $2.50 a year. (Mo.)

Modelmaker, The. Wauwatosa, Wis. $1.50 a year. {B-Mo.}

Popular Homecraft. 919 N. Michigan Ave., Chicago, Ill. $3.00 a year. (B-Mo.)

Popular Mechanics Magazine. 200 E. Ontario St., Chicago, Ill. $2.50 a year. (Mo.)

Popular Science Monthly. 353 Fourth Ave., New York, N. Y. $1.50 a year. (Mo.)

Books and Pamphlets:

Boats, Airplanes and Kits, by Armand J. LeBerge. Manual Arts. $2.00.

Boys' Book of Model Airplanes, by Francis Collins. Appleton, 1929. $2.00.

Building s Model Railroad, by A. S. Coolidge. Macmillan, 1929. $2.00.

Building and Flying Model Aircraft, by P.E. Garber. Ronald Press, 1928. $2.25.

Clipper Ships Done in Cork Models, by Peter Adams. Dutton, 1929. $1.00.

Complete Model Aircraft Manual, by E. T. Hamilton. Dodd, Mead, 1933. $3.50.

Cork Ship Models and How to Make Them, by Peter Adams. Dutton, 1928. $1.25.

Making and Operating Model Railroads, by R. F. Yates. Appleton, 1938. $3.00.

Miniature Aircraft, by O. H. Day and Terrence Vincent. Manual Arts. 80 cents.

Model Boats for Boys, by C. W. Horst. Manual Arts. 90 cents.

Model Power Boats, by E. Hobbs. Modelmaker, 1939. $2.50.

Model Railroader Encyclopedia. Modelmaker, 1938. 3rd ed. $2.00.

Model Sailing Ship Fittings, by E. W. Hobbs. Spon. 35 cents.

Model Steam Engine Design, by R. M. de Vignier. Modelmaker. 50 cents.

Modelmaker, 1936, by A. C. Kaimbach. Modelmaker, 1937. $2.00.

Models Any Boy Can Build, by Joseph Leeming. Appleton, 1938. $2.25.

Racing Yachts Done in Cork Models, by Peter Adams. Dutton, 1930. $1.00.

Simple Mechanical Working Models, by P. Marshall. 10th ed. Spon, 1928. 35 cents.

Yachting with Models, by John Black. McGraw-Hill, 1939. $3.00.

PHOTOGRAPHY
(Publications for those who want to make money with a camera)

Periodicals:

American Camera Trade. 22 E. 12th St., Cincinnati, Ohio. $2.00 a year. (Mo.)

American Photography. 353 Newbury St., Boston, Mass. $2.50 a year. (Mo.)

Better Photography. 148 W. 24th St., New York, N. Y. $2.50 a year. (Mo.)

Camera, The. 153 N. Seventh St., Philadelphia, Pa, $2.50 a year. (Mo.)

Camera Craft. 425 Bush St., San Francisco, Calif. $2.50 a year. (Mo.)

Commercial Photographer. 520 Caxton Bldg., Cleveland, Ohio. $2.00 a year. (Mo.)

Everyday Photography Magazine. 67 W. 44th St., New York, N. Y. $1.50 a year. (Mo.)

Foto-Craft. 99 Hudson St., New York, N. Y. $2.50 a year. (Mo.)

Home Movies. 6060 Sunset Blvd., Hollywood, Calif. $1.00 a year. (Mo.)

Minicam. 22 E. Twelfth St., Cincinnati, Ohio. $2.50 a year. (Mo.)

Photographic Dealer. 6060 Sunset Blvd., Hollywood, Calif. $1.00 a year. (Mo.)

Photographic Retailing. 604 N. Michigan Ave., Chicago, Ill. $3.00 a year. (Mo.)

Popular Photography. 608 S. Dearborn St., Chicago, Ill. $2.50 a year. (Mo.)

Professional Photographer. 520 Caxton Blvd., Cleveland, Ohio. $2.50 a year. (S-Mo.)

U. S. Camera Magazine. 122 E. 4ind St., New York, N. Y. $2.50 a year. (Bi-Mo.)

Books and Pamphlets:

American Annual of Photography. American Photographic Pub. Co., 353 Newbury St., Boston, Mass. $2.25.

Camera in Advertising and Industry, by W. G. Briggs. Pitman, 1939. $4.00.

Cash from Your Camera, by H. R. Snyder and K. Barleben. American Photographic Pub. Co., 353 Newbury St., Boston, Mass., 1929. $1.00.

Color Photography for the Amateur, by Keith Henney. McGraw-Hill, 1938. $3.50.

Commercial Photography, by D. Charles. 2nd ed. Pitman, 1933. $3.00.

Fifty Dollars a Week with Car and Camera, by H. R. Snyder. 5th ed. Snyder, 1931. $1.50.

Fun of Photography, by Mario and Mabel Schacheri. Harcourt, Brace, 1938. $3.75.

How to Make Good Movies. Eastman Kodak Company. $2.00.

How to Make Good Pictures. 18th rev. ed. Eastman Kodak Company, 1932. 50 cents.

Making Pictures with the Miniature Camera, by Jacob Deschin. McGraw-Hill, $3.00.

Finding New Subjects for Your Camera. McGraw-Hill, 1939. $2.75.

How to Make Good Pictures. 24th rev. ed. Eastman Kodak Company, 1938. 50 cents.

News Photography, by J. Price. Industries Pub. Co., 80 Lafayette St., New York, N. Y., 1932. $2.00.

Outdoor Photography, by J. A. Dimock. Macmillan. $1.00.

Photography for Fun, by William Strong. Leisure League, 1934. 25 cents.

Photography for Fun and Money, by A. F. Collins. Appleton, 1939. $2.00.

Portrait Lighting, by F. R. Fraprie. American Photographic Pub. Co. $2.00.

Practical Amateur Photography, by W. S. Davis. Little, Brown, 1935. $2.25.

Profitable Photography with the Miniature Camera, by E. C. Buxbaum. Box Tree Press, Milwaukee, Wis. $1.00.

Put Your Camera on the Payroll, by H. R. Snyder. Snyder, 1934. 50 cents.

Ten Lessons in Camera Journalism, by H. R. Snyder. Snyder, 1934. 50 cents.

Where and How to Sell Photographs, by H. R. Snyder. Snyder, 1933. 50 cents.

POULTRY AND PIGEONS

Periodicals:

American Pigeon Journal. Warrenton, Mo. $1.00 a year. (Mo.)

American Pigeon Keeper. 20 W. Jackson St., Chicago, Ill. $1.50 a year. (Mo.)

American Poultry Journal. 536 S. Clark St., Chicago, Ill. 25 cents a year. (Mo.)

American Turkey Journal. 105 S. Third St., Grand Forks, N. D. 50 cents a year. (Mo.)

Burley Tobacco Bulletin and Poultry Fancier. Lock Box 245, Greeneville, Tenn. 50 cents a year. (Mo.)

Cackle And Crow. 116 Church St., New Haven, Conn. $1.00 a year. (Mo.)

Dixie Farm and Poultry Journal. 110 Seventh Ave., N., Nashville, Tenn. 50 cents a year. (Mo.)

Everybody's Poultry Magazine. Exchange Place, Hanover, Pa. 25 cents a year. (Mo.)

Farm Journal and Farmer's Wife. Washington Sq., Philadelphia, Pa. 50 cents a year. (Mo.)

Inland Poultry Journal. Spencer, Ind. 25 cents a year. (Mo.)

Leghorn World. Waverly, Ia. 25 cents a year. (Mo.)

National Barred Rock Journal. South Whitley, Ind. 25 cents a year. (Mo.)

New England Poultryman and Northeastern Breeder. 4 Park St., Boston, Mass. $1.00 a year. (Mo.)

Northwest Turkey News. 1800 S. W. Temple St., Salt Lake City, Utah. 25 cents a year. (Mo.)

Plymouth Rock Monthly. Waverly, Ia. 25 cents a year. (Mo.)

Poultry Herald. Metropolitan Bank Bldg., St. Paul, Minn. 25 cents a year. (Mo.)

Poultry Item. Sellersville, Pa. 35 cents a year. (Mo.)

Poultry Keeper. 337 Hampshire St., Quincy, Ill. 25 cents a year. (Mo. and B-Mo.)

Poultry Press. York, Pa, 50 cents a year. (Bi-Wkly)

Poultry Supply Dealer. 1230 W. Washington Blvd., Chicago, Ill. Controlled free distribution. (Mo.)

Poultry Tribune. Mount Morris, Ill. 50 cents a year. (Mo.)

Rhode Island Red Journal. Waverly, Ia. 25 cents a year. (Mo.)

Turkey World. Mount Morris, Ill. $1.00 a year. (Mo.)

Government Publications:

Business Records for Poultry Keepers. Farmers' Bulletin No. 1614. 5 cents.
Capons and Caponizing. Farmers' Bulletin No. 849. 5 cents.
Construction and Packing of Egg Case. Agriculture Leaflet No. 64. 5 cents.
Dressing and Packing Turkeys for Market. Farmers' Bulletin No. 1694. 5 cents.
Duck Raising. Farmers' Bulletin No. 697. 5 cents.
Farm Poultry Raising. Farmers' Bulletin No. 1524. 5 cents.
Feeding Chickens. Farmers' Bulletin No. 1541. 5 cents.
Fowl Tick and How Premises May Be Free from It. Farmers' Bulletin No. 1070. 5 cents.
Goose Raising. Farmers' Bulletin No. 767. 5 cents.
Guinea Fowl. Farmers' Bulletin No. 1391. 5 cents.
Incubation and Brooding of Chickens. Farmers' Bulletin No. 1538. 5 cents.
Marketing Eggs. Farmers' Bulletin No. 1378. 5 cents.
Marketing Poultry. Farmers' Bulletin No. 1377. 5 cents.
Methods of Packing Eggs and of Buffing and Bracing Cases of Eggs In Carload Shipments. Agriculture Department Circular No. 391. 5 cents.
Mites and Lice on Poultry. Farmers' Bulletin No. 801. 5 cents.
Poultry Houses and Fixtures. Farmers' Bulletin No. 1554. 5 cents.
Poultry Keeping in Backyards. Farmers' Bulletin No. 1508. 5 cents.
Selecting Hens for Egg Production. Farmers' Bulletin No. 1727. 5 cents.
Squab Raising. Farmers' Bulletin No. 684. 5 cents.
Standard Breeds and Varieties of Chickens. Farmers' Bulletin No. 1506. 5 cents; Farmers' Bulletin No. 1507. 5 cents.
Turkey Raising. Farmers' Bulletin No. 1409. 5 cents.

Books and Pamphlets:

Book of the Pigeon, by C. A. Naether. McKay, 1939. $2.50.
Commercial Poultry Farming, by T. B. Charles and H. O. Stuart. 3rd ed. Interstate Printing Co., Danville, Ill., 1939. $3.20.
Egg Farming, by W. C. Thompson. Orange Judd, 1936. $2.00.
How a Living Can Be Made with Poultry, by M. K. Boyer. Caspar, 1935. 50 cents.
How to Make Money Breeding Squabs, by E. C. Rice. Plymouth Rock Squab Co., Melrose, Mass., 1937. 10 cents.
Modern Poultry Management, by H. Howes. Macmillan, 1939. $1.10.
Marketing Poultry Products, by E. W. Benjamin and H. C. Pierce. 3rd rev. ed. Wiley, 1937. $4.00.

National Squab Book, by E. C. Rice. 56th ed. Squab Pub. Co., Melrose, Mass., 1939. $2.00.

New Road to Independence, by M. H. Arndt. New Era Pub. Co., Trenton, N. J., 1933. $1.00.

Poultry Breeding, by M. A. Jull. 3rd ed. Wiley, 1933. $2.75.

Poultry Enterprises, by S. Dickinson and H. R. Lewis. Lippincott, 1939. 2nd ed. $2.00.

Poultry Husbandry, by M. A. Jull. 2nd ed. McGraw-Hill, 1938. $4.00.

Practical Poultry Farming, by L. M. Hurd. Macmillan, 1928. $2.50.

Poultry Problems in Production, Marketing and Management. Lippincott, 1938. $1.00.

Poultry Science and Practice, by R. H. Waite. McGraw-Hill, 1929. $3.50.

Productive Poultry Husbandry, by H. R. Lewis. 8th ed. rev. Lippincott, 1933. $3.00.

Profitable Poultry Management, by C. E. Lee. 8th rev. ed. Beacon Milling Co., Inc., Cayuga, N. Y., 1935. 50 cents.

RADIO MECHANICS AND MERCHANDISING

Periodicals:

Electrical Merchandising. 330 W. 42nd St., New York, N. Y. $2.00 a year. (Mo.)

Electronics. 330 W. 42nd St., New York, N. Y. $5.00 a year.

Popular Mechanics Magazine. 200 E. Ohio St., Chicago, Ill. $2.50 a year. (Mo.)

Proceedings of the Institute of Radio Engineers. 330 W. 42nd St., New York, N. Y. $10 a year. (Mo.)

Radio and Electric Appliance Journal. RKO Bldg., Radio City, Rockefeller Center, New York, N. Y. $5.00 a year. (Mo.)

Radio and Television Today. 480 Lexington Ave., New York, N. Y. (Mo.)

Radio and Television Weekly. 99 Hudson St., New York, N. Y. $4.00 a year (Wkly)

Radio Craft. 99 Hudson St., New York, N. Y. $2.00 a year. (Mo.)

Radio Engineering. 19 E. 47th St., New York, N. Y. $2.00 a year. (Mo.)

Radio Jobber News. 524 E. Superior St., Chicago, Ill. (Mo.)

Radio Retailing. 330 W. 42nd St., New York, N. Y. $1.00 a year. (Mo.)

Radio-Television Retailer & Jobber. 11 W. 42nd St., New York, N. Y. $2.00 a year. (Mo.)

Service. 19 E. 47th St., New York, N. Y. $2.00 a year. (Mo.)

Government Publications:

Construction and Operation of Simple Home-Made Radio Receiving Outfit. Standards Circular No. 120. 5 cents.

Safety Rules for Radio Installations. Standards Handbook Series No.9. 10 cents.

Some Methods of Testing Radio Receiving Sets. Standards Technologic Papers No. 256. 10 cents.

Books and Pamphlets:

Breaking into Radio Servicing, by R. Eichberg. Radcraft, 1938. 50 cents.

Point-To-Point Resistance Analysis for Service Men. Raderaft, 1938. 50 cents.

Principles and Practice of Radio Servicing, by H. J. Hicks. McGraw-Hill, 1939. $3.00.

Radio Construction and Repairing, by J. A. Moyer and J. F. Wostrel. 4th ed. *McGraw-Hill,* 1933. $2.50.

Radio Handbook, by J. A. Moyer and J. F. Wostrel. McGraw-Hill, 1931. $5.00.

Radio Service Trade Kinks, by L. S. Simon. McGraw-Hill, 1939. $8.00.

Radio Upkeep and Repairs, by A. T. Witts. 3rd ed. Pitman, 1938. $2.00.

Radio's Master Encyclopedia. United Catalog Pubs., Inc., 230 Fifth Ave., New York, N. Y., 1939. $2.50.

SELLING BY MAIL

Advertising Media:

American Freeman. Haldeman-Julius Co., Girard, Kans. $1.00 a year. (Mo.)

Family Journal. 131 Varick St., New York, N. Y. $2.00 a year. (Mo.)

Good Stories. Augusta, Me. 25 cents a year. (Mo.)

Grit. Williamsport, Pa, $2.00 a year. (Wkly)

Home Friend. 1411 Wyandotte St., Kansas City, Mo. 25 cents a year. (Mo.)

Household Management Journal. Batavia, Ill. 25 cents a year. (Mo.)

Professional Journals:

Income Increaser. 177 State St., Boston, Mass. $1.00 a year. (Mo.)

Liberty Mail Order Digest. 820 Center Ave., Sheboygan, Wis. $1.00 a year. (Mo.)

Mail Order Journal. 62 W. 45th St., New York, N. Y. $1.00 a year. (Mo.)

Mail Order Review. 417 Eversham Ave., Baltimore, Md. $1.00 a year. (Mo.)

Mail Order Selling. Elburn, Ill. $1.00 a year. (Mo.)

Mail Order Trade. Gossip Printery, Holton, Kans. 50 cents a year. (Mo.)

The Schemer. Alliance, Ohio. $1.00 a year. (Mo.)

Books and Pamphlets:

Handbook on Mail Order Selling and Merchandising, by R. K. Wadsworth. Dartnell, 1928. $3.75.

How to Make Sales Letters Make Money, by F. Egner. Harper, 1937. $2.50.

How to Sell by Mail, by E. A. Buckley. McGraw-Hill, 1938. $2.00.

Letters That Sell - and Why, by Cameron McPherson. Dartnell, 1930. $3.75.

Mail-Order and Direct-Mail Selling, by S. Roland Hall. McGraw-Hill, 1928. $5.00.

Mailing Lists. Chapter 30 of the Sales Managers Handbook, by J. C. Aspley. 3rd ed. Dartnell, 1940. $7.50.

Principles of Selling by Mail, by J. H. Picken. McGraw-Hill, 1927. $3.00.

Successful Direct-Mail Methods, by J. K. Crippen. McGraw-Hill, 1936. $3.50.

SELLING METHODS

(Publications for those who want to make money selling)

Periodicals:

How To Sell. 168 N. Michigan Ave., Chicago, Ill. $1.00 a year. (Mo.)

Independent Salesman. 22 E. Twelfth St., Cincinnati, Ohio. 25 cents a year. (Mo.)

Opportunity Magazine. 620 N. Michigan Ave., Chicago, Ill. $1.00 a year. (Mo.)

Sample Case. 632 N. Park St., Columbus, Ohio. $1.00 a year. (Mo.)

Specialty Salesman Magazine. 307 N. Michigan Ave., Chicago, Ill. $1.00 a year. (Mo.)

Books and Pamphlets:

Art of Persuading People, by J. A. Worsham. Harper, 1938. $2.00.

Getting the Most Out of Salesmen, by J. C. Aspley. Dartnell, 1935. $1.50.

Go-Giver, The, by Vash Young. Bobbs-Merrill Co., 724 N. Meridan St., Indianapolis, Ind., 1934. $1.50.

How to Deliver a Sales Presentation, by R. C. Borden. Harper, 1938. $2.00.

How to Get the Order, by Harry Simmons. Harper, 1937. $2.00.

How to Make More Sales, by Harry Simmons. Harper, 1936. $2.00.

How to Win Friends and Influence People, by D. Carnegie. Simon & Schuster, 1937. $1.96.

How to Win What You Want, by Kenneth Goode. Prentice-Hall, 1939. $2.50.

I Am a Salesman, by Jack Klein. Harper, 1934. $2.50.

Knack of Selling More, by Burton Bigelow. 3 vol. McGraw-Hill, 1936. $4.00.

Knack of Selling Yourself, by James Mangan. Dartnell, 1938. $2.50.

Practical Course in Successful Selling, by Harry Simmons. Harper, 1939. $3.00.

Profitable Showmanship, by Kenneth Goode. Prentice-Hall, 1939. $2.75.

Rex Cole on Salesmanship, by Rex Cole and C. D. Frazer. Forbes, 120 Fifth Ave., New York, N. Y., 1935.$2.50.

Salesmanship for Today for Sales Managers of Tomorrow, by D. R. Osborne. Harper, 1939. $2.50.

Self-Management in Selling, by D. R. Osborne. Harper, 1931. $3.50.

Selling Is a Game, by J. McCord. Prentice-Hall, 1939. $2.00.

Showmanship in Business, by Kenneth Goode and M. Z. Kaufman. rev. ed. *Harper*, 1939. $2.75.

Sizzle Book, by E. Wheeler. Prentice-Hall, 1938. 75 cents.

Step Out and Sell, by William Holler. Dartnell, 1939. $1.50.

Steps to the Order, by J. C. Aspley. Dartnell, 1934. $1.00.

Tested Sentences That Sell, by E. Wheeler. Prentice-Hall, 1937. $3.75.

Turn Your Imagination into Money, by R. Giles. Harper, 1934. $2.50.

You Can Do Anything, by James Mangan. Dartnell, 1934. $2.50.

STAMP AND COIN COLLECTING

Periodicals:

American Philatelist. Second National Bank Bldg., Cincinnati, Ohio. $2.50 a year. (Mo.)

American Stamp Digest. 142 W. 24th St., New York, N. Y. $1.00 a year. (Mo.)

International Post. 6908 Carleton Ave., Seattle, Wash. $1.00 a year. (B-Mo.)

Mekeel's Stamp News. 31 Pierce Ave., Portland, Me. $1.00 a year. (Wkly)

Numismatist. American Numismatic Assoc., 4215 Fernhill Ave., Baltimore, Md. $2.00 a year. (Mo.)

Philatelic Gossip. Gossip Printery, Inc., Holton, Kans. $1.00 a year. (Wkly)

Stamp and Cover Collector. 109 E. Cary St., Richmond, Va. $1.00 a year. (Mo.)

Stamps. 100 Sixth Ave., New York, N. Y. $1.00 a year. (Wkly)
Western Stamp Collector. Mill City, Ore. 85 cents a year. (S-Wkly)
World Stamp Market. Gossip Printery, Inc., Holton, Kans. 50 cents a year. (Mo.)

Books and Pamphlets:

America's Story as Told in Postage Stamps, by E. M. Allen. rev. ed. McGrawHill, 1935. $2.50.

Coin Collecting, by Joseph Coffin. rev. ed. Coward, McCann, Inc., 2 W. 45th St., New York, N. Y., 1938. $1.75.

Coins Of The World, by W. Raymond and S. Mosher. Raymond Wayte, Inc., 630 Fifth Ave., New York, N. Y., 1938. $3.00.

Geography and Stamps, by Kent B. Stiles. McGraw-Hill, 1935. $3.00.

National Catalog of United States Coins. California Stamp Co., 832 Wilshire

Blvd., Los Angeles, Calif., 1934. $3.50.

Stamp Collecting, by Stanley Phillips. Dodd, Mead, 1932. $3.00.

Stamp Collecting, by Henry Renouf. Leisure League, 1934. 25 cents.

Standard Catalog of United States Coins and Currency from 1652 to Present Day, by W. Raymond, comp. Scott Stamp & Coin Co., 1 W. 47th St., New York, N. Y., 1934. $2.50.

Standard Postage Stamp Album, 1937. Scott Publications, 1 W. 47th St., New York, N. Y., 1938. $3.00.

Star Coin Encyclopedia and Premium Catalog, by B. M. Mehl. 28th ed. Caspar, 1934. $1.00.

Successful Stamp Merchandising. Weekly philatelic Gossip, Holton, Kans. 50 cents.

STORE KEEPING
(Publications for the merchant)

Periodicals:

All-Pets Magazine. 2810 S. Michigan Ave., Chicago, Ill. $1.00 a year. (Mo.)

American Druggist. 57th St. at 8th Ave., New York, N. Y. 50 cents a year. (Mo.)

Display World. 1209 Sycamore St., Cincinnati, Ohio. $3.00 a year. (Mo.)

Drug Topics. 330 W. 42nd St., New York, N. Y. $5.00 a year. (Wkly)

Electrical Merchandising. 330 W. 42nd St., New York, N. Y. $2.00 a year. (Mo.)

Furniture Age. 2225 N. Lakewood Ave., Chicago, Ill. $3.00 a year. (Mo.)

Furniture Record. 342 Madison Ave., New York, N. Y. $2.00 a year. (Mo.)

Hardware Age. 239 W. 39th St., New York, N. Y. $1.00 a year. (Ftntly)
Hardware Retailer. 130 E. Washington St., Indianapolis, Ind. $2.00 a year. (Mo.)
Hardware World. 160 N. LaSalle St., Chicago, Ill. 50 cents a year. (Mo.)
Meat Merchandising. 105 S. Ninth St., St. Louis, Mo. Controlled free distribution. (Mo.)
Milk Dealer. 509 W. Cherry St., Milwaukee, Wis. $2.00 a year. (Mo.)
Office Appliances. 20 No. Wacker Drive, Chicago, Ill. $2.00 a year. (Mo.)
Radio Retailing. 330 W. 42nd St., New York, N. Y. $1.00 a year. (Mo.)
Retail Ledger. 342 Madison Ave., New York, N. Y. $2.00 a year. (Mo.)
Retail Executive. 8 E. 13th St., New York, N. Y. $2.00 a year. (Wkly)
Retailing Home Furnishings. 8 E. 13th St., New York, N. Y. $2.00 a year. (Wkly)

Government Publications:

Aids to Retail Grocery Profits. Practical hints designed to help make more money for the grocery retailer. 1933. Domestic Commerce Series No. 71. 10 cents.
Causes of Failures Among Drug Stores. Domestic Commerce Series No. 59. 5 cents.
Costs, Markets, and Methods in Grocery Retailing. Distribution Cost Studies No. 8. 20 cents.
Costs, Sales, and Profits in Retail Drug Store. 1934. Domestic Commerce Series No. 90. 20 cents.
Department Leasing in Retail Stores. Domestic Commerce Series. (Price not given.)
Drug Store Arrangement. Domestic Commerce Series No. 57. 10 cents.
Jewelry Distribution by Retail Jewelers. Domestic Commerce Series No. 48. 10 cents.
Merchandising in City Drug Stores. Domestic Commerce Series No. 70. 5 cents.
Merchandising in Country Drug Stores. Domestic Commerce Series No. 65. 5 cents.
Prescription Department Sales Analysis in Selected Drug Stores. Domestic Commerce Series No. 61. 5 cents.
Retail Operating Costs within a Metropolitan Community. 1934. Domestic Commerce Series No. 88. 10 cents.
Store Arrangement Principles. 1938. Domestic Commerce Series No. 104. 10 cents.
Survey of Retail Management Practices. 1933. Domestic Commerce Series No. 81. 10 cents.

Books and Pamphlets:

Better Retailing. National Cash Register Company, Merchants Service, Dayton, Ohio, 1935. 10th ed., rev., 1937. Gratis.

Credit Department Salesmanship, by J. T. Bartlett and C. M. Reed. Harper, 1932. $3.50.

Displaying Merchandise for Profit, by A. E. Hurst. Prentice-Hall. $5.00

Drug Store Business Methods, by C. W. Pearson. 2nd ed. rev. Lea & Bebiger, 600 S. Washington Sq., Philadelphia, Pa., 1931. $2.75.

Fundamentals of Window Display, by C. Ellison. International Textbook Co., Scranton, Pa., 1937. $1.25.

Getting Ahead in Retailing, by N. M. Ohrbach. McGraw-Hill, 1935. $2.50.

How to Make Grocery Windows Pay. W. L. Butler, ed. Progressive Grocer, 89 Madison Ave., New York, N. Y., 1932. $2.00.

How to Open a Shop, by Alissa Keir. McGraw-Hill, 1939. $2.00.

How to Paint Signs and Show Cards, by E. C. Matthews. rev. ed. Illustrated Editions Co., New York, N. Y., 1938. $2.00.

How to Succeed in Retail Selling, by R. M. Hardy. Harper, 1938. $~2.00

How to Turn People into Gold, by K. M. Goode. 5th ed. Harper, 1937. $1.00.

Modern Food Merchandising, by C. V. Hill & Co., Inc., Trenton, N. J. 1934.

Practical Display Instructor, by R. Harman. 2nd ed. Chemical Pub. Co., 300

N. Third St., Easton, Pa., 1937. $2.00.

Principles and Practice of Show-Card Writing, by L. E. Blair. 2nd ed. McGraw-Hill, 1937. $2.50.

Problem of Retail Site Selection, by R. U. Ratcliff. Univ. of Michigan, Ann Arbor, Mich., 1939. $1.00.

Profitable Retail Advertising, by M. E. Tobias. Harper, 1930. $4.00.

Profitable Specialty Shop Operation, by G. C. Engel and M. O. Kohn. McGraw- Hill, 1938. $2.50.

Retail Flower Shop, by Robert Kilt. De La Mare. $3.50.

Retail Merchandise Control, by J. W. Wingate. Prentice-Hall, 1933. $5.00.

Retail Selling Simplified, by E. F. Hayter. Harper, 1939. $1.25.

So You Want to Open a Shop, by Alissa Keir. McGraw-Hill, 1939. $2.00.

Start Your Own Business, by H. S. Kahm. Hillman-Curl, Inc., 7-11 E. 44th St., New York, N. Y., 1937. $1.50.

Store Salesmanship, by N. A. Brisco and Others. Prentice-Hall, 1932. $2.00.

Survey of Retailing Practices. Two volumes. Dartnell, 1931. $5.00.

Ticket and Show-Card Designing, by F. A. Pearson. 2nd ed. Pitman, 1937. $1.75.

2800 Retailing Ideas, by E. Lyons. Pub. by the author, Pittstown, N. J., 1937. $3.00.

Wayside Marketing, by Schuyler Arnold. De La Mare. $1.50.

TEA ROOMS AND RESTAURANT MANAGEMENT

Periodicals:

American Hotel Journal. 203 N. Wabash Ave., Chicago, Ill. (Mo.)

American Restaurant. 5 S. Wabash Ave., Chicago, Ill. $2.00 a year. (Mo.)

Hotel Bulletin. 342 Madison Ave., New York, N. Y. $3.00 a year. (Mo.)

Hotel Management. 222 E. 42nd St., New York, N. Y. $3.00 a year. (Mo.)

Hotel Monthly. 950 Merchandise Mart, Chicago, Ill. $1.00 a year. (Mo.)

Restaurant Man, The. 1457 Broadway, New York, N. Y. $2.00 a year. (Mo.)

Restaurant Management. 222 E. 42nd St., New York, N. Y. $3.00 a year. (Mo.)

Soda Fountain Magazine. 420 Lexington Ave., New York, N. Y. (Controlled free distribution.) (Mo.)

Books and Pamphlets:

Advertising And Promotion For Hotels And Restaurants, by J. O. Dahl. The Dahls, Stamford, Conn., 1939. $3.00.

Hotel Management, by L. M. Boomer. 3rd rev. ed. Harper, 1938. $4.00.

Housekeeping Management in Hotels and Institutions, by C. M. Dahl. Harper. $4.00.

How to Get More for Your Payroll Dollar, by J. O. and C. M. Dahl. The Dahls, Stamford, Conn., 1937. $2.00.

Kitchen Management, by J. O. Dahl. rev. ed. Harper, 1934. $4.00.

Restaurant Management, by J. O. Dahl. 3rd rev. ed. Harper, 1938. $4.00.

Restaurateur's Handbook, by C. S. Faissole and L. Mackall. Harper, 1938. $2.00.

Running a Tea-Room and Catering for Profit. Pitman, 1936. $1.00.

Salads and Sandwiches, by Emory Hawcock. Harper, $3.50.

Secret of Successful Restaurants, by Alice Foote MacDougall. Harper, 1929. $3.50.

Seven Hundred Sandwiches, by F. A. Cowles. Little, Brown, 1928. $1.75.

Soda Fountain and Luncheonette Management, by J. O. Dahl. Harper, 1930. $3.50.

Tea Room Recipes, by L. Richards and N. Treat. Little, Brown, 1925. $2.00.

PUBLISHERS OF BOOKS LISTED
IN THIS SECTION

ABBREVIATION | ADDRESS

American Home — American Home, Garden City, N. Y.

Appleton D. — Appleton-Century, Inc., 35 W. 32nd St., New York, N. Y.

Barnes — A. S. Barnes & Co., 67 W. 44th St., New York, N. Y.

Barrows — M. Barrows & Company, 286 Fifth Ave., New York, N. Y.

Better Homes — Better Homes and Gardens, 17th and Locust Sts., Des Moines, Ia.

Blue Ribbon Books — 386 Fourth Ave., New York, N. Y.

Bowker — R. R. Bowker Company, 62 W. 45th St., New York, N. Y.

Caspar — Caspar, Krueger, Dory Co., 772 N. Water St., Milwaukee, Wis.

Coward, McCann — Coward, McCann, Inc., 2 W. 45th St., New York, N. Y.

Dartnell — Dartnell Corporation, 4660 Ravenswood Ave., Chicago, Ill.

Daye — Stephen Daye Press, Brattleboro, Vt.

De La Mare — De La Mare Co., Inc., 448 W. 37th St., New York, N. Y.

Dodd, Mead — Dodd, Mead & Co., 449 4th Ave., New York, N. Y.

Doubleday — Doubleday, Doran & Co., Garden City, N. Y.

Drake — Frederick J. Drake & Co., 179 N. Michigan Ave., Chicago, Ill.

Dutton — E. P. Dutton & Co., 286 4th Ave., New York, N. Y.

Eastman Kodak Company - Eastman Kodak Company, Rochester N. Y.

Funk — Funk & Wagnalls Company, 354 4th Ave., New York, N. Y.

Fur Trade Journal — Fur Trade Journal of Canada, 143 St. Leonards St., Toronto, Ontario, Canada.

Greenberg — Greenberg Publisher, Inc., 67 W. 44th St., New York, N. Y.

Harcourt, Brace — Harcourt, Brace & Co., 383 Madison Ave., New York, N. Y.

Harper — Harper & Brothers, 49 E. 33rd St., New York, N. Y.

Holt — Henry Holt & Co., 1 Park Ave., New York, N. Y.

Houghton Mifflin — Houghton, Mifflin Co., 2 Park Ave., New York, N. Y.

John Day — John Day Co., Inc., 386 4th Ave., New York, N. Y.

Judy	Judy Publishing Co., 3223 Michigan Blvd., Chicago, Ill.
Knopf	Alfred A. Knopf, Inc., 730 5th Ave., New York, N. Y.
Leisure	Leisure, 683 Atlantic Ave., Boston, Mass.
Leisure League	Leisure League of America, 30 Rockefeller Plaza, New York, N.Y.
Lippincott	J. B. Lippincott Co., 227 S. 6th St., Philadelphia, Pa.
Little, Brown	Little, Brown & Co., 34 Beacon St., Boston, Mass.
Longmans	Longmans, Green & Co., 114 5th Ave., New York, N. Y.
McBride	Robert M. McBride & Company, 4 W.16th St., New York, N.Y.
McClurg	A. C. McClurg & Co., 333 E. Ontario St., Chicago, Ill.
McKay	David McKay Co., 604-608 S. Washington Sq., Philadelphia, Pa.
McGraw-Hill	McGraw-Hill Book Co., Inc., 330 W. 42nd St., New York, N.Y.
Macmillan	Macmillan Co., 60 5th Ave., New York, N. Y.
Manual Arts	Manual Arts Press, 237 N. Monroe St., Peoria, Ill.
Methuen	Methuen & Co., Ltd., 36 Essex St., Strand, London, Eng.
Modelmaker	Modelmaker Corp., Wauwatosa, Wis.
Olsen	The Olsen Pub. Co., 505 W. Cherry St., Milwaukee, Wis.
Orange Judd	Orange Judd Publishing Co., 15 E. 26th St., New York, N. Y.
Penton	Penton Pub. Co., 1213 W. 3rd St., Cleveland, Ohio.
Pitman	Pitman Publishing Corporation, 2-6 W. 45th St., New York. N.Y.
Popular Mechanics Press	Popular Mechanics Press, 200 E. Ontario St., Chicago, Ill.
Prentice-Hall	Prentice-Hall, Inc., 70 Fifth Ave., New York, N. Y.
Putnam	G. P. Putnam's Sons, 2-6 W. 45th St., New York, N. Y.
Radcraft	Radcraft Publications, Inc., 99 Hudson St., New York, N. Y.
Ronald Press	Ronald Press Co., 15 E. 26th se, New York. N. Y.
Scribner	Charles Scribner's Sons, 597 5th Ave., New York, N. Y.
Simon & Schuster	Simon & Schuster, 386 4th Ave., New York, N. Y.
Snyder	Rossiter Snyder Publishing Co., Guildford, Conn.
Spon	Spon & Chamberlain, 120 Liberty St., New York, N. Y.
Stokes	F. A. Stokes Co., 443 4th Ave., New York, N. Y.
Stratford	Stratford Company, 289 Congress St., Boston, Mass.

Warne	Frederick Warne & Co., Inc., 79 Madison Ave., New York, N.Y.
Wiley	John Wiley & Sons, Inc., 440 4th Ave., New York, N. Y.
Winston	John C. Winston Company, 1006 Arch St., Philadelphia, Pa.

INDEX

NOTES

CPSIA information can be obtained
at www.ICGtesting.com
Printed in the USA
BVOW03s0226190717

489618BV00022B/25/P